TEXAS JUSTICE

The Legacy of Historical Courthouses

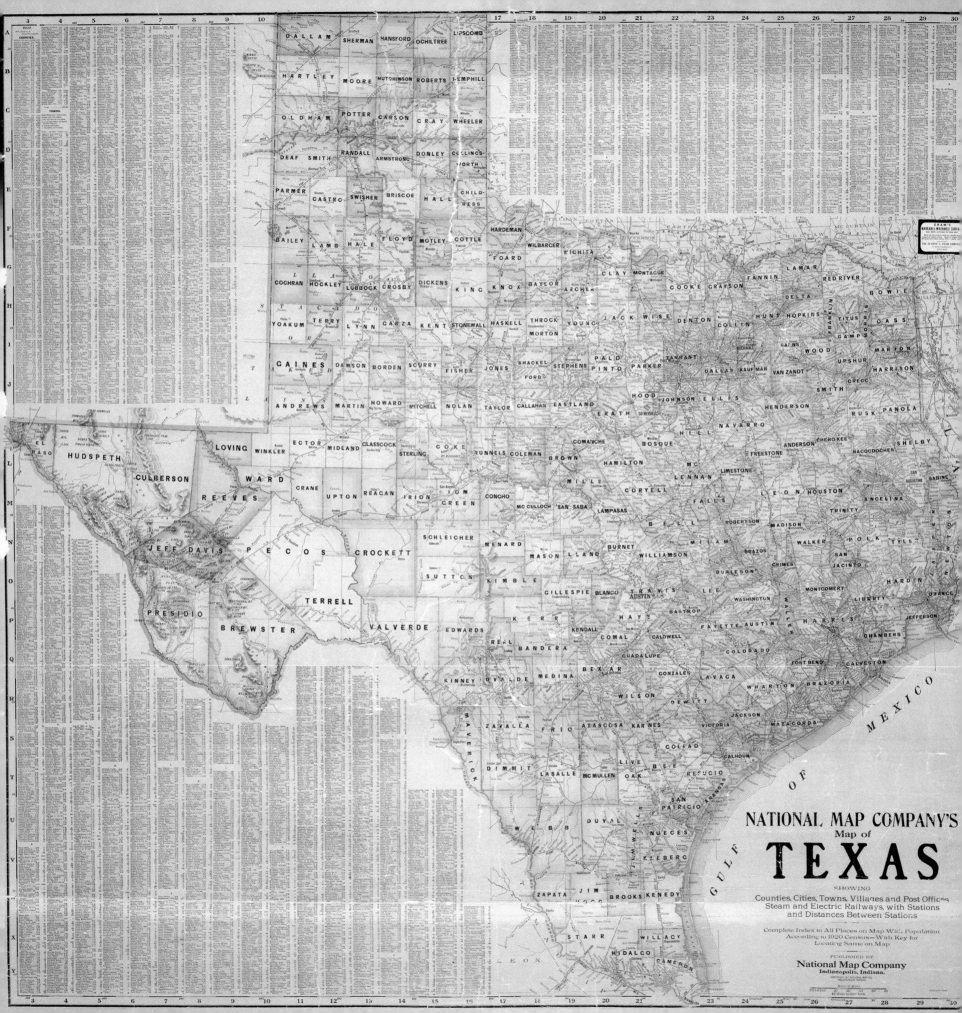

NATIONAL MAP COMPANY'S
Map of
TEXAS

SHOWING

Counties, Cities, Towns, Villages and Post Offices
Steam and Electric Railways, with Stations
and Distances Between Stations

Complete Index to All Places on Map With Population
According to 1920 Census—With Key for
Locating Same on Map

PUBLISHED BY

National Map Company
Indianapolis, Indiana.

TEXAS JUSTICE

The Legacy of Historical Courthouses

MARTANA

Foreword by Richard "Racehorse" Haynes

Photography by Texas Photographers

Red Bandana Publishing, Dallas, Texas

RED BANDANA Publishing

Red Bandana Publishing
25 Highland Park Village, 100-140
Dallas, TX 75205
www.martana.com

Printed in Malaysia

PUBLISHERS DATA

Texas Justice: The Legacy of Historical Courthouses

By Martana

Library of Congress Control Number: 2004113128

ISBN 0-9728992-1-9 (alk. paper)

History / Texana

First printing, 2004

1 2 3 4 5 6 7 8 9 10 – 08 07 06 05 04

DEDICATION

Texas Justice is dedicated to my father, Melvin (Mel) John Hanson,

who stood for justice in the Marine Corps,

who experienced injustice in his lifetime,

and who sometimes was on the other side of justice—I salute you in the heavens above,

and thank you for all that I am,

all that I am not,

and for all that I will be.

FOREWORD

Texas Justice! Two words that reflect the rich and colorful history of courthouses, judges, lawyers and law officers that have shaped and influenced the quality of life under law in every community in the Lone Star State. Dubbed "Racehorse" by a junior high school coach, I have been privileged to practice law for almost fifty years. Even after almost half a century, I still get a thrill every time I walk into a Texas Courthouse. I can still feel and sense the high drama and emotion of by-gone trials, history-making judges, lawyers and law officers, cases involving everything from accusations of murder, kidnapping and cattle rustling. You name it and Texas Courthouses have seen them all. Like all courtroom veterans, *Texas Justice* reminds me of how far we have come from the trial of Jack Ruby for the killing of Lee Harvey Oswald, million-dollar disputes over oil rights and the trials of serial killers like Henry Lee Lucas—to mention just a few of the landmark trials that have taken place in Texas Courthouses. *Texas Justice* gives us insight into how the legal system has changed, and how it has not changed since the time Texas became a Republic. Congratulations to Martana. Martana has captured some of Texas' Historical Courthouses in all of their majesty, and the bigger-than-life cases, judges, lawyers and lawmen who have and are serving justice for Texans with every strike of the gavel.

Richard Haynes

Richard "Racehorse" Haynes

INTRODUCTION

My inspiration for Texas Justice came to me while I was attending the first Texas Courthouse Rededication for Shackelford County in Albany, Texas, in 2001 by the Texas Historic Courthouse Preservation program. This Lone Star beauty was truly a symbol of the Texas heritage of pride, freedom, prosperity and protection for all Texans. As I walked the halls of the courthouse that day, I thought about the famous trials of crime and passion; love and war; murder and innocence that had been tried right here, and the Texas law legends who tried these cases. So, I decided to create a book that would celebrate the architectural grandeur of our Lone Star beauties and the famous cases that were tried within their walls. From the hanging gallows of Austin County to the electric chair; from horse thieves of Coryell County to the corporate raiders; these Texas Courthouses have seen the likes of them all! *Texas Justice* unveils nearly 100 of Texas' 254 county courthouses, of which 234 have the distinction of being a Historical Courthouse and 84 of these Historic Courthouses have the double crown of being a National Register Property. The Architectural styles include Art-Deco, Second Empire, Texas Renaissance and Beaux-Arts, just to name a few. I applaud Dale Sellers of Phoenix 1 for his Texas pride in insisting on retaining the integrity of the buildings by duplicating materials used in the original structures. In *Texas Justice: The Legacy of Historical Courthouses,* you will tour Texas Courthouses through the eyes and words of Texas legal legends, judges and lawmakers as they share the lore of the past and the present-day law. From small-town lawmakers to big-time super lawyers, they reveal the heart and fierce persistence to uphold the law every time they face that twelve-man-jury. I hope that this book is an introduction to the rich heritage of Texas Justice and an inspiration to save and restore our majestic treasures for future generations to enjoy. After all, we are our past, we are creating our present and the future will be told through the democracy of our government in small towns and metropolitan cities across the Lone Star State in our Texas Courthouses.

MARTANA

Table of Contents

Austin
County Courthouse

"Whenever men take the law into their own hands, the loser is the law. And when the law loses, freedom languishes."

~ DAVID'S FAMOUS TEXAS JUSTICE SAYING

"Death by Lethal Injection"

A Famous Texas Case as Told by
DAVID ROSE
CONLEY ROSE, P.C.

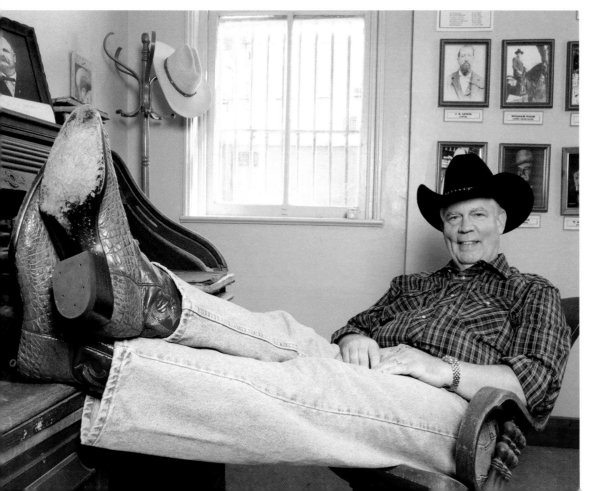

It began Sunday evening, April 4, 1976, when the Katy police dispatcher notified law officers that a man had attempted to pay for his room at the Brookshire Days Inn with a stolen credit card. Patrolman Mark Frederick and his partner, Patrolman Jack Reichert, were on duty on Interstate Highway 10 when they received the radio report. About an hour later, they spotted the vehicle and began pursuit. The suspect took the Sealy exit and pulled to a stop. Patrolman Frederick approached the suspect's car. When he came to the window, the suspect pulled a pistol and fired a fatal shot at point-blank range, hitting Patrolman Frederick in the arm, the bullet then passing through his heart. Patrolman Reichert jumped from the patrol car firing six shots as the suspect drove away.

Patrolmen from Sealy and Eagle Lake were notified and began pursuit. They found the suspect's car abandoned about four miles from Sealy with six bullet holes in it and a tire shot out, but no suspect. In the car was a 9 mm Browning automatic pistol of the same caliber which had killed Patrolman Frederick. A high-powered rifle, a sawed-off shotgun and a rubber mask were found in the trunk.

Thus began one of the most massive manhunts in Texas, involving up to 500 officers, several helicopters and numerous tracking dogs. However, primarily due to the heavy rain, the suspect could not be tracked. The sheriff reported that he had just returned from funeral services for the slain patrolman on Tuesday, April 6, when a call was received that a man had been seen in the El Pleasant area about ten miles from Sealy. A man fitting the description of the suspect was spotted running into a small wooded area. Law enforcement immediately surrounded the area. The dogs began flushing out the suspect while the helicopter hovered overhead. The three-day manhunt ended at 4:45 p.m. with the arrest of Billy George Hughes, Jr., about seven miles from where he had abandoned his vehicle.

It turned out that twenty-four-year-old Hughes from Montgomery, Alabama, had previously been arrested in 1974 for obtaining money under false pretenses, but the charge was dropped. In 1975, he pleaded guilty to threatening to bomb banks that had refused to grant him loans and spent two months in the Springfield Missouri Institution. He then received a three-year probated sentence and returned to Alabama and began roaming around the country in violation of his probation. He testified that he had been in New Orleans and was heading toward the West Coast just prior to the shooting. The day of the murder he had been drinking heavily on Galveston Beach.

Hughes was indicted in 1976 by the Austin County grand jury for capital murder in *The State of Texas vs. Billy George Hughes, Jr.* The trial took place in Bay City on a change of venue from Austin County due to extensive publicity. The state prosecutors were up against Robert Scardino of Houston and L.L. "Pop" Warner of La Grange. Hughes pleaded innocent by reason of insanity with the defense doctor testifying that Hughes was a "paranoid schizophrenic."

In September, 1976, after a four-day trial, the jury deliberated less

". . . ONE OF THE MOST MASSIVE MANHUNTS IN TEXAS . . . 500 OFFICERS, SEVERAL HELICOPTERS AND NUMEROUS TRACKING DOGS."

than three hours before denying the insanity plea and finding Billy George Hughes, Jr. guilty of capital murder. Furthermore, after about an hour of deliberation, the jury unanimously ruled that Hughes be put to death. District Judge G. P. Hardy, after hearing the decision of the jury, told Hughes in an empty courtroom, "Your sentence is death." Sheriff T.A. Maddox pointed out that this was the speediest trial in years where the death penalty was assessed.

During the course of his time behind bars, Hughes appealed his conviction nearly a dozen times and was the fourth-longest serving inmate of the 458 on death row. As he was being wheeled-off to execution, Hughes said, "They are executing an innocent man because things did not happen as they say they happened." After having been on death row for more than 23 years, Hughes was put to death by lethal injection in Huntsville on January 24, 2000.

Where did Austin County get its name?
IN 1823, STEPHEN F. AUSTIN OBTAINED 25 LEAGUES (4,428 ACRES PER LEAGUE) OF LAND FROM MEXICO TO SETTLE FAMILIES IN AN AREA EXTENDING FROM AUSTIN COUNTY TO THE GULF COAST. THE AUSTIN COLONY WAS THE FIRST SUCH SUCCESSFUL SETTLEMENT SITE IN TEXAS AND THEREFORE, THE COUNTY WAS NAMED AFTER HIM IN 1836.

Where is the Austin County Courthouse located?
THE COURTHOUSE IS IN THE CENTER OF BELLVILLE, TX, WHERE MAIN STREET AND HOLLAND AND BELL STREETS FORM A CIRCLE DRIVE AROUND THE COURTHOUSE.

Who designed the Austin County Courthouse?
WYATT C. HEDRICK DESIGNED THE MOST RECENT COURTHOUSE IN 1960, WHEN THE FORMER STRUCTURE WAS LOST TO A TRAGIC ACCIDENTAL FIRE. THE NEW COURTHOUSE WAS DESIGNED IN A MODERNE STYLE ARCHITECTURE CONSTRUCTED OF GRANITE AND CONCRETE.

What is the Courthouse's most unusual feature?
IT HAS A MODERN ARCHITECTURAL STYLE THAT IS UNUSUAL TO THE AUSTIN COUNTRYSIDE SETTING.

What is the most famous case tried in the Austin County Courthouse?
ANOTHER INTERESTING CASE WAS WHEN A 15-YEAR-OLD HELD UP A BANK WITH A TOY GUN AND RAN OFF WITH A BAG OF MONEY THAT HE HID UNDER HIS BED UNTIL HE WAS NABBED BY THE POLICE.

Where do you hang your hat?
IN HOUSTON, TX, WHERE I FOUNDED THE LAW FIRM CONLEY ROSE. CONLEY ROSE WAS FORMED ON APRIL 1, 1991, AND OPENED ITS AUSTIN OFFICE ON MAY 1, 1994, AND ITS DALLAS OFFICE ON JULY 1, 2000. THE FIRM CURRENTLY HAS FIFTY PROFESSIONALS, MAKING IT THE LARGEST LEGAL FIRM IN TEXAS FOCUSING EXCLUSIVELY ON INTELLECTUAL PROPERTY MATTERS.

Believe it or not!
THE REPUBLIC OF TEXAS BEGAN IN SAN DE FELIPE DE AUSTIN IN AUSTIN COUNTY. THIS SITE WAS SELECTED AS THE CAPITOL OF THE REPUBLIC WHEN THE TEXAS CONGRESS FIRST MET IN AUSTIN IN NOVEMBER, 1839!

Where did Baylor County get its name?

AFTER DR. HENRY W. BAYLOR, WHO WAS AN INDIAN FIGHTER, TEXAS RANGER CAPTAIN, SURGEON AND MEXICAN WAR VETERAN IN 1879. SEYMOUR, TX, IS ALSO HOME TO THE ANNUAL COWBOYS' REUNION, NOW KNOWN AS THE SETTLER'S REUNION.

Where is the Baylor County Courthouse located?

THE FIRST COURTHOUSE WAS BUILT BY LOCAL ROCK MASONS IN 1879 ON MAIN STREET. THE ARCHITECTS OF THE 1968 MODERN BUILDING WERE PIERCE, NORRIS & PACE.

Who designed the Baylor County Courthouse?

THE FIRST COURTHOUSE WAS BUILT IN 1879 BY LOCAL ROCK MASONS AND HAD A GRAND DOME. THE ARCHITECTS OF THE 1968 MODERN BUILDING WERE PIERCE, NORRIS & PACE.

What is the Courthouse's most unusual feature?

ITS UNUSUALLY MODERN, GEOMETRIC STYLE OF ARCHITECTURE INCLUDING A FLAT ROOF; ERECTED AS THE NEW COURTHOUSE IN 1968 ON THE SAME LOCATION AS THE 1879 COURTHOUSE.

What is the most famous case tried in the Baylor County Courthouse?

BURK BURNETT MURDER TRIAL—SAMUEL BURK BURNETT (1849-1922) WAS A PROMINENT OILMAN, RANCHER AND BANKER, WHO OWNED THE LARGEST CATTLE EMPIRE IN TEXAS HISTORY.

Where do you hang your hat?

JAMES W. COLLIER, ATTORNEY, P.C., STAYS BUSY IN AZLE, TX, AS A PRACTICING ATTORNEY, MEDIATOR AND TRIAL CONSULTANT. HE HAS A TITLE COMPANY OFFICE, A CONFERENCE CENTER AND IS A SHAREHOLDER IN THE CONCILIATION INSTITUTE, INC., AN A.D.R. FIRM. MR. QUISENBERRY ENGAGED IN THE PRIVATE PRACTICE OF LAW FOR THIRTEEN YEARS, BUT IS NO LONGER ACTIVELY PRACTICING. HE ASSUMED THE BENCH IN 1995 WHERE HE REMAINS TODAY. JUDGE QUISENBERRY MAINTAINS AN ACTIVE CIVIL AND CRIMINAL DOCKET IN PARKER COUNTY, TX. HE WAS APPOINTED BY TEXAS GOVERNOR RICK PERRY TO THE NEWLY CREATED 415TH DISTRICT COURT IN EARLY 2004.

Believe it or not!

WHEN THE HISTORIC COURTHOUSE BURNED, COURT WAS TEMPORARILY HELD IN A SUPERMARKET DOWN THE STREET ...UNBELIEVABLE!

"File today, Don't delay!"
~ JIM'S FAMOUS TEXAS JUSTICE SAYING

"Property Owners Just Say No!"

A Famous Texas Case as Told by
JIM COLLIER
LAW OFFICES OF JAMES W. COLLIER, P.C.
and
JUDGE GRAHAM QUISENBERRY
ATTORNEY AT LAW

In a case that can now fondly be called, "Property Owners Just Say No!", Jim Collier and his former law partner, now Judge Graham Quisenberry, were representing twelve land owners in Baylor County who, coincidentally, paid most of the taxes in the county. The two lawyers brought a school bond election contest to prohibit the school district from issuing bonds and raising taxes to pay them.

The original plaintiff in the election suit died in 1990. At the time of the lawsuit, virtually all residents of Baylor County were in favor of reasonable improvements to the Seymour schools. Over time, the taxpayers, of whom the plaintiff was one, became mistrustful of the school administration because of perceived extravagance and wasting of money, hence, the conduct of the election itself became an object of suspicion. So, this rancher and some of his friends hired Collier and Quisenberry, a two-man firm in Fort Worth, to even the playing field. The ranchers thought the election (and the following tax increase) had been crammed down their throats and wanted some relief.

The two lawyers filed an election protest, something neither had done before. The lawyers couldn't find a similar case in Texas. They called all their legal mentors and buddies to get tips, but not one had experience with such a case. The case took some

Baylor County Courthouse

wild turns that the young guns never expected. This situation might not sound too glamorous or interesting, but every person in Baylor County was technically a party to the case. When they discovered that fact, Collier and Quisenberry facilitated the filing of almost 300 individual "pro-se" answers, which baffled the other side. The school district's lawyers just couldn't deal effectively with that many parties. Collier and Quisenberry had no problem with it because of Collier's experience in complicated bankruptcy matters. The school district's lawyers tried to scare off some of the individuals with claims for attorney fees, but only a few folks withdrew their answers.

Talk about a mass of people! The lawsuit generated thousands of pages of law-related documents that were primarily handled in-house by a two-man law firm. One of the legal research assistants is now a district judge, as is the plaintiff's

> **". . . THEY WERE ABLE TO NAME EVERY PERSON IN BAYLOR COUNTY AS A PARTY TO THE CASE."**

lawyer, Mr. Quisenberry.

Eventually, after multiple heated depositions and hearings, the other side was overwhelmed and the case settled on favorable terms. The settlement saved millions in bond expenditures. According to the settlement agreement, the old high school could be demolished. It was. The property upon which it stood could be sold to offset capital expenditures. It never was. The new high school was built and the ranchers saved a bundle on taxes.

Jim Collier and Judge Graham Quisenberry just chalked it up to the experience of being two good lawyers with a solid, committed client.

Bell
County Courthouse

"The Day the Bell County Clock Tower Chimed in Italy"

A Famous Texas Case as Told by

BILL MESSER & JIM BOWMER
MESSER, POTTS, MESSER, P.C.
NAMAN, HOWELL, SMITH AND LEE

Our story tellers, Bill Messer and Jim Bowmer, are the products of families that have resided in Bell County since its founding. Bill Messer's family came to the county in the 1850s. They have ranched there continuously ever since. Furthermore, every generation has held public office and attended Belton schools, so one might certainly say that they are a product of Bell County institutions.

The remodeling of the Bell County Courthouse in 1999 returned it to its original 1885 style and detail and reminds us of the great history of this building. The previous 1950 "modernization" was necessitated by general deterioration, including a malfunctioning clock, but it masked the original brilliance of the structure. It so happens that this 1950 overhaul was accomplished during Judge W.A. Messer's service as county judge. However, he was not the last in his family to have been witness to the changing character of the courthouse.

In 1978, Bill Messer was campaigning for his first elective office as state representative when at a senior citizens' center in Temple, he struck up a conversation with an elderly woman whom he did not know. But she certainly knew his family. In animated fashion, the woman complimented Mr. Messer on both the Messer and Burton sides of his family; she had been acquainted for a number of years with several members of Bill's extended family.

As he brought the conversation to a conclusion, Messer asked the lady for her vote, but she replied, "Oh, no.

> *"If you always tell the truth, it's not hard to remember what you said."*
>
> ~ BILL'S FAMOUS TEXAS JUSTICE SAYING

I cannot vote for you." Mr. Messer said, "Well, I understand that my opponent is a ten-year incumbent and I can appreciate your loyalty to him." "I don't care to vote for him," she responded, "but I promised your grandfather when he took the bell tower off the courthouse that I would never vote for a Messer as long as I live. So I'm very sorry; I cannot vote for you."

The malfunctioning courthouse clock of the 1950s precipitated an exchange that resulted in a truism that has been often repeated in Bill Messer's family ever since. Messer's grandfather walked down the steps of the courthouse on his way to lunch. The clock began to chime and he stopped to look up at the face of the clock, as did a man sitting on the curb (Belton was "wet" at this time in its history and had a number of downtown saloons. The inebriate on the curb was something of a town drunk). The clock chimed once, twice …six times, seven times …eleven, twelve, thirteen, fourteen and fifteen. As he looked down to continue on

"THE CLOCK CHIMED ONCE, TWICE . . . SIX TIMES, SEVEN TIMES . . ."

JUDGE W.A. MESSER

his way, the clock still chiming, the town drunk, with wonder on his face, stated this truth: "You know it ain't never been so late before."

This notorious clock has been noted by many, even before this time. In 1943, Captain Henry Waskow, a farm boy from just north of Belton, leading his troops in the Monte Cassino fighting in Middle Italy, got a letter from his brother August, who was fighting elsewhere in Italy, saying, "I'm all right. Don't worry about this tough old bird and I'll hear the courthouse clock strike before you do." Henry's death in battle a couple of days after getting his brother's letter was poignantly described by Ernie Pyle in a Pulitzer Prize winning column, making Henry one of the most famous and best loved heroes of World War II and the epitome of the foot-soldier. So, in spirit at least, Henry heard the clock on this historic Bell County Courthouse chime before his brother August did when August returned home safely.

Where did Bell County get its name?
FROM GOVERNOR PETER HANSBOROUGH BELL, A VETERAN OF THE SAN JACINTO BATTLE, MEXICAN-AMERICAN WAR AND CIVIL WAR AND A TEXAS RANGER.

Where is the Bell County Courthouse located?
THE PRESENT BUILDING IS IN BELTON, TX, AT THE SOUTHEAST CORNER OF MAIN STREET AND CENTRAL AVENUE, WHICH IS THE THIRD COURTHOUSE IN BELL COUNTY BUILT ON THE SAME SITE.

Who designed the Bell County Courthouse?
JASPER N. PRESTON AND SONS DESIGNED THE 1884 HISTORIC COURTHOUSE IN A RENAISSANCE REVIVAL STYLE OF SANDSTONE, WHICH ORIGINATED IN GREEK AND ROMAN ARCHITECTURE AND IS ON THE NATIONAL REGISTER OF HISTORIC BUILDINGS.

What is the courthouse's most unusual feature?
IN 1999 THE STATUE, DOME AND CLOCK TOWER OF THE COURTHOUSE WERE REPLACED WITH REPLICAS OF THOSE FROM THE ORIGINAL STRUCTURE AND IS NOW ON THE NATIONAL REGISTER OF HISTORIC BUILDINGS. ON THE SOUTHWEST CORNER OF THE COURTHOUSE SQUARE STANDS A STATUE OF PETER HANSBOROUGH BELL, THE GOVERNOR WHO CREATED BELL COUNTY.

What is the most famous case tried in the Bell County Courthouse?
GEORGE HORNSBY WAS TRIED AND SENTENCED TO DEATH BY HANGING FOR THE CLAW-HAMMER MURDER OF WEALTHY BUSINESSMAN J.N. WEATHERBY TO STEAL HIS ENORMOUS DIAMOND STICK PIN. HORNSBY WAS CONVICTED LARGELY ON THE TESTIMONY OF A TEEN-AGED ACCOMPLICE, WHO LATER RECANTED AND THEN RECANTED HIS RECANTING. THOUSANDS OF BELL COUNTY RESIDENTS SIGNED A PETITION TO GOVERNOR PAT M. NEFF ASKING HIM TO COMMUTE THE DEATH SENTENCE, BUT GOVERNOR NEFF REFUSED AND HORNSBY WAS PUBLICLY HANGED IN 1922. HIS LAST WORDS, AND THOSE ON HIS TOMBSTONE, WERE "I AM INNOCENT." THE LASTING EFFECT WAS THAT IT BROUGHT TO A HEAD THE GROWING TEXAS REVULSION AGAINST PUBLIC HANGINGS AND HELPED PROD THE LEGISLATURE TO PASS A BILL SUBSTITUTING THE ELECTRIC CHAIR FOR THE HANGMAN'S NOOSE – SPONSORED BY BELL COUNTY'S STATE SENATOR.

Where do you hang your hat?
FOURTH-GENERATION BELL COUNTY ATTORNEY BILL MESSER HANGS HIS HAT IN BELTON AND AUSTIN. JIM BOWMER IS AFFILIATED WITH NAMAN, HOWELL, SMITH AND LEE.

Believe it or not!
DURING THE MID TO LATE 1860S, THE FAMED CHISHOLM TRAIL CUT THROUGH CENTRAL BELL COUNTY, ALONG A ROUTE BETWEEN THE PRESENT-DAY CITIES OF BELTON AND SALADO, TX!

Where did Bexar County get its name?

NAMED FOR VICEROY BALTHASAR MANUEL DE ZUNIGA Y GUZMAN SOTOMAYOR Y SARMIENTO, SECOND SON OF THE DUKE OF BEXAR IN 1718.

Where is the Bexar County Courthouse located?

IN DOWNTOWN SAN ANTONIO'S MAIN PLAZA, ACROSS THE STREET FROM SAN FERNANDO CATHEDRAL, WHERE GENERAL SANTA ANA DIRECTED HIS TROOPS AND OBSERVED THE ACTION IN THE BATTLE OF THE ALAMO.

Who designed the Bexar County Courthouse?

J. RIELY GORDON, A 27-YEAR-OLD ARCHITECT AND RESIDENT OF SAN ANTONIO DESIGNED THIS MAJESTIC 1897 HISTORIC COURTHOUSE AND NATIONAL REGISTER PROPERTY MADE OF STUNNING RED GRANITE. THE BEXAR COUNTY COURTHOUSE WAS REDEDICATED ON APRIL 4TH 2003, BY THE TEXAS HISTORICAL COMMISSIONS' TEXAS COURTHOUSE PRESERVATION PROGRAM.

What is the Courthouse's most unusual feature?

THE ONLY REMAINING ROMANESQUE REVIVAL STYLE STRUCTURE IN THE SAN ANTONIO AREA AND ITS DISTINCTIVE BEEHIVE TOWER.

What is the most famous case tried in the Bexar County Courthouse?

"LA CHANSA DE APOLINAR" MEANS "NOT A CHANCE IN HELL." IN 1921, CLEMENTE APOLINAR WAS A HOMELESS 29-YEAR-OLD MEXICAN AMERICAN WHO ESCAPED FROM AN ASYLUM AND ATTACKED A YOUNG BOY HERDING CATTLE WITH HIS YOUNGER BROTHER. APOLINAR CRUSHED 14-YEAR-OLD THEODORE BERNHARD'S SKULL AND GOUGED OUT HIS EYES. HE WAS CONVICTED BY A WHITE JURY LESS THAN A MONTH AFTER THE KILLING AND ORDERED "HANGED BY THE NECK UNTIL DEAD." A NINE-DAY INSANITY HEARING UPHELD THE CONVICTION. JUDGE S.G. TAYLOE PRONOUNCED HIS FIRST DEATH SENTENCE AND APOLINAR WAS THE LAST MAN HANGED IN BEXAR COUNTY IN THE JAIL HOUSE GALLOWS!

Where do you hang your hat?

SAN ANTONIO, RC BAR 7 RANCH AND NICHOLAS AND BARRERA, MAYBE THE OLDEST, UNCHANGED PARTNERSHIP, BOASTING 47 YEARS IN THE PRIVATE PRACTICE OF LAW. ANTHONY NICHOLAS' SON, STEPHEN, AND MY SONS, ROY JR. AND BOBBY, PRACTICE WITH THE FIRM. FOLLOWING CLOSE BEHIND ROY JR. IS HIS SON, ROY, III, AN ATTORNEY WITH THE FIRM OF JONAS AND TUGGE, AND ROY JR.'S TWINS, MARK, A SECOND YEAR STUDENT AT HARVARD LAW, AND MARISSA, A SECOND YEAR STUDENT AT BAYLOR LAW.

Believe it or not!

DURING RENOVATION / EXPANSION PROJECTS AT THE BEXAR COUNTY COURTHOUSE, CREWS UNCOVERED A GRAVESITE AND TWO AQUEDUCTS USED TO PROVIDE WATER FROM THE CENTRAL PART OF THE CITY TO SURROUNDING AREAS!

"I am 'not guilty,' I have been found 'not guilty' and what's more, I'll never do it again."

~ ROY'S FAMOUS TEXAS JUSTICE SAYING

"A Black Eye or Russian Roulette?"

A Famous Texas Case as Told by

ROY R. BARRERA, SR.

NICHOLAS AND BARRERA, P.C.

In over 53 years of practice, I have tried many criminal jury cases, both as a prosecutor in the District Attorney's office under Austin F. Anderson and Hubert Green, Jr., from 1951 to June, 1957, and as a defense lawyer from 1957 to the present. I have also tried and participated in numerous civil jury trials. Most of these trials have been of great interest and excitement to me as a trial lawyer.

One case that I investigated and participated in the prosecution of has left lasting memories with me. It was a case of police officer abuse, civil rights violations and obstruction of justice. This case was an example of a cover-up and official indifference to the killing of a black citizen by a police officer and an acquittal by an obviously prejudiced jury.

In 1954, John W. Caldwell, a black bar operator of "The Spot," was shot in the left temple by Police Officer O.R. Graves. Graves reported that he killed Caldwell in self-defense when Caldwell tried to cut him with a knife. This happened in the small back-office of "The Spot" in the presence of vice officers Myron Hubble and James Seibrecht.

It was reported that Caldwell was a whiskey "bootlegger" and that the police were attempting to have Caldwell open an office safe, which he refused to do. While the two vice officers were searching immediately outside the small back-office, they heard Caldwell curse Officer Graves and heard the shot, but did not see the shooting. They also heard the knife fall on the floor, apparently from Caldwell's hand, where it was found and photographed by homicide investigators. Caldwell was pictured sitting in a lean-back chair, left arm on the chair rest and the right arm hanging down with the right hand open, over the knife on the floor.

The Eastside community and its black leaders, Valmo Bellinger, G.J. Sutton, Archie Johnson, Reverend Claude Black and others, were incensed and appeared before the City Council, asking for the officers' suspension and a full investigation. They were answered with platitudes, generalities and assurances by the Chief of Police that he believed his officers report on the matter.

Bexar
County Courthouse

Although I was an assistant D.A., I was assigned to the investigation along with Investigator Joe Hester. I called in all three officers for sworn statements on their allegations of "justifiable homicide." Following their lawyers' advice, they refused to even swear to their skimpy police reports. We got busy and checked all vice reports by the officers on that day and found one case of aggravated assault. The officers were called to a bar where a knife had been used and given to them as evidence. The description of the knife fit the one found under Caldwell's hand. The original owner and user of that knife confirmed it was his and that Hubble and Seibrect had confiscated it from him.

> "[GRAVES] HAD BEGUN 'PLAYING RUSSIAN ROULETTE' WITH CALDWELL TO FRIGHTEN HIM INTO OPENING THE SAFE."

At the funeral home, where I first saw the body of Caldwell in the casket, I discovered an almost imperceptible "black eye" on the same side of the bullet entry wound on the temple. The medical examiner had overlooked this contusion, as it was not in his autopsy report. I called the medical examiner to have him confirm the "black eye," and he did. Although I suggested the impact of the bullet as the cause, he assured me it was a blow by a blunt instrument, "like a fist."

The Justice of the Peace coroner returned a ruling of justifiable homicide. The media headlines were unbelievable with charges and countercharges as we developed the facts regarding the planted knife and discovered a black witness who had been "relieving" himself behind the small office who overheard a "click" and then Caldwell say "I guess you're going to have to kill me because I don't know the combination to the safe." He heard the shot and ran away.

As the results of our investigation surfaced, the two vice officers, with their lawyers, came into the D.A.'s office and asked for and received immunity from prosecution in exchange for their cooperation and the truth of the events. This exchange for immunity was done without my knowledge and I certainly would not have agreed to it. I felt that our investigation was 95% complete and that all three could be indicted and convicted for murder and/or accomplices, obstruction of justice and other related offenses without their cooperation.

The officers admitted Graves had put his gun to Caldwell's temple after expelling all rounds but one in Caldwell's presence and had begun "playing Russian roulette" with Caldwell to frighten him into opening the safe. All three were present when the gun went off on the second trigger pull. All three panicked and that gave way to planting the knife and the self-defense cover story. Our investigation revealed that the vice officers, on their earlier aggravated assault case, made their report and substituted another knife for the one planted on Caldwell. After many legal and factual maneuvers, O.R. Graves was indicted for murder and because of the "black eye," we alleged a beating prior to the shooting. The case moved on a "change of venue" to Atascosa County, Texas.

Graves testified that he "played Russian roulette" with Caldwell, but misjudged the turn of the cylinder. He testified that the gun discharged on the second trigger pull; he believing that he still had three more before discharging and that he did not intend to kill Caldwell. The medical examiner reneged on the "black eye" by a fist and stated the bullet impact as the cause of the contusion. Graves admitted under cross examination that he had been negligent in doing what he did. We asked the Atascosa County District Judge for a lesser and included offense of "negligent homicide" in the charge to the jury. The judge finally consented to it, though he did not want to. After deliberating for about an hour, a "fair and impartial jury" of Atascosa citizens returned a verdict of "not guilty." The judge thanked the jury for their verdict and excused them. For the State, we were shocked! And the fifty to seventy-plus black citizens, friends and family of J.C. Caldwell were stunned into silence. Once more they were subjected to the bottom line; "That's the way it was fifty years ago."

I have retained lasting memories of that incident, its investigation and the verdict.

THE STATE OF TEXAS · COUNTY OF BEXAR

Tom Rickhoff, Judge
Probate Court 2
Bexar County Courthouse
100 Dolorosa STE 117
San Antonio, Texas 78205-3002
210-335-2580
210-335-2029 Fax

Dear Martana,

Every active trial lawyer in San Antonio suffers memories of Roy Barrera Sr. besting them in court. Roy was a redoubtable prosecutor to us law students in the 60's from the Supreme Court decision in Alcorta v Texas. I was doomed to contend with him in the mid 70's. Coming from the Organized Crime Strike Force of Department of Justice, opposing the finest lawyer's the Mafia could hire, I thought I was ready for the local legend. My father, a career trial lawyer and judge, visited my inaugural prosecution in San Antonio of a corrupt federal inspector. Roy was defending and selected an all Hispanic jury, I co operated…his client was Anglo. Roy's opening statement lapsed into a Spanish proverb about how the powerful mean beast eats the little helpless ones, and I think it contained some hilarious reference to testiscles but Dad and I were the only non Spanish speakers in the courtroom so I couldn't be sure. After Roy and the judge enjoyed a further exchange in Spanish I was able to observe that out of courtesy to visiting Yankees like myself federal trials are conducted in the King's English. After the acquittal the jury wrote "the prosecutor was trying too hard to get this little defendant", and my Dad said Roy was the finest trial lawyer he had seen.

In the 80's, while presiding judge I assigned myself the trial of another District Judge and Roy opted to exclude himself when his co-counsel brought a most serious quo warranto to remove me from office. He may have assumed I therefore trusted him when later he dumped in my lap a one armed, 69 year old, chicken farmer for sentencing. Woodrow waltzed into a local hospital and frightened nurses when he kept one bullet in his six shooter--after unloading the other five in his brother's chest as he laid in his hospital bed. Roy passed on jury sentencing, life was the max, and I gave Woodrow ten years probation and made him work in a nursing home. Roy presented the widow as a witness who explained the deceased did not want to live; suffered from severe Alzheimer's and the legislature should have allowed a way of ending such pain. When I asked what sentence to give she said, "God will guide you." I didn't feel any special intervention; except from Roy who covered me with a great record. Woodrow served admirably and later ran for office.

I thought I was the star of the resulting 60 minutes special while Roy, due to his subdued ego, would have a bit part. Later, the paper reported that after the segment aired my wife told me, "Well you didn't say anything . . .but at least you didn't say anything stupid." Roy had taken Ed "the gourmet" Bradley out for Mexican food so his far more profound comments aired. "We must all accept that people should be allowed to go to their end in dignity." Will someone please shoot me!

Sincerely,

Tom Rickhoff

"Emma 'Straight Eight' Oliver & Judge McCrory"

A Famous Texas Case as Told by
ROY R. BARRERA, JR.
NICHOLAS AND BARRERA, P.C.

As the abundance of landmark and otherwise interesting trials in the Texas Justice book attest to, there is certainly no shortage of entertaining material concerning Texas court cases. However, it is safe to say that in the majority of these, the interest lies in the facts of the cases itself, the character of the defendant or the prowess of the attorneys involved. This was not the situation in Emma "Straight Eight" Oliver's San Antonio murder trial in 1951.

Emma Oliver was certainly a newsworthy figure, as she had been charged with and found guilty of murder. As if that were not dramatic enough, this was, in fact, her third murder conviction. This particular trial I speak of resulted in Emma being sentenced to death. All of this news, however, would quickly take a backseat when rumors began to surface about the corruption of the case itself and the judge accused of being at the heart of it all.

Not long after the verdict was read, the papers were printing stories about the possibility that Judge W.W. McCrory had entered into a deal with the District Attorney, Hensley, ultimately affecting the overall outcome of the case. It was reported that Judge McCrory had entered into a verbal agreement with Hensley that the judge would overrule the request for a new trial; if in return; Mr. Hensley would join Judge McCrory in a request for clemency. Indeed, Judge McCrory did deny the request for a new trial and ultimately, the board of pardons did recommend clemency for Emma Oliver, but the question of whether or not either of these things were part of this supposed deal was the debate and most importantly whether this deal had occurred before or after the request for a new trial had been denied.

With enough information to suggest that such a deal did indeed exist, the bar association formed a committee to begin investigating. When they announced the formation of such a committee, they also let it be known that ten practicing attorneys could, under oath before a judge of a court of record, present causes against Judge McCrory. These causes would then be heard by the Supreme Court which would ultimately have the power to remove him. Solving the issue was greatly complicated by the fact that D.A. Hensley died prior to the investigation. It seemed the judge himself was the sole authority on the issue. The most important issue for the investigation committee to resolve was two

SAN ANTONIO TEXAS · A Constructive Force in the Community

NEWSPAPER

PRICE 5 CENTS

38 PAGES

the Associated Press

WEDNESDAY, JUNE 6, 1951

Deal Probed

fold; 1) if there was such an intentional and binding deal made between the judge and the D.A. and 2) most importantly if there was such a deal, if it occurred before or after the judge had made the decision to overrule the motion for a new trial.

A major piece of evidence the investigation committee focused on was actually a letter written by the judge to the board of pardons and paroles. In this letter, the judge expressly states that he did make a deal with Hensley, but to the opposite effect. In the letter, he says the deal was that they would let the case go to the Court of Appeals where they were certain it was to be upheld, and at that point, they would jointly ask that the governor commute the sentence to life imprisonment. Also taken as evidence was the testimony of Sheriff Owen W. Kilday who testified that he heard the judge state the contrary; the reason he refused the new trial was because of a deal that he made with Hensley. The judge would then later go on to say that there never was such a deal and that any conversation between he and Hensley on the issue was certainly not to be interpreted by either party as anything more than discussion.

The judge went even further in his own defense to say that the whole scandal had been spun by Attorney Bernard Ladon and his go-to-boy, Jesse Oppenheimer. McCrory contested that he and Ladon had a long standing feud and that it was his request that led the San Antonio Bar Association to create the investigation committee. The judge continued by saying that it was his understanding that they were hard pressed to find lawyers to even serve on that committee and those that were serving had never even practiced in the judge's court.

With all of the, "he said, she said, oh no he didn't say. . ." in this case, the committee certainly had their work cut out for them. After it was all said and done, the Bar Association made their findings public. They stated that while there were reports of the alleged deal, the judge denied this under oath, and more importantly, there was no evidence that this deal was made before the motion to deny a new trial. It was their recommendation that there be no censure of Judge McCrory—an interesting end to a bizarre twist in an already newsworthy case.

". . . THE PAPERS WERE PRINTING STORIES ABOUT THE POSSIBILITY THAT JUDGE W.W. McCRORY HAD ENTERED INTO A DEAL WITH THE DISTRICT ATTORNEY . . ."

Censure In Oliver Case Inquiry

The San Antonio Bar Association made public Wednesday...

Top Gun & Legal Eagle
Robert J. "Bobby" Barrera

★ RECEIVED AN ACQUITTAL IN A CAPITAL MURDER TRIAL WHEREIN A MOTHER CONFESSED TO SMOTHERING HER 15-MONTH-OLD CHILD TO DEATH WITH A PILLOW—THIS WAS THE 2ND CHILD WHICH SHE WAS ACCUSED OF KILLING IN THE SAME MANNER

★ SAT 1ST CHAIR WITH FATHER, ROY BARRERA, SR., IN A HIGH-PROFILE AGGRAVATED SEXUAL ASSAULT CASE OF A SAN ANTONIO POLITICAL POWERBROKER THAT RESULTED IN AN ACQUITTAL

★ CLIMBED 19,500 FEET TO THE PEAK OF MOUNT KILIMANJARO TO WATCH THE SUN RISE OVER THE AFRICAN CONTINENT

★ ATTAINED SEVEN BOW HUNTING TROPHY RECORDS, RANKING IN THE TOP TEN IN THE WORLD FOR EACH SPECIES

★ TOOK A SIX-MONTH CROSS-COUNTRY "WALK-ABOUT" PHOTOGRAPHING AFRICAN WILDLIFE

★ BUILT BY HIS OWN HAND, UTILIZING OLD BARN LUMBER AND TIN, A TWO-STORY LOFT CABIN AT THE FAMILY RANCH

★ PRESIDENT OF SAN ANTONIO YOUNG LAWYERS ASSOCIATION

★ INVITED BY PRESIDENT GEORGE W. BUSH TO PARTICIPATE IN THE INAUGURAL CELEBRATION

★ FLEW ON AIR FORCE II WITH PRESIDENT GEORGE BUSH ON A "GET OUT THE VOTE" TEXAS TOUR

Brazoria County Courthouse

"Showdown at the Courthouse"

A Famous Texas Case as Told by

SCOTT D. LASSETTER
WEIL, GOTSHAL & MANGES

More than sixty years ago, H.H. Dow chose this steamy land along the Texas Gulf Coast to build what would become the largest chemical plant in North America. Since then, Brazoria County's huge chemical production has been matched only by its record for producing huge plaintiffs' verdicts. Defense lawyers nationwide know its reputation well and few are willing to become the next notch on the courthouse wall.

One notable exception is Scott Lassetter, a trial lawyer who earned his spurs trying and winning the ugliest of cases in the nastiest of venues all across America. More than any other place, however, Mr. Lassetter built his reputation in Brazoria County with an unparalleled record of sixteen straight gritty defense verdicts. This record of winning against all odds led to Mr. Lassetter being named by the Texas Lawyer as its "Go-To Lawyer" of 2002, the number-one rated personal injury trial lawyer in the State of Texas, and featured in profiles in *The Wall Street Journal, The National Law Journal, The American Lawyer,* and *Texas Monthly's* Guide to "Super Lawyers."

With great success comes even greater challenges and word soon spread that Mr. Lassetter was the lawyer to call when the stakes couldn't be higher. Until 1996, General Motors had settled all lawsuits alleging defects in the door latches it had used for more than a decade. The plaintiffs' bar had amassed a treasure trove of inflammatory documents authored by GM engineers that detailed

"One Riot, One Ranger."
~ Scott's Famous Texas Justice Saying

problems with the latch, as well as crash tests which showed doors opening at an alarming rate.

Now GM was set for trial in a case involving an 18-year-old girl who had been severely brain damaged in a tragic accident in which her door had come open. The settlement demand was astronomical and non-negotiable. Trial was only a few months away and GM wanted Mr. Lassetter. The venue was Brazoria County. "Plaintiffs verdicts are glorified in the media as though David has beaten Goliath yet again," says Mr. Lassetter, "but real justice often means having the courage to fight cases built on sympathy. It's hard, but the truth is a powerful weapon."

Mr. Lassetter wasted no time. First, he studied the accident. Physical evidence indicated that the plaintiff had tried to speed around the big truck in her path. Mr. Lassetter also concluded from the plaintiff's injury pattern that she had not worn her seatbelt. These were important new defenses. Next, Mr. Lassetter learned everything possible about the product. He studied every test, talked to the engineers involved and buried himself in charts and films. He tested competitors' door latches and determined that GM's latch performed better than most. Finally, Mr. Lassetter confirmed his theories by reproducing the accident. He ran a series of crash tests and showed that the young girl had been speeding, accelerated rather than braked and was not wearing her seatbelt. Most importantly, high-speed films proved that the door had come open after the girl was already injured.

"PLAINTIFFS VERDICTS ARE GLORIFIED IN THE MEDIA AS THOUGH DAVID HAS BEATEN GOLIATH YET AGAIN. . ."

Word of the showdown at the courthouse spread through Brazoria County like wildfire. For three weeks, damaging evidence about the GM latches was introduced, but it was the defense that got stronger with each passing day. A unanimous verdict was sealed: the door latch was found to be free of defects and no damages were awarded. Mr. Lassetter had beaten the odds once again.

Two months later, a different lawyer took a similar case to trial. The jury in that case found the latch defective and assessed damages against GM in the amount of $150 million. General Motors soon hired Mr. Lassetter to lead the defense of door latch cases nationwide. To this day, Mr. Lassetter has yet to see his winning streak broken despite many trials in hot spots ranging from Alabama all the way to Chicago—and he still likes trying cases in Brazoria County.

Where did Brazoria County get its name?
BRAZORIA COUNTY IS NAMED FOR THE BRAZOS RIVER, WHERE STEPHEN F. AUSTIN SETTLED HIS TEXAS COLONIES.

Where is the Brazoria County Courthouse located?
THE COUNTY SEAT WAS MOVED FROM THE CITY OF BRAZORIA IN 1897 TO THE RAILROAD TOWN OF ANGLETON, WHICH IS CURRENTLY WHERE THE COURTHOUSES ARE LOCATED.

Who designed the Brazoria County Courthouse?
THE 1897 HISTORIC COURTHOUSE IS NOW A MUSEUM AND LIBRARY AND WAS DESIGNED BY EUGENE T. HEINER IN THE ITALIAN RENAISSANCE STYLE. THE HISTORIC COURTHOUSE OF 1940 WAS DESIGNED BY LAMAR Q. CATO IN A MODERNE STYLE OF INDIANA GRANITE AND LIMESTONE.

What is the Courthouse's most unusual feature?
ITS CONJOINED BUILDINGS OF THE 1940 AND THE NEW 1976 COURTHOUSES, BUILT 36 YEARS APART, BUT MADE INTO ONE BUILDING OF BRICK AND STONE. THE 1976 STRUCTURE IS EXTREMELY CONTEMPORARY IN BRICK, WHILE THE OTHER SIDE OF THE BUILDING WAS BUILT IN INDIANA GRANITE AND LIMESTONE AND WAS ERECTED IN 1940 MODERNE STYLE.

What is the most famous case tried in the Brazoria County Courthouse?
TURNER V. GENERAL MOTORS ESTABLISHED THE DOCTRINE OF "CRASHWORTHINESS" IN TEXAS PRODUCTS LIABILITY LAW. THIS CASE SET THE STAGE FOR THE TRIAL STORY WE TELL IN TEXAS JUSTICE.

Where do you hang your hat?
IN HOUSTON, TX, WHERE I AM THE MANAGING PARTNER OF THE HOUSTON OFFICE OF WEIL, GOTSHAL & MANGES DEFENDING CORPORATIONS IN LAWSUITS ALLEGING SUCH THINGS AS PRODUCT DEFECTS, CORPORATE FRAUD AND PATENT INFRINGEMENT, WITH DAMAGES OFTEN IN THE MANY BILLIONS OF DOLLARS.

Believe it or not!
MR. LASSETTER WAS A RODEO COWBOY BEFORE HE WENT TO LAW SCHOOL!

Where did Brown County get its name?

NAMED IN HONOR OF HENRY STEVENSON BROWN, AN EARLY TEXAS MERCHANT AND FAMOUS INDIAN FIGHTER.

Where is the Brown County Courthouse located?

IN BROWNWOOD, THE HEART OF TEXAS, TWENTY-FIVE MILES FROM THE EXACT GEOGRAPHIC CENTER OF THE STATE.

Who designed the Brown County Courthouse?

UNKNOWN. THE ORIGINAL COURTHOUSE FOR THE COUNTY WAS A FRONTIER LOG CABIN. THE CURRENT HISTORICAL CLASSICAL REVIVAL BRICK COURTHOUSE WAS COMPLETED IN 1917 AND WAS TECHNICALLY A "REPAIR" OF THE ORIGINAL 1884 COURTHOUSE WHICH REPLACED THE 1880 COURTHOUSE DESTROYED IN A FIRE.

What is the Courthouse's most unusual feature?

THE MASSIVE VAULT LOCATED IN THE HEART OF THE COURTHOUSE IS THE ONLY ORIGINAL FEATURE SURVIVING FROM THE 1884 STRUCTURE.

What is the most famous case tried in the Brown County Courthouse?

IN 1993, A BROWN COUNTY JURY CONVICTED AND SENTENCED RICKY MCGINN TO DEATH IN THE AX-MURDER AND RAPE OF HIS 12-YEAR-OLD STEP-DAUGHTER. SEVEN YEARS LATER, GOVERNOR GEORGE W. BUSH GRANTED THE CONVICTED MURDERER'S DEATH SENTENCE A THIRTY DAY POSTPONEMENT DUE TO CLAIMS OF INNOCENCE. MCGINN'S APPEAL WAS DENIED AND HE WAS EXECUTED ON SEPTEMBER 27, 2000, BY LETHAL INJECTION.

Where do you hang your hat?

IN DALLAS, TX, AND AT MY HILL COUNTRY RANCH IN KATEMCY, TX. PRESENTLY CEO OF CONSOLIDATED RESTAURANT COMPANIES, INC. ("CRO"), WHICH OWNS 140 RESTAURANTS IN 17 STATES AND CANADA. CRO HAS 6,500 EMPLOYEES AND OPERATES SUCH WELL KNOWN BRANDS AS III FORKS, SILVER FOX, COOL RIVER, CANTINA LAREDO, EL CHICO, SPAGHETTI WAREHOUSE, GOOD EATS AND LUCKY'S.

Believe it or not!

AS A TRIBUTE TO BROWNWOOD'S CRITICAL ROLE AS THE HOME OF THE LARGEST WORLD WAR II ARMY BASE IN THE NATION, GENERAL DOUGLAS MACARTHUR BEQUEST HIS FULL COLLECTION OF WAR MEMORABILIA TO THE COMMUNITY!

"The most important thing in life is finding a game worth playing. Then once you have found the game, play it as though your life depends upon it."

~ JOHN'S FAMOUS TEXAS JUSTICE SAYING

"The Outlaw & the Sheriff with a Vengeance"

A Famous Texas Case as Told by

JOHN D. HARKEY JR.

JOHN D. HARKEY JR. P.C.
ATTORNEY AT LAW

John Wesley Hardin, born in 1853, was the son of a Methodist preacher, but became one of the most infamous Texan outlaws in Brown County history. A member of the notorious Doolin gang, Hardin killed his first man at the age of twelve. This would begin his lifelong relationship with crime and his run from the law. At fifteen, in Polk County, he shot and killed a black man as a result of an argument on the street. In 1871, Hardin hired on as a cowboy on the Chisholm Trail where he killed seven people on the journey and then three more in Abilene, Kansas.

Hardin's streak of murders continued through his adulthood. It was not until 1873 that he was personally wounded for the first time. Shot in the stomach while arguing over a gambling debt, he found it more difficult to run from authorities and finally surrendered himself to the Smiley County, Texas, sheriff. Hardin soon learned however that the state police were in route to take him into custody. He made a hasty escape to Gonzales. While in Gonzales, he became involved in a family feud between the Taylor and Sutton families and led the Taylor faction in killing members of the Sutton clan and their supporters. With these latest murders, the Texas Governor personally took interest in capturing Hardin and enlisted the help of law enforcement officials state wide to catch the outlaw. Brown County sheriff Charles Webb accepted this challenge with a vengeance and swore that he would personally find and kill the fugitive Hardin.

Brown
County Courthouse

Webb rode to Comanche where he understood Hardin was betting at a horse track. The sheriff was smart and knew it would be disastrous to approach the outlaw alone while he was with his friends. Enlisting the help of several Brown County residents, he patiently waited at Jack Wright's saloon where Hardin had planned his 21st birthday celebration. When Hardin arrived at the saloon, a brawl ensued; the sheriff convinced him he was not there to start trouble. As Hardin reholstered his gun, the sheriff drew. Hardin instinctively reacted, shot and killed Webb before he could even fire his gun. Hardin fled. His gang was apprehended and transported to the jail. Later that night, Brown County residents stormed the jail and lynched three men.

"AS HARDIN REHOLSTERED HIS GUN, THE SHERIFF DREW."

Hardin fled to Alabama, where he became a saloonkeeper and adopted a new alias. The Texas Rangers were, however, on his trail and captured him, returning him to Texas to stand trial. Hardin served nineteen years before being pardoned in 1894. While in prison, he unsuccessfully attempted to escape dozens of times. He began to study theology and law and was elected superintendent of the prison's Sunday school. Following his release, Hardin was admitted to the bar and reportedly became a fine lawyer and law abiding citizen until his death.

Cameron
County Courthouse

ROGGE DUNN RIDES THE CAMERON
COUNTY TRAIN FOR JUSTICE.

"Prejudice v. Justice"

A Famous Texas Case as Told by
ROGGE DUNN
CLOUSE DUNN HIRSCH LLP

Few places lie deeper in the Deep South than Brownsville, located closer to the equator and further from the Mason-Dixon Line than any place in Texas. It is also the southernmost point in the continental United States.

In 1910, less than half a century after the abolition of slavery and with a melting pot brewing Mexican and American cultures, one would expect Brownsville to be a racially hostile environment. Racial harmony, which is now prized in present day Cameron County, was not always the case in the early part of the 20th century.

But location and timing are not everything. Texas towns are defined by the character of their residents and the quality of their chili. While few have the guts to bring Cameron County's chili to the test, the character of its residents was tested in the winter of 1910 at the murder trial of Marcellus Dougherty.

At one o'clock in the afternoon of April 23, 1909, a train carrying Mr. F. Brewer pulls into Brownsville. Brewer is a black man working as a Pullman porter on the train. He is a proud, stout and robust 34-year-old man. By two o'clock he is scuffling with Marcellus Dougherty in the middle of the main boulevard. Dougherty is 50 years old, weak and partially disabled. Dougherty is a lifelong Brownsville resident.

Unarmed, Brewer grabs Dougherty's right hand, which is holding a pistol. As they struggle, Brewer manages to break free and starts to run away. Before Brewer can escape, Dougherty fires his blue-barrel .44, hitting Brewer in the chest. Brewer gasps "I am shot," stumbles down the

> *"A young lawyer knows the law;
> an old lawyer knows the exceptions."*
>
> ~ ROGGE'S FAMOUS TEXAS JUSTICE SAYING

street and collapses in front of two buggies. Dougherty has no injuries. This is what eyewitness Henry Klause, a long-time friend of defendant Dougherty, saw and will testify to at trial.

The authorities seek a first degree and second degree murder conviction. The defendant wants an acquittal based on self-defense.

The case seems clear cut, even in the Deep South of the early 1900s. However, variations in the eyewitness testimony require the jury to search for truth and justice.

The defendant relies on Al Carpenter's testimony, which appears to be based on prejudice rather than fact. Carpenter testifies that "the negro" ran away from Dougherty but then turned, bent forwards and ran towards him. Carpenter says "the favorite way of a negro to fight is to butt a man with his head; and from what I have seen in the South, that's the way they do it; that's what it looked like to me."

Jury deliberations are heated. At first, several jurors refuse to even consider a guilty verdict. If the jurors embrace Carpenter's biased testimony, they can easily acquit Dougherty based upon a reasonable doubt. Will they choose to convict a white, lifelong local resident who killed an out-of-towner African-American who is a total stranger? Somehow justice

> ## "TEXAS TOWNS ARE DEFINED BY THE CHARACTER OF THEIR RESIDENTS AND THE QUALITY OF THEIR CHILI."

prevails in the jury room. One by one, the jurors agree that Dougherty is guilty of second degree murder. The Texas Court of Criminal Appeals affirms their guilty verdict.

Thus, in 1910, the citizens in the southernmost part of our state and country showed the world the strength of Texas justice. Faced with an opportunity to choose between prejudice and justice, they chose to uphold justice. It all happened in the Cameron County Courthouse nearly 100 years ago. Then, as today, the citizens of Cameron County are able to celebrate diversity and justice, proud not only of their strong chili, but of their strong character.

Where did Cameron County get its name?

FROM A LEADER OF THE MIER EXPEDITION, SCOT EWEN CAMERON, WHO WAS A SCOT HIGHLANDER PROMINENT IN THE TEXAS REVOLUTION. DURING THE INFAMOUS BLACK BEAN AFFAIR, CAMERON GOT A WHITE BEAN, BUT WAS SHOT BY SANTA ANNA ON THE WAY TO MEXICO CITY IN 1843.

Where is the Cameron County Courthouse located?

THE HISTORICAL 1912 COURTHOUSE IS LOCATED IN BROWNSVILLE, TX, AT THE CORNER OF 11TH AND MONROE STREETS. CAMERON COUNTY HAS HAD THREE COURTHOUSES: 1812, 1912 AND THE CURRENT ONE.

Who designed the Cameron County Courthouse?

ATLEE B. AYRES DESIGNED THIS BEAUTIFUL HISTORIC COURTHOUSE TEXAS RENAISSANCE AND CLASSICAL REVIVAL STRUCTURE OF BRICK AND TERRA COTTA IN 1912.

What is the courthouse's most unusual feature?

ITS STUNNING STAINED GLASS DOME AND THE OPEN ROTUNDA WHICH TRAVELS UP THROUGH THREE FLOORS.

What is the most famous case tried in the Cameron County Courthouse?

THE TRIAL OF FREDA "SUSIE" MOWBRAY FOR THE MURDER OF HER HUSBAND IN 1987. IT WAS BELIEVED THAT SHE KILLED HER HUSBAND TO COLLECT HIS $1.8 MILLION INSURANCE POLICY, BUT SHE CLAIMED HE KILLED HIMSELF BECAUSE OF FINANCIAL PROBLEMS, AND THIS WAS HIS THIRD ATTEMPT. IN 1988, SHE WAS SENTENCED TO LIFE IN PRISON, BUT AN APPEALS COURT OVERTURNED THE CONVICTION IN 1997 AND THE JURY FOUND HER "NOT GUILTY."

Where do you hang your hat?

IN DOWNTOWN DALLAS WHERE MR. DUNN IS ONE OF ONLY TWENTY ATTORNEYS IN TEXAS WHO IS BOARD CERTIFIED IN BOTH CIVIL TRIAL LAW AND LABOR AND EMPLOYMENT LAW. HE REPRESENTS CORPORATIONS AND INDIVIDUALS IN CASES INVOLVING COMMERCIAL DISPUTES, EMPLOYMENT LAW, PARTNERSHIP ISSUES, ARBITRATIONS AND CLASS ACTIONS. HE HAS WON MORE THAN $200 MILLION IN VERDICTS AND SETTLEMENTS FOR HIS PLAINTIFF CLIENTS, INCLUDING A $58 MILLION VERDICT FOR ACTUAL DAMAGES IN NEW ORLEANS. THIS CASE SET THE RECORD AS THE LARGEST PRODUCTS LIABILITY VERDICT IN LOUISIANA HISTORY.

Believe it or not!

THE LAST BATTLE OF THE WAR BETWEEN THE STATES WAS FOUGHT IN BROWNSVILLE, NEARLY FIVE WEEKS AFTER CONFEDERATE GENERAL ROBERT E. LEE SURRENDERED!

Camp
County Courthouse

"Shoot-Out at the Train Depot"

A Famous Texas Case as Told by

MICHAEL P. SETTY
MICHAEL P. SETTY ATTORNEY AT LAW

The most notorious legal incident in Camp County history took place in 1885 and involved two timeless themes; the "love triangle" and the "courthouse turf war." Annie Collins Smart (age 19), wife of M. D. "Dallas" Smart (age 40) visited her parents in Arizona and while there, met U.S. Army Lieutenant John W. Heard (age 25) from Mississippi. Annie Smart returned home to Camp County and Lt. Heard took a furlough and soon arrived in Pittsburg. Upon his arrival, he began "visiting" Annie Smart while her husband was at work.

Dallas Smart quickly asked his friend, Camp County Sheriff James D. Stafford, to arrest Lt. Heard. He arrested him that day, charging him with a robbery that took place in Sulphur Springs. Unfortunately for the sheriff, Heard had an alibi and he was forced to release him.

Dallas Smart then asked a group of friends to "visit" with Heard. This resulted in Heard quickly leaving for the depot to board a train and depart Pittsburg. Late that evening, however, Dallas Smart and his group of friends came armed to the depot for a confrontation with Lt. Heard. After a discussion, Smart shot Lt. Heard, the bullet passing through the lapel of Lt. Heard's coat and leaving powder burns on his neck. Lt. Heard shot at Dallas Smart one time, that shot going through Dallas Smart's heart, killing him instantly. Two men in Dallas Smart's group then fired nine shots at Lt. Heard, all missing him.

Lt. Heard quickly turned himself over to Camp County officials. The next day, Camp County Judge M.N. Brooks conducted a preliminary hearing and ruled Heard was justified in killing Smart. Judge Brooks ordered that Lt. Heard be released and placed on the next train out of Pittsburg. Sheriff

"The Code of East Texas: Do unto others before they can do it to you."

~ MIKE'S FAMOUS TEXAS JUSTICE SAYING

Stafford, upset with Judge Brooks' ruling, re-arrested Lt. Heard on the train and took him to Gilmer (in Upshur County) to be held for the death of Dallas Smart. The sheriff was then ordered by Judge Brooks to release Lt. Heard.

Judge Brooks' actions caused considerable controversy in Camp County. Under Texas law at the time, County Judges could conduct preliminary hearings, thereby allowing an individual to avoid trial. Sheriff Stafford wrote the Texas Attorney General attempting to get a ruling that Judge Brooks could not release Lt. Heard without bail. Sheriff Stafford also contacted Mississippi authorities and had Lt. Heard arrested and held pending a determination by the Texas Attorney General. On March 3, 1885, the Texas Attorney General determined that County Judge Brooks was acting in the capacity of a magistrate and, therefore, had acted properly. Lt. Heard was again released.

Heard soon returned to the military, where he faced a Court Martial on three charges of "conduct unbecoming of an officer." (Sheriff Stafford was reportedly behind these charges). One charge involved Lt. Heard telling

"UPON HIS ARRIVAL, HE BEGAN 'VISITING' ANNIE SMART WHILE HER HUSBAND WAS AT WORK."

Annie Smart's father, "if you procure a divorce of your daughter from her husband, I will marry her." Lt. Heard was acquitted by the U. S. Army.

In July, 1885, Sheriff Stafford convinced a Camp County Grand Jury to present a bill against Lt. Heard for the murder of Dallas Smart. The case was tried in the old Camp County Courthouse before a district judge and jury in December, 1885. The jury was sent out that night and after fifteen minutes deliberation, returned a verdict of "Not Guilty".

Sheriff Stafford did, however, get the last laugh in his battle against Judge Brooks. In 1886, the sheriff arrested Judge Brooks for accepting a bribe. After trial of the bribery charge, Sheriff Stafford took Judge Brooks into custody to transport him to the penitentiary. Judge Brooks shot and killed himself while in the custody of Sheriff Stafford.

Where did Camp County get its name?

CAMP COUNTY WAS NAMED FOR COLONEL JOHN L. CAMP, A LAWYER, JUDGE, CONFEDERATE COLONEL IN THE 14TH TEXAS REGIMENT, MEMBER OF THE CONSTITUTIONAL CONVENTION OF 1866 AND TEXAS SENATOR IN 1874.

Where is the Camp County Courthouse located?

IN PITTSBURG, TX, CAMP COUNTY IS THE PROUD BIRTHPLACE OF RACING LEGEND AND CAR DESIGNER CARROLL SHELBY AND HOME TO BO PILGRIM OF PILGRIM'S PRIDE CHICKEN.

Who designed the Camp County Courthouse?

SMITH AND PRAEGER OF PARIS (TEXAS THAT IS!) DESIGNED THE HISTORIC COURTHOUSE IN 1928. IT IS A TEXAS RENAISSANCE STYLE WITH CLASSICAL REVIVAL ELEMENTS AND PRAIRIE SCHOOL INFLUENCE.

What is the courthouse's most unusual feature?

EACH SIDE OF THE COURTHOUSE HAS AN INVITING COLUMNED PORCH ENTRANCE THAT WELCOMES VISITORS.

What is the most famous case tried in the Camp County Courthouse?

JEFF HAGEN V. TEXAS OIL AND GAS CORPORATION WAS TRIED IN THE 1970S AND CERTIFIED AS A CLASS ACTION. LOCAL LAWYERS REPRESENTED LOCAL MINERAL INTEREST OWNERS AGAINST TEXAS OIL AND GAS CORPORATION AND OTHERS, ALLEGING THEY HAD ARTIFICIALLY RAISED PRODUCTION AND SALE COSTS TO REDUCE ROYALTIES PAID TO THE INTEREST OWNERS. IT RESULTED IN A JUDGMENT FOR THE PLAINTIFFS IN EXCESS OF $1 MILLION AND A FIASCO IN THE LOCAL DISTRICT CLERK'S OFFICE ATTEMPTING TO SEND OUT NET CHECKS TO ALL MEMBERS OF THE PLAINTIFF CLASS.

Where do you hang your hat?

I MOVED TO CAMP COUNTY AND ESTABLISHED MY LAW PRACTICE IN 1977. SINCE 1980, I HAVE OFFICED ON COLLEGE STREET, IN PITTSBURG, TX. MY PRACTICE HAS PRIMARILY BEEN A GENERAL CIVIL PRACTICE, WITH PARTICULAR EMPHASIS ON REAL ESTATE, PROBATE, BANKING, BUSINESS AND MUNICIPAL MATTERS.

Believe it or not!

AROUND 1901, BURRELL B. CANNON, A LOCAL, BUILT AN AIRCRAFT CONSISTING OF FABRIC-COVERED WINGS AND POWERED BY AN ENGINE THAT TURNED FOUR SETS OF PADDLES. HE BASED HIS DESIGN ON A DESCRIPTION IN THE BOOK OF EZEKIEL. HE ATTEMPTED TO FLY IT NEARLY ONE YEAR BEFORE THE WRIGHT BROTHERS SUCCESSFUL FLIGHT IN NORTH CAROLINA!

Where did Cass County get its name?

CASS COUNTY WAS ORIGINALLY NAMED IN 1846 FOR LEWIS CASS, A U.S. SENATOR FROM MICHIGAN WHO FAVORED THE ANNEXATION OF TEXAS. HE WAS KNOWN AS A NORTHERN MAN WITH SOUTHERN PRINCIPLES UNTIL HE RESIGNED HIS POST AS SECRETARY OF STATE WHEN PRESIDENT JAMES BUCHANAN DID NOT REINFORCE THE FORTS IN CHARLESTON, SOUTH CAROLINA. WHEN WORD OF HIS ACTIONS REACHED TEXAS, THE NAME OF THE COUNTY WAS CHANGED TO DAVIS IN HONOR OF JEFFERSON DAVIS. IT WAS CHANGED BACK TO CASS IN 1871.

Where is the Cass County Courthouse located?

IN "MUSIC CITY, TEXAS" (AKA LINDEN, TX)—JUST A TWO-STEP AWAY FROM THE MUSIC CITY TEXAS THEATER. LINDEN IS HOME TO SUCH MUSICAL LEGENDS AS DON HENLEY, SCOTT JOPLIN AND T-BONE WALKER.

Who designed the Cass County Courthouse?

COUNTY JUDGE CHARLES AMES DESIGNED THE 1866 HISTORIC CASS COUNTY COURTHOUSE IN ITS BRICK CLASSICAL REVIVAL STYLE. IT FEATURES TWO-STORY GABLED PORCHES SUPPORTED BY COLUMNS ON ITS NORTH AND SOUTH SIDES. 1866.

What is the courthouse's most unusual feature?

ITS AGE—THE COURTHOUSE IS THE OLDEST COURTHOUSE IN CONTINUOUS USE IN THE STATE OF TEXAS AND THE ONLY REMAINING ANTEBELLUM COURTHOUSE!

What is the most famous case tried in the Cass County Courthouse?

THE MOST RECENT FAMOUS CASE TRIED IN CASS COUNTY WAS WHEN KIM LAIRD FACED CAPITAL MURDER CHARGES IN THE FEBRUARY 2000 DEATH OF 1-YEAR-OLD MICHAEL SHANE ANDREWS JR., WHO WAS IN HER CARE. LAIRD WAS FOUND NOT GUILTY. LAIRD WAS REPRESENTED BY MR. CARNEY'S GOOD FRIENDS, DONALD DOWD, AN ATTORNEY IN LINDEN, TX, AND CORKY STOVALL OF HUGHES SPRINGS, TX.

Where do you hang your hat?

ATLANTA, TX, WHERE I AM SEMI-RETIRED FROM THE PRACTICE OF LAW TO SPEND MORE TIME WITH MY WIFE, CHILDREN AND GRANDCHILDREN AND TO TRAVEL AND PLAY GOLF. I PRACTICED LAW AS A GENERAL PRACTITIONER FOR 36 YEARS WITH THE FIRM MY GRANDFATHER STARTED, CARNEY & MAYS

Believe it or not!

CASS COUNTY WAS THE HOME OF THE LAST AMERICAN ENLISTED SERVICEMAN KILLED IN ACTION JUST HOURS BEFORE THE PARIS PEACE ACCORDS WERE SIGNED ON JANUARY 27, 1973, ENDING U.S. INVOLVEMENT IN THE VIETNAM WAR. A PLAQUE ON THE COURTHOUSE LAWN HONORS THOSE WHO LOST THEIR LIVES IN WAR!

"Justice is best served when a lawyer is fair and honest with his clients, works hard and is well prepared and does the very best he can to represent his client."

~ HOWARD'S FAMOUS TEXAS JUSTICE SAYING

"Just Walking My Dog, Judge"

A Famous Texas Case as Told by
HOWARD CARNEY JR.
HOWARD CARNEY, JR., ATTORNEY AT LAW

In my experience as an attorney, I have tried some very exciting and high-profile criminal cases that I will never forget and this is one of them. While this burglary case that I tried many years ago may not be a famous case, it certainly teaches us a valuable lesson and the facts and the result were very interesting.

I was a hard working general practitioner with a very successful law career, involved in many different types of cases I was court appointed to defend an indigent elderly man for burglary. This particular, somewhat eccentric, elderly man was arrested inside a building in Atlanta, Texas, late at night, wearing gloves with a garbage bag in his pocket, after the burglar alarm went off. As the circumstances pertaining to his arrest were seemingly obvious, it appeared to be an open and shut case for the State. Like a rat in a cage, it appeared that this burglar had been cornered. However, this elderly gentleman insisted that he was not guilty and there would be no plea bargaining in his case; he wanted a jury trial.

We picked a jury and the State prosecutors proved they arrested this man in the building wearing gloves, with a garbage bag in his pocket after the burglar alarm went off. When the time came, my client, the defendant, testified and he had a logical response for all of the accusations. His story went something like this:

He said that he had been out walking his dog late at night and he saw a hole or opening in this building. As he thought of it, he felt it was his civic duty to go in and investigate to make sure that there was no criminal activity going on in the building. That is just what he

Cass
County Courthouse

did and as he entered the building through the opening, he inadvertently set off the buildings security system. The alarm was still sounding when the police arrived. As for the suspicious gloves that he was wearing, he said he had gloves on because it was a cold winter night. Not at all an act with criminal intent, he was simply trying to keep warm. He said he had a garbage bag in his pocket because he picked up cans on the road.

As he was being arrested that night, he tried to explain his situation to the police but they would not accept his explanation. This gentleman had no prior criminal history and thankfully the jury believed

> "... HE FELT IT WAS HIS CIVIC DUTY TO GO IN AND INVESTIGATE TO MAKE SURE THAT THERE WAS NO CRIMINAL ACTIVITY GOING ON IN THE BUILDING."

everything he said and found him not guilty. Our former district judge, who is now on the Court of Appeals, has told me that he has used this case as an example on several occasions at various speaking engagements to illustrate the point that everything is not always as it appears to be.

Where did Chambers County get its name?

AFTER INDEPENDENCE, BOTH CHARLES WILCOX AND GENERAL THOMAS JEFFERSON CHAMBERS TRIED TO CLAIM OWNERSHIP OF THE TOWN. GENERAL CHAMBERS NAMED THE TOWN CHAMBERS, TO HONOR HIMSELF, ALTHOUGH IT WAS NOT THE POPULAR CHOICE FOR ALL TOWNS' PEOPLE. IN 1865, CHAMBERS WAS KILLED AT HOME BY AN ASSASSIN.

Where is the Chambers County Courthouse located?

ON THE WEST CORNER OF WASHINGTON AVENUE AND STONEWALL STREETS IN ANAHUAC, TX, WHICH, IN 1989, WAS NAMED THE "ALLIGATOR CAPITAL OF THE WORLD" BY THE TEXAS LEGISLATURE, DUE TO THE FACT THAT IT WAS HOME TO MORE ALLIGATORS THAN PEOPLE!

Who designed the Chambers County Courthouse?

IN 1936, CORNELL G. CURTIS DESIGNED THE HISTORIC COURTHOUSE IN THE CONTEMPORARY STYLE OF LIMESTONE AND CONCRETE. IN 1875, A HORRIBLE FIRE DESTROYED ALL RECORDS IN THE OLD LOG COURTHOUSE.

What is the courthouse's most unusual feature?

AIR CONDITIONING! CHAMBERS COUNTY LAYS CLAIM TO BEING THE FIRST COURTHOUSE THAT WAS AIR CONDITIONED AND ON A SMOLDERING TEXAS SUMMER AFTERNOON, YOU WOULD FIND THE LOCAL POPULATION LINGERING IN ITS HALLS JUST TO STAY COOL!

What is the most famous case tried in the Chambers County Courthouse?

THE MURDER TRIAL OF BENNY JOHNSON WHO WAS INDICTED IN 1943 FOR THE MURDER OF LEONA FRANSSEN AND HER BROTHER, RALPH MALEY. JOHNSON WAS CONVICTED TEN DAYS AFTER THE INDICTMENT; THE TRIAL LASTED ONLY TWO DAYS. HE WAS ELECTROCUTED IN 1944, LESS THAN A YEAR AFTER THE INDICTMENT. THE MURDER AND TRIAL IS THE SUBJECT OF THE BOOK MURDER AT THE COVE BY KENDON CLARK.

Where do you hang your hat?

IN THE HOUSTON OFFICE OF PHELPS DUNBAR LLP, WHICH WAS FOUNDED IN 1854 IN NEW ORLEANS AND HAS OFFICES TODAY THROUGHOUT THE GULF COAST. FOR THE PAST THIRTY YEARS, MY PRACTICE HAS EXCLUSIVELY INVOLVED THE TRIAL OF CIVIL CASES INVOLVING EVERYTHING FROM BREAST IMPLANTS TO SALT DOME STORAGE WELLS.

Believe it or not!

THE ANAHUAC COURTHOUSE WAS THE FIRST TEXAS COURTHOUSE THAT WAS AIR CONDITIONED—AN ENGINEERING MARVEL FOR 1937!

"You may be able to beat the rap, but you can never beat the ride."

~ PATRICIA'S FAMOUS TEXAS JUSTICE SAYING

"Justice is Served for Dinner"

A Famous Texas Case as Told by

PATRICIA HAIR

PHELPS DUNBAR L.L.P.

In Texas, justice is not always administered exclusively from the courthouse, as demonstrated by the fate of Solomon Barrow, one of the earliest American settlers in what is now Chambers County and Patricia Hair's great, great, great uncle. This case is referred to as, "The Case of Justice Served for Dinner."

With his brothers, Ben "the Bear Hunter" and "Bully" Reuben Barrow, Solomon emigrated in the 1820s from Louisiana to the Anahuac area, which was then a part of Mexico. The Barrow brothers settled in different portions of the county, receiving land grants from the Mexican government, planting oak trees and establishing families so that many of the current residents of Chambers County can trace their roots to one of the brothers. Solomon settled in the portion of the county west of the Trinity River and prospered, fathering eleven children and establishing a homestead overlooking Galveston Bay.

Unfortunately, Solomon discovered his wife's brother cooking a hog that Solomon believed he owned and the ensuing argument ended with Solomon shooting and killing his brother-in-law. His wife never spoke to

Chambers
County Courthouse

Solomon again. Imprisoned by the Mexican authorities in Anahuac, Solomon was visited by his brother Ben "the Bear Hunter", who was reputed to ride the fastest horse in the territory. Ben conveniently left the horse untied in front of the jail. During the visit, Solomon ran out of the prison, jumped on the waiting horse and escaped to hide with his pet raccoon in a deep thicket near his home. He was sustained by a slave woman who prepared and brought him food that he shared with his raccoon. One day after sharing a particularly tasty soup, Solomon observed his raccoon die suddenly. His own demise followed shortly, the apparent poisoning victim of his

"ONE DAY AFTER SHARING A PARTICULARLY TASTY SOUP, SOLOMON OBSERVED HIS RACCOON DIE SUDDENLY."

slave, who took the initiative to administer a little Texas justice on her own.

When the Barrow brothers immigrated to Texas, it was truly a frontier where different cultures mingled and the absence of a strong government, police protection and healthcare meant that individuals had to be resourceful, self-reliant and independent. These traits that permitted Chambers County's early settlers just to survive have enabled it to prosper today.

ANAHUAC IS THE ALLIGATOR CAPITAL OF TEXAS, SO DON'T BE SURPRISED UPON ENTERING THE COURTHOUSE AT BEING GREETED BY THE TRADITIONAL CHAMBERS COUNTY "YARD DOG."

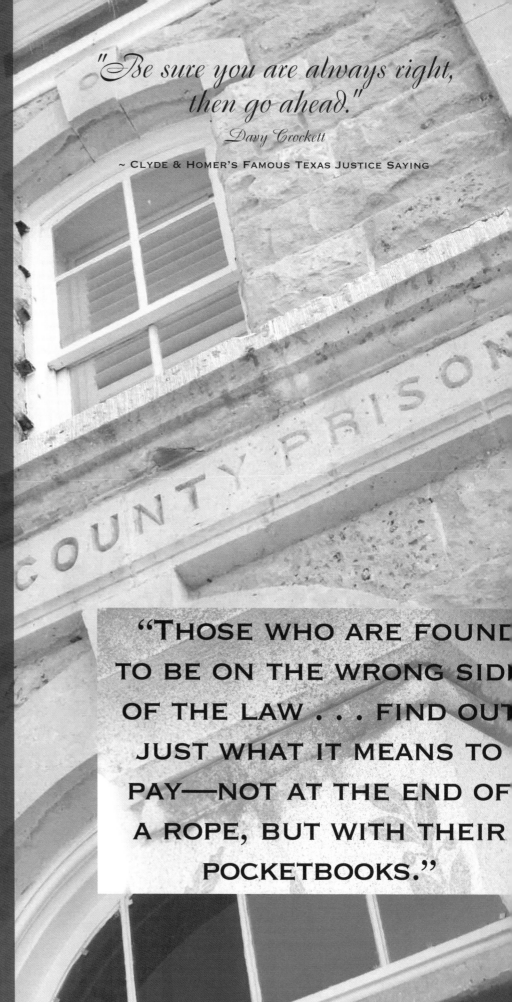

Where did Collin County get its name?

WHEN THE COUNTY WAS ORGANIZED IN 1846, COLLIN McKINNEY LENT HIS NAME, AS HE WAS ONE OF THE FIRST SETTLERS IN THE AREA AND ONE OF FIVE MEN WHO DRAFTED THE TEXAS DECLARATION OF INDEPENDENCE, AS WELL AS ONE OF 59 WHO SIGNED IT.

Where is the Collin County Courthouse located?

THE 1927 HISTORIC COURTHOUSE IS NEAR THE HISTORIC COLLIN COUNTY PRISON, ON THE DOWNTOWN SQUARE IN McKINNEY, TX.

Who designed the Collin County Courthouse?

THERE HAVE BEEN SIX COURTHOUSES TO DATE! THE 1927 HISTORIC COURTHOUSE'S ARCHITECT WAS W.A. PETERS WHO REMODELED THE 1874 HISTORIC COURTHOUSE DESIGNED BY CHARLES WHEELER IN A SECOND EMPIRE STYLE BORROWED FROM THE TIME OF NAPOLEON III OF FRANCE. THE CONTEMPORARY COURTHOUSE WAS CONSTRUCTED IN 1979 AND SITS JUST OFF THE SQUARE.

What is the Courthouse's most unusual feature?

ITS STRIKING FACADE WITH CORINTHIAN COLUMNS.

What is the most famous case tried in the Collin County Courthouse?

<u>STATE OF TEXAS V. CANDACE MONTGOMERY</u> THERE ARE MOVIES, BOOKS, ARTICLES AND LOTS OF COFFEE SHOP TALK ABOUT THIS CASE!

Where do you hang your hat?

IN PLANO AND SHERMAN, TX, WHERE CLYDE AND HOMER ARE THE FOUNDING PARTNERS OF SIEBMAN, REYNOLDS, BURG & PHILLIPS, LLP. FOUNDED IN 1991, THE LAW FIRM REPRESENTS CLIENTS THROUGHOUT NORTH AND EAST TEXAS.

Believe it or not!

IN 1980, CANDY MONTGOMERY WAS ACCUSED OF KILLING HER NEIGHBOR, BETTY GORE. AT THE TRIAL, CANDY MONTGOMERY LAID A BOMBSHELL ON THE JURY WITH A SHOCKING REVELATION THAT SHE HAD INDEED ARGUED WITH MRS. GORE OVER AN AFFAIR SHE WAS HAVING WITH MRS. GORE'S HUSBAND. IN THE FIGHT, SHE STRUCK MRS. GORE 41 TIMES WITH AN AX IN SELF-DEFENSE. THE JURY BOUGHT HER STORY AND ACQUITTED MRS. MONTGOMERY. IMMEDIATELY AFTER THE VERDICT WAS READ AND THE COURTROOM CLEARED, PART OF THE CEILING IS SAID TO HAVE FALLEN DOWN OVER THE JURY BOX. APPARENTLY SOMEBODY, OR SOMETHING, DID NOT APPROVE OF THE VERDICT. MRS. GORE... WAS THAT YOU?!

"Be sure you are always right, then go ahead."
Davy Crockett

~ CLYDE & HOMER'S FAMOUS TEXAS JUSTICE SAYING

"THOSE WHO ARE FOUND TO BE ON THE WRONG SIDE OF THE LAW . . . FIND OUT JUST WHAT IT MEANS TO PAY—NOT AT THE END OF A ROPE, BUT WITH THEIR POCKETBOOKS."

Collin
County Courthouse

"Gunfighters to Legal Paladins"

A Famous Texas Case as Told by
CLYDE SIEBMAN
& HOMER REYNOLDS, III
SIEBMAN, REYNOLDS, BURG & PHILLIPS, LLP

From real-life gunfighters of the Old West to the new breed of legal paladins, Collin County has always been a place where outlaws and lawmen, good guys and bad guys, have clashed over differing points of view about justice. And, as the old Collin County Courthouse and prison may whisper to you, outlaws beware, because in Collin County, you just never know what is going to happen. If you push your luck too far, someone might just get the modern equivalent of a rope.

Just ask those who have taken on some of the nation's largest corporations that call Collin County home. These companies, with their super-sized legal teams, account for the most substantial litigation that occurs in the county's court system. Those who are found to be on the wrong side of the law in these mammoth commercial cases often find out just what it means to pay—not at the end of a rope, but with their pocketbooks

One such case involved a Collin County telecommunications giant and its intellectual property rights. Filed in the 366th Judicial District Court and removed to the United States District Court for the Eastern District of Texas, Sherman Division, this case was tried by Clyde Siebman and a highly esteemed team of Baker & Botts lawyers, including senior trial counsel Joe Cheavens, Scott Partridge and Bob Kantner.

Siebman and the Baker & Botts team represented DSC Corporation, a technology and telecommunications company headquartered in Collin County. The company sued several former employees who were alleged to have stolen trade secrets when they left the company. DSC alleged that these employees used the trade secrets to create a start-up company with a group of others, reaching people as far away as Silicon Valley, California. The trial lasted several weeks, with the plaintiff calling over a dozen fact witnesses and several experts. At the end of the trial, a jury returned a verdict in favor of DSC with a judgment being entered in excess of $140 million.

The old Collin County Courthouse and prison have been witnesses to the settlement of the Old West and the emergence of modern Texas. A venue for real life Bonnie and Clyde escapades, the arrest and extradition of Tex Watson for his role in the Manson murders and now, home to some of the nation's most cutting edge technology related litigation, Collin County justice has always been in the spotlight. It is fitting that the justice system of Collin County, once used to protect its citizens from the likes of Sam Bass (who pulled off the first train robbery in Texas in Collin County), is now used to protect its citizens and their twenty-first century intellectual property rights. Belle Starr, obtaining her marriage license inside the old courthouse, could never have imagined what those old walls would later witness.

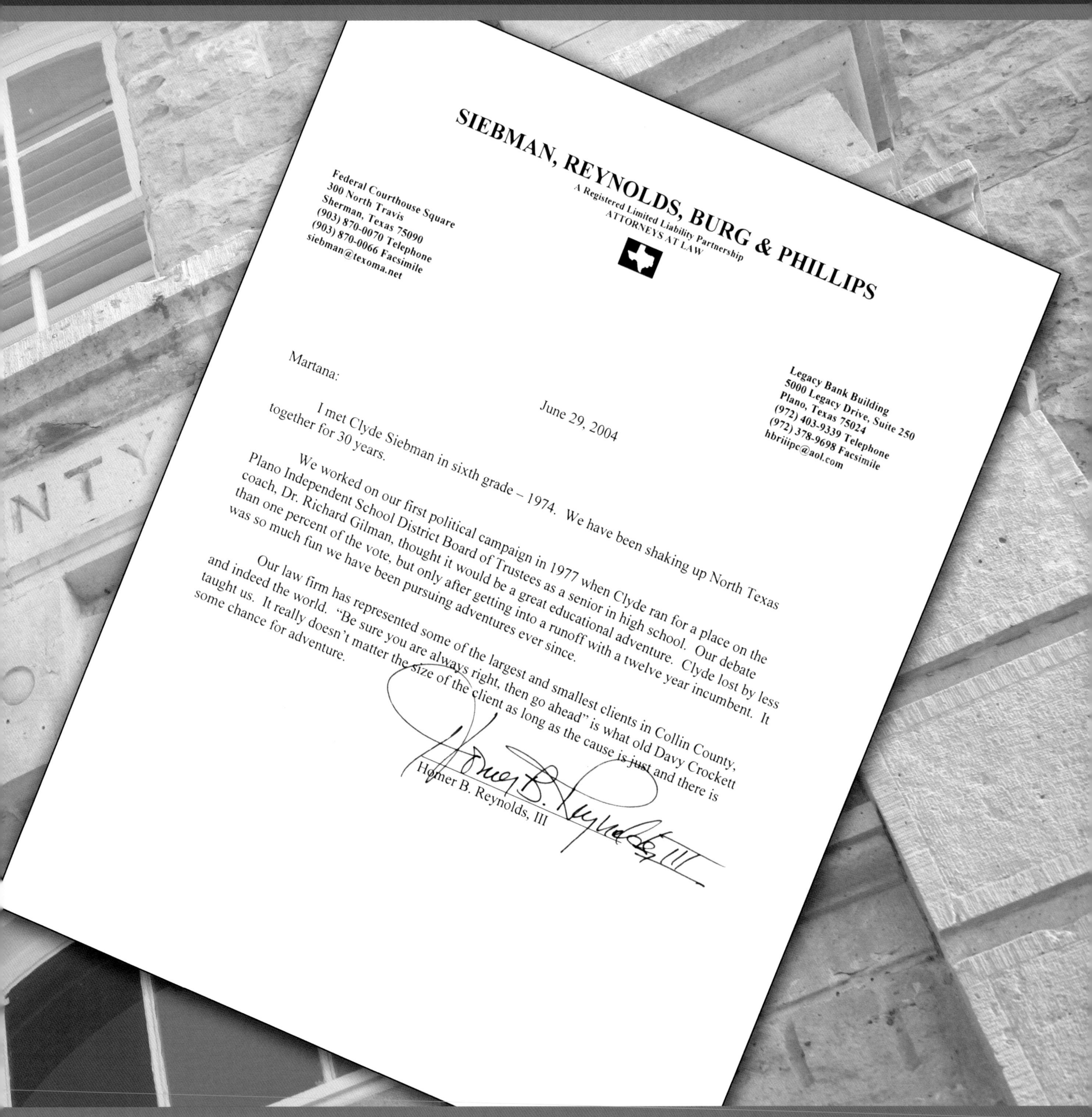

SIEBMAN, REYNOLDS, BURG & PHILLIPS

A Registered Limited Liability Partnership
ATTORNEYS AT LAW

Federal Courthouse Square
300 North Travis
Sherman, Texas 75090
(903) 870-0070 Telephone
(903) 870-0066 Facsimile
siebman@texoma.net

Legacy Bank Building
5000 Legacy Drive, Suite 250
Plano, Texas 75024
(972) 403-9339 Telephone
(972) 378-9698 Facsimile
hbriiipc@aol.com

Martana:

June 29, 2004

I met Clyde Siebman in sixth grade – 1974. We have been shaking up North Texas together for 30 years.

We worked on our first political campaign in 1977 when Clyde ran for a place on the Plano Independent School District Board of Trustees as a senior in high school. Our debate coach, Dr. Richard Gilman, thought it would be a great educational adventure. Clyde lost by less than one percent of the vote, but only after getting into a runoff with a twelve year incumbent. It was so much fun we have been pursuing adventures ever since.

Our law firm has represented some of the largest and smallest clients in Collin County, and indeed the world. "Be sure you are always right, then go ahead" is what old Davy Crockett taught us. It really doesn't matter the size of the client as long as the cause is just and there is some chance for adventure.

Homer B. Reynolds, III

Colorado County Courthouse

"The Battle of the Texas Blue Law"

LINDA L. ADDISON
A Famous Case of Texas Justice
FULBRIGHT & JAWORSKI L.L.P.

"The Battle of the Texas Blue Law" captured the national spotlight in 1984, when Linda Addison won the case that declared the law unconstitutional. Although blue laws were unpopular, powerful forces fought all efforts to repeal them, and Texas and sixteen other states still had them on the books. *USA Today* featured the Texas fight in a cover story on the nation's blue law controversy under the headline, "To Sell or not to Sell on Sunday."

The Texas Blue Law had been on the books for 120 years and seemed to be invincible at the time. The law had prohibited the sale of everything from clothing to automobiles, to toys and power tools on consecutive Saturdays and Sundays. Its purpose was to provide a common day of rest for retail employees, but, in fact, it only succeeded in restricting retail competition on Sundays and interfering with the lives of consumers who had little time to shop except on weekends.

The case focused attention on the lives of working mothers, shift workers, students working part-time, households with two wage earners, and people with two jobs. By severely limiting their shopping choices on weekends, the Texas Blue law in practice was a hardship on many Texans, as well as a frustration. A number of merchants in the Houston area defied the law by opening for business every Sunday. The Retail Merchants Association of Houston sued Linda's client Handy Dan Hardware and fifteen other Houston merchants to force

"Pigs get fat, hogs get slaughtered."

~ LINDA'S FAMOUS TEXAS JUSTICE SAYING

them to comply with the law. Linda was the lead counsel. She recommended that Handy Dan attempt what no one had done successfully before—challenge the constitutionality of the Texas Blue Law.

Linda felt that she could develop and present a compelling case demonstrating that the law was unconstitutional. The rest, as they say, is history. The judge who presided over the case was Tom Phillips, a well respected district judge who later became Chief Justice of the Texas Supreme Court. Linda was the first lawyer ever to overcome the evidentiary and legal hurdles necessary to have the law declared unconstitutional, by presenting a case that proved that the law was vague and that there was no rational relationship between the law's intent and its actual effect.

Based on the evidence and legal arguments that Linda presented, Judge Phillips declared the Texas Blue Law unconstitutional. The decision was national news. Linda was quoted in the *Wall Street Journal* and appeared on national television—PBS's "McNeil Lehrer Report"— on

". . . LINDA WAS QUOTED IN THE WALL STREET JOURNAL AND APPEARED ON NATIONAL TELEVISION—PBS'S McNEIL LEHRER REPORT . . ."

Christmas Night of that year. Emboldened by the decision, Houston retailers began opening on Sunday in open defiance of the law while the case was on appeal. The case became a catalyst for a movement to repeal the law. Even though the opponents of repeal were powerful, the Texas legislature saw the handwriting on the wall. The legislature repealed the Texas Blue Law within months of her victory. Linda became known as the "Blue Law Buster," the lawyer who made it possible for Texans to shop on Sunday.

Where did Colorado County get its name?
FROM THE COLORADO RIVER THAT RUNS THROUGH THE TOWN OF COLUMBUS, THE COUNTY SEAT. THE COUNTY WAS ORGANIZED IN 1837.

Where is the Colorado County Courthouse located?
ON THE SOUTHEAST CORNER OF WALNUT AND MILAM STREETS IN COLUMBUS, JUST WEST OF THE FAMOUS OAK TREE UNDER WHICH JUDGE ROBERT McALPIN WILLIAMSON, NICKNAMED THREE-LEGGED WILLIE, HELD THE FIRST TERM OF DISTRICT COURT OF THE REPUBLIC OF TEXAS. THE CURRENT COURTHOUSE IS THE THIRD TO STAND ON THIS SITE.

Who designed the Colorado County Courthouse?
ARCHITECT EUGENE T. HEINER DESIGNED THE HISTORIC COURTHOUSE IN 1891.

What is the Courthouse's most unusual feature?
THE COURTHOUSE HAS A LOVELY COPPER DOME DATING TO 1910 THAT REPLACED THE ORIGINAL BELL TOWER, WHICH WAS DESTROYED BY A HURRICANE IN JULY 1909. THE COPPER DOME HOUSES A STUNNING STAINED GLASS DOME THAT IS IN THE CEILING OF THE DISTRICT COURTROOM.

What is the most famous case tried in the Colorado County Courthouse?
MEXICAN FOLK HERO GREGORIO CORTEZ WAS TRIED AND CONVICTED HERE FOR THE MURDER OF SHERIFF MORRIS OF KAMES COUNTY IN JUNE 1901. CORTEZ HAD BEEN CAPTURED FOLLOWING THE LARGEST MANHUNT IN TEXAS HISTORY BY TEXAS RANGERS WHO HAD PURSUED HIM FOR ELEVEN DAYS OVER 450 MILES. A NETWORK OF SUPPORTERS AND A LEGAL DEFENSE CAMPAIGN RESULTED IN HIS PARDON BY GOVERNOR O.B. COLQUITT AFTER CORTEZ HAD SERVED EIGHT YEARS IN PRISON. THE DEBATE OVER HIS GUILT OR INNOCENCE HAS BEEN MEMORIALIZED IN A BOOK, "WITH A PISTOL IN HIS HAND," BY AMÉRICO PAREDES (1958) AND IN A 1982 MOVIE, "THE BALLAD OF GREGORIO CORTEZ," STARRING EDWARD JAMES OLMOS.

Where do you hang your hat?
ANYWHERE ONE OF MY CLIENTS HAS A "BET THE COMPANY" CASE. WHEN I'M NOT IN COURT, I REST MY BOOTS IN HOUSTON, TX, WHERE I AM A SENIOR PARTNER IN FULBRIGHT & JAWORSKI L.L.P. AND SERVE ON THE FIRM'S EXECUTIVE COMMITTEE.

Believe it or not!
JUDGE ROBERT McALPIN WILLIAMSON WAS NICKNAMED THREE-LEGGED WILLIE BECAUSE ONE OF HIS LEGS WAS DRAWN BACK AT THE KNEE AND SUPPORTED BY A WOODEN LEG. AFTER THE TOWN OF COLUMBUS WAS BURNED IN THE RUNAWAY SCRAPE IN 1836, LEAVING NO SUITABLE STRUCTURE IN WHICH TO HOLD COURT, THREE-LEGGED WILLIE CONVENED THE FIRST TERM OF DISTRICT COURT OF THE REPUBLIC OF TEXAS UNDER A LARGE OAK TREE NEXT TO THE SITE WHERE THE CURRENT COURTHOUSE NOW STANDS!

Where did Comanche County get its name?

FROM THE INDIAN TRIBE OF THE SAME NAME, WHO LIVED IN THE TERRITORY DURING THE TIME OF ITS CREATION IN 1856 IN CORA AND MOVED TO COMANCHE IN 1858.

Where is the Comanche County Courthouse located?

THE HISTORICAL 1939 COURTHOUSE IS ON THE TOWN SQUARE OF CENTRAL AVENUE AND AUSTIN STREET IN COMANCHE, TX. AS EARLY AS 1856, THE HISTORICAL "OLD CORA," THE LITTLE LOG STRUCTURE, WAS THE FIRST COURTHOUSE FOR COMANCHE IN CORA, TX. OLD CORA WAS LATER MOVED TO COMANCHE ON THE SQUARE AND IS NOW BARKS MUSEUM.

Who designed the Comanche County Courthouse?

THE AWARD WINNING WYATT HENDRICK OF FORT WORTH DESIGNED THE CURRENT 1939 HISTORIC ART DECO COURTHOUSE USING LIMESTONE FROM THE LOCAL QUARRY AND EVEN SALVAGED SOME MATERIALS FROM THE 1891 COURTHOUSE TO USE IN THE INTERIOR WALLS.

What is the Courthouse's most unusual feature?

THE LARGE STONE EAGLES THAT PERCH ABOVE THE NORTH AND SOUTH ENTRANCES OF THE COURTHOUSE, MADE BY A COMANCHE STONE CUTTER NAMED ELMER WEBB.

What is the most famous case tried in the Comanche County Courthouse?

ONE OF COMANCHE COUNTY'S EARLY TRIALS CONCERNED ASA REED, JESSE REED AND JOHN TAYLOR, WHO WERE ACCUSED OF MURDER. FOLKS FROM ALL AROUND ATTENDED THE TRIAL WHERE IT WAS FOUND THAT ASA WAS INNOCENT BECAUSE JESSE HAD DONE IT. JUSTICE COULD NOT BE SERVED, HOWEVER, BECAUSE JESSE SKIPPED TOWN AND WAS NEVER SEEN AGAIN (OR MAYBE JUSTICE WAS SERVED).

Where do you hang your hat?

AT FREIDMAN, SUDER & COOKE IN FORT WORTH, WHERE I SPECIALIZE IN COMPLICATED COMMERCIAL AND PATENT INFRINGEMENT LITIGATION.

Believe it or not!

WHEN THE NOTORIOUS JOHN WESLEY HARDIN KILLED BROWN COUNTY DEPUTY SHERIFF CHARLIE WEBB IN COMANCHE IN 1874, MANY LOCAL CITIZENS RESENTED HARDIN'S ESCAPE. IN MISGUIDED RETALIATION, A MOB OF 300 RESIDENTS OF BROWN AND COMANCHE COUNTIES STORMED THE COUNTY JAIL WHERE JOE HARDIN (BROTHER OF THE OUTLAW) AND TWO OF THE OUTLAW'S ASSOCIATES WERE BEING HELD. THE THREE PRISONERS WERE LYNCHED!

"The $10 Cooperative Investment"

A Famous Texas Case of
JONATHAN T. SUDER
FREIDMAN, SUDER & COOKE
As Told by the Honorable Judge Eldon B. Mahon

Jon Suder came to me fresh out of law school having grown up on the East Coast. I knew from the outset that Jon would make a good trial lawyer. After leaving my Court in 1986, he would always come by and share with me his trials. One such trial involved the Comanche County Telephone Company and many of the residents in that area. While this area was within my division while I served as a Federal Judge, the case was in state court; it made a great impact on the residents of Comanche County and the surrounding counties.

Many will recall that in the 50s and 60s, rural areas used cooperatives as a way to obtain electrical and telephone service. Comanche County was no exception and in the mid-60s, formed a telephone cooperative. Local residents were permitted to acquire one share in the cooperative for $10. However, that share was restricted such that there were never any dividends, the shares could never be sold and upon death, the shares were returned to the company in exchange for the original $10 investment. As that area grew, so did the phone company, eventually establishing a cellular subsidiary. Along the way, the cooperative changed to a for-profit corporation but the shareholders were never told of this fact.

Over time, many of the original shareholders passed away. As the pool of shareholders got smaller and smaller, the value of the company got larger and larger. Only those on the board (which was bestowed on a select group of local businessmen from each of the telephone exchanges in that area) knew the true value of the company.

In the mid-90s, Randy Barnett, an Abilene native, figured out that the Comanche County Telephone Company was worth millions of dollars. He quickly became a shareholder by paying his $10 and gained access to the records of the company. He then initiated a tender offer to acquire the

"I consider trial by jury as the only anchor ever yet imagined by man, by which a government can be held to the principles of its constitution."

Thomas Jefferson

~ JON'S FAMOUS TEXAS JUSTICE SAYING

Comanche
County Courthouse

company, offering each of the approximately 500 remaining shareholders a sum of $20,000, or a total of approximately $10 million. Given that most of the shareholders were senior citizens, many living on a modest income, you can imagine what this money would do for these people.

Rather than embrace what Barnett was trying to do for this area, the Board of Directors branded him as an outsider trying to steal their company and ruin the local phone service. The smear campaign resulted in Barnett literally being run out of town and his tender offer rejected. As a result,

> **"IT TOOK TREMENDOUS COURAGE . . . TO COME FORWARD AND TESTIFY AGAINST THEIR NEIGHBORS AND FRIENDS."**

Barnett and the company filed suit over what happened. The case went to trial in Tarrant County and the jury returned a verdict in favor of Jon's client. Before the verdict was read in open court, the parties reached a settlement.

One of the most interesting aspects of the trial involved the treatment of approximately 27 widows/shareholders who were not technically shareholders because the shares were in their deceased spouse's name. The company nevertheless treated them as shareholders because it needed their votes to defeat Barnett's tender offer. It took tremendous courage for some of these women to come forward and testify against their neighbors and friends. One woman explained that while she personally felt betrayed, she was more upset for her friends who recently had passed away without ever knowing what their share was worth and how that money could have changed their lives.

As a result of this lawsuit, the shareholders received what they were entitled to and this, in turn, had a huge ripple effect on the entire region as it literally pumped millions of dollars into the local economy. Clearly, justice was served.

Cooke
County Courthouse

"Did You Forget to Return the Child?"

A Famous Texas Case as Told by

RANDY J. ESSENBURG
ATTORNEY AT LAW

In September of 2003, Gainesville, Texas, made national news when an alert civilian on Interstate 35 aided police in catching a local man wanted for kidnapping his 4-year-old daughter in Kansas. Arlington man, Robert Sidney Yocum, 57, was arrested by Gainesville police officers on a felony charge of interfering with child custody.

The mother of the 4-year-old girl alerted police to her disappearance after Yocum arrived at her Kansas home to spend time with his daughter. He begged the mother to let him take the girl out for ice cream, and when she relented, Yocum took the girl, failing to bring her back home. The mother began searching for her daughter that afternoon and when no trace of Yocum or her daughter could be found, she notified Sgt. Steve Farmer with the Harper County, Kansas, Sheriff's office, around 3 p.m.

Sgt. Farmer and his team immediately produced fliers with pictures and information about the girl, her father and the circumstances of the kidnapping. In partnership with the Center for Missing Children, the information was distributed in a 600-mile radius to other agencies. It was only because of this immediate action that neighboring civilians were alerted to the kidnapping and that Yocum was eventually apprehended. Farmer and his team were extremely pleased with the results of their efforts. Although Yocum was the girl's biological father, the girl's mother had sole

> ## "*Your best thinking got you here.*"
> ~ RANDY'S FAMOUS TEXAS JUSTICE SAYING

custody and he was given no visitation rights. The two were in the process of filing for divorce.

Before 8 p.m., Gainesville Police Capt. Jim Bleything and the Gainesville Police Department received a phone call from a woman who had begun to follow a white Chevrolet Tahoe on Interstate 35. Just minutes earlier, the woman heard an alert broadcast on a radio station giving details of the kidnapping, as well as information containing the vehicle's description. When she saw a vehicle matching the description traveling south on the interstate, she immediately began to pursue it.

Without delay, the woman driver notified the Oklahoma State Police regarding the alert and the possible suspect. Her call was then transferred to the Gainesville Police Department because the vehicles would soon cross the Red River into Texas and Cooke County.

". . . AN ALERT CIVILIAN ON INTERSTATE 35 AIDED POLICE IN CATCHING A LOCAL MAN WANTED FOR KIDNAPPING HIS 4-YEAR-OLD DAUGHTER IN KANSAS."

Police officers set up barricades where they were anticipating Yocum would soon be driving on North I-35 and his car was apprehended. Officers attempted to talk to Yocum, but he and his daughter gave conflicting stories. It was not until officers spoke to the police department in Kansas that they gained a full understanding of the situation.

Yocum was arrested and placed in Cooke County Jail to await trial for the charge of aggravated interference with parental custody, which is a felony. Yocum also aggravated the charges, escalating his crime to a higher level of felony, by crossing state lines.

Where did Cooke County get its name?
COOKE COUNTY WAS NAMED FOR WILLIAM G. COOKE, A SOLDIER AND STATESMAN WHO COMMANDED A COMPANY OF THE NEW ORLEANS GREYS AT THE CAPTURE OF BEXAR IN 1835.

Where is the Cooke County Courthouse located?
ON THE SQUARE IN DOWNTOWN GAINESVILLE, TX—COOKE COUNTY SEAT AND HOME OF THE FRANK BUCK ZOO.

Who designed the Cooke County Courthouse?
PROMINENT DALLAS ARCHITECTS LANG & WITCHELL DESIGNED THE HISTORIC COOKE COUNTY COURTHOUSE IN A BEAUX-ARTS STYLE OF BRICK AND STONE IN 1911. IT WAS THE COUNTY'S FOURTH COURTHOUSE.

What is the Courthouse's most unusual feature?
A LARGE CLOCK TOWER WITH UNDERSIZED CLOCKS. THE CLOCKS WERE ADDED TO THE COURTHOUSE'S DOME IN 1920 AS A WORLD WAR I MEMORIAL.

What is the most famous case tried in the Cooke County Courthouse?
THE TRIAL OF THOMAS C. BARRETT, A MINISTER AND SELF-TAUGHT PHYSICIAN, WHO DEMANDED A JURY TRIAL FOR HIS PARTICIPATION IN THE HANGINGS OF MORE THAN FORTY MEN IN THE "UNION PEACE PARTY" OF 1862. ON OCTOBER 1, 1862, THE GROUP OF SEVERAL HUNDRED CONFEDERATE SUPPORTERS TOOK SIXTY TO SEVENTY ALLEGED UNION CONSPIRATORS INTO CUSTODY, AND A "CITIZENS' COURT" OF FIVE MEN SENTENCED 39 OF THEM TO HANG.

Where do you hang your hat?
AT MY FAMILY LAW PRACTICE IN DALLAS, TX, WHERE I SPECIALIZE IN CHILD CUSTODY CASES, BEST INTEREST OF CHILDREN, DOMICILE RESTRICTION CASES, ENFORCEMENT OF VISITATION, CHILD SUPPORT, MODIFICATIONS OF DIVORCE DECREES, PROPERTY MATTERS AND OTHER FAMILY RELATED MATTERS.

Believe it or not!
PEOPLE ATTENDING THE PARADE LAUNCHING THE GAINESVILLE COMMUNITY CIRCUS SEASON OF 1939 GOT AN EXTRA THRILL WHEN ELLIOTT ROOSEVELT, SON OF PRESIDENT FRANKLIN AND ELEANOR ROOSEVELT, APPEARED ON HORSEBACK—THOUGH HE DID NOT STAY ON THE HORSE LONG. "HE HAD RAISED HIS TEN-GALLON HAT TO WAVE TO FRIENDS, WHEN THE HORSE SHIED, CAUSING HIM TO LOSE HIS BALANCE AND SLAP THE ANIMAL WITH HIS HAT. THE ANIMAL THEN BUCKED HIM OFF!"

Corvell
County Courthouse

"The Ambush of the Horse Thieves"

A Famous Texas Case as Told by
PATRICIA KAY DUBE
PATRICIA KAY DUBE, P.C.

In December of 1889, Jim Leeper and Ed Powell, reputed horse thieves, were practicing their trade when things went desperately wrong. The duo decided to ambush a gentleman by the name of J.T. Mathis, who was accompanied by a young boy, as they rode down a deserted trail, in an attempt to steal his horse and mules. For reasons unknown, Leeper and Powell resorted to viciously attacking the man and the boy and left them for dead. A witness to the incident, Dr. Baird, tried futilely to aid the dying man after the robbers had left the scene. While the boy survived, Mr. Mathis was not so lucky. Immediately following the incident, word was out and the chase was on. With the whole town on the lookout for the fugitives, they were apprehended the very next day.

Leeper and Powell sought the representation of attorney J.L. Crain, who knew he had his work cut out for him. Crain tried to stall the case to develop a defense. The odds were against him, though, as was the judge and the rest of the town. Crain asked for a continuance of the case until the following term of court. No such luck. Things were to move right ahead in a "timely" fashion and trial was set for February 16, 1890.

Over the next two months, the rage in the town over this injustice began to rise. The judge ordered the courthouse to be heavily guarded to deter the citizens from taking mob action against Leeper and Powell. The trial commenced as scheduled and in what could have been record time, the jury returned a verdict. The defendants were found guilty of murder and sentenced to death. The defendants caused quite a stir and the jurors from this small sleepy town were not about to lie down silently. They wanted justice at the ultimate price.

The defense urged a motion for a new trial, but was struck down. As was their right, the accused appealed the original ruling, but again hit a wall when the Court of Appeals upheld the verdict. With no other options left, the last resort for Leeper and Powell was to plead and at least keep their lives, even if it meant they would be forever behind bars. During the sentencing in late July 1891, the court proved to be just as callous. Judge C.K. Bell followed the recommendation

". . . ON SEPTEMBER 29, 1891, LEEPER AND POWELL WERE MARCHED TO THE HANGING SCAFFOLDS."

of the jury and the general sentiment of the town and passed down the death sentence. Crain valiantly tried to save the lives of his clients by appealing to Governor J.S. Hogg for a stay of execution. But alas, the gavel had fallen and on September 29, 1891, Leeper and Powell were marched to the hanging scaffolds. The last moments of their lives were spent in front of a vast crowed, gleefully gathered to watch their deaths. People even went so far as to bring their children to show them what would happen to them if they flaunted the law. At two o'clock that day, the town sheriff pulled the trap and, with it, the last legal hanging in Coryell County was carried out.

Where did Coryell County get its name?
THE COUNTY WAS ESTABLISHED IN 1854 AND NAMED FOR JAMES CORYELL, A FRONTIERSMAN WHO WAS IN THE BOWIE EXPEDITION OF 1831 AND LATER BECAME A TEXAS RANGER.

Where is the Coryell County Courthouse located?
IN THE COUNTY SEAT OF GATESVILLE BUILT ON LAND THAT HAD BEEN DONATED BY RICHARD C. GRANT, AN EARLY SETTLER AND INDIAN TRADER.

Who designed the Coryell County Courthouse?
THE HISTORIC BEAUX-ARTS STYLE COURTHOUSE, BUILT OF LIMESTONE AND SANDSTONE, WAS DESIGNED BY THE RENOWNED ARCHITECT W.C. DODSON AND ERECTED IN 1897 IN CORYELL COUNTY, BY SCOTSMEN WHO, WHILE FULLY ATTIRED IN THEIR KILTS, WERE KNOWN TO PLAY THEIR BAGPIPES AT THE COURTHOUSE. THIS COURTHOUSE IS ALSO A NATIONAL REGISTER PROPERTY.

What is the Courthouse's most unusual feature?
THE TWO FIGURES OF JUSTICE ATOP THE COURTHOUSE AT EACH ENTRANCE ARE NOT BLINDFOLDED AND THEY DO NOT CARRY THE SCALES OF JUSTICE.

What is the most famous case tried in the Coryell County Courthouse?
PERHAPS NOT THE MOST FAMOUS CASE, BUT A FIFTEEN-YEAR-OLD UNSOLVED MURDER WAS PUT TO REST IN 2003. JOHN SWART, A CORYELL COUNTY APPRAISER, WAS CHARGED IN THE MURDER OF HIS WIFE. IN 1988, SHE WAS FOUND DEAD IN A BURNING CAR NORTH OF COPPERAS COVE. A YEAR-LONG INVESTIGATION BY THE CORYELL COUNTY SHERIFF'S DEPARTMENT, THE TEXAS RANGERS UNSOLVED CRIMES UNIT AND OTHER AGENCIES, FINALLY SHUT THE DOOR ON THIS HAUNTING CASE.

Where do you hang your hat?
IN THE GREAT CITY OF HOUSTON. PATRICIA KAY DUBE, P.C. IS A LITIGATION BOUTIQUE WITH AN EMPHASIS ON INSURANCE LAW, SOPHISTICATED INSURANCE COVERAGE MATTERS, PRODUCT LIABILITY LAW, CONSTRUCTION LAW, PROFESSIONAL MALPRACTICE, GENERAL CIVIL AND COMMERCIAL LITIGATION AND MATTERS INVOLVING PRESERVATION OF PRIVILEGES RELATED TO HOSPITALS, HEALTHCARE PROVIDERS, NURSING HOMES AND ASSISTED CARE LIVING FACILITIES.

Believe it or not!
MS. DUBE'S GRANDFATHER, WILLIAM JOHN DUBE, SR., OWNED A GENERAL MERCANTILE STORE, COTTON GIN AND BLACKSMITH SHOP IN THE GROVE, TX, IN CORYELL COUNTY. THE OLD GENERAL STORE AND ANCILLARY BUILDINGS ARE NOW A TOWN MUSEUM, HAVING BEEN PURCHASED BY MOODY ANDERSON OF AUSTIN, TEXAS!

Crosby
County Courthouse

"A Saturday Night Special"

A Famous Texas Case as Told by

KENT HANCE
HANCE SCARBOROUGH WRIGHT

In 1972 Kent Hance who later went on to serve West Texas as a United States Congressman was before Judge Pat Moore in Crosbyton, Texas trying a civil case. During one of the recesses, Judge Moore, the first woman judge in the South Plains of Texas, told Mr. Hance that she had been informed that Erminio Orta Yannis was in jail, charged with murder. The judge further added that Mr. Yannis had been in jail for over six months and had yet to have an attorney appointed, much less a trial. During the recess, the judge asked Mr. Hance if he would be kind enough to represent the gentleman. At this point in time, Mr. Hance had four motions pending in front of the Court and informed the Court that he would be more than happy to represent Mr. Yannis, and in fact, all he had thought about on his drive over from Lubbock was the possibility of trying a murder case in Crosbyton, Texas.

As soon as the civil case was over and Judge Moore had ruled against all four of Mr. Hance's motions, she officially appointed him the attorney of record in the case of *State of Texas vs. Erminio Orta Yannis*, Cause No. 1585. The case was set for trial two months later.

In the meantime, Mr. Hance had two law students interview the defendant. One of the law students, Bill Haltom, who is now a practicing attorney in Albuquerque, New Mexico, informed Mr. Hance that the shooting was an accident. The gun, a .25 caliber automatic, accidentally went off and shot the deceased, Frank Robledo. On the day of the trial, Mr. Hance voir dired the jury panel and told them that the defense would show that it was an accident. One of the first witnesses called was a pathologist who testified that there were two bullets. Mr. Hance showed no sign of panic, but later admitted that he wanted to lean over to the jury and say, "Would you believe self-defense?"—or explain that accidents do run in spurts, especially when you are shooting a Saturday night special.

Later in the trial, Sheriff Fletcher Stark was testifying when Mr. Hance asked him about the deceased. Sheriff Stark testified that the deceased was one of the sorriest men to ever live in the county, was a trouble-maker and deserved to be shot. The jury was out less than thirty minutes and found Mr. Yannis not guilty.

". . . MR. YANNIS HAD BEEN IN JAIL FOR OVER SIX MONTHS AND HAD YET TO HAVE AN ATTORNEY APPOINTED, MUCH LESS A TRIAL."

The foreman of the jury later told Mr. Hance that the rumor in the county was that the Sheriff had been telling everyone at the coffee shops to be sure and let Mr. Yannis go if they got on the jury.

Judge Pat Moore paid Kent Hance the sum of $75.00 per day plus she had the defendant sign over the gun to Mr. Hance. It was her thought that if the defendant got the gun back, he'd probably just shoot someone else. It seems that everyone was happy except Mr. Robledo. May he rest in peace.

Where did Crosby County get its name?

IT WAS NAMED FOR TEXAS LAND COMMISSIONER STEPHEN CROSBY, WHO WAS A MEMBER OF THE "KNOW-NOTHING" PARTY WHEN CROSBY COUNTY WAS ORGANIZED IN 1886. THE KNOW-NOTHING PARTY WAS AN ANTI-CATHOLIC, ANTI-FOREIGNER SECRET SOCIETY, ALSO KNOWN AS THE AMERICAN ORDER.

Where is the Crosby County Courthouse located?

IN CROSBYTON, TX, AT BERKSHIRE AVENUE AND ASPEN STREET ON THE SOUTHWEST CORNER.

Who designed the Crosby County Courthouse?

THIS HISTORICAL 1914 COURTHOUSE WAS DESIGNED BY THE M.H. WALLER & CO. OF FORT WORTH, TX.

What is the Courthouse's most unusual feature?

ITS TEXAS RENAISSANCE STYLE OF ARCHITECTURE, WITH ELEMENTS OF CLASSICAL REVIVAL, FEATURING FOUR CLASSICAL COLUMNS THAT MAKE FOR AN IMPOSING FACADE AND FORM A NARROW AND INTIMATE PORTICO.

What is the most famous case tried in the Crosby County Courthouse?

ON JULY 12, 1998, "THE MEANEST MAN IN LORENZO," LARRY MCCLAREN, A DISGRUNTLED COTTON FARMER, HAD APPARENTLY REACHED THE END OF HIS WITS WHEN HE SHOT AND KILLED TWO OF HIS NEIGHBORS CLARENCE GREGORY, 70, AND HIS SON LOYD GREGORY, 42. MR. MCCLAREN PREVIOUSLY HAD SEVERAL RUN-INS WITH COUNTY RESIDENTS DURING THE YEARS AND IT IS BELIEVED THAT ONE OF THOSE DISPUTES WITH THE GREGORYS PROBABLY LED UP TO THE SHOOTINGS. HE WAS KNOWN TO COMMONLY THROW ROCKS AT THE VEHICLE OF PEOPLE PASSING BY, AS WELL AS TO TRY TO RUN THEM OFF THE ROAD.

Where do you hang your hat?

AT THE LAW FIRM OF HANCE SCARBOROUGH WRIGHT IN AUSTIN, TX—OUR CAPITOL CITY OFFICE IS LOCATED DOWNTOWN ON CONGRESS AVENUE.

Believe it or not!

MR. HANCE WAS "AWARDED" THE ALLEGED MURDER WEAPON, A SMALL HANDGUN, IN THIS CASE. HE KEEPS IT IN HIS DESK DRAWER TO THIS DAY!

Where did Dallas County get its name?

DALLAS COUNTY WAS NAMED AFTER GEORGE MIFFLIN DALLAS WHO WAS AN AMERICAN STATESMAN, DIPLOMAT AND A TOP GRADUATE OF HIS 1810 CLASS AT PRINCETON.

Where is the Dallas County Courthouse located?

IT IS IN DOWNTOWN DALLAS, ON THE CORNER OF JEFFERSON AND JACKSON STREETS, NEAR THE INFAMOUS "GRASSY KNOLL" WHERE PRESIDENT JOHN F. KENNEDY WAS ASSASSINATED

Who designed the Dallas County Courthouse?

THE HISTORIC COURTHOUSE, "OLD RED" WAS BUILT IN 1891 BY ORLOPP AND KUSENER IN THE ROMANESQUE REVIVAL STYLE OF ARCHITECTURE. GARGOYLE-LIKE FIGURES WITH A SERPENT'S BODY, A BAT'S WING AND THE HEAD OF A LION ADORN EACH CORNER OF THE BUILDING.

What is the Courthouse's most unusual feature?

THE BRIGHT RED COLOR OF THE STONE USED TO CONSTRUCT THE BUILDING STANDS OUT BRILLIANTLY AGAINST THE TEXAS BLUE SKIES.

What is the most famous case tried in the Dallas County Courthouse?

WHILE DALLAS COUNTY HAS ITS FAIR SHARE OF FAMOUS COURT CASES, ONE STANDS OUT. THAT IS, THE JACK RUBY TRIAL FOR THE MURDER OF LEE HARVEY OSWALD IN 1963. RUBY FIRED HIS HANDGUN AS OSWALD WAS BEING TRANSFERRED IN THE BASEMENT GARAGE OF DALLAS POLICE HEADQUARTERS; THE KILLING WAS BROADCAST ON LIVE TV. RUBY WAS ARRESTED, TRIED AND SENT TO PRISON; HE DIED THERE OF CANCER IN 1967.

Where do you hang your hat?

IN DALLAS, TX, WHERE I PRACTICE LAW AT THE LAW OFFICES OF FRANK L. BRANSON. SPECIALIZING IN PERSONAL INJURY AND MEDICAL NEGLIGENCE, WE BRING THE SKILLS AND MAKE THE FINANCIAL RESOURCES AVAILABLE TO PUT OUR CLIENTS ON AN EQUAL FOOTING WITH THEIR ADVERSARIES.

Believe it or not!

MR. BRANSON HAS AN EXTENSIVE GUN COLLECTION THAT INCLUDES GERONIMO'S RIFLE AND BAT MASTERSON'S PISTOL AND CANE!

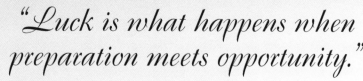

"Luck is what happens when preparation meets opportunity."

Darrell K. Royal,
Former Head Coach, University of Texas Longhorns

~ FRANK'S FAMOUS TEXAS JUSTICE SAYING

"Spinning Yarns on Texas Courthouses"

A Famous Texas Tale as Told by

FRANK BRANSON
THE LAW OFFICE OF FRANK L. BRANSON

Texas Monthly recently published a poll and named the top 100 lawyers in Texas. The magazine referred to them as Texas Super Lawyers. One of those was Dallas trial lawyer, Frank Branson. Already recognized by *D Magazine* as one of the best lawyers in Dallas, and by *Forbes* as one of the most successful trial lawyers in the country, Mr. Branson has also been named each year for more than a decade by *The Best Lawyers in America* as one of the nation's outstanding personal injury trial lawyers.

We have asked this nationally-recognized trial lawyer, who has spent over a third of a century in the courtrooms of Texas, to be our representative from Dallas County. Before he begins his tale, we'd like to tell you a little bit about him. He was raised in Fort Worth, the son of a high-school football coach. He graduated from Texas Christian University in 1967, from Southern Methodist University Law School in 1969 and thereafter received his Masters of Law from SMU with a concentration in Legal Medicine.

Mr. Branson's reputation has been built on championing the causes of underdogs whose lives have been devastated by defective and dangerous products, such as automobiles with defective tires, drug companies that prey on the unsuspecting public by manufacturing and selling dangerous and defective drugs and trucking companies that send poorly maintained trucks driven by unqualified drivers out on the highways of this state and cause catastrophic injuries to Texas families.

He has also championed the causes of people who have been rendered brain-damaged, blinded and paralyzed by doctors and

Dallas
County Courthouse

hospitals who failed to live up to the responsibility of their chosen profession. During his practice he has represented people in every walk of life including such recognizables as "Spanky" of "Spanky and Our Gang" in a dispute over the use of his name and Southwest Airlines in its dispute with the City of Fort Worth and American Airlines over its rights to use Love Field.

We've asked this legendary lawyer to spin us some yarns about Texas courthouses:

"The first Dallas courthouse was a frame building erected in 1851. In 1855, work was begun on a two-story brick courthouse at a cost of $7,400. The current courthouse was completed in 1966 at a cost to the taxpayers of about $13.5 million.

In the 152 years since our first courthouse was built, there's been a lot of activity conducted in the name

"... TONAHILL HAD A PAIR OF CUFFLINKS MADE THAT WOULD EACH FIRE A BULLET."

of justice, some of it sad, some of it courageous, some of it humorous and some of it tragic.

For example, in 1925, a brave Dallas sheriff named Schuyler Marshall turned fire hoses on a crowd and he and his deputies killed one man and wounded four others in an attempt to prevent two men from being lynched for rape and murder.

In March of 1964, the Dallas courthouse saw the

Top Gun & Legal Legend
Frank Branson

★ LISTED AS ONE OF THE BEST LAWYERS IN HIS FIELD IN EVERY EDITION OF THE <u>BEST LAWYERS IN AMERICA</u> SINCE 1987

★ RECIPIENT OF THE SOUTHERN TRIAL LAWYERS ASSOCIATION WAR HORSE AWARD

★ NAMED ON MULTIPLE OCCASIONS AS ONE OF THE 'THE BEST LAWYERS IN DALLAS' BY <u>D MAGAZINE</u>

★ NAMED BY <u>TEXAS MONTHLY</u> AS ONE OF TEXAS' SUPER LAWYERS IN 2003 AND 2004

★ NAMED BY <u>FORBES</u> AS ONE OF THE MOST SUCCESSFUL TRIAL LAWYERS IN THE COUNTRY

★ CONTRIBUTOR OF MULTIPLE ARGUMENTS TO 'MILLION DOLLAR JURY ARGUMENTS'

★ <u>NATIONAL LAW JOURNAL</u> ARTICLE, 'THE WIZARD OF SHOW-AND-TELL'

★ <u>ASSOCIATED PRESS</u> ARTICLE, 'LAWYER GIVES VICTIMS BEST SHOT WITH VIDEO HARDBALL'

★ HONORED WITH 'LEGEND SEMINAR' BY TEXAS TRIAL LAWYERS ASSOCIATION

★ MEMBER OF THE BOARD OF GOVERNORS OF THE ASSOCIATION OF TRIAL LAWYERS OF AMERICA; PAST PRESIDENT OF DALLAS TRIAL LAWYERS ASSOCIATION, DALLAS CHAPTER OF AMERICAN BOARD OF TRIAL ADVOCATES, AND SOUTHERN TRIAL LAWYERS ASSOCIATION; DIRECTOR EMERITUS OF THE TEXAS TRIAL LAWYERS ASSOCIATION; EXECUTIVE BOARD MEMBER OF SOUTHERN METHODIST UNIVERSITY DEDMAN SCHOOL OF LAW; FORMER MEMBER OF TEXAS SUPREME COURT ADVISORY COMMITTEE; FORMER PROSECUTOR FOR GRIEVANCE COMMITTEE OF STATE BAR OF TEXAS; MEMBER OF INTERNATIONAL ACADEMY OF TRIAL LAWYERS; FELLOW OF INTERNATIONAL SOCIETY OF BARRISTERS

trial of Jack Ruby, a man convicted of killing Lee Harvey Oswald, the believed assassin of President John F. Kennedy. A number of interesting things occurred during the course of that trial. Marvin Belli, the self-proclaimed "King of Torts," came to Dallas with a unique, but risky defense of Jack Ruby, contending that Mr. Ruby could not control his actions because of a rare form of epilepsy. Famous Dallas District Attorney, Henry Wade, prosecuted the case and during the course of the trial continued to intentionally refer to the suave and sophisticated Melvin Belli as "Mr. Belly." The mispronunciation seemed to highlight the red sash that Mr. Belli wore about his rather substantial waist throughout the trial.

However, To Belli's credit, he retained, as co-counsel, one of Texas' legendary trial lawyers, Joe Tonahill, who (among his many talents) was considered a prankster of the first order. Mr. Tonahill, recognizing the potential danger in defending an assassin of an assassin of a President, thought it wise to arm himself with a pistol during the trial as he had done in the past when trying notorious cases in his hometown of Jasper. Mr. Belli insisted that Tonahill, who stood 6'6" and weighed 280 pounds, not arm himself during the trial (this was obviously in the days before metal detectors!). While appeasing Belli, Tonahill had a pair of cufflinks made that would each fire a shot. Legend has it that one weekend during the trial, while contemplating their next move and imbibing in the grape, Tonahill could stand it no more and fired one of his cufflinks in the hotel room at The Fairmont, scaring the be-Jesus out of Belli! Shortly before his death, knowing that I was an avid gun collector, Joe honored me with the legendary set of cuff shooters.

On another occasion in our courthouse, two lawyers were trying a case before the Honorable Joe Bailey Humphrey, who, by that time was up in his years. The two lawyers had begun to argue among themselves

over a point of law. When they couldn't agree on the answer to the legal question, they turned to the court for a decision and found that Judge Humphrey was no longer on the bench. One lawyer said to the other, "And where is the old S.O.B.?" at which point Judge Humphrey's head popped up over the Judge's bench and he said, "I'm here. I was just tying my shoe!"

Back in the early 1970s, Dallas County added microphones just in front of the bench where the lawyers would stand and argue their legal points to the court. The microphones were, in fact, hooked up to the jury box. A week after they were installed, I happened to be in trial on a worker's compensation case. My opponent was C.L. Mike Schmidt who is a good lawyer and a little older than I was with more experience. During the middle of trial, we were arguing a point of law at the bench while I was facing the jury and Mike had his back to them. Mike decided he didn't like the direction the argument was taking the court, so he bent over near me, cupped his hands and said directly into the microphone, "I'm going to whip your ass when this case is over with!" I could see the reaction of the jury who could hear what Mike was saying and I sat back and said, "Mr. Schmidt, I'll accept your offer but I don't think Juror No. 8 heard you. You might want to repeat it," at which point the judge realized what had just occurred and granted a mistrial. Following the trial, Mike and I agreed to continue our mutual admiration of each other in the local saloon and after a few drinks began a friendship which has now lasted easily three decades!"

Where did Delta County get its name?

THE COUNTY WAS NAMED FOR ITS TRIANGULAR SHAPE- THE SAME SHAPE AS THE GREEK LETTER DELTA. THE TOWN OF COOPER, WHICH IS THE COUNTY SEAT, WAS NAMED AFTER SENATOR L. W. COOPER, FOUNDER OF THE COUNTY.

Where is the Delta County Courthouse located?

ON THE NORTHWEST CORNER OF FIRST STREET AND DALLAS AVENUE IN THE COUNTY SEAT OF COOPER, TX.

Who designed the Delta County Courthouse?

HOOK SMITH DESIGNED THE 1940 FOUR-STORY MODERNE BRICK HISTORIC COURTHOUSE THAT WAS FUNDED BY THE WORK PROJECTS ADMINISTRATION . THE COST TO BUILD THE COURTHOUSE WAS $110,450.

What is the courthouse's most unusual feature?

FOLLOWING THE CIVIL WAR, CONFEDERATE AND UNION VETERANS PLANTED PECAN TREES IN FRONT OF THE COURTHOUSE TO SYMBOLIZE THE END OF THE TURMOIL AND A NEWFOUND PEACE WITH EACH OTHER.

What is the most famous case tried in the Delta County Courthouse?

WILLIAM PRESTON LONGLEY WAS AN INFAMOUS TEXAN OUTLAW TRIED FOR A NUMBER OF THINGS IN THE DELTA COUNTY COURTHOUSE. IN FEBRUARY OF 1876, LONGLEY ENDED UP IN THE DELTA COUNTY JAIL AGAIN AFTER ARGUING WITH A MAN OVER A GIRL. IN JUNE, HE BURNED HIMSELF OUT OF THE JAIL AND SOON AFTER MURDERED A REVEREND WHILE THE REVEREND WAS MILKING A COW. LONGLEY WAS EVENTUALLY HUNG IN LEE COUNTY, TX, FOR ANOTHER ONE OF HIS CRIMES.

Where do you hang your hat?

AT THE LAW FIRM OF ADKERSON & HAUDER IN DOWNTOWN DALLAS, TX, LOCATED IN BRYAN TOWER. MY PARTNER, BERNIE E. HAUDER AND I, ARE PLEASED TO BE AV RATED BY MARTINDALE-HUBBELL AND LISTED AMONG BEST'S DIRECTORY OF RECOMMENDED INSURANCE ATTORNEYS. TEXAS LAWYER PUBLISHED A FRONT PAGE ARTICLE HIGHLIGHTING THE FIRM AS ONE OF TEXAS' BEST FIRMS TO HANDLE LARGE LIABILITY CASES. WE HAVE EXTENSIVE EXPERIENCE REPRESENTING CLIENTS IN STATE AND FEDERAL TRIAL AND APPELLATE COURTS AND BEFORE THE TEXAS WORKERS' COMPENSATION COMMISSION.

Believe it or not!

HANGING GALLOWS USED TO BE UPSTAIRS IN THE COURTHOUSE. THE GALLOWS WERE UP A NARROW STAIRCASE WITH A JAIL DOOR AT THE TOP, WITH ONE SMALL WINDOW IN THE DOOR. JUDGE NOBLE THOMPSON SAID THAT LONG AGO, THE STATE OF TEXAS ACTUALLY HUNG PEOPLE UP THERE!

"Despite the usual corporate fear of Texas juries, our clients continue to have the confidence in this law firm to 'seek truth and justice' at the Courthouse."

~ DARRELL'S FAMOUS TEXAS JUSTICE SAYING

"The Small Town Underdog"

A Famous Texas Case as Told by

DARRELL G. ADKERSON
ADKERSON & HAUDER

As a co-chair to President George W. Bush's Economic Advisory Council of Texas, Attorney Darrell Adkerson is knowledgeable about the environment and the effects of toxins on nearby communities and its residents. More importantly, he knows how to defend the businesses who set up shop in Texas towns, where the environment is a sensitive subject to all who are concerned. Mr. Adkerson handled a precedent setting case where a man goes up against a town.

The Plaintiff had been an employee of the Holly Carburetor Company, located in Delta County. The former employee of the plant decided that his extensive liver and lung damage was due to his strenuous work environment. His gastroenterologist and lung doctors even testified he suffered permanent liver and lung damage from working around toxins. He further claimed he was completely disabled as a result of his employment and that he could never work again and could only lift five pounds. The suit was for approximately $25 million and if the Holly Carburetor Company lost the case, the plant would be closed. The economic impact on this small town would be devastating; hundreds of Delta County residents would lose their jobs if this case were not won.

Mr. Adkerson was brought in to defend Delta County's main source of income, the Holly Carburetor Company. The odds were slim. This small town didn't stand a chance, but in true Texas style, the Holly Carburetor Company and Mr. Adkerson were willing to go the extra mile to see that justice was served. Mr. Adkerson decided to argue the case alone, with no local counsel and

Delta
County Courthouse

he felt that the case he had against the former employee was strong because of what he found in his research. The plaintiff had four attorneys and the Delta County attorney as local counsel.

Not only did Mr. Adkerson discover that the claimant even mowed his own lawn (hardly a job for the disabled), but that he had prior medical treatment for years, that bordered on the side of him being a full-fledged hypochondriac. The claimant had been going to a Choctaw Indian hospital in Oklahoma for over fifteen years prior his residency in Delta County, and well before his employment with Holly. His illnesses were not due to his employment and exposure to toxins, but due to many other documented possibilities. The Holly Carburetor Company was found not liable and Mr. Adkerson won this landmark case for Delta County, allowing the plant's doors

> "... HUNDREDS OF DELTA COUNTY RESIDENTS WOULD LOSE THEIR JOBS IF THIS CASE WERE NOT WON."

to stay open and saving the company millions. This case was unique in that the jury answered affirmatively as to whether the plaintiff intentionally misrepresented his physical condition before being hired by Holly. This was a first for Texas history, as far as anyone knows. To this date, Mr. Adkerson goes down in Delta County history as being the "under-dog" who won in the case of "Home Townin' Gone Bad in Delta County."

Denton County Courthouse

"Serial Killer in Denton"

A Famous Texas Case as Told by
DONALD H. FLANARY, JR.
THE FLANARY GROUP, P.C.

Henry Lee Lucas is one of the best known serial killers in America. This story hits home in Denton County, where he was charged and convicted of murdering two county residents.

Lucas was conditioned by his environment to become capable of killing another. Born in 1936, he had a home life of poverty, perversion and many forms of abuse. Both of Lucas' parents were alcoholics, his mother a part-time prostitute and his father a quadriplegic. The nine children were put in charge of running the family still, where they made moonshine.

One night in 1960, Lucas and his mother were out drinking when they began to argue. They returned home, where the argument continued well into the night. By daybreak, Lucas' mother was dead. The argument had reached its climax when Lucas swung at her with a pocket knife. He proceeded to stab her several more times. According to his confession, after she was dead he had sex with her corpse. Lucas was apprehended shortly after the murder and convicted; however, Lucas served only ten years for this murder and he was released in 1975.

Lucas became a drifter, finding his way to Florida. Here he befriended Ottis Toole, a transvestite. Toole himself was a rooky criminal with an interest in arson and the two became close friends. Toole quickly invited Lucas to live with him at his mother's house, where he befriended Becky Powell, the 12-year old niece of Toole.

An odd relationship grew between Lucas and Becky, and after they were all kicked out of Toole's mother's house, the duo headed west together. They even posed as husband and wife and they eventually ended up in Texas. In Ringgold, they found employment looking after the elderly Kate Rich and they moved into her home. This did not last long, though, as Rich's family was wary of Lucas and Becky.

Their next stop was in Stoneburg, Texas, where they were taken in by a man by the name of Moore, who ran a sort of church and halfway house. While Lucas described this as one of the best points in his life, Becky was not so happy. Becky wanted to go back to Florida and, quite simply, Lucas did not. While Lucas told Moore that he and Becky were leaving to head back towards Florida, it seems Becky never made it. She was never seen alive again.

The story began to unravel when, a month later, the elderly Ms. Rich went missing. Witnesses reported seeing her with Lucas on the day of her disappearance and an investigation was opened. Shortly after his arrest Lucas wrote the following… "To Whom It May Concern, I, Henry Lee Lucas, to try to clear this matter up, I killed Kate Rich. I have tried to get help so long and no one will help. I have killed for the past ten years and no one will believe it." Lucas was not done at the end of this confession, however; he went on to tell the authorities that he had murdered Becky Powell, as well.

He told investigators that he and Powell had been arguing about returning to Florida. Becky was so upset that she slapped Lucas; he responded by stabbing her in the chest. He then dismembered her and returned two weeks later to bury her body. In both cases Lucas led

" . . . BECKY NEVER MADE IT. SHE WAS NEVER SEEN ALIVE AGAIN."

investigators to the scene, where they found skeletal remains and other evidence to corroborate his story. Lucas was charged with first degree murder and, during his trial, admitted to having killed over 100 women.

Henry Lee Lucas was found guilty of murder in both cases and is serving two life sentences. Since his arrest the number of murders he has confessed to have reached nearly 600; however, nearly all of these are now thought to be false confessions. With his street smarts and attention to detail, Lucas was able to feed investigators enough details that they believed him. He later claimed that these false confessions were his way of making the investigators look incompetent.

What is true, despite his various stories and hoaxes, is that he is guilty of murdering his mother, Kate Rich and Becky Powell, and will be remembered by Denton County residents for years to come.

"Do right and fear no one."
~ DON'S FAMOUS TEXAS JUSTICE SAYING

Where did Denton County get its name?
FROM JOHN BUNYAN DENTON WHO WAS AN EASTERN FANNIN COUNTY METHODIST PREACHER, INDIAN FIGHTER AND LAWYER WHO WAS KILLED IN A RAID AGAINST INDIANS IN THE BATTLE OF VILLAGE CREEK IN NORTHERN TARRANT COUNTY ON MAY 22, 1841. IN 1846, THE TEXAS LEGISLATURE FORMED DENTON COUNTY OUT OF WHAT HAD BEEN A MUCH LARGER FANNIN COUNTY.

Where is the Denton County Courthouse located?
KNOWN AS THE COURTHOUSE-ON-THE-SQUARE IN DENTON, TX, IT IS BOUNDED BY OAK AND HICKORY, AND FORT WORTH DRIVE AND DALLAS DRIVE.

Who designed the Denton County Courthouse?
W.C. DODSON DESIGNED THIS SPECTACULAR 1896 HISTORICAL COURTHOUSE OF STONE MIXING SECOND EMPIRE ELEMENTS WITH ROMANESQUE REVIVAL. THIS COURTHOUSE HAS THE HONOR OF ALSO BEING A NATIONAL REGISTER PROPERTY.

What is the courthouse's most unusual feature?
IT HAS EIGHTY PINK GRANITE PILLARS AND THERE IS A MUSEUM WITHIN THE COURTHOUSE LOCATED ON THE SECOND FLOOR.

What is the most famous case tried in the Denton County Courthouse?
THE MURDER TRIAL OF HENRY LEE LUCAS FOR THE MURDER OF BECKY POWELL

Where do you hang your hat?
AT THE FLANARY GROUP ON JACKSON STREET IN DALLAS, TX.

Believe it or not!
MR. DENTON WAS A CAPTAIN IN A COMPANY LED BY EDWARD H. TARRANT. AFTER LEADING A VALIANT CHARGE AGAINST THE INDIANS OF KEECHI VILLAGE, MR. DENTON WAS WOUNDED AND DIED. HE IS BURIED ON THE SOUTHEAST SIDE OF DENTON COUNTY'S COURTHOUSE LAWN!

Where did Eastland County get its name?

FROM ONE OF ITS FIRST SETTLERS, CAPTAIN WILLIAM MOSBY EASTLAND, WHO WAS A VICTIM OF THE BLACK BEAN EPISODE AT SALADO, TX, WHILE ON THE MIER EXPEDITION IN 1873.

Where is the Eastland County Courthouse located?

IN THE CENTER OF A CLASSIC TOWN SQUARE AT THE INTERSECTION OF COMMERCE AND LAMAR STREETS IN EASTLAND, TX. IT IS ONE OF FOUR COURTHOUSES IN EASTLAND COUNTY: 1874, 1875, 1897 AND 1928.

Who designed the Eastland County Courthouse?

ARCHITECTS LANG AND WITCHELL DESIGNED THE HISTORIC COURTHOUSE IN 1928 OF A MODERNE-ART DECO STYLE OF STONE WHICH WAS HOME TO "OLD RIP."

What is the courthouse's most unusual feature?

DEFINITELY THE DETAILED ART-DECO STYLE OF THE COURTHOUSE ITSELF—MOST UNUSUAL!

What is the most famous case tried in the Eastland County Courthouse?

THIS WOULD HAVE TO BE THE LEGENDARY CASE ABOUT THE SANTA CLAUS BANK ROBBERY—A CASE THAT LED TO ONE OF THE MOST FAMOUS MAN-HUNTS OF ALL TIME. ON DECEMBER 23, 1927, MARSHALL RATLIFF (WEARING A SANTA SUIT), HENRY HELMS, ROBERT HILL AND LOUIS DAVIS HELD UP THE FIRST NATIONAL BANK IN CISCO, TX. CHIEF BEDFORD AND DEPUTY GEORGE CARMICHAEL WERE MORTALLY WOUNDED IN THE SHOOTOUT THAT FOLLOWED. AT THE END OF IT ALL, DAVIS WAS SHOT AND KILLED, HILL SERVED FIFTEEN YEARS IN JAIL, HELMS RECEIVED THE DEATH PENALTY AND RATCLIFF WAS HUNG BY A MOB.

Where do you hang your hat?

I HAVE BEEN WITH VINSON & ELKINS, IN DALLAS, TX, LOCATED IN THE HEART OF DOWNTOWN BIG D ON ROSS STREET, FOR FIVE YEARS AND AM CO-HEAD OF THE DALLAS LITIGATION PRACTICE. I HANDLE A VARIETY OF LARGE COMMERCIAL BUSINESS DISPUTES, WITH AN EMPHASIS ON ACCOUNTING MALPRACTICE AND SECURITIES FRAUD!

"The Brazilian Silver Mine Speculation"

A Famous Texas Case as Told by
Karen Hirschman
VINSON & ELKINS LAW FIRM

My association with the Eastland County Courthouse was a case in which I represented Ernst & Young LLP ("E&Y"), sued by its former audit client, Sunshine Mining and Refining Company, headquartered in Dallas. Sunshine, a publicly traded mining company, had invested in a silver prospect in Brazil called the Pirquitas Mine.

It had planned a "road show" in London and several other cities in Europe to generate interest in the investment, which was scheduled to take place in May of 1999. A few days before the "road show" was set to begin, E&Y resigned as Sunshine's auditor, saying it would not be auditing Sunshine's upcoming 1999 financial statements.

Sunshine hired new auditors, but ended up postponing the "road show" until the fall. The fall offering was not successful, Sunshine claimed, because of changes in market conditions (including a significant drop in silver prices). Without the funds from the offering, Sunshine said, it was unable to pay its debts and stave off bankruptcy while waiting out the depressed silver market. Sunshine sought $250,000,000 in damages — alleged lost profits it claimed it

Believe it or not!

OLD RIP, KNOWN IN EASTLAND COUNTY, TX, AND BEYOND AS "THE MIRACLE HORNY TOAD" HAS BEEN A PART OF TEXAS FOLKLORE FOR SEVERAL YEARS. HE WAS NAMED FOR RIP VAN WINKLE BECAUSE

JUST LIKE VAN WINKLE, OLD RIP WAS LOST TO THE WORLD FOR MORE THAN TWENTY YEARS. IN THIS CASE, OLD RIP WAS ENCLOSED IN THE EASTLAND COUNTY COURTHOUSE STRUCTURE AS IT WAS BEING BUILT IN 1897. THIRTY-ONE YEARS LATER AS THE RUBBLE OF A FIRE ALLOWED WORKERS TO TAKE APART THE CORNERSTONE, THE HORNY TOAD WAS FOUND, STILL ALIVE! AN IMMEDIATE SENSATION ENSUED AS OLD RIP BECAME AN INSTANT LEGEND. HE WAS TAKEN TO WASHINGTON, D.C. TO VISIT THE PRESIDENT AND SEEN IN PICTURES ACROSS THE COUNTRY. UNFORTUNATELY, A YEAR LATER, OLD RIP DIED OF PNEUMONIA SHORTLY AFTER THE NEW COURTHOUSE WAS BUILT. HIS BODY RESIDES IN A GLASS CASE IN THE CENTER OF THE CURRENT EASTLAND COUNTY COURTHOUSE!

Eastland County Courthouse

would have realized had it been able to raise the money to develop the Pirquitas Mine.

After two years of discovery, some thirty depositions and thousands upon thousands of pages of produced documents, the trial judge, The Honorable David Gibson, granted E&Y's Motion for Summary Judgment. Sunshine appealed and the case was assigned to the Eastland Court of Appeals. In a unanimous opinion by Judges Arnot, Wright and McCall, the Eastland Court found there was no evidence E&Y caused the damage Sunshine sought. The Court concluded Sunshine had failed to present any admissible evidence that the stock offering would have been successful if E&Y had not resigned.

"SUNSHINE SOUGHT $250,000,000 IN DAMAGES . . ."

Statements by Sunshine personnel and investment bankers that they believed the offering would have been successful were nothing more than speculation and conjecture. Even the evidence by Sunshine that it had been very successful in raising money in the past was insufficient. The Court did not find evidence identifying any investor who would have purchased stock or that a sufficient amount of stock would have been purchased in order for the offering to be considered successful.

The opinion is very important in Texas jurisprudence, as it holds plaintiffs to a high standard of proof of causation if damages are based upon the purchasing decisions of third parties. In concluding Sunshine had not met the standard, the Court observed that its stock offering was an "inherently speculative undertaking given its historically deteriorating financial condition and the depressed silver market." My partner, Marie Yeates, argued the appeal in the Eastland County Courthouse — a beautiful and imposing structure and the perfect environment for the argument of an important case such as this one.

Ellis
County Courthouse

"The Path of the Mystery Bullet"

A Famous Texas Case as Told by

C.L. MIKE SCHMIDT
THE SCHMIDT FIRM, LLP

Texas is a state that is known as a mecca of hunting and sport shooting. It is a right of passage for a young boy to be taught by his father how to shoot and to get his first deer in his teen years. This was the famous case on The Learning Channel with Trey Cooley and his father, Butch. Trey grew up around guns, learned to hunt at a young age and competed in pistol competitions. His father, Butch, an ex-State Trooper of 21 years, actually worked as a judge in some of these competitions and spent many hours at the shooting range.

It was the morning of September 29th that Butch awoke Trey to ask if he wanted to help him at one of the competitions he was judging. Even though it was a Saturday morning, this junior high school student agreed to work as a score card runner for the day and he accompanied his father to the Dallas Pistol & Revolver Club. While watching the competition, Trey decided to take a break and go cool off inside a building that housed the air gun range. A couple of moments later screams rang out as two women in the building watched young Trey slump over and fall to the ground unconscious with blood dripping from his temple.

Butch and others ran over and were shocked to find that Trey had been shot by an apparent stray bullet. Trey was rushed to the hospital where he only remained alive for six hours. It was a mysterious accident with a fatal result that left everyone wondering "how?" Trey was seated in a safety zone, surrounded by experienced shooters, at a range that had apparently ample safety measure to guard against such catastrophes.

The family hired attorney C.L. Mike Schmidt to represent

hem and figure out how this accident happened and who was at fault. Mr. chmidt put together a team of experts who were able to reconstruct the recise events that resulted in Trey's death. The first expert, Larry Fletcher, s a ballistics expert who analyzed the bullet and using barrel marks and wax esidue, was able to determine what gun had fired the fatal bullet. The gun vas a .45 caliber pistol that belonged to Dan Smith. On the day in question, Mr. Smith had been shooting in a pistol competition on a range directly behind he air gun building. It was also determined that the gun had been altered to re more easily and could easily have "doubled" or fired a second shot as the gun was recoiling up and to the left. This would have aimed the bullet owards the air gun building.

> " . . . AS TWO WOMEN IN THE BUILDING WATCHED YOUNG TREY SLUMP OVER AND FALL TO THE GROUND UNCONSCIOUS WITH BLOOD DRIPPING FROM HIS TEMPLE."

However, the bullet should have been stopped by the eye brow boards above the shooter, the protective berm behind the range or the wooden baffles above the berm. Why did all of these safety measures fail? What computer reconstructions created by the forensic animator and the accident reconstruction creator revealed is that the shooter was not on the 25 yard shooting line. He was firing at the target from fifteen yards, making the safety measures obsolete! What was worse is that shooters in he competition were required to shoot from twenty-five, twenty and ifteen yards! Further, there was a gap between the baffles and the berm, and the baffles were not even backed with concrete or steel as required. All of these factors were a recipe for disaster.

At fifteen yards, Mr. Smith's gun "doubled," sending a bullet up and to he left of the target. Unbelievably, the bullet then traveled 3 inches over the berm and under the baffles. It then entered the air gun building where it went hrough the siding, into a storage room, passed one inch from a broom and teel pipes, passed through a wall into the indoor range, grazed a ceiling tile and came back down as it barreled towards Trey Cooley. It was Mr. Schmidt's incredible team with their technology and investigation that were able to piece ogether the path of the mystery bullet and obtain a favorable recovery for such a great loss in the Cooley family.

Where did Ellis County get its name?

THE COUNTY WAS ESTABLISHED AROUND 1849 AND NAMED FOR RICHARD ELLIS, WHO SIGNED THE TEXAS DECLARATION OF INDEPENDENCE. THE COUNTY SEAT, WAXAHACHIE, IS KNOWN AS "GINGERBREAD CITY" AND THE "MOVIE CAPITAL OF TEXAS" SINCE FOUR ACADEMY AWARD FILMS, INCLUDING PLACES IN THE HEART, TENDER MERCIES AND BONNIE & CLYDE WERE SHOT ON LOCATION THERE.

Where is the Ellis County Courthouse located?

APPROXIMATELY THIRTY MILES SOUTH OF DALLAS, ON THE WAXAHACHIE TOWN SQUARE, AT THE CORNER OF MAIN AND ROGERS STREETS.

Who designed the Ellis County Courthouse?

THE RENOWNED J. RIELY GORDON DESIGNED THE HANDSOME HISTORIC COURTHOUSE AND NATIONAL REGISTER PROPERTY IN 1896 IN THE ROMANESQUE REVIVAL STYLE OF SANDSTONE AND GRANITE. THE ELLIS COUNTY COURTHOUSE WAS REDEDICATED ON OCTOBER 4TH 2002, BY THE TEXAS HISTORICAL COMMISSIONS' TEXAS COURTHOUSE PRESERVATION PROGRAM.

What is the Courthouse's most unusual feature?

THE ORNATE STONE CARVINGS EVIDENT ON ITS FOUR PORCHES, EACH OF WHICH FACES A TRUE COMPASS POINT. THE NORTH PORCH HAS TWELVE FACES, INCLUDING THE "GREEN MAN", AN ANCIENT FIGURE PREVALENT IN EUROPEAN ARCHITECTURE. IT ALSO HAS A COLOSSAL TOWER!

What is the most famous case tried in the Ellis County Courthouse?

IN JULY OF 2003, A YOUNG WAXAHACHIE BOY WAS TRIED FOR THE ATTEMPTED MURDER OF A 16-YEAR-OLD MAYPEARL GIRL. THE GIRL SAID THE BOY COAXED HER OUT OF HER HOME BEFORE KNOCKING HER TO THE GROUND UNCONSCIOUS. HE THEN DRUG HER TO A NEARBY FIELD AND ATTEMPTED TO STRANGLE HER, LEAVING BEHIND WHAT HE BELIEVED WAS HER DEAD BODY, HAVING NO IDEA THAT SHE WAS STILL ALIVE.

Where do you hang your hat?

THE SCHMIDT FIRM IN DALLAS, TX. SINCE 1992, THE SCHMIDT FIRM HAS LIMITED ITS PRACTICE TO THE REPRESENTATION OF PLAINTIFFS INVOLVED IN BOTH TRADITIONAL PERSONAL INJURY AND WRONGFUL DEATH LITIGATION INVOLVING MEDICAL MALPRACTICE, AVIATION, NURSING HOME ABUSE, TRUCKING, CONSTRUCTION AND MASS TORT LITIGATION INVOLVING PHARMACEUTICALS AND MEDICAL DEVICES.

Believe it or not!

IN 1989, ELLIS COUNTY WAS CHOSEN FOR THE SUPERCONDUCTING SUPERCOLLIDER, A 54-MILE TUNNEL IN WHICH ELECTRICALLY CHARGED PROTONS ACCELERATE FOR COLLISION EXPERIMENTS. ALTHOUGH, "SUPER CLYDE" WAS DEFUNDED IN 1993, THERE ARE FOURTEEN MILES OF TUNNEL, A MAGNET-DEVELOPMENT COMPLEX, THE SUPERCOLLIDER CENTRAL FACILITY AND THE LINEAR ACCELERATOR THAT WERE ALREADY BUILT!

Where did Erath County get its name?

ERATH COUNTY WAS NAMED FOR GEORGE B. ERATH, ONE OF THE ORIGINAL SURVEYORS OF THE AREA. ERATH FOUGHT IN THE TEXAS REVOLUTION AND, IN 1845, BECAME ONE OF THE FIRST STATE SENATORS.

Where is the Erath County Courthouse located?

IN THE COUNTY SEAT, STEPHENVILLE ON WEST WASHINGTON STREET. IN 1856 JOHN M. STEPHEN OFFERED TO DONATE LAND FOR A COURTHOUSE AND TOWN SITE IF THE TOWN WAS NAMED "STEPHENVILLE" AND MADE A COUNTY SEAT.

Who designed the Erath County Courthouse?

BUILT IN 1892, THIS ROMANESQUE REVIVAL HISTORIC COURTHOUSE WAS THE DESIGN OF RENOWNED ARCHITECT J. RIELY GORDON, AN ARCHITECT OUT OF SAN ANTONIO. THIS PROPERTY IS ALSO A NATIONAL REGISTER PROPERTY. THE ERATH COUNTY COURTHOUSE WAS REDEDICATED ON AUGUST 20TH 2002 BY THE TEXAS HISTORICAL COMMISSIONS' TEXAS COURTHOUSE PRESERVATION PROGRAM.

What is the courthouse's most unusual feature?

IT WAS CONSTRUCTED FROM WHITE LIMESTONE QUARRIED FROM THE LEON RIVER AND RED SANDSTONE FROM THE PECOS RIVER. WHILE MOST TEXAS COURTHOUSES HAVE THE TOWER OFF TO ONE SIDE, HERE THE TOWER IS IN THE CENTER.

What is the most famous case tried in the Erath County Courthouse?

"THE CASE OF OLD MAN SNOW." THIS INFAMOUS ERATH RESIDENT WAS INDICTED AND EXECUTED FOR THE TRIPLE HOMICIDE OF HIS WIFE, STEP-MOTHER AND STEP-SON IN 1926. AFTER OLD MAN MURDERED HIS STEP SON, HE CUT-OFF THE HEAD AND PUT IT IN A BAG A CELLAR. WHEN IT WAS SNIFFED-OUT BY HUNTERS, IT WAS STILL PRESERVED ENOUGH FOR LOCAL AUTHORITIES TO HAVE IT EMBALMED AND PUT ON DISPLAY FOR IDENTIFICATION. THIS IS HOW THE VICTIM WAS IDENTIFIED AND OLD MAN SNOW WAS CONNECTED TO THE MURDER.

Where do you hang your hat?

MY LAW OFFICE, FOREMAN, LEWIS & HUTCHISON, IS IN GRAPEVINE, TX. WE ARE ALL AGGRESSIVE AND SKILLED TRIAL LAWYERS WHO ARE COMMITTED TO PROTECTING THE RIGHTS OF INDIVIDUALS.

Believe it or not!

THE COUNTY IS BEST KNOWN FOR THE TOWN OF DUBLIN, WHERE DR. PEPPER IS STILL MADE THE OLD FASHIONED WAY!

"Justice for the poor, the injured, the forgotten, the voiceless, the defenseless and the damned."

Gerry Spence

~ SUSAN'S FAMOUS TEXAS JUSTICE SAYING

"Fighting Discrimination One County at a Time"

A Famous Texas Case as Told by
SUSAN E. HUTCHISON
FOREMAN, LEWIS & HUTCHISON, P.C.

Every Texas town has at least one diner that the locals consider to be an extension of their own home. One of the things that make these local diners special is the atmosphere. It is relaxed; no one is putting on airs. The dress is work clothes, often Dickies or overalls. The parking lot is full of pickups — not BMWs. The tables and vinyl-cushioned booths are as worn and comfortable as Grandma's kitchen table. The waitresses in these diners are extra friendly. They work long hours with a cheerful smile, usually greeting their guests as "honey" or "sugar." Their labor is a labor of service.

The atmosphere in one such diner in Erath County was much more friendly to the dining guests than it was to the staff. In our diner, the term "honey" was often used by the male owner in addressing a waitress we will call "Nancy." Sometimes it was even used as he touched her inappropriately. Nancy had worked in this diner for several years, but when she complained no one in power listened or seemed to care. This job was important to Nancy and her lack of education and a tough economy left her little opportunity to just walk away. Her family lived week to week on her income and she felt trapped, helpless and with little choice but to endure the injustice she was suffering.

Enter Susan Hutchison. Susan is affable and friendly to those who know her. But facing an injustice in the courtroom, Susan is a pit bull—a true warrior

Erath
County Courthouse

 Foreman, Lewis
& Hutchison P.C.
Warriors for Justice.com

for justice. She is, as *Texas Monthly* has called her, a "Texas Super Lawyer." Susan empowered Nancy and told her story—when on her own Nancy would have had no voice. The management and the team of lawyers their insurance company hired, denied,

> "... SHE FELT TRAPPED, HELPLESS AND WITH LITTLE CHOICE BUT TO ENDURE THE INJUSTICE SHE WAS SUFFERING."

delayed and ultimately sought to destroy Nancy. But Susan fought back. She fought them in the courthouse of Erath County and in the end, justice prevailed for Nancy and Susan. Nancy's story was heard and she was able to regain her dignity. Changes were made and Nancy and those who spend their days serving others were finally served themselves—with a large portion of Texas justice.

Falls
County Courthouse

"The Obedient Son"

A Famous Texas Case as Told by

RICHARD A. "RICK" DODD
CAPPOLINO, DODD & KREBS
ASSOCIATED ATTORNEYS

It was the early 1900s in Falls County, Texas. It was a happy time for folks in general. The population of the region was growing thanks to an increase in farming in the area and the county was reaping the benefits of having two railroads running through it. Marlin, the county seat, was a well-known tourist spot, attracting visitors from all over the nation to visit its spring. It was a quaint place with a sense of naiveté to it. No one suspected an innocent young boy was about to turn the town upside down.

The little boy I speak of was named Bus and for him those days were not peaceful at all. In fact, it was a confusing time for Bus. All he wanted in life was to please his mother. Despite his best efforts, this proved a difficult challenge for Bus. His mother was prone to exaggeration. Once, when she was particularly displeased with Bus' cousin, she told Bus, "I won't be satisfied until that boy's head is hung from my front porch." It was a creative way to let Bus know she was unhappy with something her nephew had done.

Bus, in his endless pursuit to please his mother, took her a little too literally. Not long after his mother's comment, Bus lured his cousin to a nearby creek, where he murdered him and cut off his head. He then took the head and did not hang it, but simply placed it on his mother's front porch.

The decapitated head remained on the porch for a short time before being taken to the creek for burial. The

> *"Justice is in the eye of the beholder."*
> ~ RICK'S FAMOUS TEXAS JUSTICE SAYING

cousin's headless body was taken to the Marlin funeral home, where it was laid out for friends and family to pay their respects. The head was later reunited with the body and the cousin received a proper burial.

Bus was apprehended for his crime. He was tried, convicted and sentenced, receiving 99 years in jail. Bus did not begin serving his sentence right away

"I WON'T BE SATISFIED UNTIL THAT BOY'S HEAD IS HUNG FROM MY FRONT PORCH."

because he managed to slip through the fingers of the Falls County sheriff. After the escape, he enjoyed a few days of freedom, although not in the best of conditions. It turns out that Bus was living under his friend's porch during that time and eating the family's leftovers to survive. When Bus was recaptured, he served only two years in Huntsville before being pardoned by the Governor. After all, he only did what his mother wanted.

A good lesson is to watch what you say in front of youngsters. You never know when they might take you seriously!

Where did Falls County get its name?
FROM THE BRAZOS RIVER FALLS NEAR THE CENTER OF THE COUNTY WHEN THE COUNTY WAS ORGANIZED IN 1850. THE FALLS ON THE BRAZOS ARE A POPULAR TOURIST ATTRACTION FOR THE AREA.

Where is the Falls County Courthouse located?
ON THE SQUARE IN MARLIN, TX. THE FIRST COURTHOUSE WAS A LOG CABIN; IT WAS USED FOR COUNTY BUSINESS AND COURT, SCHOOL, CHURCH, MEETING PLACE FOR POLITICAL AND COMMUNITY MEETINGS AND DANCE HALL.

Who designed the Falls County Courthouse?
ARTHUR E. THOMAS DESIGNED THE PRESENT MODERNE STYLE HISTORIC COURTHOUSE IN 1939 OF STONE, BRICK AND CONCRETE. IT WAS CONSTRUCTED AFTER THE HISTORIC STRUCTURE OF 1887 WAS DECLARED UNSAFE.

What is the Courthouse's most unusual feature?
ITS ENTRY, WHICH INCLUDES PINK GRANITE STEPS AND DECORATIVE ELEMENTS MADE FROM AUSTIN SHELLSTONE.

What is the most famous case tried in the Falls County Courthouse?
IN 1902, THE HEIRS OF S.S. WARD SUED WILLIAM M. RICE FOR 1,280 ACRES OF LAND. THE TRIAL WAS A DAVID AND GOLIATH STORY, PITTING TEXAS LANDOWNERS AGAINST A NEW YORK MILLIONAIRE. THE RULING WAS OVERTURNED, BUT THE CASE WAS SENT BACK FOR RETRIAL, WHERE IT WAS TEMPORARILY HELD UP BY THE DEATH OF RICE AND THEN SETTLED WITH A COMPROMISE.

Where do you hang your hat?
IN CAMERON, WHICH IS IN THE MIDDLE OF CENTRAL TEXAS. I GREW UP ON A SHARE-CROP COTTON FARM BETWEEN CAMERON AND MARLIN AND HAVE BEEN IN PRIVATE PRACTICE FOR OVER TWENTY YEARS, REPRESENTING VICTIMS OF WRONGDOERS AGAINST SUCH ENTITIES AS BIG INSURANCE AND CORPORATIONS.

Believe it or not!
IN 1892, HOT MINERAL WATER WAS FOUND DURING A SEARCH FOR AN ARTESIAN WELL AND SOON THE BETHESDA BATHHOUSE, MAJESTIC BATHHOUSE, IMPERIAL HOTEL AND TORBETT HOSPITAL WERE FOUNDED. THE HILTON HOTEL EMPIRE BUILT THEIR EIGHTH HOTEL IN MARLIN, THE FALLS HOTEL, WHICH HAD A TUNNEL UNDER THE STREET TO THE BATHHOUSE. THE NEW YORK YANKEES USED TO SUMMER IN MARLIN FOR THE HEALTH BENEFITS OF THE HOT MINERAL WATER!

Where did Fannin County get its name?

THE COUNTY WAS ORGANIZED IN 1838 AND NAMED FOR JAMES W. FANNIN, WHO WAS MASSACRED WITH HIS SOLDIERS AT GOLIAD.

Where is the Fannin County Courthouse located?

IN THE COUNTY SEAT OF BONHAM ON WEST SAM RAYBURN DRIVE.

Who designed the Fannin County Courthouse?

THE ORIGINAL 1889 BUILDING WAS DESIGNED BY THE ARCHITECTS W.C. DODSON & DUDLEY; HOWEVER, AFTER TWO EXTENSIVE RECONSTRUCTION PROJECTS, ONE IN 1929 AND ANOTHER IN 1965, THE ORIGINAL STRUCTURE IS IMPOSSIBLE TO RECOGNIZE.

What is the courthouse's most unusual feature?

THE CLOCK THAT STRIKES ON THE HOUR AND CHIMES ON THE HALF HOUR, ALONG WITH THE STATUE OF JAMES BUTLER BONHAM.

What is the most famous case tried in the Fannin County Courthouse?

IN 1863, GENERAL HENRY MCCULLOCH, WHO WAS COMMANDER OF THE NORTHERN DISTRICT OF TEXAS, HAD HIS OFFICE ON THE SECOND FLOOR OF THE COURTHOUSE. GENERAL MCCULLOCH, UNDER ORDER FROM HIS SUPERIORS, ORDERED WILLIAM QUANTRILL, A CONFEDERATE GUERILLA TO SURRENDER. HE WAS ARRESTED AND IMPRISONED IN THE COURTHOUSE. WHEN GENERAL MCCULLOCH WENT FOR THE EVENING MEAL, WILLIAM QUANTRILL ESCAPED FROM THE COURTHOUSE. AFTER HIS ESCAPE HE JOINED HIS MEN AT THE HOTEL ACROSS THE STREET AND THEY FLED THE DISTRICT AND CROSSED THE RED RIVER BY WAY OF THE TOLBERT FERRY. WHEN MCCULLOCH DISCOVERED QUANTRILL WAS MISSING HE SENT HIS TROOPS AFTER HIM BUT IT WAS TOO LATE FOR HE WAS ALREADY IN INDIAN TERRITORY.

Where do you hang your hat?

SULPHUR SPRINGS, TX, AT THE J-B WELD COMPANY, WHERE WE PRODUCE A COLD WELD PRODUCT TO REPAIR MANY PRODUCTS WHICH IS SOLD HERE IN THE UNITED STATES AS WELL AS IN FOREIGN COUNTRIES.

Believe it or not!

JAMES BUTLER BONHAM, A DISTANT RELATIVE OF MARY BONHAM'S, WAS AN ATTORNEY AND DURING A TRAIL A LADY CLIENT OF HIS WAS INSULTED BY A MAN CONCERNED WITH THE CASE. BONHAM PROCEEDED TO THRASH THE MAN IN THE PRESENCE OF THE COURT AND IN A CONTROVERSY WITH THE JUDGE, HE THREATENED TO PULL HIS NOSE!

"The future is tomorrow."
~ MARY'S FAMOUS TEXAS JUSTICE SAYING

"The Messenger of the Alamo"

A Famous Texas Case as Told by
MARY BONHAM
CEO OF J-B WELD COMPANY

Mary Bonham's roots in Fannin County stretch all the way back to 1835, and James Butler Bonham, a distant cousin to her husband. The story of this legendary man has not only been passed down in her family, but is one that all Texas should remember.

The town of Bonham in Fannin County was first called Bois d'Arc when it was founded in 1843. Soon after however, it had its name changed to Bonham, and for good reason. The city was renamed after Alamo defender James Butler Bonham himself. Seemingly fearlessly devoted to his country, during the Battle of the Alamo, Bonham rode through Mexican lines twice, requesting aid from Gonzales and escorting the Gonzales volunteers back to the Alamo.

The county itself is named after James Fannin, who was massacred with his men at the battle of Coleto Creek. This was a day in Texas history that quite possibly could be considered one of the most tragic of all time. On March 27, 1836, General Santa Anna ordered the execution of some 380 Texas army soldiers who were prisoners of war. The men were under Colonel Fannin's command, and they had surrendered to the Mexican army on March 20. Fannin had received assurances from the Mexican field commander, Gen. Jose Urrea, that the Texans would eventually be paroled and sent to New Orleans. Although Urrea probably had good intentions, Santa Anna overruled him and commanded that the prisoners be slaughtered.

Fannin
County Courthouse

Despite the atrocities that have occurred here, James Butler Bonham once said that this part of the country was the garden spot of the world and the best prospect for health he ever saw. Mary Bonham still relishes these words and she, too, sees this place in a different light, having such a personal connection to the past. She nostalgically says, "It is great to live in a land of plenty where our forefathers fought and died to pave a way for us to have a life of freedom. The future they gave us allows us to be able to see the past through their history and to look to the future as our beloved ones did in their time. As I look to the days of old, I realize how rugged the way of life was for the ones who walked and rode so hard to save our country and we must continue, as they did, to fight for our rights."

Before arriving in Texas, James Butler Bonham was

"HE WAS KNOWN AS THE MESSENGER OF THE ALAMO."

already a very accomplished man. Not only a great war hero, Bonham was admitted to the bar in 1830 and began to practice law at Pendleton, South Carolina. In 1834, he received word from William Barret Travis, a boyhood friend, urging him to come to Texas. He arrived with the Mobile Grays in December of 1835. It was just a year later in 1836 that James Butler Bonham was the last one to ride into the Alamo with a white flag flying. He was known as the messenger of the Alamo.

Fort Bend
County Courthouse

"Carrie Nation Against the Saturn-Faced Rummies"

A Famous Texas Tale as Told by

DIANA MARSHALL
THE MARSHALL LAW FIRM

Texas has honestly earned its reputation for having a population with more than its share of colorful personalities—and many of these bigger-than-life Texas personalities have historically been trial lawyers. True enough, most of these courthouse kings and their cronies were men, until recent history. But, there was a time in Fort Bend County when the local advocates gathered in hiding to share a brew and a few exaggerated war stories, because they lacked the courage to face one particular woman, the legendary Carrie Nation.

Even in Texas, neither men nor women come much stronger or more colorful than did the hatchet-wielding temperance crusader, Carrie Nation. Carrie Amelia Moore Nation, who came to be known as Carrie Nation, was an advocate, though she never claimed to be a lawyer. Carrie was a resident of Richmond, Texas, working as manager of a hotel near the site of the original Fort Bend County Courthouse when she launched her campaign to rid society of the evils of alcohol.

As those of us who congregated after hearings and trials in Fort Bend County would later learn, Carrie Nation's saloon smashing campaign failed to have a lasting effect on reducing the number of the County's watering holes. Though she may have failed to purge forever the detestable drink from her beloved Fort Bend County, Carrie Nation fought harder, longer and louder for what she believed than any modern-day advocate has ever matched.

"'Half of the greatest trial lawyers in America live in Texas, and the other half are buried here.'

In saying this, I call for a moment of loving reflection to remember just a few of the magnificent lawyers who served with honor in the courthouses of Texas: Curtis Brown, Ralph Carrigan, Tom Stovall, Joe Tonahill, Jim Kronzer, Shirley Helm, Bill Blanton and Warren Burnett."

~ Diana Marshall

Where did Fort Bend County get its name?
ORGANIZED IN 1838, FORT BEND COUNTY WAS NAMED BY EARLY SETTLERS FOR A LOG FORT BUILT IN THE BEND OF THE BRAZOS RIVER. THE COUNTY SEAT BECAME KNOWN AS FORT BEND OR "FORT SETTLEMENT."

Where is the Fort Bend County Courthouse located?
IN RICHMOND, TX, ON THE CORNER OF JACKSON AND FOURTH STREETS, ON THE BRAZOS RIVER FOURTEEN MILES SOUTHWEST OF HOUSTON.

Who designed the Fort Bend County Courthouse?
THE SILVER-DOMED COURTHOUSE WAS DESIGNED IN 1908 IN THE BEAUX-ARTS STYLE BY C.H. PAGE AND BROTHER ARCHITECTS. THIS HISTORIC COURTHOUSE ALSO HAS THE HONOR OF BEING A NATIONAL REGISTER PROPERTY.

What is the Courthouse's most unusual feature?
BUILT IN 1908 OF BRICK WITH A GORGEOUS ROTUNDA, THE COURTHOUSE WAS NEARLY IDENTICAL TO THE HAYS COUNTY COURTHOUSE BUILT THE YEAR BEFORE IN SAN MARCOS. THE FORT BEND COURTHOUSE WAS DIFFERENT FROM THE HAYS STRUCTURE IN THAT THE FORT BENDERS BOUGHT THE KIT THAT INCLUDED CLOCK FACES.

What is the most famous case tried in the Fort Bend County Courthouse?
DAN LEACH, A 21-YEAR-OLD TEXAS MAN, WAS PROMPTED TO CONFESS TO THE MURDER OF HIS GIRLFRIEND, AFTER SEEING THE CONTROVERSIAL MOVIE, "THE PASSION OF CHRIST". LEACH CONFESSED THAT HE MADE IT LOOK AS IF HIS 19-YEAR-OLD PREGNANT GIRLFRIEND, ASHLEY NICOLE WILSON, HAD COMMITTED SUICIDE. THIS MURDER CASE IS CURRENTLY BEING TRIED IN THE FORT BEND COUNTY COURT, LOCATED IN RICHMOND, TEXAS.

Where do you hang your hat?
THE MARSHALL LAW FIRM IN DOWNTOWN HOUSTON, TX. WE HAVE SIX ATTORNEYS WHO FUNCTION AS A TRIAL TEAM ON MAJOR LITIGATION. IN ADDITION, THE ATTORNEYS INDIVIDUALLY HANDLE ALL TYPES OF LAWSUITS IN HARRIS AND THE SURROUNDING COUNTIES.

Believe it or not!
FORT BEND COUNTY IS THE BURIAL PLACE OF JANE LONG, "THE MOTHER OF TEXAS!"

Carrie Moore was born in Kentucky in 1846, to a family that uprooted constantly, always searching for an escape from hard times. Perhaps Carrie's fearless constitution developed from having withstood difficult times as a child and from having to grow up quickly while her mother battled a debilitating problem with mental illness. Even before she took to the hatchet, Carrie was imposing, standing almost 6-feet-tall and reportedly weighing 180 pounds.

Carrie's life went from bad to worse when she married Dr. Charles Gloyd in 1867. As fate would have it, Dr. Gloyd practiced more drinking than medicine and while Carrie was pregnant with their daughter, her alcoholic husband passed away. Carrie resolved never to be left again to the mercy of a man possessed of the demon drink, earned her teaching certificate and found work as a teacher.

In 1877, Carrie married David Nation, a colorful character who worked simultaneously as a lawyer, a newspaper correspondent and a minister. They moved to Texas and purchased a cotton plantation near Houston. When the plantation failed, Carrie turned to working to manage a hotel in Richmond and David returned to the paper, the law and the pulpit. Together they launched a life of crusade and controversy and it all started in Fort Bend County, Texas.

Carrie Nation felt "divinely ordained to forcefully promote temperance," and for those who were not persuaded by her divine message, there was always the hatchet. Carrie and her female army waged ferocious attacks on the inns of non-believers, smashing barrels and bottles, with a battle cry of, "Smash, ladies, Smash!" New York prize-fighter John L. Sullivan reportedly ran and hid when Carrie Nation charged into his saloon on her divine mission, hatchet in hand.

For many people, even the Temperance Union, Carrie Nation was too violent, too radical. Carrie even claimed that she had mystical experiences through which God spoke to her. Carrie was devoid of the civility that prompts most of today's Texas trial lawyers to refer to their adversaries as, "my worthy opponent." Not Carrie Nation, she referred to her opponents as, "rum-soaked, whiskey-swilled, Saturn-faced rummies." Though Carrie Nation was a tireless advocate for temperance, her mystical experiences taught her nothing about moderation.

Top Gun & Legal Legend
Diana Marshall

★ NAMED BY TIME MAGAZINE AS ONE THE TOP 5 WOMEN TRIAL LAWYERS IN AMERICA

★ FEATURED BY THE HOUSTON PRESS AS ONE OF FOUR "WOMEN MEN FEAR"

★ FELLOW, THE AMERICAN COLLEGE OF TRIAL LAWYERS

★ FELLOW, THE AMERICAN BOARD OF TRIAL ADVOCATES

★ MEMBER OF THE AMERICAN LAW INSTITUTE

★ J.D., THE UNIVERSITY OF TEXAS LAW SCHOOL

★ BOARD CERTIFIED, CIVIL TRIAL LAW, TEXAS BOARD OF LEGAL SPECIALIZATION

★ SMITHSONIAN INSTITUTE, "THE AMERICAN TRIAL LAWYERS-PERFORMANCE" PERMANENT COLLECTION TRIAL EXHIBITION

★ COURT TV, "ANATOMY OF A TRIAL"

★ SINGER/HARMONICA PLAYER FOR COUNTRY BAND OF CITY LAWYERS NAMED "THE TEXAS BAR FLIES"

"CARRIE NATION FELT 'DIVINELY ORDAINED TO FORCEFULLY PROMOTE TEMPERANCE,' AND FOR THOSE WHO WERE NOT PERSUADED BY HER DIVINE MESSAGE, THERE WAS ALWAYS THE HATCHET."

DIANA MARSHALL WITH HER BAND, THE TEXAS BARFLIES, JUDGE DAVID HITTNE UH PROFESSOR DAVID CRUMP,& LAWYER MAX ADDISON.

JOHN V. SINGLETON, JR.
Senior United States District Judge, Retired
314 NORTH POST OAK LANE • HOUSTON, TEXAS 77024
713/957-2469 • FAX: 713/956-0262
ARBITRATION, MEDIATION, LITIGATION COUNSELING

Dear Martana,

You have asked me for a few courthouse tales about Diana Marshall. Now, that is an easy task. When Diana first appeared in my Court, she was preceded by a nickname, "The Odessa Contessa." One of my dear friends, George Cire, admitted that he started one hearing obviously still livid about the prior case, and Diana innocently asked him if he knew that other Judge named Cire who was wise, patient and had a good sense of humor. Cire said he told her, "Fortunately for you, I know him well." He was in my office within minutes laughing about the event. Soon thereafter, I had the pleasure of meeting the Odessa Contessa. Diana gave a fine argument, and, in open Court, I jokingly gave Diana my "blessing," and said, "If I wasn't already married, I'd marry you," to which she responded, "Your Honor, I shall pray for your wife's good health and long life."

While it is true that Diana is a very gifted showboat of a lawyer, she also loves to celebrate the success of others. When her Baker & Botts partner Harold Metts was elected President of the Houston Bar, Diana conspired with Metts to concoct a country band for his reception. Thus was born "The Texas Barflies," consisting of David Crump, Max Addison, U.S. District Judge David Hittner, and, of course, Diana. The Texas Barflies made their funny and surprising debut, and President Metts thought the band sounded much better than it had in rehearsal—Diana had secretly unplugged Judge Hittner's microphone for the performance.

While Diana's sense of humor serves her well, it has occasionally gotten her into a bind. Judge Hittner loves to tell the story about the time Diana saw Judge Lynn Hughes getting cash at an airport ATM machine. Thinking it would be funny, she walked up behind him and said, "You'll only need about a hundred dollars." When he turned around, the man was not Judge Hughes. On another occasion, in the early 70's, a judge referred to Diana only as "Lady" and to her male opponent as "Counsel." In front of the jury, Diana finally objected and sweetly asked him if he would refer to both counsel, equally, as "Lady." The jury laughed uncontrollably, but Diana got a small fine. A reporter happened to be present and the story became a Texas legend.

As often is the case in Texas, Diana's nickname, "The Odessa Contessa," was given to her because it is an opposite statement of her true nature, like tall Texans nicknamed "Tiny." She lacks any air of self-importance, privilege or superiority. Diana does not create or understand any distance between herself and others. Following final argument in a trial in Fort Bend County, Judge Charles Dickerson claims that he again instructed the jurors not to talk to the lawyers, and one raised her hand and asked, "Does that go for Diana?"

Diana became a lawyer in the early 70's, when few women appeared as attorneys in Texas courthouses; yet, she was completely at home in the courthouse. Judge Red James said he picked on her as the only female at a big docket call and called on her first to "announce your appearance," and she said, "among this crowd, it is better." As President of the State Bar, Lynne Liberato called Diana an "icon," and Houston attorney Ralph Balasco was quoted as saying that Diana made "one giant leap for womankind." I would add that Carrie Nation had to use an axe to make her point in Fort Bend County. Diana has never needed an axe. True to the great heritage of Texas trial lawyers, Diana Marshall uses her remarkable, gentle wit, impeccably crafted into wisdom.

Where did Franklin County get its name?

THE COUNTY WAS NAMED AFTER BENJAMIN CROMWELL FRANKLIN, AN EARLY RED RIVER COUNTY SETTLER AND THE REPUBLIC OF TEXAS' FIRST APPOINTED JUDGE.

Where is the Franklin County Courthouse located?

THE 1912 COURTHOUSE IS ON THE NORTH SIDE OF THE PUBLIC SQUARE AT THE CORNER OF DALLAS AND KAUFMAN STREETS. IMMEDIATELY NORTH OF THE COURTHOUSE ON BUSINESS HIGHWAY 37 IS THE 1912 JAIL WHERE JAIL CELLS FROM AN EARLIER 1878 JAIL ARE STILL INTACT.

Who designed the Franklin County Courthouse?

L.L. THURMAN OF DALLAS DESIGNED THE LIMESTONE HISTORIC COURTHOUSE IN A CLASSICAL REVIVAL STYLE IN 1912. THIS CURRENT STRUCTURE, THE COUNTY'S THIRD COURTHOUSE, HAS COLUMNED PORTICOS AND A CLOCK TOWER WITH BEAUTIFUL INTRICATE WORKINGS.

What is the courthouse's most unusual feature?

THE AMOUNT OF SURVIVING HISTORIC FABRIC, SUCH AS ORIGINAL PLASTER INTERIOR TREATMENTS, LIGHT FIXTURES, ORNATE CEILING TILES AND AN ORIGINAL E. HOWARD CLOCK.

What is the most famous case tried in the Franklin County Courthouse?

THE CAPITAL MURDER TRIAL OF MICHAEL RODRIGUEZ, A MEMBER OF THE FAMED "TEXAS SEVEN" WHO SLAYED IRVING POLICE OFFICER AUBREY HAWKINS ON CHRISTMAS EVE 2000. RODRIGUEZ WAS SENTENCED TO DEATH IN MAY 2002 BY A TWELVE PERSON FRANKLIN COUNTY JURY.

Where do you hang your hat?

MR. HICKS HAS A GENERAL COMMERCIAL PRACTICE IN MOUNT VERNON, TX, WITH AN EMPHASIS IN REAL ESTATE AND PROBATE. HE IS ACTIVE IN COMMUNITY LIFE, SERVING AS AN OFFICER IN HIS CHURCH, FIRST UNITED METHODIST CHURCH OF MT. VERNON, IN ROTARY INTERNATIONAL (YOUTH EXCHANGE OFFICER FOR HIS DISTRICT); HAS HOSTED OVER FIFTY EXCHANGE STUDENTS SINCE 1987) AND ACTIVE IN LOCAL PRESERVATION ORGANIZATIONS. HE SERVES ON STATE COMMITTEES OF THE TEXAS HISTORICAL COMMISSION AND THE TEXAS PARKS AND WILDLIFE DEPARTMENT.

Believe it or not!

THERE WERE TWO OTHER MT. VERNONS IN TEXAS AND SO THE TOWN HAD TO USE THE POST OFFICE NAME "LONE STAR" UNTIL THE MT. VERNON IN LAMAR COUNTY WASTED AWAY!

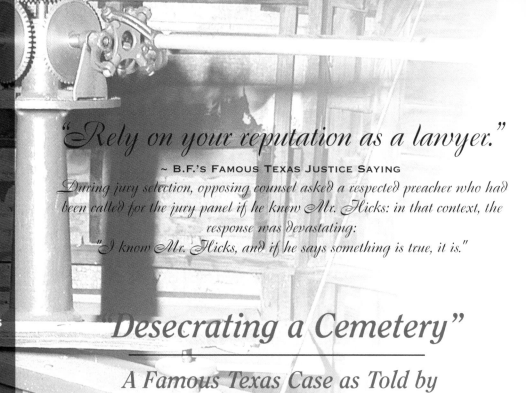

"Rely on your reputation as a lawyer."

~ B.F.'S FAMOUS TEXAS JUSTICE SAYING

During jury selection, opposing counsel asked a respected preacher who had been called for the jury panel if he knew Mr. Hicks: in that context, the response was devastating:
"I know Mr. Hicks, and if he says something is true, it is."

"Desecrating a Cemetery"

A Famous Texas Case as Told by

B.F. HICKS

B.F. HICKS LAW OFFICE

I have come to be known in many circles as an expert in "cemetery law." I drafted the Model Operating Manual for Small Cemeteries which is distributed widely through the Texas Historical Commission and have also prepared model articles and by-laws for non-profit cemetery associations.

There are approximately 50,000 small rural cemeteries in Texas; often the cemetery is the last physical evidence of a once thriving community. With development expanding into rural areas, we have instances of developers destroying cemeteries—bulldozing tombstones or removing graves. I am currently acting as a facilitator for a "summit on cemetery preservation" sponsored by the Texas Historical Commission to work toward preservation in this year 2004. I am currently serving on three state level committees. It is with this insight that I was involved in the following case.

In the late 1980s, the prominent labor lawyer, Otto B. Mullinax of Dallas, had acquired property in Franklin County. I was the county attorney for ten years from 1978 through 1988. There was a large rural cemetery which adjoined the Mullinax farm. The cemetery took in about two acres; graves were on half of the land and a wooded area with a spring was in the adjacent cemetery enclosure.

There had possibly been a church and parsonage near the spring and the burials had started beside the churchyard. In any event, it had evolved into a park like setting and was a beautiful acre of land used by the public as a park. Local citizens took great pride in this beautiful cemetery. Mr. Mullinax came in, bulldozed back a lot of brush and the fence lines and erected a new fence which resulted in the cemetery being restricted only

Franklin
County Courthouse

to the area with actual graves facing a farm-to-market road and the adjacent acreage including the valuable fresh water spring (also road frontage land) being enclosed within his pasture fence.

The local citizenry was outraged and I brought charges for cemetery desecration. We had a warrant issued and Mr. Mullinax ultimately arrived for his jury trial. My reputation for picking a jury was cinched in my rural home county when we got a guilty verdict in about thirty minutes. I had to overcome two defenses; that Mr. Mullinax had desecrated a cemetery—thus confirming the concept that a cemetery involves more

> "WITH DEVELOPMENT EXPANDING INTO RURAL AREAS, WE HAVE INSTANCES OF DEVELOPERS DESTROYING CEMETERIES—BULLDOZING TOMBSTONES OR REMOVING GRAVES."

than just the area taken in by actual graves and that Mr. Mullinax had intended to offend the public sensibilities through his wanton land grab.

The case was overturned on appeal (Texas Court of Appeals) because of the issue of "intent" in an opinion, which now makes it almost impossible to prosecute any cemetery desecration case with the subjective requirements for finding intent. Mr. Mullinax has now passed away and his heirs got this ill-gotten gain of land. And I am still defending cemeteries.

SALLIE ANN ENNIS
FLOWERS
BORN SEPT. 20, 1850
DIED CIRCA 1888

WIFE OF BERRY I. FLOWERS

Galveston
County Courthouse

"A Reclusive Millionaire"

A Famous Texas Case as Told by

TONY BUZBEE
THE BUZBEE LAW FIRM

In November of 2003, New York millionaire Robert Durst was acquitted for killing his 71-year-old neighbor, Morris Black. Prosecution claimed that Durst, who openly admitted to walking around Galveston smoking marijuana dressed as a woman, had the intent to murder and steal Morris Black's identity. They believed this was his way of escaping the attention of New York prosecutors who suspected he might be involved with his first wife's disappearance in 1984. The two neighbors had apparently become good friends in the previous months leading up to the murder.

Durst professed that the two were good friends, but the relationship became troublesome when Black began acting erratically and abusively. He claimed that the two had been involved in an argument one night when they fought over a gun that then discharged in Black's face. Durst admitted to shooting, cutting up the dead body of his neighbor and dumping it into the Galveston Bay in a state of panic, but adamantly protested it was an act of defense the whole time.

Durst also claimed he did not remember using saws and an axe to cut up the body. However, he told jurors of his vivid memories of cleaning up the mess. When investigators scoured his apartment, only 22 specks of visible blood were found on the wall. Shockingly, the jury came back with a verdict of not guilty. When interviewed after the five days of deliberating, the jury said they acquitted Durst on the basis of inconsistency from the prosecution.

"At my back I always hear, time's winged chariot hurrying near, and yonder all before us lie, the vast desert of eternity."

Andrew Marvell, to his Coy Mistress

~ TONY'S FAMOUS TEXAS JUSTICE SAYING

"IN MARCH OF 2004, DURST'S CASE MADE GALVESTON HEADLINES AGAIN WHEN THE POPULAR TELEVISION SHOW 'LAW & ORDER,' PROFILED HIS CASE."

Where did Galveston County get its name?
ORGANIZED IN 1887, THE COUNTY WAS ORIGINALLY NAMED BAHÍA DE GALVEZTON FOR THE SPANISH GOVERNOR OF LOUISIANA BERNARDO DE GALVEZ.

Where is the Galveston County Courthouse located?
ON THE CORNER OF 21ST AND BALL, JUST NEAR GALVESTON'S FAMED BEACHES.

Who designed the Galveston County Courthouse?
RAYMOND R. RAPP, JR., AND BEN J. KOTEN & ASSOCIATES DESIGNED THE CURRENT COURTHOUSE IN 1966 IN A MODERNE STYLE OF CONCRETE AND STEEL.

What is the Courthouse's most unusual feature?
THE 1966 STRUCTURE IS INCREDIBLY MODERN, MADE OF CONCRETE—ODD FOR A CITY AS STEEPED IN HISTORY AS GALVESTON.

What is the most famous case tried in the Galveston County Courthouse?
CHESTER LEE WICKER WAS TRIED AND CONVICTED OF CAPITAL MURDER OF A WHITE WOMAN, SUZANNE KNUTH, WHO HAD BEEN BURIED ALIVE. THE ACLU ATTEMPTED BUT FAILED TO HALT WICKER'S EXECUTION BY LETHAL INJECTION ON AUGUST 26, 1986.

Where do you hang your hat?
THE BUZBEE LAW FIRM, WHICH IS HEADQUARTERED IN THE RESTORED 1910 ICE COLD STORAGE BUILDING ON GALVESTON'S INDUSTRIAL WATERFRONT, IS A SMALL FIRM THAT TRIES BIG CASES. THE BUZBEE LAW FIRM HAS OBTAINED MORE THAN $230 MILLION IN SETTLEMENTS AND VERDICTS IN THE LAST FIVE YEARS. THE FIRM REPRESENTED SPAIN'S BASQUE PROVINCE IN ONE OF THE BIGGEST OIL SPILLS IN EUROPEAN HISTORY. BUZBEE WAS LEAD COUNSEL IN A ONE-OF-A-KIND ANTITRUST CASE FILED ON BEHALF OF ALL OFFSHORE DRILLING WORKERS, WHICH SETTLED FOR $75 MILLION. BUZBEE HAS BEEN NAMED ONE OF THE TOP FIVE COMMERCIAL LITIGATORS FOR PLAINTIFFS IN THE STATE OF TEXAS BY TEXAS LAWYER MAGAZINE AND HAS BEEN NAMED A RISING STAR AND SUPERLAWYER BY LAW AND POLITICS MAGAZINE AND TEXAS MONTHLY.

Believe it or not!
AT ONE TIME, GALVESTON WAS THE LARGEST CITY IN TEXAS. IN 1900, A FORCE FIVE HURRICANE HIT GALVESTON, KILLING MORE THAN 5,000 PEOPLE, CAUSING THE CITIZENS TO RAISE THE SEA LEVEL OF GALVESTON BY MORE THAN FIFTEEN FEET!

Top Gun & Legal Legend
Tony Buzbee

★ SUMMA CUM LAUDE GRADUATE OF UNIVERSITY OF HOUSTON LAW CENTER, WHERE HE GRADUATED #2 IN HIS CLASS

★ GRADUATED FROM TEXAS A&M UNIVERSITY WITH A BACHELOR OF SCIENCE IN PSYCHOLOGY, WHERE HE WAS NAMED DISTINGUISHED NAVAL GRADUATE, DISTINGUISHED STUDENT AND OUTSTANDING NROTC SENIOR

★ NAMED TEXAS LAWYER TOP 5 "GO TO" LAWYERS IN PLAINTIFF'S COMMERCIAL LITIGATION

★ NAMED TEXAS MONTHLY "RISING STAR" IN THE AREA OF ADMIRALTY AND TRANSPORTATION LAW

★ RECENTLY NAMED A "SUPER LAWYER" BY TEXAS MONTHLY AND LAW & POLITICS MAGAZINE IN THE FIELD OF BUSINESS LITIGATION

★ RECENTLY, MR. BUZBEE SETTLED A CLASS ACTION FOR ALL OFFSHORE DRILLING WORKERS IN THE GULF OF MEXICO, TOTALING MORE THAN $75 MILLION. HE HAS BOTH THE HIGHEST BENCH AND JURY VERDICTS EVER ENTERED INTO GALVESTON FEDERAL COURT

★ SERVED IN THE MARINE CORPS INFANTRY AND MARINE RECON UNITS IN SAUDI ARABIA, KUWAIT AND SOMALIA

★ EARNED THE NAVY COMMENDATION MEDAL FOR MERITORIOUS SERVICE DURING HIS MILITARY TENURE

★ HAS SERVED ON THE BOARD OF DIRECTORS FOR THE UNIVERSITY OF HOUSTON LAW ALUMNI FOUNDATION, AND IS A BOARD MEMBER OF JESSE TREE, AND IS A MEMBER OF THE BUSINESS DEVELOPMENT COMMITTEE OF HOMETOWN BANK OF FRIENDSWOOD

Although Durst was given a not guilty verdict on murder charges, he still served two sentences for shop lifting a sandwich and skipping bail. When Durst was picked up for shoplifting a sandwich he had hundreds of dollars in his pocket. His family still operates a billion dollar foundation in New York.

In March of 2004, Durst's case made Galveston headlines again when the popular television show Law & Order, profiled his case. The tagline of the episode read "Ripped from the Headlines." Defense attorneys found the program ridiculous, saying it was "pure science fiction." There were some inconsistencies in the program that became controversial, such as the suggestion that a romantic relationship existed between fictional defendant Eli Madison (the character based on Durst) and his neighbor. The program ended with Madison being convicted of murder in the disappearance of his wife after being acquitted of killing his neighbor.

Three months after Robert Durst's acquittal on murder charges, he was indicted on a charge of tampering with evidence. The charge was based on the fact that Durst tampered with evidence by dismembering Morris Black's body and dumping it into Galveston Bay in 2001. Durst's bail was set at $3 billion, but later reduced as this amount was found to be unconstitutional by an appeals court. As of July 2003, his case was still pending.

SUSAN E. CRISS
JUDGE

212TH JUDICIAL DISTRICT COURT
GALVESTON COUNTY
www.co.galveston.tx.us/judgecriss
GALVESTON COUNTY COURTHOUSE
722 MOODY
GALVESTON, TEXAS 77550
(409) 766-2266
FAX (409) 765-2610

MELISSA EWING
COURT COORDINATOR

DALE W. LEE
OFFICIAL COURT REPORTER
(409) 766-2264

Dear Texas Justice,

Tony Buzbee is one of the most successful trial lawyers in the Houston and Galveston area. It is my pleasure to have gotten to know him over the years. I think he has enjoyed a high level of success for several reasons.

Tony is a master of strategy as well as a very effective public speaker. The combination of these two talents make him an exemplary litigator.

His fiercely competitive nature makes him a strong advocate for his clients. Tony fights hard against all odds to see that his clients get justice. His reputation precedes him and his opponents are well aware that he prepares every case as if it will go to trial.

Tony believes in our system of justice and that everyone deserves equal access to that system.

And finally he loves being a trial lawyer and that shows in his dynamic prescence in the courtroom.

Sincerely,

Susan Criss

Where did Grayson County get its name?

GRAYSON COUNTY WAS NAMED FOR PETER WILLIAM GRAYSON, AN EARLY TEXAS ENTREPRENEUR, DIPLOMAT AND GOVERNMENT OFFICIAL WHO FOUGHT TO RELEASE STEPHEN F. AUSTIN FROM A MEXICO CITY PRISON IN 1834.

Where is the Grayson County Courthouse located?

THE COURTHOUSE IS LOCATED ON THE SQUARE IN DOWNTOWN SHERMAN, SIXTY MILES NORTH OF DALLAS.

Who designed the Grayson County Courthouse?

VOELCKER AND DIXON WERE THE ARCHITECTS WHO DREW UP THE PLANS FOR THIS HISTORIC COURTHOUSE IN 1936 AFTER THE ORIGINAL BUILDING WAS BURNED DOWN BY AN ANGRY MOB.

What is the Courthouse's most unusual feature?

THE MOST UNUSUAL FEATURE IS A JAPANESE HOWITZER, IN PLACE OF THE WWI CANNON THAT FORMERLY STOOD ON THE CORNER NEXT TO THE STATURE OF THE CONFEDERATE SOLDIER. THE BUILDING IS 1936 MODERN-STYLE ARCHITECTURE, BUILT OF CONCRETE AND LIMESTONE.

What is the most famous case tried in the Grayson County Courthouse?

WHILE NOT A TRIAL, THE MOST FAMOUS COURT APPEARANCE OCCURRED IN THE 1970s WHEN CHARLES "TEX" WATSON, A MEMBER OF THE CHARLES MANSON FAMILY, WAS ARRESTED AND ARRAIGNED IN GRAYSON COUNTY BEFORE HE WAS EXTRADITED TO CALIFORNIA. HE WAS KNOWN AS MANSON'S GUNMAN, AS HE SHOT AND REPEATEDLY STABBED ALL OF HIS VICTIMS. HE WAS CONVICTED OF MULTIPLE MURDERS AND WAS SENTENCED TO DEATH. HOWEVER, CALIFORNIA ABOLISHED THE DEATH PENALTY BEFORE HE COULD BE EXECUTED.

Where do you hang your hat?

IN SHERMAN, TX, WITH WIFE SANDY AND TWO DAUGHTERS, SAMANTHA AND DANIELLE. FORMERLY THE ELECTED GRAYSON COUNTY DISTRICT ATTORNEY FOR TWELVE YEARS, JARVIS IS NOW IN PRIVATE PRACTICE. ALTHOUGH HE HANDLES FAMILY LAW AND CIVIL CASES, THE MAJORITY OF HIS PRACTICE IS CRIMINAL DEFENSE. HE IS LICENSED TO PRACTICE IN STATE AND FEDERAL COURT, BOTH IN GRAYSON COUNTY AND THROUGHOUT TEXAS.

Believe it or not!

THE ORIGINAL 1847 COURTHOUSE WAS BURNED DOWN BY TWO DRUNKEN MEN ATTEMPTING TO SETTLE A BET ON WHETHER OR NOT A GOOSE LIVED UNDERNEATH THE COURTHOUSE!

"Justice is worth fighting for."

~ BOB'S FAMOUS TEXAS JUSTICE SAYING

"The Unbelievable Shot"

A Famous Texas Case as Told by

BOB JARVIS

ROBERT T. JARVIS, P.C.

Richard C. Hicks, a well-respected rancher who was always willing to lend a hand to a neighbor, had lived in the Fannin County area his entire life. It was a shock to the community when he was arrested, charged and indicted with the capital murder of a police officer from Whitewright, Texas. With Bob Jarvis and co-counsel, Michael Wynne from Sherman, representing him, his trial was moved to Grayson County. They were up against Fannin County prosecutors and the Texas Attorney General's "Death Team" which had never lost a death penalty case.

The state believed that a drunken Hicks led the police officers on a high-speed chase, then pulled off into a pasture where, in total darkness, he shot a 30/30 rifle with iron sights over 220 yards up hill, into the half-open squad car window, and into the police officer's head. The first bullet supposedly entered and exited both windows of the patrol car; the second entered the patrol car through the half-opened window and struck the officer who was sitting in the driver's seat. After several extensive searches by state and federal officers, the bullet that caused the death was never found. Officers then claimed that the white pickup left the field and drove to Hicks' house. Five hours later, the Grayson County Sheriff's Office Special Response Team stormed the home and arrested Hicks who was asleep in his underwear and tee shirt.

After each officer testified in carefully-scripted direct testimony, Jarvis began a rapid-fire cross-examination and pointed out the many discrepancies in the officer's testimony and how the investigation had been poorly handled by law enforcement. Several police officers, including a Texas Ranger, had testified there were five long-barreled guns on a rack, including the murder weapon, in Hicks' home. When Jarvis produced photographs of that very gun rack, the courtroom sat in silence when he slowly counted out only four on the rack. Further, Jarvis pointed out that there were three different versions of the search warrant which indicated forgery and tampering, at a minimum. In the end, there was not a single piece of physical evidence that positively showed Hicks was even in the pasture where the shooting occurred. The mud on his boots did not match the soil and the tire tracks in the field did not match his pickup truck. Even the dirt found on his pickup

Grayson
County Courthouse

truck was inconclusive. The only "eye witness" was the victim's brother, who was in his first week as a police officer, and riding with the victim the night of the shooting. Mike Wynne was successful in getting the brother to admit that he misidentified the type of pick up truck and the license plate, and also that he was unable to identify who fired the fatal shot. The jury kept waiting for some piece of physical evidence to tie Hicks to the murder, but it never came.

Switching from offense to defense, Jarvis and Wynne brought forth their own experts. They described the difficulty of shooting that size of target not once, but twice, with that gun at that distance. The star witness was Dr. Linda Norton, who testified very plainly that it was just as likely that his own brother shot the police officer accidentally. During closing arguments, the large, old courtroom echoed with Jarvis' demands of proof that his client had committed the murder. Jarvis dared

> **"JARVIS DARED THE PROSECUTORS TO PICK OUT ANY PIECE OF EVIDENCE . . . TO SHOW HIS CLIENT WAS ACTUALLY AT THE SCENE, MUCH LESS GUILTY OF MURDER."**

the prosecutors to pick out any piece of evidence from the multiple boxes in the courtroom to show his client was actually at the scene, much less guilty of murder. The prosecutors could not answer the challenge.

Each day, for three weeks, the courtroom had been packed. On one side were law enforcement officers with black tape over their badges demanding justice, and on the other was a man, his family and friends with yellow ribbons demanding the same. On the last day of trial, after less than three hours of deliberations, the jury reached a verdict. The courtroom became silent as Hicks, Jarvis and Wynne stood to receive the verdict. The courtroom erupted with a shout when the verdict was read by Judge Webb Baird, "not guilty."

Gregg County Courthouse

"The Slant-Hole Oil Well Scandal"

A Famous Texas Case as Told by

JOHN M. SMITH

HARBOUR, SMITH, HARRIS & MERRITT

In 1962, the "slant-hole scandal" brought unfavorable national attention to Gregg County, the fifth largest producer of oil in Texas, located in the East Texas Oil Field, and lost millions for many local investors.

Oil was discovered in Gregg County in 1931, bringing a boom to the county's residents just as the rest of the country and much of Texas was facing the Great Depression. In only a few weeks after oil was discovered, the population of the county increased from16,000 to more than 100,000. By 1935, bank deposits in the town of Longview had grown from $500,000 to over $10 million. A new jail, courthouse, roadway, and hospital were all built in the early 1930s. Longview and the rest of Gregg County were booming and there was no sign that the good fortune would end.

The streak of growth continued for years, until 1962, when a scandal erupted in the county. One billion dollars worth of oil had started being produced by independent operators in 1948. By slanting nearly 400 oil wells, the operators were able to obtain oil from larger industrial owned pools. Obviously illegal, the practice was tolerated by city officials for almost eighteen years.

"If you show me a lawyer that does not worry about his case, then I'll show you a lawyer that I can beat every time."

~ JOHN'S FAMOUS TEXAS JUSTICE SAYING

"TO THIS DAY NOT ONE OF THE 'OIL PIRATES' . . . WAS EVER PROSECUTED FOR THEIR CRIMES."

In the following year, 1963, Longview (the largest city in Gregg County) began to transform from a centralized city into a suburban sprawl. During this period, land inspectors found approximately 380 deviated wells in the East Texas Field and shut them down. Unfortunately, this shut down was not before an estimated $100 million in oil was stolen over several decades. To this day not one of the "oil pirates"—mostly leading citizens of east Texas communities who built their fortune on the stolen oil—was ever prosecuted for their crimes.

Where did Gregg County get its name?
FROM GENERAL JOHN GREGG, A CONFEDERATE SOLDIER WHO BECAME A LOCAL HERO IN THE CIVIL WAR AS A SECESSION CONVENTION DELEGATE AND A DELEGATE TO THE PROVISIONAL CONFEDERATE CONGRESS.

Where is the Gregg County Courthouse located?
IN THE TOWN SQUARE OF LONGVIEW, TX, JUST A BLOCK AWAY FROM THE FIRST NATIONAL BANK, THE PLACE OF THE LAST RAID OF THE DALTON GANG. IN 1894, BILL DALTON AND HIS OUTLAW GANG ROBBED THE BANK AND THEN SHOT THEIR WAY OUT OF TOWN ON HORSEBACK. THE ROBBERY RESULTED IN THE ULTIMATE CAPTURE OF THE GANG, ENDING ITS REIGN OF CRIME AND VIOLENCE.

Who designed the Gregg County Courthouse?
ARCHITECTS VOELCKER AND DIXON DESIGNED THE HISTORICAL GREGG COUNTY COURTHOUSE OF 1932 USING AN ART DECO STYLE. THE BUILDING WAS CONSTRUCTED OF TERRA COTTA (HARD BAKED CLAY), BRICK AND MARBLE, CREATING A REDDISH RED-YELLOW HUE ON THE STRUCTURE.

What is the Courthouse's most unusual feature?
TODAY'S GREGG COUNTY COURTHOUSE, THE FIFTH IN THE CITY OF LONGVIEW, WAS BUILT TO MEET THE GROWING NEEDS OF THE COUNTY FOLLOWING THE EAST TEXAS OIL BOOM. IT REPLACED A RED BRICK COURTHOUSE THAT WAS BUILT IN 1897.

What is the most famous case tried in the Gregg County Courthouse?
STATE OF TEXAS VS. JIM NITE. A MEMBER OF THE FAMOUS DALTON GANG, NITE WAS INDICTED FOR HIS INVOLVEMENT IN THE 1894 ROBBERY OF THE FIRST NATIONAL BANK, THE MURDER OF GEORGE BUCKINGHAM AND CHARLIE LEARNED, GOOD CITIZENS OF LONGVIEW, TX, AND THE SHOOTING OF J.W. MCQUEEN, WHO WAS SHOT THROUGH THE HIP, AND ACCORDING TO THE INDICTMENT, "THEREBY RENDERED A HELPLESS CRIPPLE FOR LIFE." HE WAS SENTENCED TO TWENTY YEARS IN PRISON, ONLY TO LATER BE PARDONED BY TEXAS GOVERNOR OSCAR B. COLQUITT. NITE WAS LATER KILLED IN A TULSA, OK, SALOON FIGHT.

Where do you hang your hat?
IN LONGVIEW, TX, WHERE OUR FIRM PRACTICES GENERAL AND CIVIL TRIAL LAW AND ESTATE PLANNING.

Believe it or not!
A DOWNTOWN PARK IN KILGORE, TX, HAS REPLICATED OIL DERRICKS MARKING THE SPOT KNOWN AS THE, "WORLD'S RICHEST ACRE!"

Where did Grimes County get its name?

THE COUNTY WAS NAMED FOR JESSE GRIMES IN 1846, ONE OF STEPHEN F. AUSTIN'S COLONISTS, A SIGNER OF THE TEXAS DECLARATION OF INDEPENDENCE AND A TEXAS SENATOR.

Where is the Grimes County Courthouse located?

IN THE COUNTY SEAT OF ANDERSON, A TOWN WHICH HAS NEVER HAD A POPULATION OVER 500.

Who designed the Grimes County Courthouse?

THE HISTORIC COURTHOUSE WAS DESIGNED IN 1893 BY F.S. GLOVER IN ITALIANATE STYLE OF STONE AND BRICK. THIS BEAUTIFUL COURTHOUSE IS ALSO A NATIONAL REGISTER PROPERTY. THE GRIMES COUNTY COURTHOUSE WAS REDEDICATED ON MARCH 2ND 2002 BY THE TEXAS HISTORICAL COMMISSIONS' TEXAS COURTHOUSE PRESERVATION PROGRAM.

What is the Courthouse's most unusual feature?

AS THE COURTHOUSE IS AN ITALIANATE STRUCTURE, IT IS UNUSUAL IN COMPARISON TO MOST OF TEXAS' HISTORIC COURTHOUSES. THE COURTHOUSE WAS RESTORED IN 2002, BUT STILL INCORPORATES THE EAST WALL AND FOUNDATION WALLS OF AN EARLIER COURTHOUSE DESTROYED BY FIRE.

What is the most famous case tried in the Grimes County Courthouse?

IN THE 1930S, BARROW PARKER, ONE OF BONNIE AND CLYDE'S GANG MEMBERS, WAS TRIED AND CONVICTED OF HIS CRIMES IN GRIMES COUNTY. IT IS SAID THAT CONTRARY TO POPULAR BELIEF, BONNIE AND CLYDE WERE NOT LOVERS, BUT FRIENDS, AND PARKER WAS BONNIE'S TRUE BEAU.

Where do you hang your hat?

IN HOUSTON, TX. PROCTOR & NAGORNY, P.C. LIMITS ITS PRACTICE TO CIVIL DEFENSE LITIGATION, DEFENDING MEDICAL PROFESSIONALS, HOSPITALS, NURSING HOMES, DENTISTS, NURSES, PRODUCT MANUFACTURERS, PREMISE OWNERS/LESSORS AND TRANSPORTATION COMPANIES AT THE TRIAL AND APPELLATE LEVELS. ADDITIONALLY, THE ATTORNEYS HAVE EXPERIENCE REPRESENTING CLIENTS BEFORE PROFESSIONAL BOARDS WHERE CONTINUED PROFESSIONAL LICENSURE IS AN ISSUE.

Believe it or not!

THE FIRST COURTHOUSE, MADE OF CEDAR LOGS, BURNED DOWN IN 1838. THE SECOND COURTHOUSE, A WOODEN BUILDING ERECTED IN 1849, WAS LITERALLY BLOWN DOWN BY HIGH WINDS. THE THIRD COURTHOUSE, A ROCK STRUCTURE BUILT ON THE PRESENT SITE IN 1850, BURNED IN 1890. THE FOURTH COURTHOUSE, BUILT IN 1891, WAS DESTROYED BY FIRE IN 1893!

"Well behaved women rarely make history."

~ LORI'S FAMOUS TEXAS JUSTICE SAYING

"The Blind Bingo Player"

A Famous Texas Case as Told by
LORI D. PROCTOR
PROCTOR & NAGORNY, P.C.

As a medical malpractice defense attorney, Lori Proctor has rarely had exposure to private investigators, secret photographs or other clandestine evidentiary matters arising in high profile cases. However, sometimes doing your homework really makes all the difference at trial. Ms. Proctor defended a Texas doctor at trial who was accused of causing blindness in a patient following laser surgery to treat diabetic retinopathy.

According to the doctor, the surgery went just as it should have and the patient should have had no complications. There was a chance the surgery would not improve his vision, but there was no reason in the surgeon's mind that the patient's vision should have deteriorated as a result of the procedure. The stories of the plaintiff and the physician were quite simply diametrically opposed.

While her client did carry insurance which would have paid a portion of a settlement or judgment, the plaintiff was suing for punitive damages and if recovered, the Texas doctor's life savings would have been depleted. The plaintiff's attorney was considered to be a "master of trial" and spoke frequently around the state regarding litigation tactics.

On a hunch, Ms. Proctor hired a private investigator to follow and observe the plaintiff to ascertain his true activity level and find out if he was living as a person who was "blind." The case proceeded to trial without the plaintiff or his attorney being aware of the investigator's findings. During the trial, the plaintiff would appear each day as if he could not see or identify the people who were greeting him. However, before lunch and

Grimes
County Courthouse

at the end of the day when he was tired, he was observed peeking at the clock on the far wall of the courtroom to see how much longer before the trial day would end!

The investigator, an attractive, petite woman, testified that while observing the plaintiff, he drove a motor home to Galveston, helped her change a staged flat tire on the side of the road and the coupe de gras; played sixteen hands of bingo at a bingo parlor, all at the same time! The bingo playing was caught on more than one occasion by the investigator and the film was shown to the jury. The plaintiff re-took the stand and tried to explain that the bingo parlor had installed special lighting for him, which allowed him to see the cards — only under that light. Fortunately, the jury

> **"... Ms. Proctor hired a private investigator to follow and observe the plaintiff ... and find out if he was living as a person who was 'blind'."**

did not buy this and the Texas doc was exonerated.

Undaunted, however, the "blind" plaintiff began a pro se course of suing everyone involved in the case, including the judge, the bailiff, the court reporter, his own attorney and Ms. Proctor, filing pages of hand written documents lodging various complaints in various courts. It took years, but ultimately all of the cases were dismissed and the doctor is still in practice, with his hard earned savings intact!

Hardeman County Courthouse

DEDICATED TO THE MEMORY OF
THE LAST GREAT COMANCHE
CHIEF, QUANAH PARKER. HE
PRONOUNCED THIS BLESSING ON
"HIS" TOWN QUANAH, TEXAS:
"MAY THE GREAT SPIRIT SMILE
ON YOUR LITTLE TOWN, MAY THE
RAIN FALL IN SEASON, AND IN
THE WARMTH OF THE SUNSHINE
AFTER THE RAIN, MAY THE
EARTH YIELD BOUNTIFULLY. MAY
PEACE AND CONTENTMENT BE
WITH YOU AND YOUR CHILDREN
FOREVER."

"A County Seat Won in the Wash"

A Famous Texas Case as Told by
TOBY GOODMAN
TEXAS HOUSE OF REPRESENTATIVES
GOODMAN, CLARK AND BECKMAN

As we all have learned in our middle school American history classes, the expansion of the American railroad opened up the west in a way never previously imagined. As travel and trade were facilitated, new settlements popped up and commerce expanded rapidly. Building a railroad was a huge financial effort that required many years and a lot of manpower. Hundreds of men spent a good part of their lives laying down the tracks, fighting off Indian attacks as they moved westward. These railroad workers resided for long periods of time in the settlement closest to the railroad. This lead to what might be the equivalent of a college town today. The local settlers were often overrun and nearly outnumbered by these transient workers. They would come into town pack the boarding houses, fill the bars and most importantly, get their laundry done. While that fact may seem inconsequential, it proved to be the key factor in the election of 1890 that moved the county seat of Hardeman County from Margaret to Quanah, Texas.

While Hardeman County had been formed 42 years earlier in 1858, at that point it was still a remote location on the edge of Indian Territory. It was not until some time after the Civil War that the county was organized and settled. Finally, in 1884 that happened, but the principle inhabitants were cattle rustlers heading to "safe" Indian Territory across the Red River. At this time Margaret, situated across the Pease River, was the county seat. With the majority of Hardeman County lying between the Red River and the Pease River, this made Margaret relatively far removed. A year after the organization, the railroad came to town and drastically effected the area. It was the Fort Worth and Denver, who in 1885 laid out the site for Quanah on the other side of the Pease River from Margaret.

The naming of Quanah was of great importance, as it was named after the famed Comanche Indian Chief, Quanah Parker. Quanah was the bi-racial son of a Comanche warrior and a white settler who was captured and raised by the Indians. Not only did he have the blood of two cultures, but when his father was killed and his mother captured by Texas Rangers, he was taken in by a different Comanche band. It would be an error to think that all Comanche's were "created equal" as there were several bands that each kept to themselves and interacted little with one another. However, Quanah learned at an early age to adapt to his surroundings and make the best of things.

When the Indians were further encroached upon, it was Quanah who brought not only the Comanche bands together, but the Cheyennes, Arapahoes and Kiowas, as well. As the Indians were moved to the reservations, he was elected Chief of all Comanche bands, successfully uniting them. He spoke up for his people's rights and helped them to adjust to the white man's world while keeping their heritage and traditions. He believed in educating the youths in schools and doing business with the white man to ensure a better future for his people. When the city of

"QUANAH WAS THE BI-RACIAL SON OF A COMANCHE WARRIOR AND A WHITE SETTLER WHO WAS CAPTURED AND RAISED BY THE INDIANS."

REPRESENTATIVE GOODMAN'S FATHER, JOHNNIE GOODMAN, IS A NATIVE OF HARDEMAN COUNTY AND A VETERAN OF WWII AND THE KOREAN WAR.

Quanah was named, he was a very wealthy man who counted such people as Theodore Roosevelt among his friends.

The city of Quanah would grow in importance, too, as had the man it was named after. In an odd turn of events, there was an election in 1890 to move the county seat of Hardeman from Margaret to Quanah. Prior to the election, it was decided that only residents of the town could vote. However, one only had to prove that they had their laundry done in town for six weeks to establish residency there. This then would include all of the railroad workers as voting residents, and the election of Quanah as county seat was won.

"*Compromise and settlement are always better than trial.*"

~ TOBY'S FAMOUS TEXAS JUSTICE SAYING

Where did Hardeman County get its name?

HARDEMAN COUNTY WAS NAMED AFTER TWO EARLY MATAGORDA LEGISLATORS, BAILEY AND THOMAS JONES HARDEMAN. IT WAS STILL SPARSELY SETTLED WHEN THE COUNTY WAS ORGANIZED IN 1884.

Where is the Hardeman County Courthouse located?

THE COURTHOUSE IS LOCATED IN THE TOWN OF QUANAH, NAMED AFTER QUANAH PARKER, THE LAST, AND SOME SAY GREATEST, CHIEF OF THE COMANCHES.

Who designed the Hardeman County Courthouse?

R. H. STUCKEY WAS THE ARCHITECT WHO DESIGNED THE HISTORIC 1908 COURTHOUSE.

What is the Courthouse's most unusual feature?

ITS BEAUX-ARTS STYLE AND THE NATIVE AMERICAN MONUMENT TO QUANAH PARKER ON THE COURTHOUSE GROUNDS.

What is the most famous case tried in the Hardeman County Courthouse?

JANUARY 2002, STEVEN LYNN HUGUELEY WAS TRIED IN HARDEMAN COUNTY FOR THE MURDER OF A CORRECTIONS OFFICER. PRIOR TO THIS TRIAL, HUGUELEY WAS NOT ELIGIBLE FOR RELEASE FROM PRISON UNTIL 2057, AFTER BEING FOUND GUILTY OF THE MURDER OF HIS MOTHER IN 1986. HE IS NOW ON DEATH ROW IN TENNESSEE.

Where do you hang your hat?

IN ARLINGTON, TX, AT THE FIRM OF GOODMAN, CLARK AND BECKMAN WHERE HE IS THE FOUNDING MEMBER. MR. GOODMAN HAS STRONG TIES TO HARDEMAN COUNTY, WHERE HIS GRANDPARENTS LIVED AND HIS FATHER GREW UP. MR. GOODMAN IS A SEVEN-TERM MEMBER OF THE TEXAS HOUSE OF REPRESENTATIVES.

Believe it or not!

CHIEF QUANAH WAS STILL RESIDING IN THE TOWN WHEN IT WAS NAMED AFTER HIM!

Harris
County Courthouse

"Superman Nets $8.5 Million"

A Famous Texas Case as Told by

JOHN M. O'QUINN
O'QUINN, LAMINACK & PIRTLE

The trial resulting from the death of "Superman 1024" in Bay City, Texas, was a landmark verdict, publicized as far away as San Francisco, California. Superman was a world famous 4-year-old Santa Gertrudis bull and was also considered a pet by his owner, Dan Wendt. Dan loved Superman. He loved his bull as much as you or I would love our faithful dog or cat. Much to Mr. Wendt's dismay, Superman dropped dead about five minutes after he was sprayed with a Diamond Shamrock insecticide, Vapona. This is an insecticide which is twelve times as potent as other chemicals used to keep flies and ticks off cattle. The event was devastating to Dan and caused him much grief. You might say because I "humanized" Superman, the jury felt pity for Dan, as well as wanting to punish the big corporation for marketing, without warning, an insecticide that was overly toxic to animals.

The trial of Superman is one of my favorite cases because of the message sent to the big corporations that make, sell and use toxic chemicals; to reduce the toxic effects of chemicals to the highest extent. Even though Superman was an animal, his life had value. The jury was appalled that Diamond Shamrock had put making money first and safety second. They decided to send a message loud and clear that safety was to be first and that Diamond Shamrock needed to adopt "safety first" as its business plan.

When the verdict was announced, the news spread like a wildfire across not only Texas, but the nation. Clearly this was a landmark victory. The verdict was written about in a Matagorda County newspaper article of *The Daily Tribune* Tuesday, December 11, 1984, stating, "Jury awards $8.5 million in death of Superman." The news was further

To those who say that justice goes only to the rich and the powerful, this Texas attorney says,

"*Remember the heroes of our youth, like the Lone Ranger and Robin Hood, who helped the poor and the weak, obtain justice against the bullies.*"

~ JOHN'S FAMOUS TEXAS JUSTICE SAYING

". . . SUPERMAN DROPPED DEAD ABOUT FIVE MINUTES AFTER HE WAS SPRAYED WITH A DIAMOND SHAMROCK INSECTICIDE, VAPONA."

Where did Harris County get its name?

FROM JOHN RICHARDSON HARRIS, THE FOUNDER OF HARRISBURG, TEXAS, AND A MERCHANT WHO MANAGED A SMALL FLEET OF SCHOONERS THAT TRADED BETWEEN NEW ORLEANS AND THE GULF COAST OF TEXAS.

Where is the Harris County Courthouse located?

IN HOUSTON, TX, ON THE CORNER OF PRESTON AND CAROLINE STREETS, ON WHAT IS REFERRED TO AS "COURTHOUSE SQUARE"—AN AREA WHERE FIVE COURTHOUSES HAVE STOOD.

Who designed the Harris County Courthouse?

LANG, WINCHELL & BARGLEBAUGH DESIGNED THE HISTORIC 1910 BEAUX-ARTS COURTHOUSE THAT IS MADE OF GRANITE AND BRICK, STILL SERVING AS THE CIVIL COURTS BUILDING AND LISTED AS A NATIONAL REGISTRY PROPERTY.

What is the Courthouse's most unusual feature?

THE COURTHOUSE HAS BEEN ON THE SAME BLOCK SINCE 1838. THE CURIOUS FACT IS THAT DURING THE CIVIL WAR, THE UNFINISHED BUILDING SERVED AS A PRISONER OF WAR CAMP. THERE ARE RUMORS THAT THERE WERE NUMEROUS DEATHS AND UNION PRISONERS ARE STILL BURIED IN THE COURTHOUSE BLOCK. THERE HAS NEVER BEEN AN EXCAVATION TO PROVE THE TRUTHS OF THIS TALE.

What is the most famous case tried in the Harris County Courthouse?

PENNZOIL V. TEXACO- IN 1987, TEXACO INTERFERED WITH THE AGREEMENT BETWEEN PENNZOIL AND THE GETTY ENTITIES FOR THEIR OWN ECONOMIC GAIN, AND AS A RESULT, PENNZOIL SUFFERED DAMAGES OF $7.53 BILLION. PENNZOIL WAS AWARDED PUNITIVE DAMAGES OF $3 BILLION.

Where do you hang your hat?

IN HOUSTON, TX, WHERE I AM THE MANAGING PARTNER AT MY FIRM, O'QUINN, LAMINACK & PIRTLE, WHERE I AM ALSO KNOWN AS "THE MIGHTY QUINN." SINCE 1981, OUR HOUSTON-BASED LAW FIRM HAS BUILT A REPUTATION FOR TAKING A RESULTS-ORIENTED APPROACH TO CIVIL TRIAL LAW "MY FIRM WORKS WITH OUR CLIENTS AND CHARGES A FEE ONLY IF WE WIN."

Believe it or not!

THE EPOCHAL BATTLE AT SAN JACINTO THAT ESTABLISHED THE INDEPENDENT LONE STAR REPUBLIC HAPPENED IN HARRIS COUNTY ON APRIL 21, 1836, WHEN THE MEXICANS AND SANTA ANNA WERE DEFEATED FOR CONTROL OF TEXAS. SAN JACINTO DAY IS CELEBRATED EACH YEAR ON APRIL 21!

announced in *The Houston Post* article, Wednesday, December 12, 1984, "No bull! Jury awards $8.5 million," and in the *Houston Chronicle* article, Thursday, December 13, 1984, "Man 'floored' by jury award in his suit over death of bull." Cities big and small were hearing the news. The *Tyler Morning Telegraph* article, Thursday, December 13, 1984, read, "Bull's Death Nets $8.5 Million," and the *San Francisco Chronicle* article, Thursday, December 13, 1984, printed, "Rancher Awarded $8.5 Million in Death of His Bull." Everyone was talking, and for good reason.

This verdict was the biggest verdict ever in America for the death of an animal, even a champion race horse. It was awarded by a six-man, six-woman jury in the 130th State District Court in Bay City against Diamond Shamrock and Medina Valley Artificial Insemination, Inc. Diamond Shamrock was ordered to pay Dan Wendt, a local Bay City rancher, 65% of the $1.5 million in actual damages for the death of his purebred registered Santa Gertrudis bull, "Superman 1024," and $7 million in exemplary damages as a monetary fine for punishment. Medina Valley was ordered to pay the remaining 35% of the actual damages for spraying the Vapona too near to Superman, which then got on his skin.

Exemplary damages were defined in the jury's instructions as those awarded to "set an example to others and as a penalty or by way of punishment to deter similar wrongs in the future." This verdict was a major victory from two standpoints: besides being the biggest verdict ever in America for the death of any animal, more importantly, this decision was notable because of the punitive damages. There has been, and always will be, a growing concern in our country about the spread of chemicals particularly toxic chemicals. This verdict sent out a message that chemical companies are going to have to be more responsible for their products.

"Superman," the 2,700-pound bull, died at the Medina Valley Artificial Insemination Laboratory near San Antonio on May 1, 1981, almost immediately after being sprayed with Vapona. As counsel to the owners of Superman, I, along with local attorney Bert M. Huebner, argued that Vapona was to be used only in surface applications in animal pens. Further argument was made that Diamond Shamrock's instruction label on the chemical was confusing and contradicting and did not explicitly tell Medina Valley this. Diamond Shamrock knew the chemical was dangerous, but chose to do nothing about it. Diamond Shamrock knew if consumers knew how unnecessarily dangerous its insecticide was, it could not sell much of it. Diamond Shamrock put monetary gains before consumer safety.

As most defense attorneys for large corporations always do in their closing arguments, they tried to shift the blame onto someone else. They argued that the labeling on the chemical was adequate and they refocused the attention to the Medina Valley laboratories. Diamond Shamrock attorneys unsuccessfully argued that Medina Valley laboratories allowed untrained, unsupervised workers to spray "Superman" and three other bulls, who also died after being sprayed with the Vapona. Trained or untrained, supervised or not, these arguments failed to address the fact that labeling on the product was inadequate because the container did not specify how the potent chemicals should be used. While this was a regrettable loss for owner Dan Wendt, it turned out to be a good lesson taught to irresponsible and greedy chemical producers.

And that's no bull!

RICHARD HAYNES & ASSOCIATES, P.C.

RICHARD HAYNES

J. BLAKE HAYNES
JOSEPH L. LANZA
SHARON R. LEVINE

LAWYERS

4300 SCOTLAND
HOUSTON, TEXAS 77007-7394
TELEPHONE: **713/868-1111**
FACSIMILE: 713/863-9934

Dear Martana,

It was a classic courtroom confrontation. A Texas rancher, represented by the "Tall Guy", suing an international corporation, represented by a cadre of big firm trial lawyers, for money damages.

The jury was selected, the parties presented their evidence, the lawyers argued their cases, and the jury deliberated. Their verdict, judgment for the rancher. The damage awarded, eight million dollars.

The lawsuit was over the death of a prize bull. An eight million dollar verdict for a dead bull!

The legal community buzzed with excitement. Prior to trial, some legal pandits predicted that because of the legal team representing the corporation the "Tall Guy" would have an uphill and difficult time establishing liability, and even if he did, the prospective damages would be too minimal to warrant his courtroom efforts.

After the verdict, the question was: How in the hell did the "Tall Guy" get an eight million dollar jury verdict for a dead bull? The answer: The "Tall Guy" was able to demonstrate to the jury the pain, agony, and anguish suffered by the rancher at the death of his bull. The "Tall Guy" humanized the bull, showing the jury how a bull can be more than "market value", this was a family pet, and the death of the bull was almost like losing a member of the rancher's family.

Fortunately for America, law schools from time to time graduate academic wizards. The "Tall Guy" was one of these rare lawyers. Valedictorian of his class, Editor of Law Review and State Moot Court Champion. It was no surprise that upon graduation he was embraced by a prestigious law firm.

It was brief however, as the "Tall Guy" started his own firm specializing in representing plaintiffs in personal injury and business dispute litigation. The "Tall Guy's" intelligence, work ethic and genuine care for his clients have resulted in literally ten of millions of dollars in jury verdicts and settlements and the unbridled appreciation of his many clients.

I respect and admire the "Tall Guy". I love him like a brother; in fact, I call him "Bro". The "Tall Guy" is John M. O'Quinn, the trail lawyer's trial lawyer.

Richard Haynes
Richard "Racehorse" Haynes

"Tobacco Giants Pay 'Til the End of Time"

A Famous Texas Case as Told by

JOHN M. O'QUINN
O'QUINN, LAMINACK & PIRTLE

The small East Texas city of Texarkana is typically a quiet urban place of homes, schools and small businesses. However, in 1996-1998, Texarkana was host to the biggest trial in the history of Texas, and the biggest case of my life.

The lawsuit began in a Texarkana courtroom with a number of lawyers, including myself, up against tobacco giants, such as Phillip Morris (Marlboros) and R.J. Reynolds (Camels). The State of Texas selected and hired me and my law firm and four other law firms to sue the nation's largest tobacco companies in an effort to recover the costs of treating patients with illnesses resulting from smoking. Texarkana was literally taken over by lawyers and reporters. Hundreds of witnesses were called and over 50,000 exhibits were assembled. The state alone commandeered a gymnasium in a former psychiatric hospital in Texarkana in order to fill it with 4,000 boxes of trial-related documents.

Texas Attorney General Dan Morales hired five private attorneys to handle the tobacco lawsuit. The attorneys were myself and John Eddie Williams from Houston; Walter Umphrey and Wayne Reaud of Beaumont; and Harold Nix of Daingerfield. Robert Ries, a Dallas attorney, represented Harris County and the Harris County Hospital District, which spends millions of local tax dollars each year treating people with low income, many with illnesses associated with tobacco.

The largest counties and hospital districts in Texas estimated that they spent $95 million on smoking-related damages in 1996 alone. Total health care costs were more than $5 billion for all local governments over the previous forty years. A number of claims were made against the tobacco companies, including allegations that tobacco companies had violated federal and state anti-trust laws, federal anti-racketeering laws and the Texas Deceptive Trade Practices Act and was negligent in designing and marketing its products and is liable for the fact that cigarettes are unreasonably dangerous and defective products.

Morales understood when filing the suit that it was considered more than a gamble. However, our legal team forced the tobacco industry to make a settlement that earned for the state of Texas and counties the present value of fifty years of payments and is estimated to be $17.3 billion in a series of annual payments of $1 billion, that averages $750 million a year, more or less, a year for a total of $50 billion over the next fifty years beginning in 1998. This sum was based on an average of $750 million dollars a year to be paid to the state as long as tobacco companies are in the business of selling cigarettes.

And as Ms. Pam Burns, my legal assistant and a smart lady, tells me, these payments will go on for a long, long time because cigarette companies will likely sell cigarettes "till the end of time."

"THE STATE ALONE COMMANDEERED A GYMNASIUM . . . IN TEXARKANA IN ORDER TO FILL IT WITH 4,000 BOXES OF TRIAL-RELATED DOCUMENTS."

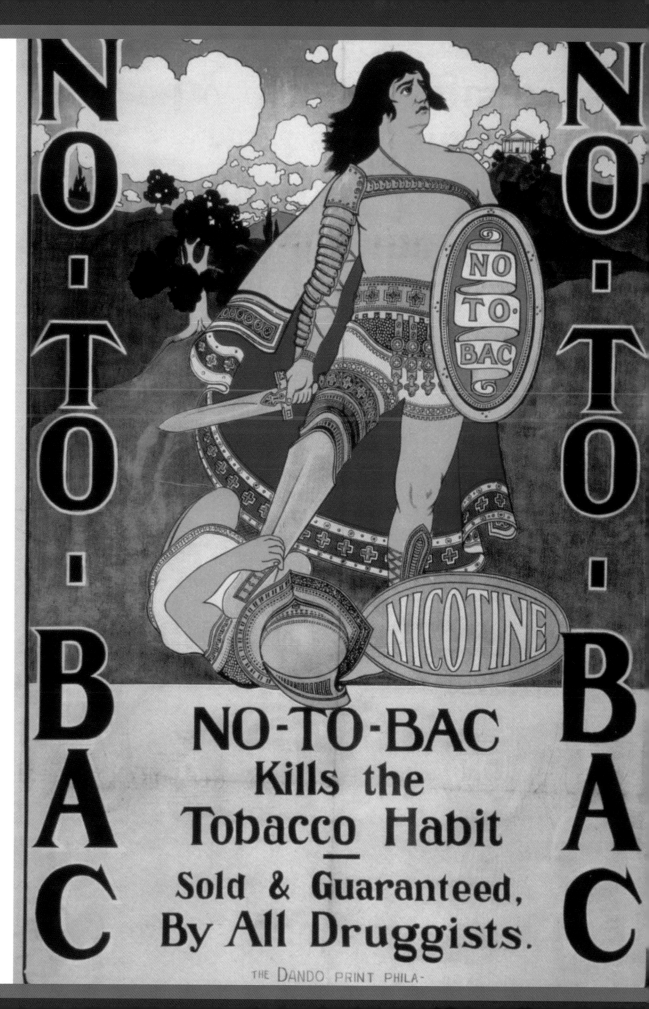

Where did Harrison County get its name?
IN 1842 FROM THE TEXAS REVOLUTIONARY LEADER, JONAS HARRISON, WHO WAS ONE OF THE FIRST SETTLERS AND A DISTINGUISHED LAWYER.

Where is the Harrison County Courthouse located?
IN MARSHALL, TX, AT THE CORNER OF WEST HOUSTON AND FRANKLIN STREETS.

Who designed the Harrison County Courthouse?
THE ORIGINAL HISTORIC COURTHOUSE WAS DESIGNED C. 1899 BY J. RIELY GORDON, ARGUABLY THE MOST PROLIFIC COURTHOUSE ARCHITECT IN TEXAS, WITH 1920 ADDITIONS DESIGNED BY C.G. LANCASTER. THIS RENAISSANCE REVIVAL STRUCTURE IS MADE OF GRANITE, MARBLE AND STONE AND HAS THE DISTINCTION OF BEING A NATIONAL REGISTER PROPERTY.

What is the Courthouse's most unusual feature?
THE ORIGINAL COURTHOUSE NOW SERVES AS HARRISON COUNTY'S HISTORICAL MUSEUM AND THE CURRENT COURTHOUSE, BUILT IN 1964, IS LOCATED ACROSS THE STREET.

What is the most famous case tried in the Harrison County Courthouse?
THE BARRYMORE SHOOTING. IN 1879, MAURICE BARRYMORE WAS PASSING THROUGH MARSHALL WITH HIS ACTING TROUPE. WHILE DINING AT THE RAILROAD RESTAURANT WITH A MALE FRIEND AND THE FRIEND'S FEMALE COMPANION, JIM CURRIE, A DRUNKEN RAILROAD DETECTIVE, INSULTED THE WOMAN. IN THE FRACAS THAT FOLLOWED, THE FRIEND WAS KILLED AND BARRYMORE WOUNDED. CURRIE WAS TRIED FOR MURDER IN MARSHALL, BUT HE WAS FOUND NOT GUILTY ON GROUNDS OF INSANITY. HIS APPEARANCE AT THE TRIAL BROUGHT HIM NATIONAL ATTENTION FROM HARPER'S AND LESLIE'S ILLUSTRATED NEWSPAPER. AFTER THE TRIAL, BARRYMORE WAS REPORTED AS SAYING, "TEXAS IS A NO MAN'S LAND WHERE SUDDEN DEATH LURKS IN EVERY BISTRO."

Where do you hang your hat?
AT THE FIRM'S OFFICES IN THE RENAISSANCE TOWER, DOWNTOWN DALLAS WHERE MR. BUETHER IS PARTNER, SPECIALIZING IN PATENT AND COMMERCIAL LITIGATION AND CHAIR OF THE INTELLECTUAL PROPERTY/LITIGATION SECTION.

Believe it or not!
MARSHALL IS ONE OF TEN CITIES AWARDED THE TITLE OF "ALL AMERICAN CITY" BY THE NATIONAL MUNICIPAL LEAGUE IN 1976!

"... moderation in the pursuit of justice is no virtue."

Barry Goldwater, Acceptance Speech, Republican Presidential Nomination (July 16, 1964)

~ ERIC'S FAMOUS TEXAS JUSTICE SAYING

"Monsanto v. Crum & Forster"

A Famous Texas Case as Told by
ERIC BUETHER
GODWIN GRUBER

Although Harrison County is not one of the largest counties in Texas population-wise, it has been the home of some of the biggest lawsuits in Texas history. Eric Buether was involved in two of them.

In 1990, Buether represented Monsanto in a lawsuit against its insurance company Crum & Forster in the Harrison County state court in Marshall charging the insurance company with bad faith. Monsanto found out that Crum & Forster had secretly purchased a 50% interest in the claims of homeowners being asserted against Monsanto in a toxic tort lawsuit and then increased the damages sought from Monsanto in that case 20 fold to half a billion dollars. Crum & Forster did this while denying coverage of the homeowner's lawsuit under an insurance policy it issued to Monsanto. Monsanto won the homeowners' lawsuit and then sued Crum & Forster for violating an insurer's duty of good faith and fair dealing. After a four month trial, the Harrison County jury found Crum & Forster guilty of bad faith and awarded Monsanto damages totaling $71 million. The damages award was upheld on appeal and the case set a precedent for the duty of good faith owed by insurance companies.

Harrison
County Courthouse

"[MONSANTO'S INSURER] SECRETLY PURCHASED A 50% INTEREST IN THE CLAIMS OF HOMEOWNERS [AGAINST IT] . . ."

Immediately after the Crum & Forster verdict, Buether sued Xerox in Marshall federal court for violating the antitrust laws by refusing to sell spare parts needed by independent service companies to service Xerox copiers and printers. One irony was that Xerox owned Crum & Forster. Xerox eventually settled the antitrust lawsuit for $260 million and agreed to discontinue its refusal to deal policy. Marshall turned out to be a venue that Buether and Xerox would never forget, but obviously for diametrically opposite reasons.

Where did Hemphill County get its name?

FROM REPUBLIC OF TEXAS JUSTICE JOHN HEMPHILL. CANADIAN WAS NAMED FOR THE NEARBY RIVER. CANADIAN, TX, WAS ORIGINALLY KNOWN AS "HOGTOWN" AND LATER BECAME KNOWN AS "DESPERADO CITY" AS WELL AS "RODEO TOWN."

Where is the Hemphill County Courthouse located?

ON MAIN STREET IN CANADIAN, TX, AT THE CENTER OF THE ANNUAL 4TH OF JULY CELEBRATION.

Who designed the Hemphill County Courthouse?

THE TEXAS RENAISSANCE STYLE HISTORIC COURTHOUSE WAS BUILT IN 1909 AT A COST OF $31,278.00 DOLLARS BY ARCHITECT R.G. KIRSCH CO. AND CONTRACTOR GILCOAT AND SKINNER.

What is the Courthouse's most unusual feature?

THE ITALIAN STYLE TOWER AND DOME WITH THE JAIL DIRECTLY BEHIND IT.

What is the most famous case tried in the Hemphill County Courthouse?

THAT WOULD BE WHEN 77-YEAR-OLD IMOGENE FRENCH WAS MURDERED IN 1999. THE CASE WENT ON, UNSOLVED, FOR 19 MONTHS UNTIL FORENSIC SCIENTISTS DISCOVERED A SINGLE FINGERPRINT. THE PRINT BELONGED TO A TRUCKER WHO HAD BEEN IN CANADIAN ON THE DAY OF THE MURDER.

Where do you hang your hat?

ON LOUISIANA ST. IN HOUSTON, TX, WHERE I SPECIALIZE IN CRIMINAL LAW (CERTIFIED BY THE TEXAS BOARD OF LEGAL SPECIALIZATION IN CRIMINAL LAW SINCE 1986). I HAVE SUCCESSFULLY DEFENDED INDIVIDUALS AND CORPORATIONS ACCUSED OF A WIDE RANGE OF OFFENSES FROM WHITE COLLAR CRIME TO MURDER, IN STATE AND FEDERAL COURTS THROUGHOUT TEXAS AND LOUISIANA. MY CLIENTS COME FROM DIVERSE BACKGROUNDS: PLAIN HARD-WORKING FOLKS; POLICEMEN; SCHOOL TEACHERS; NURSES; DOCTORS; LAWYERS; BUSINESS EXECUTIVES AND LARGE PUBLICLY TRADED COMPANIES.

Believe it or not!

HEMPHILL COUNTY WAS THE SCENE OF THE BUFFALO WALLOW BATTLE IN 1874, WHERE TWO SCOUTS AND FOUR SOLDIERS HELD OFF A FORCE OF COMANCHES AND KIOWAS TWENTY TIMES THEIR NUMBER!

"Bull!"

Mr. Durham has several pair of hand-made boots with "Bull" engraved on the tops. During trial he has been known to start his final summation [after the State or Government has opened] with the comment: "Ladies and gentlemen, this is what you should think of the prosecutor's case..." as he is revealing the engraving on the tops of his boots!

~ DOUG'S FAMOUS TEXAS JUSTICE SAYING

"The Doolin Gang Swindle"

A Famous Texas Case as Told by

DOUGLAS M. DURHAM

LAW OFFICE OF DOUGLAS M. DURHAM

Hemphill County's history is rich in Texan imagery—cowboys, cattle ranches and shootouts. Hemphill County lies in the rolling plains on the eastern edge of the Texas panhandle. The terrain is as rugged as any cowboys and Indians movie you've ever seen, with two major rivers and dozens of creeks. Beginning in the 1870s, buffalo hunters entered the panhandle, and by 1878, every last one of the great southern herd had been killed. At the same time, the original residents of the area, Indians, were overtaken and transported to reservations in "Indian Territory." In the earlier Red River War of 1873-1874, the United States Army had defeated the panhandle tribes the Comanches and Kiowas, who, themselves, had already driven the Apaches out of the region.

The county was soon settled when a railroad was laid through the area to connect Dodge City, Kansas, with other cities in Texas. Early settlers of the county established what are said to be the first rodeos, giving the Hemphill County town of Canadian the name "Rodeo Town," which is still used today. The county's first sheriff, Thomas T. McGee, was an authentic cowboy, having roamed all over the country, roping cattle and driving herds to Dodge City for ranches across the South. In 1886, McGee bought stock in the PO Ranch and soon became foreman of the property. He was soon after elected the first sheriff of Hemphill County. McGee and his sidekick, deputy sheriff, Vastine Stickley, operated a wagon yard and livestock stable located in the town of Canadian until 1893.

The following year, a local man by the name of George Isaacs sent five envelopes reported to contain $5,000 each from Kansas City to his home in Canadian by train. After the train

Hemphill
County Courthouse

arrived in Canadian that evening, the money-filled envelopes were transferred to the Wells Fargo safe located in the railroad station. Shortly following the transfer of the money, shots were heard outside the station. Only seconds earlier, Sheriff McGee had stepped out onto the train platform, unknowingly placing himself directly in the line of fire. McGee suffered from multiple bullet wounds and died later that night. George Isaacs' envelopes were soon opened and found to contain a total of only $500. Isaacs and his three accomplices, known collectively as the Doolin gang, had set up a scheme to swindle Wells Fargo for thousands of dollars, but it had all gone horribly wrong.

The Doolin gang had been riding high over the past few years with a string of successful robberies and shootouts. Their reputation as the most formidable gang around was escalating and their crimes were becoming bolder. The attempted robbery

> "THE DOOLIN GANG HAD BEEN RIDING HIGH OVER THE PAST FEW YEARS WITH A STRING OF SUCCESSFUL ROBBERIES AND SHOOTOUTS."

of the Wells Fargo safe in Canadian would be the end of their winning streak. Isaacs was immediately charged with McGee's murder, convicted the following year and sentenced to life in prison, serving in Huntsville Penitentiary. It was rumored that he later escaped prison and fled to Mexico. The rest of the gang was also tried and sent to prison. Some say that in the late summer, under a full moon, Sheriff McGee can be seen walking next to the railroad tracks in downtown Canadian.

Hidalgo
County Courthouse

"The Oil & Gas Pipeline Street Rental Case"

A Famous Texas Case as Told by

BENJAMIN L. HALL III, PH.D., J.D.
THE HALL LAW FIRM

The case was styled "City of Edinburg v. Southern Union Gas Company, et al." The case was destined to make history because it pitted a Texas municipality against the most powerful industry in Texas—oil and gas. The controversy involved a claim by the City that oil and gas pipelines were traversing city rights-of-way without the operators and owners of such lines paying "street rentals" for the use of public property.

Historically, oil and gas companies, rather than purchasing title to the public property on which their pipes ran, would pay a "rental fee," generally based upon a percentage of the gross receipts generated from such lines within the city, for the right to use public property. Typically, such rentals have been the third or fourth largest source of revenue in cities' budgets. However, over time, many pipeline companies failed to make their timely payments, if any payments at all. The "Edinburg case," as it came to be called, tested once and for all, the legitimacy of municipalities collecting rentals for the unpaid subterranean occupations.

After nearly four years of pre-trial proceedings, which were characterized by at least two attempts by the pipeline companies to get the Texas Legislature to pass new legislation to ban such lawsuits, the case was finally slated for trial in the Hidalgo county seat—the city of Edinburg itself. In fact, the Hidalgo courthouse is located just across the street from Edinburg's city hall.

UNDAY
WEEKEND EDITION
August 16, 1998
Vol. 84, No. 130
25 Cents Daily

THE EDINBURG
DAILY

South Texas' only ind...

"The justice system in the Valley really wants to punish bad conduct."

~ BEN'S FAMOUS TEXAS JUSTICE SAYING

Jury awards S... to city in fran...

Jury next to decide

". . . MANY PIPELINE COMPANIES HAD FAILED TO MAKE THEIR TIMELY PAYMENTS, IF ANY PAYMENTS AT ALL."

Twelve able-bodied Hidalgo county residents heard nearly three months of evidence in the case. The trial was presided over by Judge Mike Westergren, from Corpus Christi, Texas. The defendants had moved to disqualify any Hidalgo county judge because of an alleged bias they might have because the outcome of the case could conceivably lessen their tax liability—a spurious charge if ever there was one. Nevertheless, under the watchful guidance of Judge Westergren, the case lumbered on to a final verdict of nearly $13.4 million. The City had won. The City had proved that the pipeline operators had reneged on paying their fair share.

The lead trial counsel for the City was Benjamin L. Hall, III, an ordained Pentecostal minister, who is also a graduate of Harvard Law School and holds Ph.D. and M. Div. degrees from Duke University. Hall was also the immediate past City Attorney for Houston when the case was tried.

Where did Hidalgo County get its name?
THE COUNTY WAS NAMED IN 1852 AFTER MIGUEL HIDALGO Y COSTILLA, WHO GALLANTLY LED MEXICO TO INDEPENDENCE FROM SPAIN.

Where is the Hidalgo County Courthouse located?
THE ORIGINAL 1886 HISTORIC COURTHOUSE BUILDING IS LOCATED IN HIDALGO, TX. THE CURRENT COURTHOUSE IS LOCATED IN THE COUNTY SEAT OF EDINBURG, TX.

Who designed the Hidalgo County Courthouse?
THE ORIGINAL HISTORIC COURTHOUSE BUILT IN 1886 WAS DESIGNED BY THE ARCHITECT S.W. BROOKS IN THE NEOCLASSICAL STYLE IN BRICK.

What is the Courthouse's most unusual feature?
THIS FABULOUS LONE STAR BEAUTY IS NOW A COMMERCIAL BUILDING FILLED WITH SPECIALTY SHOPS.

What is the most famous case tried in the Hidalgo County Courthouse?
DEMOCRAT ANDERSON BAKER BECAME COUNTY TREASURER IN 1907 AND SHERIFF IN 1912. HIS ELECTION AND THAT OF OTHER DEMOCRATIC CANDIDATES INITIATED THE HIDALGO COUNTY REBELLION. FARMERS AND BUSINESSMEN FORMED THE GOOD GOVERNMENT LEAGUE IN 1928 AND SENT 2,000 TELEGRAMS PETITIONING FAIR ELECTIONS TO PRESIDENT CALVIN COOLIDGE. THEY CHARGED "BAKERITES" HAD THROWN AWAY THE WESLACO BALLOT BOX. THE BAKERITES SAID BALLOTS WERE THROWN OUT BECAUSE THE RETURNS WEREN'T SEALED. FIVE-HUNDRED PEOPLE CARRIED A PETITION SIGNED BY 5,700 VOTERS TO PROTEST SEATING DEMOCRATIC CANDIDATES. IN 1930, A FEDERAL GRAND JURY IN HOUSTON INDICTED BAKER AND OTHER DEMOCRATIC REPRESENTATIVES.

Where do you hang your hat?
AT MY FIRM NEAR THE SHORES OF THE BUFFALO BAYOU (A.K.A. "THE HOUSTON SHIP CHANNEL"). FROM THIS PERCH, I CAN ALMOST HEAR THE HISTORICAL VOICES OF THE FOUNDERS OF THIS SIGNIFICANT STATE. MY SPECIALTY OF LAW IS PERSONAL INJURY AND COMMERCIAL LITIGATION.

Believe it or not!
THE EDINBURG VISITOR CENTER IS THE HAUNTED 1928 SOUTHERN PACIFIC RAILROAD STATION. THERE ARE SAID TO BE GHOSTS ROAMING THE STATION, INCLUDING A CONDUCTOR TO TRANSPORT PASSENGERS TO THE FATHOMS OF HELL ON HIS "DEATH TRAIN"!

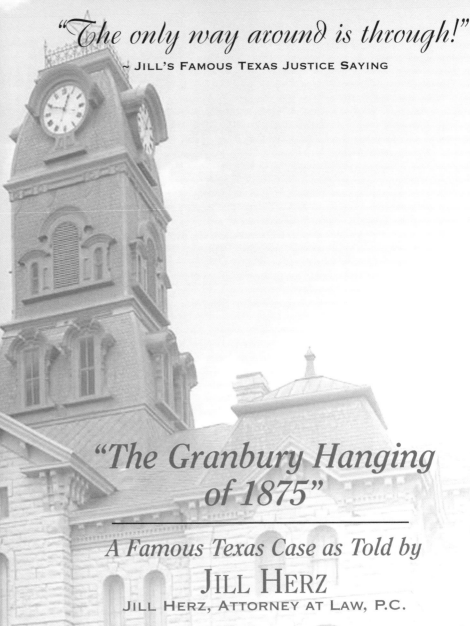

Where did Hood County get its name?
THE COUNTY WAS ORGANIZED IN 1866 AND NAMED FOR CONFEDERATE GENERAL JOHN B. HOOD.

Where is the Hood County Courthouse located?
ON THE SQUARE IN GRANBURY, TX. ITS DOWNTOWN NEIGHBORS INCLUDE GRANBURY LIVE, AN ART DECO THEATER AND THE GRANBURY OPERA HOUSE. BUILT IN 1886, THE OPERA HOUSE REOPENED IN 1975.

Who designed the Hood County Courthouse?
W.C. DODSON DESIGNED THE LIMESTONE HISTORIC COURTHOUSE IN 1890 IN A SECOND EMPIRE STYLE WITH ROMANESQUE DETAILING.

What is the courthouse's most unusual feature?
THE CLOCK TOWER IS ONE OF THE MOST UNUSUAL ARCHITECTURAL FEATURES. BOTH THE CLOCK AND BELLS ARE REGULARLY HAND-WOUND TO THIS DAY. ADDITIONALLY, THE COURTHOUSE AND ITS SURROUNDING SQUARE WERE THE FIRST IN TEXAS TO BE LISTED IN THE NATIONAL REGISTER OF HISTORIC PLACES.

What is the most famous case tried in the Hood County Courthouse?
THE TRIAL OF NELSON "COONEY" MITCHELL, THE ONLY MAN TO LEGALLY HANG IN HOOD COUNTY.

Where do you hang your hat?
ALTHOUGH I CALL DALLAS HOME, I REPRESENT INDIVIDUALS THROUGHOUT TEXAS FOR INJURIES OR DEATH RESULTING FROM AUTOMOBILE COLLISIONS, CONSTRUCTION SITE ACCIDENTS, INADEQUATE SECURITY, DOG/ANIMAL ATTACKS, DEFECTIVE PRODUCTS, NURSING HOME ABUSE/NEGLECT, MEDICAL MALPRACTICE AND OTHER ACTS OF NEGLIGENCE.

Believe it or not!
LOCAL LEGEND HAS IT THAT THE INFAMOUS OUTLAW JESSE JAMES IS BURIED IN GRANBURY CEMETERY IN HOOD COUNTY TEXAS. THE OUTLAW CAME TO THE AREA IN THE EARLY 1900S, NEARLY TWENTY YEARS AFTER STAGING HIS OWN DEATH IN MISSOURI, USING THE NAME J. FRANK DALTON. HE DIED AT THE AGE OF 103, AND WAS BURIED UNDER THE ALIAS J.W. GATES, ON THE PLOT OF HIS FRIEND SAM RASH, A DISTANT RELATIVE OF THE CURRENT HOOD COUNTY JUDGE, THE HONORABLE ANDY RASH!

"The only way around is through!"
~ JILL'S FAMOUS TEXAS JUSTICE SAYING

"The Granbury Hanging of 1875"

A Famous Texas Case as Told by

JILL HERZ
JILL HERZ, ATTORNEY AT LAW, P.C.

In the early 1870s, Nelson "Cooney" Mitchell and his family moved to Hood County and settled along the banks of the Brazos River, a place later known as Mitchell Bend, just south of Granbury. When the Truitt family moved to the area, Cooney helped them settle in the bend by carrying the note to the Truitt property.

The Mitchell-Truitt feud began in 1874. The civil lawsuit between the Mitchells and the Truitts arose from a dispute over the money under the note for the Truitt property. In March of 1875, the Hood County Courthouse mysteriously burned down, along with all of the county's land records and deeds. Although arson was suspected, the culprit was never found.

When the Truitts prevailed at trial, Bill Mitchell (Cooney's son) and an accomplice ambushed, shot and killed Sam and Isaac Truitt and wounded their brother James. They fled from the county immediately after the shooting. Cooney Mitchell and William Owens were arrested the next day—although neither appears to have been involved in the shooting, they were tried and

Hood
County Courthouse

convicted amid public outrage over the Truitt boys' killing. Cooney Mitchell was sentenced to death by hanging and William Owens got life in prison.

On October 9, 1875, Cooney Mitchell was publicly hanged in Granbury. By most accounts, Cooney Mitchell was almost eighty years old at the time of the hanging. It's been reported that more than 2,000 people witnessed the hanging. Because the jailhouse did not have gallows at the time, Cooney was hanged on an improvised scaffold made from a wagon, two poles, a crossbar and a rope. His was the only legal execution ever carried out in Hood County.

Five years later, William Owens was pardoned and released from prison. Cooney Mitchell's son, Bill, returned to Texas seventeen years later. Bill had held a grudge against James Truitt, a young minister, whose

> "... Cooney was hanged on an improvised scaffold made from a wagon, two poles, a crossbar and a rope."

trial testimony had helped to convict Bill's father. Upon his return to Hood County, Bill walked into James Truitt's house and shot him to death in front of his family. Afterwards, he again fled to New Mexico, where he lived under the alias of Bill "Baldy" Russell. After several years at large, Bill was apprehended and sentenced to prison. After serving just two years, he escaped from prison and was never heard from again.

Hopkins
County Courthouse

"A Benchmark Case"

A Famous Texas Case as Told by
COY C. JOHNSON
JOHNSON LAW FIRM, P.C.

I have tried many kinds of cases in my forty-plus years of practicing law, but worker's compensation cases are what I have become known for all over Northeast Texas. The late Judge Jim Noble Thompson presided over the civil docket in Hopkins County for many years during my practice.

On one particular Monday, I announced ready on five worker's compensation cases. Judge Thompson informed me that all five juries would be selected Tuesday

After a long day on Tuesday, all five juries were picked. On Wednesday, we finished the first worker's compensation case by 5:00 p.m., with the jury returning with a verdict of total and permanent disability. On Thursday, we finished the second worker's compensation case by the end of the day, with this jury returning the same verdict. On Friday, after learning about the verdicts earlier in the week, the insurance companies decided to accept my earlier settlement demands. They had had enough of Hopkins County that week.

Early in my career, I represented a man injured by a toxic substance while working for a railroad company. During my opening statement, I made a production of putting on gloves and taking a jar out of my briefcase containing a sample of the toxic substance. I sat it on the edge of the table, leaving it for the jury to ponder. I would point at it and refer to it, but it was too dangerous to pick up again. The jury believed it to be dangerous, as well, and returned a verdict in our favor.

In one worker's compensation case, the defense attorney scribbled all week on a black board to make notes as he cross examined my witnesses. Every strong point of his case was written on that board and I knew he would use this against me during closing argument. During the lunch break, I erased the board. When the defense lawyer discovered this,

Trial attorneys want the jury to see things their way. I want the jury to know that I represent the victims, the injured, and those who cannot speak for themselves. One quote I use near the beginning of my jury arguments is, as the great prophet Isaiah said,

"Come let us reason together."

~ COY'S FAMOUS TEXAS JUSTICE SAYING

he came unglued and complained to Judge Thompson. I responded that the board was not in evidence and I needed the board to write on during my jury argument. The judge agreed and so did the jury who followed my suggestions and wrote the same answers on their verdict.

The case that stands out above all others is the case I tried in 1989. Early one morning, police were notified by a customer that a convenience store was unattended. The police soon learned that the lone female employee had been abducted and murdered. After years of investigation, the case remains an unsolved murder.

The lady's family asked for my help in seeking damages from the owner of the convenience store. The company was sued for its failure to have proper security and for other acts of negligence. A jury was selected and the case was tried in the Hopkins County Courthouse. The company's President never made an appearance at the trial. Prior to jury summation, I placed a chair behind the Defendant's counsel table. During my jury summation, I

"DURING MY JURY SUMMATION, I POINTED TO THE 'EMPTY CHAIR' TO DEMONSTRATE THE COMPANY'S DISREGARD FOR THIS GRIEVING FAMILY."

pointed to the "empty chair" to demonstrate the company's disregard for this grieving family. The jury was so angry that it awarded the family $4.7 million in damages. This was the largest verdict ever rendered in Hopkins County, but the repercussions go far beyond those numbers.

This case was appealed to the Texas Supreme Court on two different occasions where I was unsuccessful in maintaining the jury's verdict. Based on the "causation" issue, the Court overturned the jury's verdict. This is a benchmark case in Texas law and is studied in Texas law schools today.

The family lost a wife, mother and daughter and the decision of the Court resulted in the family not being compensated for their loss. For me, the failure to obtain a successful result for deserving clients is still a lingering hurt in an otherwise long and satisfying career.

Where did Hopkins County get its name?
THE DAVID HOPKINS FAMILY, EARLY SETTLERS TO THE AREA WHO IMMIGRATED IN 1840. HOPKINS COUNTY IS ALSO KNOWN AS THE "DAIRY CAPITAL" OF TEXAS.

Where is the Hopkins County Courthouse located?
LOCATED A HOP, SKIP AND A JUMP FROM THE ST. CLAIR MUSIC BOX COLLECTION, WHICH IS ONE OF THE WORLD'S MOST EXPENSIVE, INCLUDING MORE THAN 200 MUSIC BOXES.

Who designed the Hopkins County Courthouse?
JAMES RIELY GORDAN, ARCHITECT OF THIRTEEN COURTHOUSES IN THE STATE OF TEXAS. THE ROMANESQUE REVIVAL STYLE HISTORIC COURTHOUSE WAS CONSTRUCTED IN 1894 OF RED GRANITE AND SANDSTONE TRIM AND WAS EMBELLISHED WITH A TOWER, TURRETS, BALCONIES AND STONE CARVINGS. THE HOPKINS COUNTY COURTHOUSE WAS REDEDICATED ON DECEMBER 7TH 2002 BY THE TEXAS HISTORICAL COMMISSIONS' TEXAS COURTHOUSE PRESERVATION PROGRAM.

What is the Courthouse's most unusual feature?
BEFORE THE BUILDING WAS COMPLETE, A PETITION WAS CIRCULATED BY CITIZENS ASKING FOR A CLOCK. COMMISSIONER AT THE TIME, R. CARPENTER, SAID OF THE CLOCK, "GET UP AT SUN UP; GO TO BED AT DARK AND EAT WHEN YOU ARE HUNGRY, AND YOU DON'T NEED NO DAMN CLOCK."

What is the most famous case tried in the Hopkins County Courthouse?
A TEXAS STATE REPRESENTATIVE WAS TRIED AND CONVICTED FOR CATTLE THEFT IN HOPKINS COUNTY IN THE EARLY 80S, BRINGING NATIONAL MEDIA ATTENTION TO OUR COUNTY. THE REPRESENTATIVE BROUGHT THE CATTLE UP HERE FROM THE HOUSTON AREA AND SOLD THEM UNDER A FICTITIOUS NAME, BUT HE CAME AND PICKED UP THE CHECK HIMSELF.

Where do you hang your hat?
WITH HARD WORK AND FAMILY SUPPORT, I GRADUATED FROM BAYLOR LAW SCHOOL IN 1963. SINCE THAT TIME, I HAVE BEEN TRYING CASES IN HOPKINS COUNTY AND THE NORTHEAST TEXAS AREA.

Believe it or not!
IN 1851, THE GOVERNMENT OF HOPKINS COUNTY CONTRACTED TO BUILD THE COUNTY'S FIRST PERMANENT COURTHOUSE, BUT LACKED FUNDS TO PAY FOR THE JOB. THAT IS, UNTIL AN EARLY SETTLER OBSERVED THAT OUT-OF-STATE CATTLE GRAZERS IN THE COUNTY WERE IN VIOLATION OF TEXAS LAW BECAUSE GRASS WAS ONLY FREE TO TEXAS CITIZENS. THE CATTLE WERE SOLD AT PUBLIC AUCTION. THE SALES BROUGHT IN $1,772.46—ENOUGH TO BUILD THE COURTHOUSE!

Where did Hunt County get its name?

IN 1846 FROM MEMUCAN HUNT, SECRETARY OF THE TEXAS NAVY AND FREEDOM FIGHTER. HUNT ALSO RAN UNSUCCESSFULLY FOR THE VICE-PRESIDENT OF TEXAS.

Where is the Hunt County Courthouse located?

THE COURTHOUSE IS LOCATED IN GREENVILLE, TX, WAS NAMED AFTER GENERAL THOMAS GREEN AND WAS THE SITE FOR GREENVILLE'S FIRST SCHOOL IN 1847.

Who designed the Hunt County Courthouse?

THE 1929 HISTORIC COURTHOUSE WAS DESIGNED IN CLASSICAL REVIVAL TO ART DECO TRANSITIONAL ARCHITECTURE OF BRICK AND STONE BY C.H. PAGE JR. AND BROTHER.

What is the Courthouse's most unusual feature?

ITS CLASSICAL STYLE COLUMNS, WHICH LED TO AN INTRICATE TERRA COTTA DETAILED CEILING.

What is the most famous case tried in the Hunt County Courthouse?

IN MARCH 2000, BILL GALLOWAY WAS CONVICTED BY A HUNT COUNTY JURY OF THE CAPITAL MURDER OF DAVID LOGIE, IN HUNT COUNTY, TX. HE AND THREE OTHER ACCOMPLICES FROM SOUTH DAKOTA WERE RUNNING A ROBBERY SCHEME WHERE THEY WOULD INVITE MEN INTO THEIR HOTEL ROOM TO ROB AND MURDER THEM.

Where do you hang your hat?

IN FORT WORTH, TX, AT THE LAW OFFICES OF STEVEN C. LAIRD, P.C., THIS IS A PROFESSIONAL CORPORATION THAT CONCENTRATES PRIMARILY IN MEDICAL MALPRACTICE, SERIOUS PERSONAL INJURY AND WRONGFUL DEATH CASES.

Believe it or not!

THE FIRST NAME PROPOSED FOR GREENVILLE, THE HUNT COUNTY SEAT, WAS "PINCKNEYVILLE," IN HONOR OF THE FIRST GOVERNOR OF TEXAS, JAMES PINCKNEY HENDERSON!

"Service & Sacrifice Built Our Courthouse"

A Famous Texas Tale as Told by
STEVEN C. LAIRD
LAW OFFICES OF STEVEN C. LAIRD, P.C.

The county seat of Hunt County is Greenville, my hometown. Like many children growing up in rural Texas, the courthouse square was the center of the universe as far as I was concerned. I knew of the capitols in Austin and Washington, D.C., and I had heard of the Supreme Court, but in my mind, there could be nothing as important as the business that went on inside that old courthouse.

My memories of the courthouse square are typical of what you might see in a Rockwell painting: homecoming parades, elections and dime stores. These activities in and around the courthouse and the stores on the square etched in my mind the importance of community, commerce and citizenship; values that still run strong in Hunt County.

Hunt County—which was named for Memucan Hunt, a legislator and secretary of the navy—and the city of Greenville—named for Thomas Jefferson Green, a soldier and legislator—were named in memory of servicemen. These men were representative of the spirit of that budding community much as the courthouse is representative of all that is Hunt County. It is only fitting for the Hunt County courthouse to commemorate those who provided the freedom for which it plays guardian.

The walls on the main floor of the courthouse are covered with plaques bearing the names of Hunt County residents who fought in America's wars. One cannot walk through the courthouse without being struck by the number of people from this rural county who answered our country's call. Like so many from all over this land, their sacrifices give meaning and significance to having a courthouse in the first place. It is one thing to pursue your legal rights in a court of law, but it's quite another to pass between the names of hundreds of local citizens who fought to preserve that right.

Among those servicemen who have a special place in the hearts of Hunt County residents is Audie L. Murphy, the most decorated soldier of World War II. Audie Murphy was a soldier,

Hunt
County Courthouse

an actor, a songwriter and a poet. During the war, Murphy showed gallantry and charisma. He battled the Germans at Anzio, fought his way out of an ambush in Salerno and staved off numerous bouts with malaria. At one point, Murphy turned down a promotion to remain with his men. For all of these reasons, Audie Murphy has become a symbol of patriotism, honor, courage and loyalty for all Americans. But for the people of Hunt County, Murphy is a symbol of the heroic ideal that the walls of courthouse enshrine as a local and national hero.

> **"MY MEMORIES OF THE COURTHOUSE SQUARE ARE TYPICAL OF WHAT YOU MIGHT SEE IN A ROCKWELL PAINTING . . ."**

After the war, Murphy penned the following poem that I am reminded of as I walk through this old courthouse:

> *Freedom flies in your heart like an eagle*
> *Let it soar with the winds high above*
> *Among the spirits of soldiers now sleeping*
> *Guard it with care and with love.*

The service and sacrifice of those who went before us give meaning to the justice we seek inside our courtrooms. Nowhere is this more evident to me than in the hallways of this old courthouse. I cannot walk through these halls without stopping in front of the plaque honoring those Hunt County residents who served in World War II. There I find my own father's name among the many servicemen, and I pause for a moment with thoughts of pride for our heroes and the courthouse.

Jack
County Courthouse

"Third Time's a Charm"

A Famous Texas Case as Told by
JEFF KEARNEY
THE KEARNEY LAW FIRM

Mr. Kearney was involved in one of the most notorious murder trials ever tried in the Jack County Courthouse. Mr. Kearney defended Mrs. Pamela Loffland, the wife of a socially prominent Fort Worth businessman, who was accused of hiring her hairdresser to kill her husband. The prosecution contended that Mr. Kearney's client was having an affair with the hairdresser during the time the murder plot was conceived and carried out. The case went on for several years and took many interesting twists and turns before it was finally concluded.

Mrs. Loffland's husband was allegedly kidnapped and taken deep into the woods of Parker County, just west of Fort Worth, where he was shot and killed. Because the body was found in Parker County, the charges were originally filed there. Due to extensive pre-trial publicity and high public interest, Mr. Kearney was concerned that his client could not receive a fair trial in Parker County and therefore requested a change of venue. Judge Harry Hopkins of Parker County agreed and moved the trial to Jack County. Even though the judge's jurisdiction was limited to Parker County, he decided to go with the case and preside over it in the Jack County Courthouse.

The trial in Jack County was certainly one of the most interesting cases tried in that courthouse. On day two of the trial, Judge Hopkins opened the proceedings with an announcement that surprised all the participants and spectators. The judge informed everyone that he had failed to apply for and receive a special designation to legally preside over the trial in Jack County. Proclaiming that he did not have the authority to proceed, Judge Hopkins declared a mistrial, discharged the jury and stated that the trial would be rescheduled when he was properly assigned to the case. As the jurors were filing out of the courtroom, one of them, a local barber named Elvis, approached Mr. Kearney and seemed very sympathetic to the defendant's position. The prosecutors did not see this exchange.

By the time a second trial was scheduled, the defense had learned that the judge was not required to declare a mistrial and Mr. Kearney filed a Writ of Habeas Corpus alleging double jeopardy. The District Clerk was legally required to serve the writ on the Jack County Sheriff. The sheriff refused to open his door to accept the writ, so the clerk, relying on an old Texas Statute, got a hammer and nailed the writ to the sheriff's door.

It was later determined that the second trial could proceed. When the jury panel was brought in, one of its members was the same local barber named Elvis. Both

". . . ALLEGEDLY KIDNAPPED AND TAKEN DEEP INTO THE WOODS OF PARKER COUNTY. . . ."

sides questioned whether the same person could sit on two juries in the same case. When it was determined that he could, he was selected and served as a juror in the second trial. The second case was tried to conclusion and the jury, unable to reach a unanimous verdict, hung eight to four in favor of acquittal. A second mistrial was declared.

Ultimately the case was settled with a plea bargain. Mrs. Loffland was not required to admit any guilt and received deferred adjudication probation with no conviction ever being entered on her record. Texas Justice was served in a very unusual way in this case.

Where did Jack County get its name?
It was named for brothers Patrick C. and William H. Jack in 1857, gallant commanders of the Texas Revolution for independence.

Where is the Jack County Courthouse located?
On Jacksboro's Town Square, on the corner of Farm Roads U.S. 380 and 281—the two roads that put Jacksboro on the map, opening the town up as a center for commerce and trade.

Who designed the Jack County Courthouse?
The architects, Voelcker & Dixon designed this Moderne style Historic Courthouse of stone in 1940.

What is the Courthouse's most unusual feature?
There have been four courthouses built, one in 1858, 1871, 1886 and the most recent one in 1940—the rock of the 1886 courthouse was salvaged and used to build City Hall.

What is the most famous case tried in the Jack County Courthouse?
Without an army presence during the Civil War, Indian raids plagued the area and residents were forced to flee eastward. The famous "Warren Wagon Train Raid" occurred on May 18, 1871, and chiefs Satanta and Big Tree were tried and sentenced to be executed on September 1, 1871. The sentence was later changed to life imprisonment to prevent further Indian uprising.

Where do you hang your hat?
The Kearney Law Firm is located in downtown Fort Worth on Main Street. The firm specializes in representing individuals and corporations in state and federal trials and appeals. Jeff Kearney is board certified in criminal law by the Texas Board of Legal Specialization.

Believe it or not!
During the Civil War, there were only 37 slaves in the county and the county's residents voted 76 to 14 against secession!

Jefferson
County Courthouse

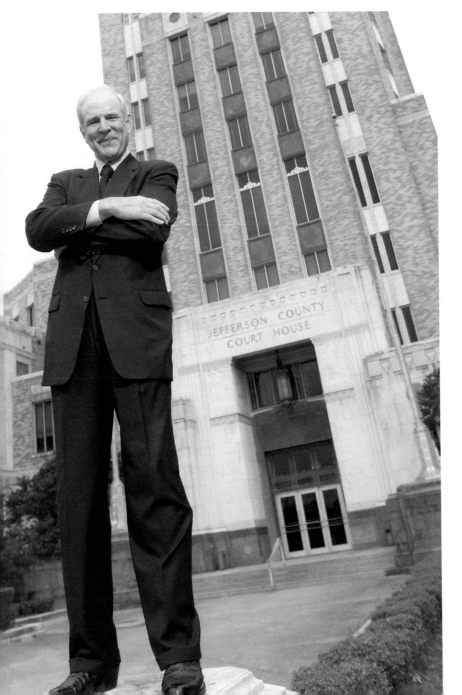

"The Widow Maker"

A Famous Texas Case as Told by
GILBERT T. ADAMS
LAW OFFICES OF GILBERT T. ADAMS, P.C.

As a young lawyer practicing less than a handful of years, I had the privilege to represent the Harlee Williams family in a challenging and deserving case. Harlee's wife Tullah made the appointment, accompanied by her husband, Harlee.

The Williams were concerned when they received notice from Harlee's employer's workers compensation insurance company that Mr. Williams' benefits were about to end. He was coming close to the end of the statutory benefits of 401 weeks at $49.00 a week. She was desperate and didn't know how she and Harlee and a family of eleven were going to face the future.

Harlee's scarred forehead overlay obviously displaced skull fragments. Soon, I learned about the devastating effect of his frontal lobe injury, the occasional epileptic seizures. After years as a responsible and productive husband and father, he was now totally unable to work and too incompetent to take care of himself. His spouse and children were constantly concerned about his whereabouts, as well as how to manage and care for him. The family tried to eke out an existence.

I wanted to know what happened, how it happened and whether or not this was a preventable injury. There was nothing I could do about the soon-to-end Texas Workers Compensation benefits. The law is the law. I began my investigation by literally trying to pull information out of Mrs. Williams and exploring and revising Harlee's shattered mind and recollections. Gradually, I began to understand what had happened. Harlee had stopped his Chevrolet 2-ton truck at a rural filling station to get some gas. While his helper Kirby Hadnot was filling up, Harlee walked around the truck checking it over. He noticed that the outside tire on the rear dual drive axle appeared to need some air. He got the air hose out and was starting to add air to the tire when there was a sudden explosion. By the time Kirby got to him, Harlee was laying on the ground his head bleeding and his body shaking uncontrollably. Kirby thought Harlee was dying. The station attendant called the ambulance and fortunately, Harlee's life was saved, but his future and the future of his family became a nightmare.

> *"No man is above the law and no man is below it. Nor do we ask any man's permission when we require him to obey it."*
>
> *Theodore Roosevelt*

~ GILBERT JR.'S FAMOUS TEXAS JUSTICE SAYING

I realized I was faced with a serious dilemma. I only had a few weeks before the statue of limitations would forever bar the Williams from filing a products liability lawsuit against the seller and manufacturer of the unreasonably dangerous two-piece truck wheel. The vehicle was manufactured by General Motors and was a 1962 model and had been scrapped. The wheel that had exploded had been scrapped as well. Eventually, I was able to get Kirby to locate a wheel "exactly like" the one that had exploded.

Intensive research revealed that the industry had given a technical designation of "RH5 °" to this two-piece truck wheel. This two-piece truck wheel had been nicknamed "The Widow Maker" for its propensity to suddenly and unexpectedly separate during tire inflation or while just driving down the road. Research revealed that numerous people had been injured or killed by these hazardous wheels.

Obviously there were a number of hurtles to overcome, not the least of which was the identity of the manufacturer. General Motors had manufactured the vehicle, but I didn't know if the wheels were the ones that had originally come with the truck. I also discovered that there were several manufacturers of the "RH5 °" wheels including Firestone, Kelsey Hayes and Bud. Without the wheel, how could I ever establish the manufacturer or the condition of the wheel?

"HE GOT THE AIR HOSE AND WAS STARTING TO ADD AIR TO THE TIRE WHEN THERE WAS A SUDDEN EXPLOSION . . . HARLEE WAS LYING ON THE GROUND TWITCHING IN HIS BLOOD . . ."

As time was short, there was no reasonable alternative other than to sue General Motors, Firestone, Kelsey Hayes and Bud. Of course, they promptly hired some of the state's biggest law firms and best lawyers to defend their clients. It is a rare case indeed in which a plaintiff is contending that a product was defective but is unable to produce the defective product for inspection and analysis to determining who the manufacturer is, whether it has been built to specifications and whether it was misused while in the market place.

Where did Jefferson County get its name?
IN 1837 FROM THOMAS JEFFERSON, A LAWYER, AUTHOR OF THE DECLARATION OF INDEPENDENCE, THE THIRD PRESIDENT OF THE UNITED STATES AND A FOUNDER OF THE DEMOCRATIC PARTY.

Where is the Jefferson County Courthouse located?
ON PEARL STREET IN BEAUMONT, THE BANKS OF THE NECHES RIVER, THE SHIP CHANNEL AND PORT THAT PROVIDES THE ECONOMIC FOUNDATION FOR THE CITY OF BEAUMONT.

Who designed the Jefferson County Courthouse?
IN 1932, THE COUNTY'S FOURTH COURTHOUSE WAS DESIGNED BY FRED C. STONE AND A. BABIN OF ARCHITECTURE IN THE MODERNE STYLE WITH ART DECO ACCENTS IN STONE AND BRICK AND DESIGNATED AS A HISTORIC COURTHOUSE.

What is the Courthouse's most unusual feature?
ITS ART DECO ARCHITECTURE; THE TALL AND TOWER-LIKE APPEARANCE WITH INTERIOR MARBLE DETAILING. THIS FOURTEEN-STORY LONE STAR BEAUTY IS A NATIONAL REGISTER PROPERTY.

What is the most famous case tried in the Jefferson County Courthouse?
THE BRAVEST JURY IN AMERICAN HISTORY LET JUSTICE ROLL LIKE A MIGHTY RIVER FOR THE HORRENDOUS DEATH OF A YOUNG MOTHER OF THREE, CINDY COFFEY. SHE WAS POISONED TO DEATH BY A DEFECTIVE DRUG IMPORTED FROM FRANCE BY WYETH PHARMACEUTICALS. ON APRIL 27, 2004, THE JURY'S VERDICT OF $1.013 BILLION SET A NEW HIGH-WATER MARK FOR THE VALUE OF HUMAN LIFE IN AMERICAN JURISPRUDENCE.

Where do you hang your hat?
IN THE LAW FIRM FOUNDED BY MY FATHER IN 1930, LOCATED IN THE ADAMS BUILDING, CALDER AVENUE AT THIRD STREET, BEAUMONT, WHERE WE SPECIALIZE IN DEFENDING LIBERTY AND PURSUING JUSTICE.

Believe it or not!
ANTHONY LUCAS, MINING ENGINEER BORN IN AUSTRIA, ENVISIONED STRIKING OIL AT SPINDLE TOP NEAR BEAUMONT IN 1901. THE HEIGHT OF THE WOODEN OIL DERRICK, THE LUCAS GUSHER, WAS 64 FEET. IT THREW A STREAM OF BLACK GOLD ALMOST 200 FEET INTO THE AIR AT A FLOW OF 100,000 BARRELS A DAY — MORE THAN ALL OF THE OTHER PRODUCING OIL WELLS IN THE UNITED STATES COMBINED!

At best, there were only two witnesses who had seen the wheel. The manufacturers of "RH5 °" wheels were not very proud of their products. They placed little indiscreet stamps on the wheels and painted over them so their visibility took a Sherlock Holmes inspection to identify who the manufacturer was, year of manufacture and the size of the wheel. The size was important because the manufacturers would assert that there had been a mismatch of the size of the rim base and the side ring.

After prodigious study and consulting with one of the top experts in the country, I believed that I would be able to establish a case if this two-piece truck wheel was unreasonably dangerous because of its design. That meant that every "RH5 °" wheel in the marketplace would have to be unreasonably dangerous. This is a very heavy burden to convince a jury of, especially when you do not have the specific product. I had other challenges as well. The accident had occurred in 1969. The vehicle had been sold to Harlee Williams about a year before his fatal injury. I had to establish that the wheel had not been misused but was in substantially the same condition as it was when it left the manufacturer, assuming it was on the Chevrolet truck when it was originally sold in 1962.

Tracing back to its inception, I found that the "RH5 °" wheel was designed and multiple patents were issued in the late '40s. Thereafter, both Firestone and Kelsey Hayes sought patents, participated in and settled litigation so that both Firestone and Kelsey Hayes could make the rim base. Firestone retained the exclusive right to build the side rings. The side ring is what separated and exploded into Harlee Williams' body.

The only two witnesses to Harlee's injury were Harlee and Kirby Hadnot. Harlee was brain damaged and could provide only limited information. I was very concerned about tendering Harlee Williams for his deposition considering his mental state. But after considering all the factors, I decided to do so. At the beginning of the deposition, I introduced each of the lawyers and identified the parties whom they represented. Phil Johns of Baker and Botts, who represented Firestone, began the questioning. When Harlee was asked who manufactured the wheel, he couldn't remember the manufacturer's name, but he pointed to Preston Shirley and said, "I can't remember the name of the company," but pointing to Mr. Shirley, "he represents them." Kyle Wheelus who represented Bud, and G.I. Low, who represented General Motors, were noticeably amused if not relieved.

Within thirty days of his deposition, Harlee Williams died. His wife told how she had fixed his lunch and he had gone to the bedroom to take a nap. Later, Harlee was found dead. Harlee's neurosurgeon testified that Harlee had a seizure and regurgitated, inhaled his vomit and smothered to death. The seizure, of course, was a residual of his brain injury from the tire explosion.

After Harlee passed away, the defendants next noticed the only

surviving witness: Kirby Hadnot. Tragically, within a few months, Kirby was killed in an automobile accident. At the trial, the jury only had the benefit of Harlee Williams' and Kirby Hadnot's written deposition transcripts. Videotaped depositions while customary today, were unavailable in the mid 1970s. The plaintiffs' wheel design engineer, Dr. Paul Youngdhl, also appeared in person and there was an excerpt from a 1952 Firestone film.

The defendants had various defenses including a serviceable and satisfactory design. After all, the wheel had been in use since the 1950s and had been included as original equipment on Ford, Chevrolet and Dodge Trucks for many years. They explained that the separation was not the result of a design defect, but a result of either improper mounting by a tire station or allowing the air pressure to get so low that the two multi-piece rim portions became misaligned. The defendants' case included an internationally renowned engineer named Howard Simpson who was completely adamant in his testimony that anyone who was assembling the "RH5 °" wheel could clearly tell when the two pieces were properly aligned.

When I showed him a portion of the 1952 16-millimeter film originally produced by Firestone, together with engineering data and material from Kelsey Hayes, Howard Simpson became noticeably uncomfortable and irritated that he had not been provided this material from these defendants because it refuted his testimony and destroyed the defense's strategy. As Dr. Simpson left the witness stand near where I was standing, he stopped momentarily, shook my hand and whispered to me, "I wish you luck, but not too much."

When the jury came back with a verdict in favor of the plaintiffs, it was a joyous moment in the life of the Williams family. Through the years, I would learn that Harlee's children grew up to be members of the City Council and contributing members of the society. They frequently expressed their gratefulness that I took their dad's case and pursued it when there was seemingly no other place to turn.

Due in a significant part to Harlee Williams' injury, death and the courageous Texas jury, the "Widow Maker" "RH5 °" wheel is no longer installed by GM, Ford and other truck manufacturers. Instead of multiple wheels, these defendants install safer one-piece truck wheels. This virtually eliminated multi-piece wheel explosions and has saved countless lives; thus, the end of the "Widow Maker" and the grisly list of other injuries, deaths and lawsuits which were its progeny.

I learned that families and the public are enthralled with the advocate that takes the part of the underdog. They rely upon plaintiff lawyers to defend the widow, the orphan, the helpless and the incompetent against those with great economic and political leverage. Through it all, the advocate is expected to and does oppose and overcome any obstacle. In all events, he is expected to try and to try hard.

Top Gun & Legal Legend
Gilbert T. Adams

★ PRESIDENT OF THE TEXAS TRIAL LAWYERS ASSOCIATION

★ FOUNDER AND FACULTY MEMBER OF THE TEXAS COLLEGE OF TRIAL ADVOCACY

★ PRESIDENT OF LAMAR UNIVERSITY ALUMNI ASSOCIATION

★ PRESIDENT OF THE SOUTHEAST TEXAS TRIAL LAWYERS ASSOCIATION

★ EXECUTIVE COMMITTEE AND BOARD OF GOVERNORS OF THE ASSOCIATION OF TRIAL LAWYERS OF AMERICA

★ NATIONAL AND INTERNATIONAL AUTHOR AND LECTURER

★ RANCHER, OUTDOORSMAN AND WILDLIFE CONSERVATIONIST

SAN JACINTO BUILDING
595 ORLEANS STREET
SUITE 500
BEAUMONT, TEXAS 77701

RICHARD J. CLARKSON
SENIOR APPELLATE SCHOLAR
ATTORNEY AT LAW

http://www.texasappellateattorney.com
lawoffice@texasappellateattorney.com

PHONE (409) 833-7713
FAX (409) 833-8991

Dear Martana,

There has been a Gilbert Adams practicing law in Beaumont since 1930. This firm is in its third generation. Over the past 35 years this Gilbert Adams – like his father – has tried a wide variety of cases from the austere courtrooms of rural Texas to the imposing State and Federal Courthouses of urban areas.

Gilbert Adams has dedicated his life to the pursuit of justice and compassion for the powerless. By any measure, he is one of the most dedicated and effective lawyers on the frontline struggle for justice.

Whether winning means a noteworthy verdict or extraordinary settlement, Gilbert Adams knows how to win cases using key elements of a trial, precision, discovery focus groups, voir dire, opening statement, the latest technology to enhance comprehension of the evidence, presenting witnesses, cross examinations and summation.

Believing that the profession involves teaching others and mentoring younger attorneys, he was a founder and faculty member of the Texas College of Trial Advocacy and has been for decades a writer and lecturer at state, national, and international professional conferences.

The next generation Gilbert Adams III (like his father and mother Marilyn), his sisters Mary Margaret Groves, Caroline Faubus, and Catherine are all attorneys. His youngest sister Juliana has even begun her law school objective. Gilbert Adams III's wife Tonya is also a lawyer.

To their credit, the Adams' give their lives and financial resources to numerous civic, political, conservation, and non-profit organizations. Gilbert continues to leave his mark on our local and national landscape.

As a fourth-generation Texan, Gilbert continues to leave his mark on our local and national landscape.

Sincerely,

Richard J. Clarkson

Richard J. Clarkson

Johnson
County Courthouse

"Texas Rangers to the Rescue"

A Famous Texas Case as Told by
DONNA J. SMIEDT
LAW OFFICE OF DONNA J. SMIEDT

In 1985, Johnson County was absorbed in the rescue of a kidnapped 13-year-old girl. Johnson County police, DPS troopers, Texas Rangers and even the FBI were involved in the attempt to rescue the girl. This case was even on Court TV.

Amy McNiel was abducted from her brother, Mark's Jeep as he drove her to school one morning. Three people in a car ran her brother's Jeep off the road before pointing a shotgun at Mark's head and then taking Amy. The kidnappers then instructed Mark to return to his parent's house, about a mile away, where they could soon expect a phone call. What the parents did not know was that the kidnappers had attempted to abduct Amy the previous Tuesday, but mistakenly showed up at the wrong house.

When Mark informed his parents of his sister's abduction, Amy's father, Neil, immediately phoned Johnson County sheriff, Eddy Boggs. The sheriff and two FBI agents instantly went to the McNiel house. Texas Ranger Bill Guinn also soon arrived, and by this time, the parents had received the first ransom demand. Guinn called his departmental captain and twelve additional Texas Rangers soon arrived at the scene.

The kidnappers asked for $100,000 ransom. It was late Friday night and all banks were closed, so in a rush to get the money, Don McNiel requested that a local bank open its doors. The bank was opened and the money was obtained. But it was not until Saturday afternoon when the kidnappers finally alerted Amy's father to where he could drop the money.

FBI officers equipped Don's limo with radio devices so they could follow him every step of the way throughout the cash drop. Also, two agents would accompany Don in the car. First, the kidnappers instructed Don to go to Dallas, then to Tyler, then to Mount Pleasant. The abductors had been high on speed for a week and were extremely paranoid. The Dallas and Tyler drops had been unsuccessful because they did not feel the locations were safe. Their demands were many times unrealistic, requiring the limo to travel at speeds over 100 miles an hour to reach a location on time.

Early Sunday morning, the limo was on its way to Mount Pleasant when things began to go wrong. First, the radio equipment in the car went haywire; failing to transmit any signals, then the limo broke down on I-30 about half a mile from where they were to meet the kidnappers. Don waited for hours for contact from the kidnappers, but heard nothing.

Finally, the kidnappers' stolen Thunderbird was spotted on I-30 with Amy sitting in the backseat. Ranger Joe Wiley began pursuing the vehicle, headed east of Mount Pleasant. However, the kidnappers began firing at Wiley's car and soon disabled it. Additional officers continued the pursuit and followed the car until it arrived at a farmhouse in Saltillo. The kidnappers had planned to bring Amy into the house and also take the residents hostage.

However, before they could make it to the house, the officers

"THE KIDNAPPERS ASKED FOR $100,000 RANSOM."

apprehended them. After a shootout lasting two to three minutes, all but two of the five suspects surrendered, while the others were wounded while attempting to escape. Amy was rescued and reunited with her parents.

All the kidnappers were charged with aggravated kidnapping and held at the Johnson County Jail. Judge John MacLean tried the case and the courtroom was packed with reporters, the most MacLean had ever seen in his courtroom.

All five of the kidnappers were prosecuted and given sentences ranging from ten years to life in prison. Years later, the leader of the kidnapping ring escaped from prison, but was captured seven days later.

Where did Johnson County get its name?
FROM COLONEL MIDDLETON T. JOHNSON, A HERO OF THE MEXICAN WAR, WHO ALSO SERVED ON THE TEXAS FRONTIER AND IN THE CIVIL WAR, AND WHO LATER BECAME A LEGISLATOR.

Where is the Johnson County Courthouse located?
THE COURTHOUSE IS LOCATED IN THE PUBLIC SQUARE, IN THE HEART OF DOWNTOWN CLEBURNE, TX.

Who designed the Johnson County Courthouse?
LANG & WITCHELL OF DALLAS DESIGNED THE HISTORIC 1913 TEXAS RENAISSANCE COURTHOUSE OF BRICK AND CONCRETE. THE PRAIRIE STYLE ELEMENTS WERE POPULAR IN THE EARLY 20TH CENTURY.

What is the Courthouse's most unusual feature?
THE CLOCK TOWER THAT TOWERS ABOVE THE REST OF THE BUILDING AND THE GORGEOUS ATRIUM INSIDE THE COURTHOUSE.

What is the most famous case tried in the Johnson County Courthouse?
THE SLEEPY LITTLE TOWN OF CLEBURNE, TEXAS, MADE NATIONAL NEWS WHEN A BURLESON SCHOOLTEACHER ARRESTED FOR SELLING "OBSCENE DEVICES" APPEARED AT HER FIRST HEARING IN COUNTY COURT. THE WOMAN HAD BEEN HOSTING A "TUPPERWARE-STYLE" ADULT TOY PARTY WHEN SHE WAS ARRESTED BY TWO UNDER-COVER POLICE OFFICERS; TEXAS LAW PROHIBITS THE SALE OF SUCH DEVICES. FOLLOWING A MAELSTROM OF NATIONAL AND LOCAL PUBLICITY, THE JOHNSON COUNTY DISTRICT ATTORNEY DISMISSED ALL OF THE CHARGES.

Where do you hang your hat?
IN ARLINGTON, TX, WHERE MY LAW FIRM IS LOCATED IN AN OLD HOUSE THAT I CONVERTED INTO AN OFFICE. IT SITS ON APPROXIMATELY ONE ACRE OF LAND IN OLD SOUTH ARLINGTON; ONCE FARM LAND THAT WAS ORIGINALLY OWNED BY LONGTIME ARLINGTON RESIDENT, KELLY ELLIOT. I AM ONE OF APPROXIMATELY FIVE BOARD CERTIFIED FAMILY LAW ATTORNEYS PRACTICING IN ARLINGTON AND I LIMIT MY PRACTICE TO FAMILY LAW, INCLUDING DIVORCE, CUSTODY, MODIFICATION, CHILD SUPPORT, PATERNITY AND ADOPTION.

Believe it or not!
JOHNSON COUNTY WAS HOME OF CHAPPARAL AUTOMOBILE FROM 1911 TO 1912. THE COMPANY MADE A TOTAL OF NINE CARS IN ITS TWO-YEAR EXISTENCE. ONE OF THOSE CARS REMAINS ON DISPLAY AT SIX FLAGS OVER TEXAS IN ARLINGTON!

Where did Jones County get its name?
FROM A DOCTOR NAMED ANSON JONES, WHO HOLDS THE HONOR OF BEING THE LAST PRESIDENT OF THE REPUBLIC OF TEXAS. YOU WILL ALSO HEAR ANSON CALLED "JONES CITY."

Where is the Jones County Courthouse located?
ON SOUTH COMMERCIAL STREET IN ANSON, TX, THE SITE OF THE OLD FORT PHANTOM HILL.

Who designed the Jones County Courthouse?
ELMER G. WITHERS DESIGNED THE 1910 HISTORIC COURTHOUSE IN A BEAUX-ARTS STYLE.

What is the Courthouse's most unusual feature?
THE STATUE ON THE CLOCK TOWER IS LADY JUSTICE. THE CLOCK ITSELF HAS RUN CONTINUOUSLY SINCE THE BUILDING WAS FINISHED IN 1910.

What is the most famous case tried in the Jones County Courthouse?
IN 1927, MRS. CLYDE BAKER BOUGHT SOME STRYCHNINE PILLS FROM A LOCAL PHARMACY, CLAIMING SHE WAS BUYING THEM TO KILL RATS. AS IT TURNED OUT, SHE WAS PLANNING TO KILL HER ESTRANGED HUSBAND INSTEAD. HAVING HEARD THAT HE HAD BEEN UNDER THE WEATHER, SHE MAILED THE PILLS TO HIM ALONG WITH A NOTE STATING SHE KNEW HE HAD BEEN SICK AND THAT THE PILLS WOULD HELP HIM. MR. BAKER TOOK THE PILLS AS INSTRUCTED AND DIED A RATHER UGLY DEATH. MRS. BAKER WAS FOUND GUILTY OF MURDER AND WAS SENTENCED TO LIFE IN PRISON. THIS WAS JUST ONE IN A SERIES OF STRYCHNINE POISONINGS, A FAD WHICH WOULD CONTINUE IN JONES COUNTY FOR ANOTHER TEN YEARS.

Where do you hang your hat?
IN DOWNTOWN FORT WORTH, TX, AT THE FIRM OF WESTFALL, PLATT & CUTRER. THE MEMBERS OF OUR FIRM SPECIALIZE IN DEFENDING PERSONS AND CORPORATIONS IN STATE AND FEDERAL CRIMINAL LITIGATION AND REPRESENTING PERSONS WHO HAVE LOST SUBSTANTIAL AMOUNTS OF MONEY DUE TO THEIR STOCKBROKER'S NEGLIGENCE OR FRAUD.

Believe it or not!
THE HUGE STATUE OF ANSON JONES THAT LOOKS SOUTH FROM THE COURTHOUSE HAS BEEN HIT SEVERAL TIMES BY DRUNK DRIVERS. THE COURTHOUSE SITS IN THE MIDDLE OF TRAFFIC CIRCLE AND FROM TIME TO TIME A DRUNK DRIVER WILL MISS THE CIRCLE, KEEP GOING STRAIGHT AND WIND UP IN ANSON JONES' LAP!

"There's been many a man who needed killin', but there's never been a horse that needed stealin'."
~ GREG'S FAMOUS TEXAS JUSTICE SAYING

"THE LEGEND OF GREGORIO CORTEZ LIVES ON IN A CORRIDO HEARD ALONG THE TEXAS BORDER . . ."

Jones
County Courthouse

"Blood, Sweat & Insurmountable Woes"

A Famous Texas Case as Told by

GREG WESTFALL
WESTFALL, PLATT & CUTRER

Unbeknownst to the gentle folks of Jones County, an alleged horse thief, murderer and Texas border hero is buried in a small cemetery eight miles outside of Anson.

The legend of Gregorio Cortez lives on in a corrido heard along the Texas border. Here's The Story of Blood, Sweat & Insurmountable Woes:

The year was 1901 and Mr. Cortez was accused of stealing a horse in a border town (a crime punishable by hanging). When questioned by the local Sheriff, Mr. Cortez misunderstood the Spanish translation and denied any wrongdoing (he had traded for a mare). Sheriff T.T. Morris attempted to arrest Mr. Cortez and a friend and a gun battle ensued. Sheriff Morris was fatally wounded.

Cortez fled but was caught after a hefty $1,000 reward was announced. He was jailed in San Antonio. A long legal fight (as most of them are!) began with convictions and mistrials to follow.

In 1913, Cortez was given an unusual conditional pardon by Governor O.B. Colquitt and released from jail. It was decided that he had never stolen the horse that triggered the series of events. His release was met with mixed emotions. Cortez would later fight against the Mexican Revolutionaries, perhaps out of gratitude for his release.

He was ultimately wounded and returned to convalesce in Manor, Texas. After his recovery, he lived quietly in Anson. Cortez died in 1916 at the home of a friend; he was 41 years old.

Where did Kaufman County get its name?

THE COUNTY WAS ORGANIZED IN 1848 AND NAMED AFTER DAVID SPANGLER KAUFMAN, A MEMBER OF THE CONGRESS OF THE REPUBLIC OF TEXAS AND THE U.S. CONGRESS.

Where is the Kaufman County Courthouse located?

ON KAUFMAN'S TOWN SQUARE, WHICH HAS BEEN THE CENTER OF ACTIVITY IN THE TOWN SINCE 1851.

Who designed the Kaufman County Courthouse?

IN 1956, A. WARREN MOREY AND MCGILL OF DALLAS DESIGNED A NEW COURTHOUSE AND TORE DOWN THE 1887 BUILDING TO MAKE WAY FOR THE NEW MODERNE STYLE BUILDING.

What is the Courthouse's most unusual feature?

THE MODERNE STEEL, ALUMINUM AND MARBLE ARCHITECTURAL STYLE—UNIQUE TO SMALL TEXAS TOWNS.

What is the most famous case tried in the Kaufman County Courthouse?

IN THE MID 1950s, THE SHERIFF, A MAN BY THE NAME OF JAMES BECKER, WAS SHOT JUST ABOVE HIS HEART BY A SUSPECT WHO WAS MENTALLY DISTURBED. LUCKILY THE SHERIFF LIVED TO TELL ABOUT IT. THERE WAS A MAGAZINE ARTICLE DESCRIBING THE INCIDENT ENTITLED, "CITING AT MY HEART."

Where do you hang your hat?

IN MESQUITE, TX, AT MY LAW FIRM LOCATED OFF OF LYNDON B. JOHNSON FREEWAY. MY FIRM IS A VOICE FOR THOSE INDIVIDUALS WHO HAVE BEEN CRIPPLED, MAIMED AND CATASTROPHICALLY INJURED BY CORPORATIONS, CHEMICAL COMPANIES AND OTHERS WHO PROMOTE THEIR OWN INTERESTS AND PROFIT AT THE EXPENSE OF MEMBERS OF OUR COMMUNITY.

Believe it or not!

DAVID SPANGLER KAUFMAN, FOR WHOM THIS COUNTY IS NAMED, WAS THE FIRST MAN FROM TEXAS SEATED IN THE U.S. HOUSE OF REPRESENTATIVES!

"Fellow Citizens and Compatriots…The enemy has demanded a surrender at discretion, otherwise, the garrison are to be put to the sword, if the fort is taken. I have answered the demand with a cannon shot and our flag still waves proudly from the walls. I shall never surrender or retreat."

William Barret Travis, Commander of the Alamo, February 24, 1836

~ TED'S FAMOUS TEXAS JUSTICE SAYING

"One Riot, One Ranger"

TED B. LYON

THE LAW FIRM OF TED B. LYON & ASSOCIATES

A Famous Texas Case as Told by

JUDGE GLEN ASHWORTH

Like so many residents of south Kaufman County, I still remember seeing the towering plume of smoke rising into the air on August 24, 1996. It was from this tragic pipeline explosion that two young lives were extinguished and one of the most memorable trials, not only in Kaufman County, but around the country, began. The case of <u>Smalley v. Koch</u> attracted substantial media attention, and not unlike a number of high-profile lawsuits, took on a persona of its own.

Among the cast of interesting personalities involved in this case, perhaps the two most dominant were the victim's father, Danny Smalley, and his attorney, Ted Lyon. While the probability of settlement always existed, Mr. Smalley never seemed motivated by a dollars-and-cents recovery, but rather by a vindication that could only come from his "day in court." Ted Lyon, who grew up in nearby Terrell and had served for years as our State Senator, was perfectly suited to his client's task and pursued the litigation with a "David and Goliath" approach. At one hearing, 27 defense lawyers stood on one side of the room defending Koch and only three lawyers, Ted Lyon, Mike McCauley and Marquette Wolf, stood on the other. Wolf, the youngest lawyer of the team, was clearly concerned about being out numbered, but I heard Lyon quote the old Texas Ranger saying, "In Texas the old adage is one riot —one ranger." In this case, at least, that saying held true.

Located in the heart of conservative North Texas, Kaufman County was hardly a preferred plaintiffs venue. As judge of the 86th District Court for 22 years, I had literally seen only a handful of plaintiffs verdicts. This background was no deterrent to the plaintiff's trial team. They never backed down from the challenge and at every hearing, of which there were many, they were relentless in their cause. The defense team employed a host of fine trial lawyers, associates and experts that filled several rows of the courtroom

Kaufman
County Courthouse

everyday. As the trial date neared, the preliminary matters became more and more contentious and difficult. Eventually, after days of pre-trial hearing, we began actual jury selection in October 1999.

One interesting thing I remember from the voir dire is that Mr. Lyon's wife, Donna, sat at the counsel table and served as his jury consultant. While I wondered about her qualifications at the time, her insight proved invaluable.

The trial itself was a judge's dream with outstanding lawyers presenting and defending a significant case with a professional and courteous demeanor. Each side was a credit to the profession as they developed their carefully orchestrated positions. Although the trial lasted several weeks, the defining moment came near the end of the plaintiff's case. At the conclusion of Ted Lyon's heart-felt and somber

> ## "THEY NEVER BACKED DOWN FROM THE CHALLENGE AND AT EVERY HEARING, OF WHICH THERE WERE MANY, THEY WERE RELENTLESS IN THEIR CAUSE."
> - JUDGE GLEN ASHWORTH

direct examination of Danny Smalley, he asked him what would be a fair amount of money to compensate him for his loss. Holding back tears and with the courtroom in stony silence, he replied, "they took everything I had and I want everything they have." That message resonated with the jury.

During Lyon's closing argument, the courtroom was filled with lawyers and observers from far and wide. Lyon put a watch on a screen that the jury could see and let the 45 seconds tick off that Danielle Smalley had lived after she was burned alive and did not say a word. During those 45 seconds, you could have heard a pin drop. By the end of his closing argument, there was not a dry eye in the room.

Where did Liberty County get its name?

THE ORIGINAL TOWN, VILLA DE LA SANTISIMA TRINIDAD DE LA LIBERTAD, WAS LAID OUT BY JOSE FRANCISCO MADERO ACCORDING TO THE LAWS OF THE INDIES. THE NAME WAS LATER CHANGED BY THE EARLY SETTLERS TO SIMPLY, "LIBERTY."

Where is the Liberty County Courthouse located?

IN LIBERTY, TX, ON THE TOWN SQUARE, AND IS THE SEVENTH COURTHOUSE TO OCCUPY THAT LOCATION SINCE 1831.

Who designed the Liberty County Courthouse?

ARCHITECTS CORNEIL G. CURTIS AND A.E. THOMAS DESIGNED THE HISTORIC COURTHOUSE IN 1931, IN BRICK AND CONCRETE IN A MODERNE CONTEMPORARY STYLE POPULAR AT THAT TIME FOR CIVIC STRUCTURES.

What is the Courthouse's most unusual feature?

THIS HISTORIC COURTHOUSE WAS BUILT IN 1931. ITS HISTORIC, AUTHENTIC AND WELL-PRESERVED ARCHITECTURE HAS MADE IT THE SITE OF SEVERAL MOVIE SETS. IT ALSO BOASTS THE LARGEST COURTROOM IN THE STATE OF TEXAS!

What is the most famous case tried in the Liberty County Courthouse?

VICKIE DANIEL WAS ACCUSED OF MURDERING HER HUSBAND, PRICE DANIEL JR., A DESCENDENT OF SAM HOUSTON AND SON OF THE FORMER SENATOR AND GOVERNOR, PRICE DANIEL. VICKIE CLAIMED SHE AND HER CHILDREN WERE VICTIMS OF ABUSE AND THE KILLING WAS JUSTIFIED. VICKIE WAS AWARDED THE CHILDREN IN A CUSTODY TRIAL AND ACQUITTED IN THE MURDER TRIAL.

Where do you hang your hat?

HAGANS, BOBB & BURDINE, P.C. OFFICES IN HOUSTON, TX, BUT WE HAVE ASSISTED CLIENTS IN TEXAS, THE UNITED STATES AND FOREIGN COUNTRIES WITH PERSONAL INJURY AND WRONGFUL DEATH CLAIMS, ALONG WITH CLAIMS RELATED TO INSURANCE BAD FAITH, INTELLECTUAL PROPERTY RIGHTS, AND MEDICAL AND LEGAL MALPRACTICE. WE HAVE A FULL DOCKET OF COMMERCIAL LITIGATION ON BEHALF OF COMPANIES FROM SMALL GROUPS TO FORTUNE 500 COMPANIES.

Believe it or not!

DURING VOIR DIRE OF A CASE, A MEMBER OF THE VENIRE RAISED HER HAND AND ASKED, "DOESN'T THIS CASE REALLY AFFECT EACH OF US PERSONALLY SINCE THE REMEDIATION AND REPAIR OF THE COURTHOUSE WILL REQUIRE TAX MONEY IF THE INSURANCE COMPANY DOESN'T PAY?" SHE ENDED UP ON THE JURY!

> *"The right of trial by jury shall remain inviolate."*
> *Article 1, Section 15, The Texas Constitution.*
> ~ FRED'S FAMOUS TEXAS JUSTICE SAYING

"Mold in the Jury Room"

A Famous Texas Case as Told by

FRED HAGANS
HAGANS, BOBB & BURDINE, P.C.

On the seventh day of trial, Liberty County agreed to accept $3,200,000 from its insurer to settle the lawsuit Liberty County filed against its insurance company, Texas Association of Counties Property and Casualty Self Insurance Fund ("TAC"). In the lawsuit, Liberty County alleged breach of contract and unfair claims handling practices. TAC alleged that it had sovereign immunity from all claims, particularly the extra-contractual claims. Trial began on November 18, 2002, after TAC filed a Motion to Recuse the presiding judge which was granted, after TAC objected to the first retired judge that was appointed to hear the case, after TAC's objection to the second retired judge appointed to hear the case was overruled, after TAC's Second Motion for Continuance was denied and after a Plea to the Jurisdiction was filed on the last business day before trial began.

Liberty County made a claim for the mold damage in the Liberty County Courthouse. Prior to the claim for mold, TAC had inspected the courthouse and had never identified problems. TAC hired an adjuster and engineer who recommended several types of testing. Despite its representations to Liberty County that it would determine the cause of the mold, TAC refused to authorize any of the recommended testing and denied the claim without determining the cause of the mold.

Liberty County asserted claims including breach of contract, breach of the duty of good faith and fair dealing, fraud and violations of the DTPA and the Insurance Code.

Liberty
County Courthouse

This lawsuit was filed in June of 2002 and trial began on November 18, 2002. During the trial, the defense lawyer elicited testimony that there was mold in the jury room. At the first break, after that testimony, the jury refused to go in that jury room and requested that the judge find another one.

The trial was interrupted five days into testimony when TAC obtained an automatic stay from the Beaumont Court of Appeals based on the trial court's denial of the plea to the jurisdiction. In its plea to the jurisdiction and its motion for stay, TAC claimed it was a governmental entity and as

"LIBERTY COUNTY MADE A CLAIM FOR THE MOLD DAMAGE IN THE LIBERTY COUNTY COURTHOUSE."

such, had immunity from suit and liability on Liberty's contractual and extra-contractual claims, essentially arguing that counties should not be allowed to enforce their rights under TAC's contract for insurance. Liberty County was able to have the stay lifted as to the breach of contract claims and trial resumed. Two days after the trial resumed, the matter settled for $3.2 million.

Limestone County Courthouse

"The Reporter Who Said Too Much"

A Famous Texas Case as Told by

GARY M. POLLAND
POLLAND AND ASSOCIATES

The most unique aspect of the Limestone County Courthouse is the existence of two jury boxes in each courtroom. As folklore has it, one box was intended for the jury and one was intended for the press. There is no other intelligible reason for there to be two identical boxes on opposite sides of the courtroom. Ms. Fence, Limestone County Clerk, says she never really knew why the extra box (which is now being used for computer storage) was there, but figures it being called a "press box" is good enough.

Texas justice has existed in Limestone County in a unique way: reporters and the press were originally intended to be in the courtroom and not outside it. It is for this unique reason that Mr. Polland respects and admires the Limestone County Courthouse.

Mr. Polland had the pleasure of representing Mr. Ed Wendt, a reporter and news editor for the Forward Times (the largest African-American newspaper in Texas) in the pursuit of freedom of the press. Mr. Wendt was ejected for allegedly "disrupting" a Houston City Council meeting. It's not a coincidence that Mr. Wendt had previously written hard-hitting stories about the mayor and some members of City Council.

Mr. Wendt was arrested for exercising his First Amendment rights and Mr. Polland was not about to let justice go unserved. It was at that time that "The Case of the Reporter Who Said Too Much," came into existence. Mr. Polland's courageous defense of Mr. Wendt and the First Amendment, which resulted in a "not guilty" verdict, should make all Texans proud. It is indeed the press who keeps the public informed and their place, at least in Limestone County, appears to be in the courtroom.

"No good deed goes unpunished."
— Gary's Famous Texas Justice Saying

"MR. POLLAND'S BRAVE DEFENSE OF MR. WENDT AND THE FIRST AMENDMENT, WHICH RESULTED IN A "NOT GUILTY" VERDICT, SHOULD MAKE ALL TEXANS PROUD. IT IS INDEED THE PRESS WHO KEEPS THE PUBLIC INFORMED AND THEIR PLACE, AT LEAST IN LIMESTONE COUNTY, APPEARS TO BE IN THE COURTROOM."

Where did Limestone County get its name?
IT WAS NAMED FOR THE ABUNDANT INDIGENOUS ROCK OF THE SAME NAME AND WAS ORGANIZED IN 1846. GROESBECK WAS FOUNDED BY THE RAILROAD AND WAS NAMED AFTER ONE OF THE LINE'S DIRECTORS, ABRAHAM GROESBECK.

Where is the Limestone County Courthouse located?
ON ELLIS STREET BETWEEN BRAZOS AND STATE STREETS WHERE IT STILL FUNCTIONS AS THE HEART OF LIMESTONE COUNTY AND IS KNOWN AS THE MILLION DOLLAR COURTHOUSE.

Who designed the Limestone County Courthouse?
R.H. STUCKY WAS THE ARCHITECT ON THIS HISTORIC CLASSICAL REVIVAL-STYLE COURTHOUSE, CONSTRUCTED IN 1924 OF BRICK, TILE, MARBLE AND CONCRETE.

What is the Courthouse's most unusual feature?
IT HAS CONTRASTING RED BRICK AND CONCRETE COLUMNS THAT ARE VERY DRAMATIC AND REVEAL THE CLASSICAL REVIVAL-STYLE ATTRIBUTES OF THE COURTHOUSE. ANOTHER UNIQUE ASPECT OF THE LIMESTONE COUNTY COURTHOUSE IS THE EXISTENCE OF TWO JURY BOXES IN EACH COURTROOM. AS FOLKLORE HAS IT, ONE BOX WAS INTENDED FOR THE JURY AND ONE WAS INTENDED FOR THE PRESS.

What is the most famous case tried in the Limestone County Courthouse?
ON JULY 21, 1994, HEATH LAMONT PRICE WAS CONVICTED OF SHOOTING AND KILLING A MEXIA POLICE OFFICER. THE POLICE OFFICER HAD RESPONDED TO A COMPLAINT OF A SHOPLIFTER AT A CONVENIENCE STORE. A SHORT FOOTRACE ENSUED, HOWEVER, THE POLICE OFFICER LOST THE SUSPECT. AS HE WAS RETURNING TO HIS PATROL CAR, THE OFFICER WAS SHOT AND KILLED. MR. PRICE, WHO WAS SEVENTEEN AT THE TIME OF THE MURDER, WAS TRIED TWICE, FOUND GUILTY AND SENTENCED TO LIFE IN PRISON. HE HAD NO PRIOR CRIMINAL RECORD AND THE CASE IS CURRENTLY BEING APPEALED.

Where do you hang your hat?
IN HOUSTON, TX, OFF OF RICHMOND AVENUE. I ALSO HOST A WEEKLY CABLE TELEVISION SHOW ABOUT TEXAS POLITICS CALLED <u>THE REAL DEAL</u>.

Believe it or not!
OLD FORT PARKER, A LOCAL ATTRACTION, IS SAID TO BE THE SITE WHERE CYNTHIA ANN PARKER WAS KIDNAPPED BY COMANCHE INDIANS. HER SON, QUANAH PARKER, WAS THE LAST COMANCHE CHIEF!

Where did Lipscomb County get its name?

NAMED IN 1887 AFTER A.S. LIPSCOMB, THE REPUBLIC OF TEXAS SECRETARY OF STATE, A MEMBER OF THE STATE CONSTITUTIONAL CONVENTION IN 1845, WHO RESOLVED THE TERMS OF ANNEXATION PROPOSED BY THE UNITED STATES.

Where is the Lipscomb County Courthouse located?

IN THE CENTER OF THE TOWN SQUARE IN LIPSCOMB, TX—ABOUT AS FAR NORTH AS YOU CAN GO AND STILL BE IN TEXAS.

Who designed the Lipscomb County Courthouse?

ARCHITECT WILLIAM M. RICE DESIGNED THE 1916 CLASSICAL REVIVAL STYLE HISTORIC COURTHOUSE OF BRICK FEATURING A PORTICO AND DORIC COLUMNS ACROSS THE FRONT, A STYLE WHICH WAS VERY POPULAR AT THE TURN OF THE CENTURY.

What is the Courthouse's most unusual feature?

FROM AN ARCHITECTURAL STANDPOINT, THE TRIANGULAR PEDIMENT SUPPORTED BY DORIC COLUMNS OVER THE ENTRANCE IS THE MOST IMPRESSIVE FEATURE.

What is the most famous case tried in the Lipscomb County Courthouse?

ROY "PETE" TRAXLER, NICKNAMED "PHANTOM FUGITIVE," "MODERN JESSE JAMES" AND "NOTORIOUS DESPERADO," WAS A HIJACKER, MURDERER, JAIL BREAKER AND THIEF WHO WAS TRIED AND CONVICTED IN 1936 FOR ROBBERY IN LIPSCOMB COUNTY. HE WOULD GO ON TO BREAK OUT OF THE TEXAS PRISON ONLY TO TERRORIZE TEXAS, OKLAHOMA, ARKANSAS AND NEW MEXICO FOR ANOTHER YEAR BEFORE HE WAS REELED-IN.

Where do you hang your hat?

LOCATED IN AMARILLO, THE WOOD LAW FIRM SPECIALIZES IN CIVIL LITIGATION. WE REPRESENT INDIVIDUALS, CHILDREN AND FAMILIES WHO FOLLOWED THE RULES AGAINST INSURANCE COMPANIES, CORPORATIONS AND OTHERS THAT BROKE THE RULES. HELPING PEOPLE FIND JUSTICE IS THE MOST SATISFYING PART OF THE WORK WE DO AT THE WOOD LAW FIRM.

Believe it or not!

THE COUNTY SEAT OF LIPSCOMB COUNTY, LIPSCOMB, IS ESTIMATED TO HAVE ONLY 45 RESIDENTS!

"There ain't no cowboy who can't be thro'd, and there ain't no horse that can't be rode."

~ JIM'S FAMOUS TEXAS JUSTICE SAYING

"A Herd of Missing Milk Cows"

A Famous Texas Case as Told by

JAMES WOOD

WOOD LAW FIRM, L.L.P.

The Texas Panhandle is known for its wide open spaces, cattle and colorful people. All three of these elements came together several years ago in Lipscomb County, a sparsely populated county located in the upper right corner of the Texas Panhandle, bordered on its east and north sides by Oklahoma.

The Lipscomb County courthouse doesn't get many trials. The county seat, Lipscomb, has a population of less than 45, so it's hard to even put together a jury pool there. The town of Lipscomb is so small, it doesn't have a gas station.

My association with Lipscomb County began when I was hired to represent a cattleman who leased a herd of milk cows to casual friends of a friend. My cattleman client is as honest as the eye can see out in Lipscomb County, and a on a clear day out there you can see tomorrow in the east and yesterday in the west. The couple who leased the milk cows, however, were cut from a completely different bolt of cloth.

As time passed, the cattleman began to wonder where his milk cows had gone. He couldn't find the animals in Lipscomb County where they were supposed to be and the couple he leased them to wouldn't even talk to him, much less tell him what had happened to the leased cows. The cattleman decided he needed legal help and called me. It didn't take much digging on my part to discover this wasn't a straightforward, honest milk cow leasing deal.

Lipscomb County Courthouse

Before the mess was over, lawmen from three states and the FBI were involved in the case. It turns out the couple borrowed money from an Oklahoma bank using the leased cows as collateral, then turned around and sold the leased cows to a dairy in Utah, all of this without my client's knowledge and certainly not with his consent.

When the husband and wife were finally brought to trial to settle the matter, they refused to even tell the judge their names, much less where the vagabond milk cows now resided. In open court, the couple threatened to do things that made the court reporter blush, things I can't repeat for this publication. In my experience, the average crook is not very smart and these two were no exception to the rule.

The Lipscomb County Judge wouldn't tolerate that kind of behavior and he promptly threw both of them in jail for

"BEFORE THE MESS WAS OVER, LAWMEN FROM THREE STATES AND THE FBI WERE INVOLVED . . ."

several days for contempt. Eventually, the larcenous duo finally got the message and "fessed up" to milking every illegal dime they could from the leased cows. The milk cows were ultimately found and sold, the Oklahoma bank and my client got some of their money back and the whole fandango created the most excitement at the Lipscomb County Courthouse that year.

Lubbock
County Courthouse

"Three Pistol Rounds at The Blue Front Restaurant"

A Famous Texas Case as Told by
CHUCK LANEHART
CHAPPELL & LANEHART, P.C.

Frank Wheelock, elected as the first mayor of the new city of Lubbock in 1909, insisted on strict order in his community. The mayor told city marshals "to shoot the belly off the first man that bothers you." Wheelock's advice was followed by deputy marshal William Taylor, chosen by fate to make Lubbock County history.

The events of October 19, 1912, were reported by the *Lubbock Avalanche* in restrained fashion. According to the account, J.J. Reynolds and Tom Collins were killed by three pistol rounds about 8:30 p.m. at the Blue Front Restaurant. Night watchman William Taylor was arrested and released on bond the following morning. The local newspaper reported that, "*The Avalanche* does not deem it wise at this time to give the particulars of the sad affair as no trial has been had to date and it would not be right to give out the particulars now. The affair is greatly regretted by everyone, and very little is being said about it one way or another."

The new District Attorney for the 72nd Judicial District, J.E. Vickers, knew otherwise; the public watched the case with intensity. Eager to win the first big case to be tried in Lubbock County, the young prosecutor saw that Taylor was quickly indicted for murder. The indictment was anchored by "Big Ben" Borger's eyewitness testimony. Borger told the grand jury that the victims were felled by Taylor because they laughed at the deputy and would not be quiet. DA Vickers secured a trial date within two months of the incident.

Vickers prepared his case zealously. A medical postmortem was prepared and the victims' wounds and the locations of their bodies were charted. A miniature scale model of the Blue Front Restaurant was constructed. Statements were reduced to typewritten memos. At least 25 State's witnesses were subpoenaed.

W.H. Bledsoe presented Taylor's case of self-defense, arguing that Jug Reynolds had been arrested some ten or twelve times, had numerous fights; that Tom Collins had once beaten a Negro to death and was usually drunk by six o'clock. Bledsoe subpoenaed only twelve defense witnesses, but they included powerful, influential names: Lubbock County Sheriff W.H. Flynn, Lubbock Mayor Frank Wheelock and Coleman County Sheriff W.L. Futch. The strength of the defense case was noted desperately by Vickers, as the judge refused to admit declarations the defendant made fifteen or twenty minutes after killing the victim as to how it was done.

State vs. Taylor was tried in Lubbock in early December of 1912. The Avalanche reported the verdict of the first murder trial in Lubbock County history on page thirteen of its December 13 issue in a curious, subtle fashion: "The trial of William E. Taylor for the killing of Thomas M. Collins in the Blue Front Restaurant in this City on the 19th day of October, which consumed last week, was given to the jury late Saturday afternoon. The jury after about three hours of deliberations, made

"THE AVALANCHE REPORTED THE VERDICT OF THE FIRST MURDER TRIAL IN LUBBOCK COUNTY HISTORY ON PAGE THIRTEEN OF ITS DECEMBER 13 ISSUE . . ."

known their desire to return a verdict, which was 'Not Guilty.'"

Taylor was never involved in law enforcement again. He farmed in the Lubbock area until his death in 1961. Bledsoe, Taylor's defense lawyer, is remembered for his later educational and political achievements. As State Senator, he spearheaded the 1925 establishment of Texas Technological College in Lubbock. Despite the defeat, prosecutor Vickers became a prominent trial lawyer, and was known to say: "If the facts are against you, argue the law; if the law is against you, argue the facts; if both law and facts are against you, jump on the opposing lawyer."

Where did Lubbock County get its name?

THE COUNTY WAS NAMED AFTER COLONEL THOMAS S. LUBBOCK, AN ORIGINAL MEMBER OF TERRY'S TEXAS RANGERS, A GROUP WHO DEFENDED TEXAS DURING THE CIVIL WAR.

Where is the Lubbock County Courthouse located?

IN LUBBOCK, TX, AT THE CORNER OF BROADWAY AND BUDDY HOLLY AVENUE. THE PRESENT DAY LUBBOCK WAS THE MERGING OF THE TWO TOWNS OF OLD LUBBOCK AND MONTEREY.

Who designed the Lubbock County Courthouse?

HAYNES & KIRBY DESIGNED THE 1950 MODERNE STYLE BUILDING OF LIMESTONE AND GRANITE THAT REPLACED THE 1915 COURTHOUSE.

What is the courthouse's most unusual feature?

THE ORIGINAL COURTHOUSE, WITH ITS DISTINCTIVE "CUPOLA" TOWER, WAS CONSTRUCTED WHERE THE LUBBOCK COUNTY COURTHOUSE NOW STANDS IN 1892. HOWEVER, A TERRIBLE WINDSTORM HIT THE WOOD FRAME STRUCTURE SO HARD IN 1895 THAT THE TOWER WAS BLOWN OFF AND NOT REPLACED.

What is the most famous case tried in the Lubbock County Courthouse?

IN THE LATE 1980s, DAMON RICHARDSON, KNOWN AS THE DRUG KING OF LUBBOCK, WAS CONVICTED OF ORDERING THE BRUTAL MURDERS OF THREE PEOPLE. REVELATIONS OF CORRUPTION AFTER HIS TRIAL RESULTED IN ACQUITTALS FOR HIS THREE CO-DEFENDANTS, PRISON FOR THE PATHOLOGIST WHO TESTIFIED AGAINST HIM, POLITICAL DEFEAT FOR THE DA WHO PROSECUTED HIM AND REVERSAL OF HIS DEATH SENTENCE.

Where do you hang your hat?

LUBBOCK, TX, IS HOME, AT CHAPPELL & LANEHART, PC. FIRM FOUNDER BYRON "LAWYER" CHAPPELL (1916-2000), A NOTED CRIMINAL DEFENSE ATTORNEY, WAS KNOWN AS "THE GRANDFATHER OF LUBBOCK LAWYERS." CHAPPELL DISCIPLES CHUCK LANEHART, FRED STANGL AND CHRIS BROWN STRIVE DAILY TO MEET HIS STANDARDS AS ZEALOUS AND ETHICAL DEFENDERS OF THE CITIZEN ACCUSED.

Believe it or not!

IN 1891, F.E. WHEELOCK WAS THE FIRST PERSON INDICTED FOR A FELONY CRIME IN LUBBOCK COUNTY. AFTER HIS CATTLE THEFT AND FENCE-CUTTING CHARGES WERE DISMISSED, HE ENTERED THE POLITICAL ARENA AND WAS EVEN ELECTED LUBBOCK'S FIRST MAYOR!

Where did Madison County get its name?

THE COUNTY AND THE TOWN WERE NAMED FOR JAMES MADISON, THE FOURTH PRESIDENT OF THE UNITED STATES, WHO WAS CONSIDERED TO BE THE FATHER OF THE U.S. CONSTITUTION.

Where is the Madison County Courthouse located?

IN MADISONVILLE ON THE TOWN SQUARE, AT THE CORNER OF MAIN AND ELM STREET, WHICH WAS THE CENTER OF THE TOWN'S FIRST SETTLEMENT IN 1854.

Who designed the Madison County Courthouse?

THE 1970 COURTHOUSE, THE FIFTH COURTHOUSE IN THE COUNTY, WAS DESIGNED IN BRICK AND CONCRETE BY THE ARCHITECTURAL FIRM OF DICKSON, DICKSON, BUCKLEY & BULLOCK.

What is the Courthouse's most unusual feature?

IT IS THE FIFTH COURTHOUSE MADISON COUNTY HAS SEEN, THE FIRST FOUR WERE ALL DESTROYED IN FIRES!

What is the most famous case tried in the Madison County Courthouse?

IN SEPTEMBER, 2000, RAFAEL HOLIDAY WAS ARRESTED FOR THE MURDER OF HIS TWO STEP-DAUGHTERS, AGES FIVE AND SEVEN, AS WELL AS HIS INFANT DAUGHTER. HE FORCED THE GIRLS TO GO INSIDE THEIR MOBILE HOME AND THEN, AT GUNPOINT, FORCED THEIR GRANDMOTHER TO DOUSE THE TRAILER IN GASOLINE. RAFAEL HOLIDAY WAS CONVICTED AND IS CURRENTLY ON DEATH ROW.

Where do you hang your hat?

IN HOUSTON, TX, AT THE LAW FIRM OF LOOPER, REED & MCGRAW. WE REPRESENT INDIVIDUALS AND BUSINESSES IN THE AREAS OF HEALTH CARE, TAXATION, PROBATE AND ESTATE PLANNING, FAMILY LAW, EMPLOYMENT LAW, CORPORATE FINANCE, MERGERS AND ACQUISITIONS, REAL ESTATE, OIL AND GAS, INTERNATIONAL AND OTHER COMMERCIAL TRANSACTIONS, AS WELL AS LITIGATION IN THESE AREAS.

Believe it or not!

THE SETTLEMENT OF THE FUTURE MADISON COUNTY BEGAN IN SPANISH TEXAS. SIEUR DE LA SALLE AND TWO OTHER EUROPEAN EXPLORERS, ALL MEMBERS OF HERNANDO DE SOTO'S EXPEDITION, REACHED MADISON COUNTY, FOLLOWING DE SOTO'S DEATH IN 1542. IT IS SAID THAT LA SALLE CROSSED SOUTHEASTERN MADISON COUNTY IN 1687 AND SOME BELIEVE HE WAS KILLED IN MADISON COUNTY, AT A SITE JUST SOUTH OF MADISONVILLE!

"A jury trial is a precious right, which must be preserved."
~ JIM'S FAMOUS TEXAS JUSTICE SAYING

"Big Guns and the Broken Promise"

A Famous Texas Case as Told by
JAMES L. "JIM" REED, JR.
LOOPER, REED & MCGRAW

In oil-rich Madison County, Texas, Judge Ernie Ernst presided in the case of the "Big Guns and the Broken Promise." This was not a class action suit. The case was tried to completion, with a verdict in excess of $30 million. Attorney Jim Reed represented the heirs of "Silver Dollar Jim West."

In 1953, Silver Dollar Jim signed a gas purchase contract with Lone Star Gas Company (Ensearch Corporation, a New York Stock Exchange company) regarding oil and gas property in Madison County. The agreement stated that the heirs of Silver Dollar Jim would sell gas and oil to Lone Star through 1993. However, the contract was amended by Lone Star in 1973.

The heirs had made a solemn Texan promise to sell all of the gas produced by the Madison County properties, and in return, Lone Star promised to purchase all of the gas that was produced. Lone Star's betrayal occurred when the company refused to take or pay for the gas produced by the committed properties. Lone Star further betrayed the heirs by manipulating reports they were filing with the Texas Railroad Commission during the 1970s and 1980s. The TRRC is the main body functioning to regulate oil and gas wellhead reports (a significant part of many Texans' lives!). The result of these false forms was the reduction of the amount of gas that could legally be purchased from the Madison County properties.

The reason for Lone Star's hesitancy to buy gas from the Madison County properties was the recent construction of the Oasis Pipeline. In the late 1960s, there was a

Madison
County Courthouse

perceived gas shortage along the Texas Gulf Coast. Houston Natural Gas (the company which later became Enron) was considering building the pipeline to transport gas from West Texas. An alternate gas company, Entratex, finalized this agreement and built the pipeline. Exxon, one of the largest gas companies world-wide, then came to Entratex to utilize the pipeline. The result of this pipeline was the sudden "opening up" of the gas markets in Texas.

With the assistance of Mr. Reed and John R. Bankhead serving as local counsel, the heirs claimed breach of contract, fraud and gross negligence, seeking actual and exemplary damages. The case was tried by jury and the plaintiffs were awarded over $30 million in damages. This became one of the most significant gas cases in Texas history and set the precedent that working interest owners can sell gas.

> **"THE AGREEMENT STATED THAT THE HEIRS OF SILVER DOLLAR JIM WOULD SELL GAS AND OIL TO LONE STAR THROUGH 1993."**

Mr. Reed also represented in excess of 11,400 oil and gas royalty owners in a royalty underpayment claim against Mitchell Energy Corporation and other Mitchell corporations. Similarly to the Silver Dollar Jim case, the lawsuit involved claims that Mitchell failed to reasonably market the gas and properly account for and pay royalty owners. The lawsuit was settled in 1997 for an award exceeding $27 million.

Marion County Courthouse

"How Do You Hide Two Elephants?"

A Famous Texas Case as Told by
JESSE M. "DUKE" DEWARE IV
JESSE M. DEWARE IV, P.C.

How do you hide two elephants? In 1982, I was contacted by the owners of two twenty-year-old female Indian elephants. They reported that their elephants had been abducted from their home in New Jersey. The elephants were located in 1984 and a New Jersey court had ordered that they be returned to the owners. They disappeared again.

In 1989, sightings of these elephants occurred in Marion County and were reported to the owners. A suit was filed by me on behalf of the owners at the Marion County Courthouse to enjoin the persons in possession from moving them again and for their return.

It became an emotional case much like a child custody case. The persons in possession claimed to love the elephants more than the owners and claimed that the elephants had been abused at their last home. In so many words, if the elephants, could talk, they would much rather live in Marion County than New Jersey. They also liked the weather—a lot warmer than New Jersey. Being loved was important.

The owners alleged that they were an endangered species so the persons in possession had the case transferred to the U.S. District Court for the Eastern District of Texas.

The national TV newsmagazine, Inside Edition, sent correspondents to Jefferson to cover the story. After the case was removed, Judge Tiny Garrison, the presiding judge in Marion County Courthouse, was presented a large, gold-painted shovel to commemorate his service in the case of the abducted elephants.

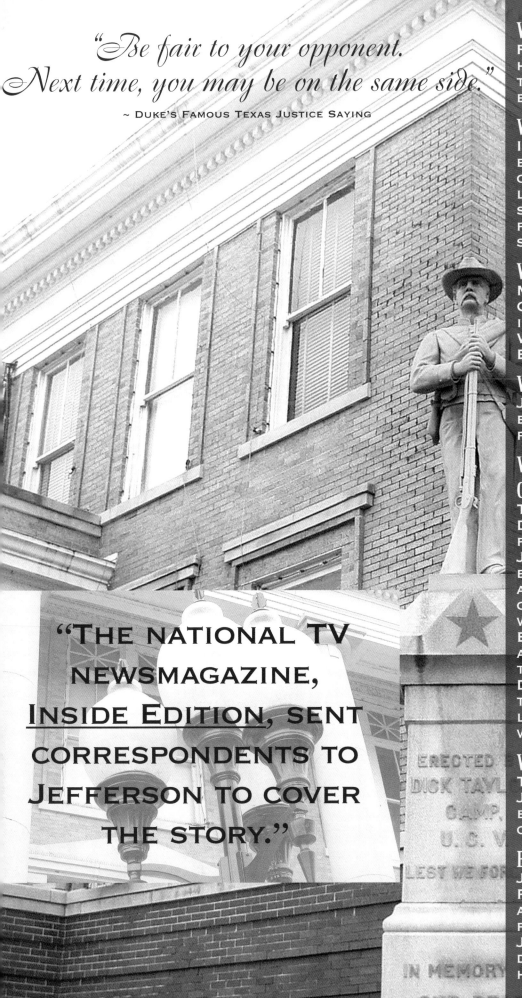

"Be fair to your opponent. Next time, you may be on the same side."
~ Duke's Famous Texas Justice Saying

"THE NATIONAL TV NEWSMAGAZINE, INSIDE EDITION, SENT CORRESPONDENTS TO JEFFERSON TO COVER THE STORY."

Where did Marion County get its name?

FROM FRANCIS MARION, A REVOLUTIONARY WAR HERO FROM SOUTH CAROLINA WHO WAS DUBBED THE "SWAMP FOX" BY THE BRITISH FOR HIS ELUSIVE TACTICS IN BATTLE.

Where is the Marion County Courthouse located?

IN JEFFERSON'S DOWNTOWN HISTORIC DISTRICT, BETWEEN DALLAS AND AUSTIN STREETS OVERLOOKING THE SITE OF AN EARLY STEAMBOAT LANDING WHERE THOUSANDS OF PIONEERS FIRST SET FOOT ON TEXAS SOIL WHEN THEY DISEMBARKED FROM STEAMBOATS AND BOARDED WAGON TRAINS TO SETTLE THE WEST.

Who designed the Marion County Courthouse?

MARION COUNTY'S HISTORIC SECOND COURTHOUSE WAS BUILT IN RENAISSANCE STYLE IN 1912 WITH THE DESIGNS OF ELMER GEORGE WITHERS, WHO ALSO DESIGNED THE UPSHUR, ECTOR AND JONES COUNTY COURTHOUSES.

What is the courthouse's most unusual feature?

JEFFERSON WAS SUBJECT TO FLOODS SO THE ELEVATED COURTHOUSE WAS CONSTRUCTED TO BE FLOOD-PROOF.

What is the most famous case tried in the Marion County Courthouse?

THE DIAMOND BESSIE MURDER TRIAL OF 1877. DIAMOND BESSIE AND ABRAHAM ROTHSCHILD FROM CINCINNATI, OHIO, MADE A VISIT TO JEFFERSON. DIAMOND BESSIE DRESSED IN AN EASTERN STYLE AND WAS YOUNG, BEAUTIFUL AND BEDECKED IN JEWELRY. ON THE THIRD DAY OF THEIR VISIT, THEY SET OFF ON A PICNIC FROM WHICH HE RETURNED AND SHE DIDN'T. DIAMOND BESSIE WAS LATER FOUND SANS DIAMONDS WITH A HOLE IN HER HEAD. MR. ROTHSCHILD WAS TRIED AND FOUND GUILTY OF THE MURDER OF DIAMOND BESSIE DESPITE THE EFFORTS OF HIS TEN ATTORNEYS AND A SUICIDE ATTEMPT THAT LEFT HIM WITH ONLY ONE EYE. THE VERDICT WOULD LATER BE OVERTURNED.

Where do you hang your hat?

THE LAW OFFICES OF JESSE M. DeWARE IV, JEFFERSON, TX, WHERE I SPECIALIZE IN REAL ESTATE TRANSACTIONS, CURING LAND TITLES AND COMMERCIAL TRANSACTIONS.

Believe it or not!

JEFFERSON IS A RAFT TOWN. A LOGJAM IN THE RED RIVER IN THE 19TH CENTURY CLOSED THE RIVER ABOVE SHREVEPORT, LOUISIANA, CREATING FAVORABLE CONDITIONS IN NORTHEAST TEXAS AT JEFFERSON FOR NAVIGATION AND ECONOMIC DEVELOPMENT. WITHOUT THE RAFT THERE WOULD HAVE BEEN NO JEFFERSON AND NO MARION COUNTY!

> *"Losing is Not an Option."*
> ~ Mark's Famous Texas Justice Saying

Where did Matagorda County get its name?
Mata and gorda is Spanish for thick brush, or shrub which came from the canebrakes that used to line the shore. This town was organized in 1837.

Where is the Matagorda County Courthouse located?
In Bay City, TX, on the town square, nestled in among the pecan trees.

Who designed the Matagorda County Courthouse?
Rusty, Martin & Vale designed the Moderne style courthouse of concrete in 1965.

What is the Courthouse's most unusual feature?
It is an unusually modern design, made of concrete and surrounded by steps.

What is the most famous case tried in the Matagorda County Courthouse?
The case of Superman the Bull was a case of John O'Quinn's that is very well known. The owner applied a fly repellent to the animal, but failed to dilute the product because of unclear instructions. When the animal died as a result, the owner sued the manufacturer of the product and won on the basis of negligence that resulted in the death of a "family pet."

Where do you hang your hat?
In Houston, TX, at the Lanier Law Firm, where I am a founder of the firm and lead litigation counsel. I earned my law degree from Texas Tech University School of Law in Lubbock in 1984 and now specialize in personal injury. My wife Becky and our five children currently live in Houston, although I am originally from Lubbock.

Believe it or not!
The need to protect their control over their slaves was used by white citizens in 1856 to justify expelling the county's entire Mexican population!

"Rubicon v. Amoco was a twentieth century David and Goliath—a story about the little guy versus the big oil company . . ."

atagorda
County Courthouse

"A Deal is A Deal"

A Famous Texas Case as Told by
W. MARK LANIER
THE LANIER LAW FIRM

Rubicon v. Amoco was a twentieth century David and Goliath—a story about the little guy versus the big oil company and like any good Texas story, it has many interesting plots, twists and turns. While Amoco orchestrated a defense bent on smothering with many lawyers and firms, delaying with continuance tactics with the court and inundating with near unlimited witnesses. We were resolute. We would fight each lawyer, each tactic, each day moving ever closer to a jury's determination. Once we got into the courthouse, the fight was twenty hours a day, seven days a week, for six weeks. In the end, exhausted physically and mentally, we saw the justice of America's jury system first hand. The relief and appreciation is as fresh as ever—over a decade later.

It was the first day of business at The Lanier Law Firm. Mark Lanier wasn't quite sure what was going to happen. But shortly, in walks Mr. John Littlejohn, from Bee, Texas. Mr. Littlejohn had a case that many other firms had turned down. It was to be one of Lanier's great successes: Rubicon v. Amoco.

Mr. Littlejohn's company, Rubicon, was in the process of contracting to pay $18 million for a couple of Amoco's oil fields in Wyoming. There was a verbal agreement for Mr. Littlejohn to buy the property. Mr. Littlejohn had undergone rigorous financial documentation in order to secure the financing which lasted almost six months. Amoco denied making the verbal agreement with Mr. Littlejohn and denied any legal obligation because the alleged agreement was not in writing.

Amoco's legal department told Mr. Littlejohn that environmental issues necessitated pulling the oil fields from the market. Then, the very next day, Amoco listed the property for sale with a New York broker for $60 million, a far cry from the $18 million negotiated and agreed to with Mr. Littlejohn. The oil fields actually had thirty years of production left

THE AMERICAN LAWYER

MARCH 2004

Top Gun & Legal Legend
Mark Lanier

★ COVER FEATURE STORY AS AMERICA'S TOP TRIAL LAWYER IN THE <u>AMERICAN LAWYER</u>

★ NAMED ONE OF THE TOP TEN TRIAL LAWYERS IN THE U.S. BY THE <u>NATIONAL LAW JOURNAL</u>

★ NAMED BY THE <u>NATIONAL LAW JOURNAL</u> AS ONE OF THE 40 BEST LAWYERS IN THE COUNTRY UNDER THE AGE OF 40

★ ONE OF THE TOP 45 ATTORNEYS IN THE COUNTRY UNDER THE AGE OF 45, ACCORDING TO <u>AMERICAN LAWYER</u>

★ IN 2002, <u>TEXAS LAWYER</u> NAMED HIM AS ONE OF THE TOP 5 "GO TO" PERSONAL INJURY PLAINTIFF ATTORNEYS IN THE STATE OF TEXAS

★ THE PUBLISHERS OF <u>LAW AND POLITICS</u> AND <u>TEXAS MONTHLY</u> NAMED HIM A 2003 SUPER LAWYER

★ FREQUENTLY THE SUBJECT OF FEATURE STORIES IN PUBLICATIONS SUCH AS <u>THE WALL STREET JOURNAL</u>, <u>BLOOMBERG NEWS</u> AND NEWSPAPERS ACROSS THE COUNTRY

with potential income of $200 million. Amoco basically told Mr. Littlejohn to go cry in his Texas beer.

Mr. Littlejohn and Mr. Lanier, with true Texas spirit, decided to sue the oil giant, Amoco, in Matagorda County. Mr. Littlejohn had missed out on several other financial opportunities and Amoco was not doing what it was supposed to do. During the midst of pre-trial, Amoco kept getting continuances through the court. It seemed the case would never actually go to trial.

With much patience and diligence and with a little help from a Mr. John O'Quinn, the case eventually went to trial. The good common sense of the Matagorda jury felt "a man's word is his bond" and found for Mr. Littlejohn. After only a day of jury deliberation, Mr. Littlejohn was awarded a $480 million verdict, the largest in Matagorda County history and one of the top three in the state!

Amoco's counsel had an air of arrogance about them and many of the jurors were put off by this. At times, the large oil company even admitted it wasn't keeping its word. An interesting sidebar of the case: one juror had a future job offer with Amoco but had not started to work; after the trial, the juror decided that he didn't want to work for the company anymore.

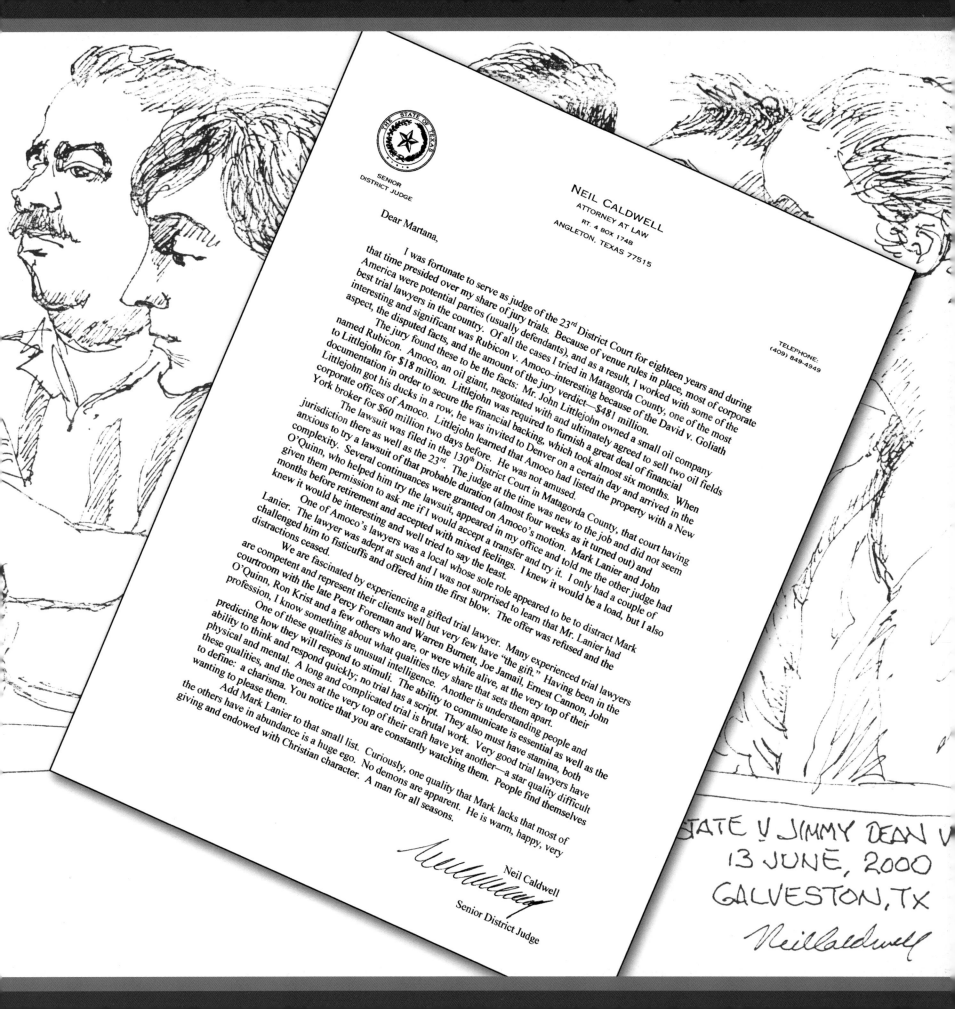

Dear Martana,

I was fortunate to serve as judge of the 23rd District Court for eighteen years and during that time presided over my share of jury trials. Because of venue rules in place, I worked with some of the best trial lawyers in the country. Of all the cases I tried and as a result, most of corporate America were potential parties (usually defendants), and as a result, most of corporate interesting and significant was Rubicon v. Amoco—interesting because of the David v. Goliath aspect, the disputed facts, and the amount of the jury verdict—$481 million.

The jury found these to be the facts: Mr. John Littlejohn owned a small oil company named Rubicon. Amoco, an oil giant, negotiated with and ultimately agreed to sell two oil fields to Littlejohn for $18 million. Littlejohn was required to furnish a great deal of financial documentation in order to secure the financial backing, which took almost six months. When Littlejohn got his ducks in a row, he was invited to Denver on a certain day and arrived in the corporate offices of Amoco. Littlejohn learned that Amoco had listed the property with a New York broker for $60 million two days before. He was not amused.

The lawsuit was filed in the 130th District Court in Matagorda County, that court having jurisdiction there as well as the 23rd. The judge at the time was new to the job and did not seem anxious to try a lawsuit of that probable duration (almost four weeks as it turned out) and complexity. Several continuances were granted on Amoco's motion. Mark Lanier and John O'Quinn, who helped him try the lawsuit, appeared in my office and told me the other judge had given them permission to ask me if I would accept a transfer and try it. I only had a couple of months before retirement and accepted with mixed feelings. I knew it would be a load, but I also knew it would be interesting and well tried to say the least.

One of Amoco's lawyers was a local whose sole role appeared to be to distract Mark Lanier. The lawyer was adept at such and I was not surprised to learn that Mr. Lanier had challenged him to fisticuffs and offered him the first blow. The offer was refused and the distractions ceased.

We are fascinated by experiencing a gifted trial lawyer. Many experienced trial lawyers are competent and represent their clients well but very few have "the gift." Having been in the courtroom with the late Percy Foreman and Warren Burnett, Joe Jamail, Ernest Cannon, John O'Quinn, Ron Krist and a few others who are, or were while alive, at the very top of their profession, I know something about what qualities they share that sets them apart.

One of these qualities is unusual intelligence. Another is understanding people and predicting how they will respond to stimuli. The ability to communicate is essential as well as the ability to think and respond quickly; no trial has a script. They also must have stamina, both physical and mental. A long and complicated trial is brutal work. Very good trial lawyers have these qualities, and the ones at the very top of their craft have yet another—a star quality difficult to define: a charisma. You notice that you are constantly watching them. People find themselves wanting to please them.

Add Mark Lanier to that small list. Curiously, one quality that Mark lacks that most of the others have in abundance is a huge ego. No demons are apparent. He is warm, happy, very giving and endowed with Christian character. A man for all seasons.

Neil Caldwell

Neil Caldwell
Senior District Judge

Maverick County Courthouse

"The Mexican Nationals, the Burning Bus & the Maquiladora"

A Famous Texas Case as Told by

MICHAEL A. CADDELL
& CYNTHIA B. CHAPMAN

CADDELL & CHAPMAN

Mr. Caddell and Ms. Chapman represented the families of thirty victims who were involved in a disaster of historic proportions and the judge presiding over the case, Amato Abascal, wore cowboy boots to the trial! "The Case of the Maquiladora" set precedence in legal history for Texas.

The community and prospective jury pools are mainly young and Hispanic in Maverick County. Most people have relatives or friends who live in Mexico. The victims in this particular case were thirty Mexican national factory workers who resided in "ejdos" or political communities in Mexico, where the main industry is farming. The workers were riding in a poorly maintained bus with an ill-equipped driver to their jobs in a makeshift factory or Mexican "maquiladora" for clothing manufacturing.

Their employer, Salant (based in Eagle Pass), provided transportation for the workers. There was a serious bus accident in northern Mexico and fourteen of the passengers riding that day burned to death. Twelve other individuals escaped, with varying degrees of physical and emotional injury. This case is extremely important because of, and in spite of, the North American Free Trade Agreement, or NAFTA, which propelled the case into the political arena.

Salant, an American company, was sued by the plaintiffs

> *"The value of a life is the same, regardless of background or national origin."*
>
> ~ Michael & Cynthia's Famous Texas Justice Saying

"THE CASE TAUGHT A STORY ON THE MORES OF HUMAN LIFE: THE LIFE OF A MEXICAN NATIONAL IS EQUALLY IMPORTANT AS THAT OF A U.S. CITIZEN."

Where did Maverick County get its name?
FROM SAM MAVERICK, A TEXAS REVOLUTIONARY, LEGISLATOR AND SIGNER OF THE TEXAS DECLARATION OF INDEPENDENCE WHO FOUGHT WITH TERRY'S TEXAS RANGERS IN THE CIVIL WAR.

Where is the Maverick County Courthouse located?
IN EAGLE PASS, TX, OFF MAIN STREET IN THE BEAUTIFUL RIO GRANDE PLAINS REGION.

Who designed the Maverick County Courthouse?
WAHRENBERGER & BECKMAN DESIGNED THE ORIGINAL HISTORIC COURTHOUSE OF BRICK AND STONE IN 1885 IN THE ROMANESQUE REVIVAL STYLE, WHICH, ALTHOUGH A NATIONAL REGISTER PROPERTY, IS CURRENTLY EMPTY DUE TO LACK OF FUNDS FOR RESTORATION.

What is the Courthouse's most unusual feature?
ITS ROMANESQUE REVIVAL ARCHITECTURAL STYLE AND RED-TILED ROOFTOP SET AMONGST A GARDEN OF PALM TREES.

What is the most famous case tried in the Maverick County Courthouse?
DICK DUNCAN WAS THE ONLY MAN TO EVER BE LEGALLY HUNG IN MAVERICK COUNTY. IN 1891, HE WAS FOUND GUILTY OF MURDERING A FAMILY OF SEVEN AND WAS SENTENCED TO A PUBLIC HANGING. THE DEFENSE CHALLENGED THE VERDICT ON THE GROUNDS THAT THERE WERE TWO "NEGROS" ON THE JURY. WHILE THIS WAS LEGAL SINCE THE END OF THE CIVIL WAR, IT WAS STILL NOT ACCEPTED AS A COMMON PRACTICE. ONE MIGHT SAY THAT EAGLE PASS WAS AHEAD OF ITS TIME. MR. DUNCAN RECEIVED ONE STAY OF EXECUTION FROM GOVERNOR HOGG, BUT HE WAS ULTIMATELY HUNG.

Where do you hang your hat?
IN HOUSTON, TX, AT THE FIRM OF CADDELL & CHAPMAN ON LAMAR STREET. CADDELL & CHAPMAN IS A TWELVE LAWYER FIRM WITH A NATIONAL PRACTICE IN COMPLEX LITIGATION. HOUSTON IS OUR HOME BASE WHERE OUR MODERN OFFICES HAVE BEEN DESIGNED BY AWARD WINNING ARCHITECT LAUREN ROTTET AND WE HAVE A LARGE MODERN ART COLLECTION IN OUR GALLERY-LIKE SPACE.

Believe it or not!
AFTER THE TEXAS REVOLUTION, MR. MAVERICK, THE COUNTY'S NAMESAKE, BECAME A WEALTHY LANDOWNER AND LEFT HIS HERD OF LONGHORNS UNBRANDED. STRAY CATTLE WERE CALLED "ONE OF MAVERICK'S." THE WORD MAVERICK IS NOW SYNONYMOUS WITH THOSE LONGHORNS AND MEANS INDEPENDENT OR UNBRANDED AND IS CONSIDERED TO BE A HIGH TEXAS COMPLIMENT!

Top Guns & Legal Legends
Michael Caddell
& Cynthia Chapman

★ TEXAS MONTHLY "SUPER LAWYERS" 2003 AND 2004 (CADDELL AND CHAPMAN)

★ TEXAS LAWYER "TEXAS IMPACT PLAYER OF THE YEAR" 1999 (CADDELL)

★ TLPJ FOUNDATION "PUBLIC INTEREST ACHIEVEMENT AWARD" 1997 (CADDELL)

★ NATIONAL LAW JOURNAL "TOP 40 LITIGATORS UNDER FORTY" 2002 (CHAPMAN)

★ NATIONAL LAW JOURNAL "TOP 50 WOMEN LAWYERS" 2001 (CHAPMAN)

★ FOUNDERS, 12-LAWYER FIRM INCLUDING THREE "TEXAS SUPER LAWYERS" AND FOUR "TEXAS RISING STARS"

★ RECOVERED OVER $3 BILLION FOR FIRM'S CLIENTS SINCE 1989

★ LEAD COUNSEL IN BRANCH DAVIDIAN LITIGATION—RESPONSIBLE FOR GETTING TRUTH OUT ABOUT WHAT HAPPENED AT WACO

★ LEAD COUNSEL—MAQUILADORA BUS ACCIDENT IN MEXICO—RECOVERED $30 MILLION AND KEYED REFORM OF LABOR SAFETY PRACTICES ALONG THE U.S.–MEXICO BORDER

★ LEAD COUNSEL—31 FOREIGN DEATH CASES INVOLVING FIRESTONE TIRE DETREADS ON FORD EXPLORERS – WON THREE EMERGENCY APPEALS TO TEXAS SUPREME COURT SEEKING TO DISMISS CASES AND SEND THEM TO VENEZUELA AND MEXICO

★ CO-LEAD COUNSEL AND CHAIRMAN OF 350-EMPLOYEE ENTITY CREATED TO ADMINISTER $1.1 BILLION POLYBUTYLENE SETTLEMENT— RESPONSIBLE FOR COMPLETELY REPLUMBING OVER 300,000 HOMES ACROSS THE UNITED STATES AT NO COST TO HOMEOWNER

★ ENDOWED CADDELL & CHAPMAN COURTROOM, RESEARCH PROFESSORSHIP, AND LAW SCHOOL FOUNDATION CONFERENCE ROOM AT UNIVERSITY OF VIRGINIA SCHOOL OF LAW

for wrongful death and personal injury in Texas state court. The company, a clothing manufacturer, attempted to deny the negligence claims despite the fact that it failed to maintain the bus properly. The bus driver was not adequately trained to drive the vehicle and the bus itself lacked basic safety features like a fire extinguisher and roof hatch.

The case taught a story on the mores of human life: the life of a Mexican national is equally important as that of a U.S. citizen. Corporations should maintain the same safety standards for maquiladora workers in Mexico as that for factory workers in the U.S. The defense counsel tried on numerous occasions to have the case sent to Mexico because of site occurrence. The defense even attempted bankruptcy proceedings on behalf of the defendant prior to the trial date.

Trial began on July 26, 1999, in Eagle Pass, Texas, where Salant's Texas division was headquartered. After only two weeks of testimony and shortly after Mr. Caddell and Ms. Chapman finished their argument, Salant became nervous and offered a settlement. The victims' families, relying heavily on the expertise of Mr. Caddell and Ms. Chapman, agreed to a $30 million public settlement (or $1 million per family affected). The families sought public recognition by the settlement to ensure that the value of the life of a Mexican national would be the same to an employer whether the employee is a Mexico or U.S. resident.

BENJAMIN A. MARTINEZ
Attorney at Law
Consultoría Internacional Jurídica

P.O. Box 2847
Eagle Pass, Texas 78853

(830) 352-0705
(830) 352-9877

Dear Martana,

After sitting as District Judge in over 100 District Courts from El Paso to Houston, Eagle Pass, Laredo, Uvalde, Hondo, San Antonio, Rio Grande Valley, Gulf Coast areas, Dallas, Sherman, Tyler and many more, I became familiar with judging lawyers in addition to judging cases of all matter of content. I say judging lawyers not as a judge but with all respect and humility, sizing them up as far as ability, integrity, and above all effectiveness in the trial of cases, from Capital cases in Houston to multi party litigations involving serious injuries to persons using defective products to handling complex business type litigation involving some of the state's most famous lawyers and litigants.

In 1998 I happened to walk into Federal Court in McAllen and was immediately spellbound by the caliber of the lawyers presenting a case involving a Hispanic businessman represented by none other than Michael Caddell and Cynthia Chapman. A year later I had the privilege of sitting at counsel table with these same lawyers in probably the most significant case involving venue in Texas of a Mexican bus crash case. The evidence proceeded on the venue issues and survived the most rigorous opposition by famous defense lawyers from all over the state. This case was of such transcendence that it was assisted by an ex-Supreme Court of Texas Justice of Hispanic descent and other big guns hired by the defense. The prosecution of this case was nothing short of magnificent and barring none a superbly presented case by Mike and Cynthia like none other that I had witnessed or had the privilege of presiding over during my entire judicial tenure of seventeen years. That case remains the most significant meting out of justice in the history of Maverick County in my opinion. The case received world wide notoriety and stands as a symbol of how the underdog can have legal representation that even the most affluent person cannot afford.

For that result and many others that Mike and Cynthia have handled and won I would never hesitate to recommend them to any client that asked my advice as to who the best lawyer or lawyers are in our state or any other state for that matter.

Benjamin A. Martinez
Retired District Judge

McLenna
County Courthouse

"The Lawyer Who Stepped on the Wrong Toes"

A Famous Texas Case as Told by
VIC FEAZELL
THE LAW OFFICE OF VIC FEAZELL

"The Case of the Lawyer Who Stepped on the Wrong Toes," would have to be the most famous case of Vic Feazell's career. The case involved accused serial killer, Henry Lee Lucas, District Attorney Vic Feazell, the Texas Rangers and Belo Broadcasting Company. Feazell had accused the historically superior Texas Rangers in 1985 of spoon-feeding bogus confessions to convicted killer, Henry Lee Lucas.

In 1983, Lucas was in a jail cell in Georgetown, Texas, where about 1,000 law enforcement officials came from across the country to question him about unsolved cases. At one point, Lucas had cleared 360 murders in 26 states and even in Canada. Lucas obligingly confessed to the crimes, including three murders in Waco. Feazell was skeptical about Lucas' claims and with help from then Attorney General Jim Mattox, Feazell got Lucas transferred to Waco. After a 1985 grand jury investigation, Feazell not only disputed Lucas' confession to the Waco murders but also accused the Texas Rangers and other legal authorities of using Lucas to clear their unsolved murders. Feazell's attack against the Texas Rangers was a mighty large siege, and Feazell took his charges to the news media. But instead of prompting an investigation of the investigators, Feazell said that he found himself the target of state and federal officials—he was accused maliciously of many things, including bribery and other improper corrupt practices. Feazell knew that his only sin was unmasking the actions of the glorified Texas Rangers.

Feazell is convinced to this day, that Lucas was innocent of most of the murders he was said to have confessed to, believing him to have never killed anyone but his mother in a drunken brawl in 1960, a charge that he had already served his sentence for at the time of his so-called confession spree. In any event, Feazell pressed his case for Lucas' innocence wherever he could—to media, journalists

"After practicing law for 25 years, I still have faith in the jury system."

~ VIC'S FAMOUS TEXAS JUSTICE SAYING

Where did McLennan County get its name?

FROM NEIL MCLENNAN, AN EARLY SETTLER IN THE COUNTY, WHO WAS KILLED IN AN INDIAN RAID IN 1838.

Where is the McLennan County Courthouse located?

IN WACO, TX, THE PROUD HOME OF THE DR. PEPPER MUSEUM AND THE TEXAS RANGER HALL OF FAME AND MUSEUM.

Who designed the McLennan County Courthouse?

J. RIELY GORDON DESIGNED THE HISTORIC COURTHOUSE IN 1902 IN A BEAUX-ARTS STYLE. IT IS BUILT OF STEEL-REINFORCED CONCRETE, A GRANITE BASE AND LIMESTONE FACADE. W.C. DODSON OVERSAW THE CONSTRUCTION WHICH IS A STUNNING NATIONAL REGISTER PROPERTY.

What is the Courthouse's most unusual feature?

ITS INTERESTING LARGE DOME TOP WITH COLORFUL STAINED GLASS PANELS THAT IS SAID TO BE INSPIRED BY SAINT PETER'S CATHEDRAL IN ROME, ITALY.

What is the most famous case tried in the McLennan County Courthouse?

THE STATE OF TEXAS V. DAVID WAYNE SPENCE. SPENCE WAS CONVICTED OF CAPITAL MURDER IN 1984 FOR THE MURDER OF THREE TEENAGERS IN A PARK AT LAKE WACO. IT BECAME KNOWN AS THE LAKE WACO TRIPLE MURDERS CASE AND WAS CHRONICLED IN AN AWARD WINNING BOOK BY CARLTON STOWERS TITLED CARELESS WHISPERS.

Where do you hang your hat?

IN AUSTIN, TX, IN THE HEART OF THE TEXAS HILL COUNTRY. MY FIRM, THE LAW OFFICES OF VIC FEAZELL, OVERLOOKS A SCENIC VIEW OF THE BEAUTIFUL TEXAS HILLS, AND IS NOT VERY FAR FROM LAKE TRAVIS AND LAKE AUSTIN.

Believe it or not!

CONVICTED SERIAL KILLER HENRY LEE LUCAS MADE ME A GIFT THAT I KEEP IN THE LOBBY OF MY FIRM—IT'S A CLOCK MADE ENTIRELY OF MATCHSTICKS!

"VIC WAS CO-COUNSEL WITH HIS FRIEND GARY RICHARDSON OF TULSA, OKLAHOMA—VIC CREDITS GOD AND GARY FOR THE VICTORIES."

CLOCK MADE BY HENRY LEE LUCAS ENTIRELY FROM MATCH STICKS.

143

and reports alike and it was at this time that Feazell's reputation became firmly set in stone; Fort Feazell is what his legal office was called.

TV news reports by Belo Broadcasting Companies' Channel 8 in Dallas, which Feazell said were fed by law enforcement officials, accused him of favoritism and corruption in cases of DWIs. In 1986, two months before Feazell faced re-election as a District Attorney, federal authorities led him, handcuffed from his office while his wife and 4-year-old son watched the arrest on TV, as agents searched their home in Waco.

Feazell won re-election despite the accusations, but several defense attorneys including two former law partners prepared to testify against him after federal authorities brought tax charges against them. There were opponents at every turn, and it would have appeared that Feazell was going down against the charges, and in a big way—he was facing eighty years in a federal penitentiary.

Despite the widespread media coverage and the countless claims against him, in 1987, a federal jury in Austin acquitted Feazell after a six-week trial. Several jurors said they believed he had been framed because of his role in unmasking the Texas Rangers. Feazell returned to Waco to resume his duties as district attorney, but the battle raged on. A year later, he was still overwhelmingly saddled with legal debts and then there was always the skeptical person who still believed what the news had said about him.

Feazell resigned and entered private practice to pursue his libel case against Channel 8. He wanted to settle the cards; to prove that he was not only innocent but had been persecuted by the media and specifically by WFAA, the Belo Corporation. The story becomes stranger than fiction, as Feazell filed a blockbuster libel suite again WFAA and investigative reporter Charles Duncan following Duncan's 10-part 1985 series portraying Feazell as a lax, corrupt prosecutor, despite the fact that Feazell's office had the highest conviction rate in the State.

Feazell asked for a staggering $63.5 million in damages! Originally he had offered to settle out of court for $3 million if an agreement was reached immediately with WFAA and Duncan. His offer also stated that the settlement would increase by $1 million at 9 a.m. on each subsequent Monday throughout the trial. Once the case went to the jury, the offer would become void, but none of the attorneys responded to this original offer. The only time a reaction came from them concerning the lesser settlement was when Feazell would catch the defending legal team off in a corner of the courthouse, laughing about it.

But in the closing argument, the jury was urged to "send a message" to Channel 8 (Belo Corporation) and to journalists throughout the country. Feazell asked that they come back with an award of not a penny less than $35 million to give him back his dignity, to pay off countless legal debt and to settle the score once and for all.

After six weeks of testimony and only five hours of deliberation, the jury filed back into a courtroom packed with

VIC FEAZELL INTERVIEWS HENRY LEE LUCAS.

Feazell supporters and a scattering of media reps and
returned a judgment that surpassed his wildest expectations.
In response to the charge given to them by visiting Judge James
Meyers, they had voted to award Vic Feazell $2 million for damage to his
business, $9 million for damage to his reputation, $6 million for humiliation
and mental suffering, $40 million in exemplary damages from Belo and $1 million
in exemplary damages from Duncan. The total was a staggering $58 million dollars! Vic
was co-counsel with his friend Gary Richardson of Tulsa, Oklahoma—Vic credits God and Gary
for the victories.

The case of "Stepping on the Wrong Toes" eventually turned into the largest libel suit ever won in
legal history. The six-year ordeal that Feazell endured ended victoriously. Feazell stays on his toes in between
legal battles by practicing Qigong and meditation. After resigning from the D.A.'s office, Feazell went on to defend Lucas
on several murder cases, all of which resulted in dismissal. Lucas' only death sentence was commuted to a life sentence by
then Governor George W. Bush. It was the only death sentence Governor Bush ever commuted. Later that year, Lucas died
peacefully in prison of natural causes. Feazell's recollections of a conspiracy are not so distant, but his victory is nonetheless sweet.

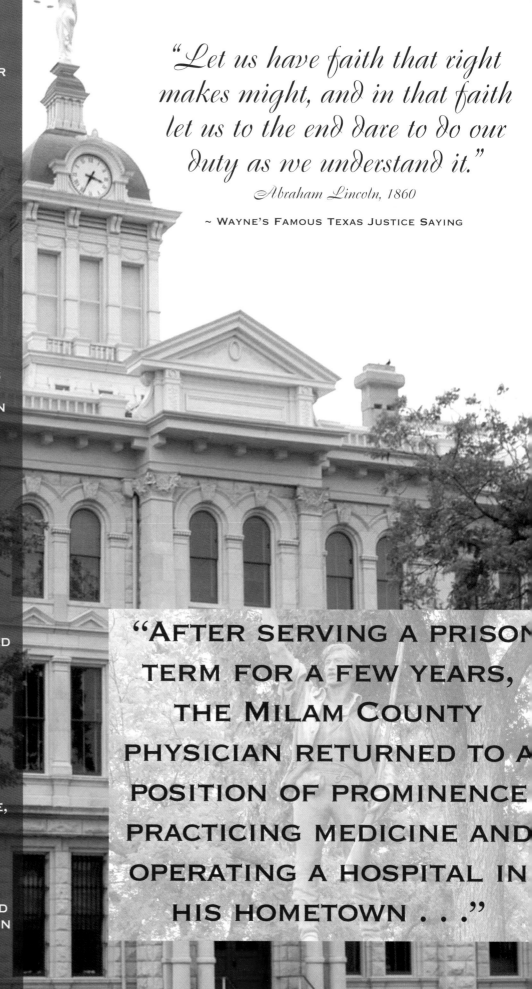

Where did Milam County get its name?

In 1837, in honor of Benjamin R. Milam, who was killed in the Siege of Bexar on December 7, 1835. Cameron is the third county seat following Caldwell and Nashville.

Where is the Milam County Courthouse located?

This National Register Property is on the "Courthouse Square" in Cameron, TX.

Who designed the Milam County Courthouse?

The Milam County Historical Courthouse was completed in 1892 by Larmour & Watson of Austin, TX, in Renaissance Revival style of stone. The Milam County Courthouse was Rededicated on July 4th 2002 by the Texas Historical Commissions' Texas Courthouse Preservation Program.

What is the Courthouse's most unusual feature?

Its history of structures; it has had six of its kind beginning in 1841 when the first courthouse was built in Caldwell, TX, then in 1846, another was built in Cameron, TX. Then again in 1856, 1871, 1876 and again in 1892 when the structure that still stands today was finally erected causing much confusion regarding Milam County's legal history.

What is the most famous case tried in the Milam County Courthouse?

While this is not the most famous case, it is another tale of murder. On December 30, 1999, a Cameron man was killed by a hit man who had been hired so that the man's wife could collect his life insurance. He later pled guilty to a murder charge that implicated both his girlfriend and the man's wife in the murder and was sentenced to life in prison.

Where do you hang your hat?

Fisher, Boyd, Brown, Boudreaux & Huguenard, L.L.P. The firm specializes in major personal injury and wrongful death cases, complex business litigation, estate and maritime cases. The firm has extensive experience in litigating medical malpractice, products liability and aviation matters.

Believe it or not!

The Milam Courthouse statue of Ben Milam pointed in earlier days to a well-known "old time watering hole." Young men would look where Ben Milam was pointing and then joke, paraphrasing our Texas hero, "Who will go with me down to the old saloon?"

"Let us have faith that right makes might, and in that faith let us to the end dare to do our duty as we understand it."

Abraham Lincoln, 1860

~ Wayne's Famous Texas Justice Saying

"After serving a prison term for a few years, the Milam County physician returned to a position of prominence practicing medicine and operating a hospital in his hometown . . ."

Milam
County Courthouse

"The Doctor's Alibi"

A Famous Texas Case as Told by
WAYNE FISHER
FISHER, BOYD, BROWN, BOUDREAUX & HUGUENARD, L.L.P.

During the evening of May 20, 1942, a physician who lived in a small town in West Texas claimed that he had received several telephone calls from a nurse he had known while attending medical school in Galveston. She had married another physician who had also been a medical student in Galveston and was, in 1942, a prominent physician in Milam County. The physician drove out around midnight to rendezvous with the nurse in response to her previous telephone calls. She was in a parked car on the roadside. As he approached her vehicle, he spoke to her briefly, but was then startled to see her husband, whom he recognized, approaching him from the rear of the car. Shots rang out and the victim fell, but managed to escape, despite being seriously wounded.

The Milam County physician was arrested the next day in Houston, Texas, and charged with assault and murder. Despite having many witnesses, including the sheriff from Caldwell in the adjoining Burleson County, confirm his alibi that he was in Milam County late on the preceding evening and that he had then traveled on to Houston, he was nevertheless convicted and sentenced to prison.

After serving a prison term for a few years, the Milam County physician returned to a position of prominence practicing medicine and operating a hospital in his hometown for the remainder of his life. Despite his conviction, the questions remained largely unanswered.

As a youngster I attended some of these proceedings and as I observed several great lawyers, including Emory A. Camp and his son, Emory B. Camp, in action in the Milam County Courthouse, I decided then and there that I would become a trial lawyer. I have never regretted that decision made so long ago.

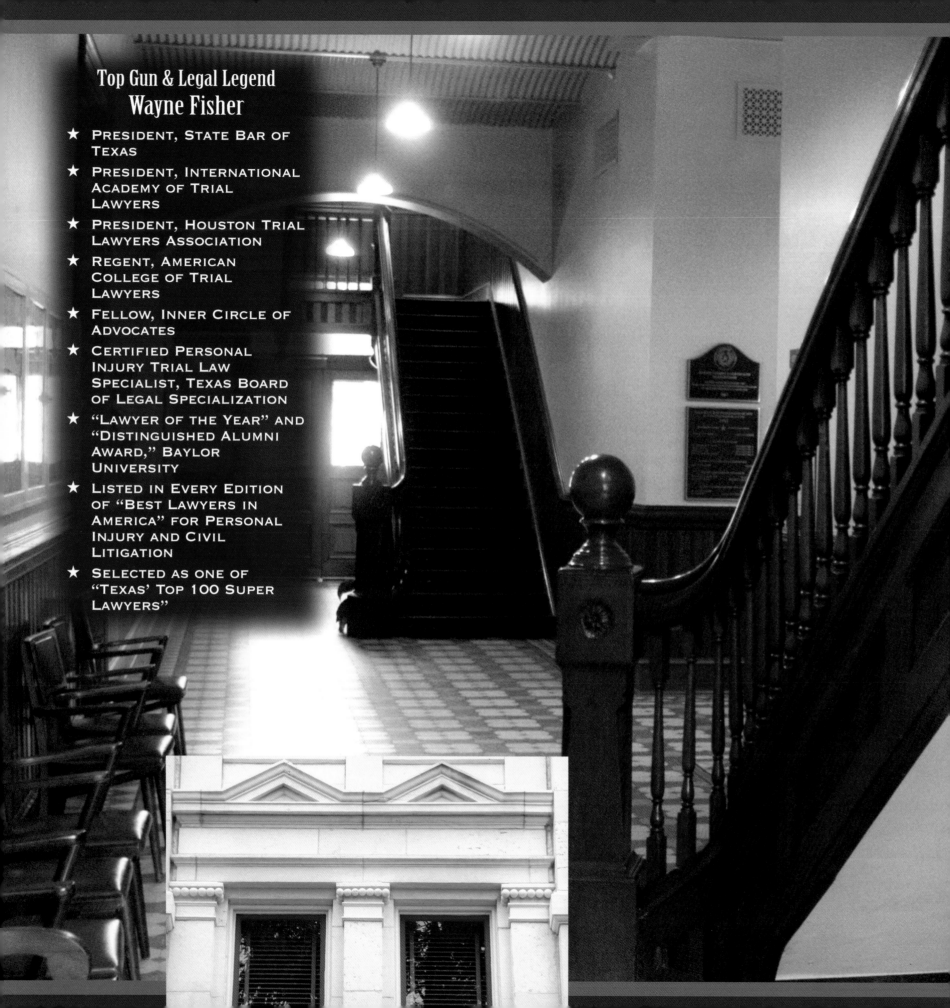

Top Gun & Legal Legend
Wayne Fisher

★ PRESIDENT, STATE BAR OF TEXAS

★ PRESIDENT, INTERNATIONAL ACADEMY OF TRIAL LAWYERS

★ PRESIDENT, HOUSTON TRIAL LAWYERS ASSOCIATION

★ REGENT, AMERICAN COLLEGE OF TRIAL LAWYERS

★ FELLOW, INNER CIRCLE OF ADVOCATES

★ CERTIFIED PERSONAL INJURY TRIAL LAW SPECIALIST, TEXAS BOARD OF LEGAL SPECIALIZATION

★ "LAWYER OF THE YEAR" AND "DISTINGUISHED ALUMNI AWARD," BAYLOR UNIVERSITY

★ LISTED IN EVERY EDITION OF "BEST LAWYERS IN AMERICA" FOR PERSONAL INJURY AND CIVIL LITIGATION

★ SELECTED AS ONE OF "TEXAS' TOP 100 SUPER LAWYERS"

McLANE GROUP

Leading the Charge

Dear Martana,

As a young boy growing up in the small town of Cameron, Texas, my classmates and I had the great fortune of getting to know almost everyone in the area. One of the best friends I made during grade and high school was Wayne Fisher, who is now one of the most respected lawyers in the State of Texas. We changed locations after graduation and continued our friendship in Waco as we tackled the challenges of college life at Baylor University.

Wayne has always been half a step ahead of me and proved such as he graduated from Baylor with honors in 1961 and embarked on what would be a tremendously successful career in personal injury and business dispute litigation. Because of my great admiration for him, we have remained close through the years and I've been very fortunate in having Wayne represent our interests in several business transactions, particularly in the sports industry.

My father always taught me that, in order to be successful in both your business and personal life, you must uphold the principles of honesty and integrity at all times. Wayne Fisher is a perfect example of someone who has never faltered in this area and we owe him a debt of gratitude for his dedication to helping others. He has ensured judgments for many who were in dire need of funds after being injured. In addition, I can't count the number of organizations who have benefited from his experience and expertise in choosing the correct path.

There is no one that I admire more than Wayne and he has proven time and time again that his door is never closed when his talents are needed. Hats off to you, Mr. Fisher, as the world is a better place because of your generosity and general ability to make any occasion a boot-stomping good time!

Drayton McLane, Jr.

Post Office Box 549 • 4001 Industrial Boulevard
Temple, Texas 76503 • 254-770-6100 • FAX 254-770-6101

Montgome
County Courthouse

"Too Much of a Good Thing"

A Famous Texas Case as Told by

TOMMY FIBICH

FIBICH, HAMPTOM, LEEBRON & GARTH, L.L.P.

At well over six-feet-tall and well over two hundred pounds, with a distinguished shock of gray hair, senior trial lawyer Paul Stallings cut a wide swath passing through his well turned-out defense team as he strode to the podium to address the Honorable Fred Edwards. After all, Stallings was the head of the litigation department at Houston's blue-ribbon firm Vinson and Elkins. It was appropriate that

> "... 'YOUR HONOR, THESE LAWYERS WANT TO TAKE THIS COURT TO SOMEPLACE WHERE NO OTHER COURT IN TEXAS HAS BEEN.' "

Stallings lead the all-star team which included the nation's top pharmaceutical lawyers from New York, Los Angeles and Washington, D.C.

Seated shoulder to shoulder at the table opposite, were counsel for the ten class members from Montgomery County who were seeking medical monitoring after having taken diet pills which were, months earlier, hastily removed from the marketplace by agreement with the FDA. Charlie

ery

"You can't stick a feather in a jaybird and make it a peacock."

~ Tommy's Famous Texas Justice Saying

Where did Montgomery County get its name?
Montgomery County was named after General Andrew Montgomery, an early settler who established a trading post that brought others to the area. In 1837, the Republic of Texas Congress named the county for its largest settlement.

Where is the Montgomery County Courthouse located?
On the corner of Davis and Main Streets in the Courthouse Square in Conroe, TX, thirty miles north of Houston.

Who designed the Montgomery County Courthouse?
Joseph Finger, Inc., designed the courthouse building in 1936 in a Moderne style constructed of limestone.

What is the Courthouse's most unusual feature?
Its architectural evolution: the original courthouse was a small, two room log building and the second was two stories tall and built of lumber, while the third was built in a Greek Revival style. The current courthouse was remodeled in 1965 with a very modern appearance.

What is the most famous case tried in the Montgomery County Courthouse?
The capital murder trial, retrial and appeal of Clarence Brandley. Brandley, a former janitor at Bellville High School, was convicted for the 1980 rape and murder of 16-year-old Cheryl Fergson. He was held on death row for nine years, only to be freed when the true murderer finally confessed in 1990. His story was made into a Showtime television movie.

Where do you hang your hat?
I am a partner in the firm of Fibich, Hampton & Leebron, LLP, in Houston, TX. We are trial lawyers specializing in representing plaintiffs that are injured by the bad conduct of others.

Believe it or not!
Montgomery County is the birthplace of the Lone Star Flag of Texas. At the request of President Mirabeau B. Lamar, Dr. Charles B. Steward of Montgomery County created the banner!

Parker, John Roberson and Tommy Fibich, all board certified in trial or appellate specialties and all three seasoned veterans of complex litigation, listened closely as Stallings intoned to the Court; "Your Honor, these lawyers want to take this Court to someplace where no other Court in Texas has been." Exchanging knowing glances, the three plaintiffs' lawyers knew exactly that was where their journey was headed.

What followed were two intense days of high-powered testimony from well credentialed medical doctors who, themselves, had written books and hundreds of articles on valvular heart disease. Judge Edwards seemed exhausted when he excused himself from the bench late on the second day. The day had been spent listening to several hours of legal testimony from prestigious law professors who had opined as to the propriety and legality of a medical monitoring class. The judge said he would return with his decision.

Meanwhile, the plaintiff's colorful local counsel, a former boxer by the name of Buddy Hopkins, was explaining to a group of Houston lawyers how the nearby town of Cut'n Shoot got its name and reputation. "People don't go around look'in for trouble, but when trouble comes it gets a warm reception in Cut'n Shoot," Buddy was heard to say. About that time, the judge came back to the bench. His brow was furrowed as he removed his glasses and rubbed his eyes. It seemed an eternity as he carefully weighed aloud his considered decision.

Ruling for the plaintiffs, this judge went where none had gone.

Buddy leaned over and whispered to the lawyer next to him, "The judge has been to Cut'n Shoot."

After that fateful day, other Senate jurisdictions and a federal judge in the national class action reached the same decision, resulting in the largest Pharmaceutical payout in United States history. The cost to Wyeth from the Fen/Phen litigation will exceed $10 billion. However, the beginning of this well-known story was at the intersection of two railroads in a small town in Texas.

Top Gun & Legal Legend
Tommy Fibich

★ 2004 ALUMNUS OF THE YEAR UNIVERSITY OF HOUSTON LAW SCHOOL

★ MEMBER, THE AMERICAN BOARD OF TRIAL ADVOCATES

★ BOARD CERTIFIED, CIVIL TRIAL LAW TEXAS BOARD OF LEGAL SPECIALIZATION

★ MEMBER ORDER OF BARONS, SCHOLASTIC HONORARY SOCIETY UNIVERSITY OF HOUSTON LAW SCHOOL

★ TEXAS SUPER LAWYER 2003 - TEXAS MONTHLY MAGAZINE

★ TEXAS SUPER LAWYER 2004 - TEXAS MONTHLY MAGAZINE

★ EXECUTIVE COMMITTEE - TEXAS TRIAL LAWYERS ASSOCIATION

★ DIRECTOR, TEXAS TRIAL LAWYERS ASSOCIATION

★ DIRECTOR, HOUSTON TRIAL LAWYERS ASSOCIATION

★ DIRECTOR, ASSOCIATION OF TRIAL LAWYERS IN AMERICA

★ J.D. UNIVERSITY OF HOUSTON SCHOOL OF LAW

FIBICH, HAMPTON & LEEBRON, L.L.P.

ATTORNEYS AT LAW

FIVE HOUSTON CENTER
1401 McKINNEY, SUITE 1800
HOUSTON, TEXAS 77010-9998

W. MICHAEL LEEBRON II
BOARD CERTIFIED, PERSONAL INJURY TRIAL LAW
TEXAS BOARD OF LEGAL SPECIALIZATION

FAX (713) 751-0025
TOLL FREE (713) 751-0030
(888) 888-0700
E-MAIL: MLEEBRON@FHL-LAW.COM

Dear Martana:

Upon graduation from Baylor Law in the early '70s, it was my good fortune to find a job at a distinguished trial firm in downtown Houston. On the first day, one of the senior partners sent me to the courthouse to try a jury case that he was relieved to dodge. However, with some luck and a fine education, the old partners were shocked to learn that the jury returned a verdict in our favor. In fact, they were so delighted; they hired a hot shot law clerk from the University of Houston to help manage the kennel full of problem cases that the partners were falling all over themselves to send our way. The new, pound manager was a young-faced kid named, Tommy Fibich.

"What do we do first?" Fibich asked. "Hell, I'm not sure...just started this career a few days ago myself," I said. Tommy shot back, "Well, in that case, let's go to the baseball game. I've often heard that great, legal minds are best sharpened while drinking beer at the domed stadium." Of course, he was right.

Since those humble beginnings, thirty years have flown by. Countless games have gone down in the score books and small fortunes have been squandered on drink. But, more importantly, thousands of unfortunate families, all victims of tragedy and death, have been given Tommy's strong, compassionate voice in solemn courtrooms throughout Texas and the nation. While the light-hearted times have been many, the heavy burden of speaking up for the voiceless became Tommy Fibich's life's work. The noble causes he has championed have not only been his hallmark but his legacy.

Just as Tommy could find basic inspiration at the baseball stadium, he has always possessed a gift for effortless simplicity when the need arose to shred a complicated legal argument. Here is an example.

National Medical Enterprises once owned hundreds of psychiatric hospitals throughout the United States. This hospital chain was notorious for hospitalizing young children in "locked" facilities when there was no sincere medical or psychiatric need for the young patient to be under such restrictive care. The hospital's unholy motive was insurance money, pure and simple. When the money ran out, the patient was summarily discharged. Tragically, severe mental and emotional trauma was visited upon the child and his family under this deleterious scheme.

Representing hundreds of these child-plaintiffs, Tommy moved the Court in Montgomery County, Texas, to consolidate fourteen or so, cases for trial to a jury. The court scheduled a hearing for the purpose of deciding whether these cases would be properly tried together. Unknown to the Judge and the plaintiffs, the hospital chain hired a respected Dean of a well known and prominent law school to be their expert witness and explain the current state of the national law regarding the disapproval of such a consolidation.

At the conclusion of the Dean's testimony (in which his credentials were developed in impressive detail and his opinions were alarmingly dismissive of the impertinent motion to consolidate), no member of Tommy's team dared take on the daunting witness. Unprepared but with an athlete's anticipation for the intuitive, Tommy rose to his feet.

"Dean Famous," he began, "have you ever heard the old law school adage that the 'A' students become professors; the 'B' students become judges; and, the 'C' students make all the money?" "Yes, I have," said the Dean. "Well," said Tommy, "since you are not only a law professor but a Dean of a prominent law school, I'd bet you were one of those 'A' students, weren't you?" "I did very well," said the Dean. "Then my next question is, why are you here?" Tommy said. The Dean feigned patience: "I am here to assist the court in understanding the state of the current national trend in the law." "Is the reason you're here because you think you are smarter than our Judge? Do you think that just because he was a 'B' student that he is incapable of reading and understanding the law, himself?" Tommy quickly responded. Flustered, the Dean said, "I don't know what grade he made." Tommy was off in a zone. "Well, Dean, it's not too often that the 'C' student gets to question the 'A' student, but I think our Judge gets the point." The District Judge could not contain a sly grin as he ordered the fourteen cases consolidated for trial. Can't imagine how much fun it would be. Sure wish we had another thirty years.

W. Michael Leebron

W. Michael Leebron II

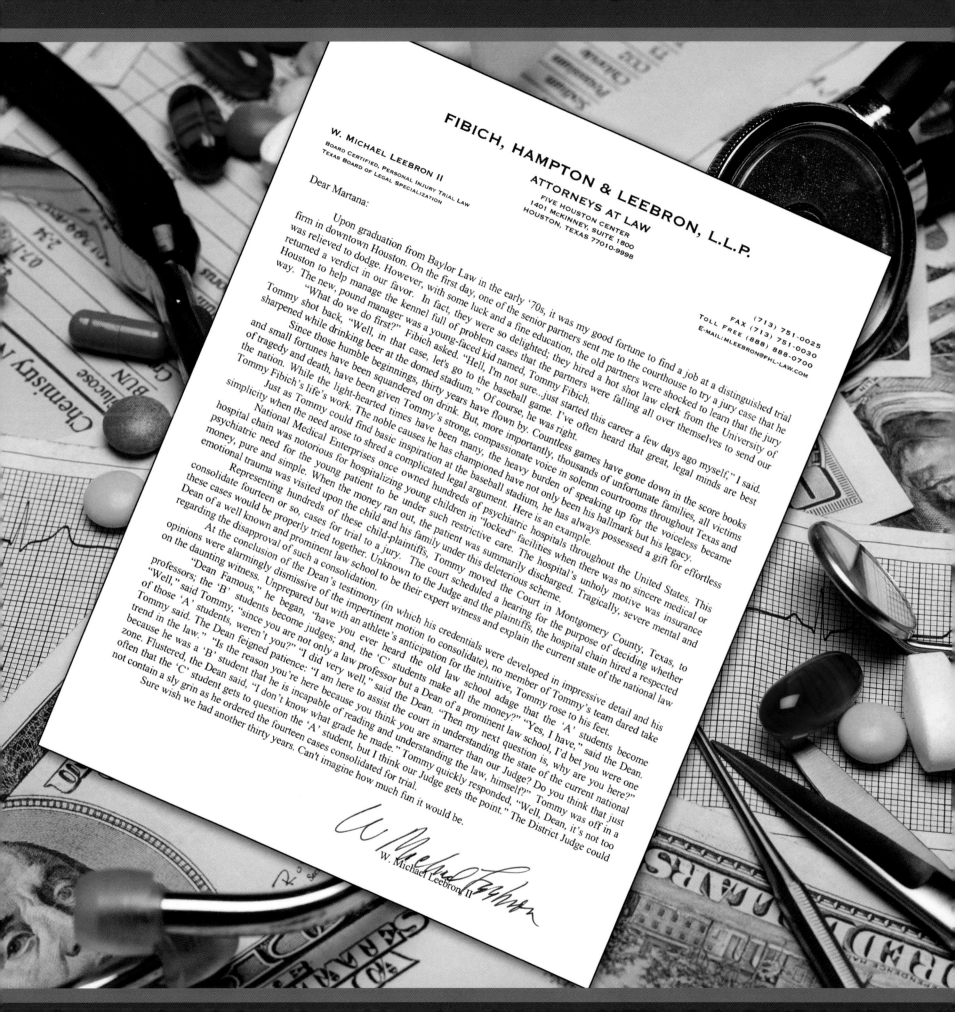

Where did Moore County get its name?
ORGANIZED IN 1892, IT WAS NAMED IN HONOR OF EDWIN W. MOORE, WHO WAS A COMMODORE OF THE TEXAS NAVY.

Where is the Moore County Courthouse located?
IN DUMAS, TX, ON THE SQUARE NEXT TO THE MEMORIAL FOR THE SHAMROCK FIRE VICTIMS OF 1955, WHEN AN OIL EXPLOSION KILLED 21 PEOPLE.

Who designed the Moore County Courthouse?
IN 1930, BERRY & HATCH DESIGNED THIS HISTORIC COURTHOUSE IN BRICK IN A MODERNE STYLE WITH EAGLES ADORNING THE CORNERS.

What is the courthouse's most unusual feature?
THE COUNTY JAIL USED TO BE LOCATED ATOP THE MOORE COUNTY COURTHOUSE.

What is the most famous case tried in the Moore County Courthouse?
"STRYCHNINE FOR BREAKFAST" TEXAS V. SARA INEZ CARAWAY IS THE MOST FAMOUS CASE FROM MOORE COUNTY, HOWEVER THERE HAVE BEEN MANY CASES IN MOORE COUNTY INVOLVE OIL AND GAS ROYALTY AND LAND DISPUTES AND MS. MCLARTY HAS REPRESENTED HER FAMILY ALONG WITH DUMAS LAWYER JIM LOVELL IN SEVERAL SUCH CASES.

Where do you hang your hat?
AT MCLARTY • ROPER • POPE, L.L.P. ON TURTLE CREEK BOULEVARD IN DALLAS, TX, WHERE I SPECIALIZE IN CIVIL TRIAL WORK, INVOLVING PERSONAL INJURY.

Believe it or not!
MARY ALICE MCLARTY'S GREAT-GRAND FATHER, W.F. BENNETT, WAS INTEGRAL TO THE FOUNDING OF DUMAS, TX, IN MOORE COUNTY. WHILE HE WAS OFFICIALLY A RANCHER, HE HELD THE POSITION OF COUNTY COMMISSIONER AND JUSTICE OF THE PEACE IN THE 1890S, AS WELL AS POSTMASTER AT ONE TIME. HER GRANDFATHER, CHARLIE BENNETT, WAS CALLED "THE MOST HONEST MAN TO COME OUT OF THE BREAKS." HER FAMILY STILL LIVES ON THE RANCH IN THE CANADIAN BREAKS IN SOUTHEASTERN MOORE COUNTY. ROWDY RHODES IS CURRENTLY MAYOR AND IS MARRIED TO MS. MCLARTY'S NIECE, CINDY (FORMERLY BENNETT) WHO IS A FIFTH GENERATION RESIDENT OF DUMAS!

"There is one way in this country in which all men are created equal—there is one human institution that makes a pauper the equal of a Rockefeller, the stupid man the equal of an Einstein, and the ignorant man the equal of any college president. That institution, gentlemen, is the court."

Atticus Finch, To Kill a Mockingbird

~ MARY ALICE'S FAMOUS TEXAS JUSTICE SAYING

"Bacon & Eggs with a Dash of Strychnine"

A Famous Texas Case as Told by
MARY ALICE MCLARTY
MCLARTY • ROPER • POPE, L.L.P.

When someone asks a resident of the town of Dumas, Texas, in Moore County what one trial standouts as memorable to them the answer is always the same, *State of Texas v. Sara Inez Caraway.* For a town that at the time of the incident did not even have a jail, the closest one being nearly four hours away, the idea of a murder taking place in their own backyard was unimaginable. So much so that it was the kind hearted people and their compassion for the grieving widow that unwittingly drove out the truth of the matter, that this widow had plotted and killed her own husband.

It was early on April 28, 1902, when W.V. Caraway, a traveling lumber salesman, returned home after a trip to his wife Sara and their five children. What greeted him were not the open arms of a tender wife, however. According to his wife, Sara, when W.V. arrived home he began complaining of heart trouble and she put him to bed to rest. After requesting his "heart tonic" to ease the pain, Sara calmly served him up a nice tall glass of Strychnine instead. She recounted that her husband complained of the bitter taste, but finished the elixir none the less. It did not take long for the man to realize that he had been poisoned and his wife immediately admitted the fact to her dying husband. As her husband agonized in front of her, Sara just watched his painful death. W.V. was begging her to give him an antidote to the poison and she finally agreed or so he thought. Sara went to the kitchen and cooked-up a batch of Strychnine-flavored bacon and eggs. She served this to him, telling him that the antidote was cooked-in. W.V. did not even finish his plate before he died.

Moore County Courthouse

This last vicious act would later prove to be the sole piece of evidence that aroused suspicion as to Sara's involvement. As there was no evidence to suggest foul play, Sara easily convinced neighbors and the authorities that her husband had died of a heart attack. After all, he was 55 at the time, which was rather mature in those days. The kind women of the town followed their nature and the very next day several of them were at Sara's house helping the grieving widow by taking care of her daily chores and watching after the children. One of the women who were helping to clean up the kitchen fed some food scraps of bacon and eggs to one of the dogs outside. It did not take long for the dog to drop dead to the ground. Suspicions were immediately aroused and

> "SARA WENT TO THE KITCHEN AND COOKED-UP A BATCH OF STRYCHNINE-FLAVORED BACON AND EGGS."

Sara was confronted. She admitted to the crime and was indicted for murder.

She received her right to a speedy trial the very next day and although she did not plead so, she was found guilty and sentenced to 99 years in the state penitentiary. Sara Caraway never did reveal the motive behind her crime. Unbelievably, she served only six years of her sentence and was released due to a potentially fatal disease by the name of Bright's disease. Incredibly enough, she would later go on to remarry a judge!

Morris
County Courthouse

"The Forty-Year Toxic Cloud"

A Famous Texas Case as Told by

HAROLD W. NIX
NIX, PATTERSON & ROACH, L.L.P.

In 1987, I was involved in the biggest case Morris County had ever seen. Suits were filed suits for 3,328 employees of Lone Star Steel Co., based in Morris County. Plant conditions at the Lone Star Steel Co., the biggest employer in the county, had given the workers "chemical AIDS."

The emissions of the factory caused by a toxic mushroom cloud that hovered ominously for forty years over the plant, seriously and dangerously affecting the immune systems of employees. These men and women spent their working lives making many of the steel products that form an integral part of our economy. But, instead of praise and wealth, many of these workers got cancer and other breathing problems caused by exposure to deadly silica and asbestos products. So, these workers and their families joined together with the lawyers of Nix, Patterson & Roach to bring the companies who made these products to justice. Their case, which came to be known as the Lone Star Steel Mill Toxic Tort Litigation, resulted in the payment of more than $90 million to these workers and their families.

Over 40% of the plant's workers were suffering from illnesses such as lung cancer, asbestosis, pleurisy, mesothelioma and silicosis. However, under state workers' compensation law, we could not technically go after the company directly in a personal injury case. If we directly targeted Lone Star's insurance company, recovery for the 3,328 employees would be limited. Worker's compensation in Texas is at a fixed rate which is far less than what the plant's employees deserved. Knowing this, we had to target every company that functioned within Lone Star's operations.

After filing suit in state court, 200 defendants and their insurance companies agreed to reach a settlement with the workers of Lone Star Steel Co. Over $90 million has been recovered to compensate the employees for their health problems.

My firm continues to fight corporate negligence affecting employee health. I was born in Daingerfield, Texas, and after attending Baylor Law School, I returned back to my home town in order to help the small town people who need it the most. I even turned down offers from defense firms in Dallas and Tyler so that I could stay in the forests of Morris County.

Several years following the Lone Star Steel Co. suit, I again fought for the rights of East Texans. Workers at the Red River Army Depot in the Texarkana area began to suffer from diseases caused by exposure to rubber products in the work place. Nix, Patterson & Roach filed suit against the manufacturers of these products to make them pay for the harm they caused these workers and their families. In the end, Nix, Patterson & Roach obtained over $47 million for 200 clients.

"OVER 40% OF THE PLANT'S WORKERS WERE SUFFERING FROM ILLNESSES SUCH AS LUNG CANCER, ASBESTOSIS, PLEURISY, MESOTHELIOMA AND SILICOSIS."

My firm currently represents employees from East Texas, as well as thousands of injured workers from areas all across the nation including Texas, Alabama, Louisiana, Mississippi, Washington, Oregon, Oklahoma and Arkansas in toxic tort litigation against those companies responsible for causing their occupational related diseases. The firm has long been at the forefront in prosecuting cases related to injuries caused by exposure to silica and asbestos. We have several employees and attorneys dedicated full-time to helping us bring these companies to justice.

Where did Morris County get its name?
FROM WILLIAM W. MORRIS IN 1875, A TEXAS LEGISLATOR AND JUDGE WHO FOUGHT TO FREE TEXAS FROM OCCUPATION.

Where is the Morris County Courthouse located?
THE HISTORIC COURTHOUSE IS AT 101 LINDA AVENUE IN THE HEART OF DAINGERFIELD, THE FOURTH OLDEST TOWN IN TEXAS. THE NEWER 1973 COURTHOUSE IS IN DAINGERFIELD ON BROADNAX STREET.

Who designed the Morris County Courthouse?
PETERSON AND STUCKEY DESIGNED THIS HISTORIC COURTHOUSE IN 1881, WITH LOTS OF CLASSICAL ELEMENTS. IT IS A TWO-STORY BRICK STRUCTURE WITH BAY WINDOWS. THE BUILDING HAS A SERIES OF WALLS BUILT IN STAIR-STEP DESIGN ALLOWING 18 OF ITS ROOMS TO HAVE CORNER WINDOWS.

What is the courthouse's most unusual feature?
THIS NATIONAL REGISTER PROPERTY IS THE OFFICES OF NIX, PATTERSON & ROACH LLP.

What is the most famous case tried in the Morris County Courthouse?
THE TRIAL OF TONY LEE WALKER. IN 1992, WALKER MURDERED AND RAPED 66-YEAR-OLD VIRGINIA SIMMONS AND MURDERED HER 81-YEAR-OLD HUSBAND WILLIE "BO" SIMMONS BECAUSE HE WANTED BEER AND MONEY FOR MORE DRUGS. WALKER WAS SENTENCED TO DIE BY LETHAL INJECTION AND WAS PUT TO DEATH IN SEPTEMBER 2002.

Where do you hang your hat?
DAINGERFIELD, MORRIS COUNTY, TX, WHERE I FOUNDED THE NIX LAW FIRM IN 1965. WE ARE ONE OF THE PREMIER PLAINTIFFS' LAW FIRMS IN THE COUNTRY. SINCE OUR FOUNDING WE HAVE GROWN FROM A ONE LAWYER, ONE ROOM SHOP TO A FIRM WITH SIXTEEN LAWYERS, STATE OF THE ART FACILITIES AND CASES THAT TAKE US ALL OVER THE WORLD. WE HAVE OFFICES IN DAINGERFIELD, TEXAS; SHREVEPORT, LOUISIANA; TEXARKANA, TEXAS AND SALTILLO, COAHUILA, MEXICO.

Believe it or not!
MORRIS COUNTY WAS A VITAL SOURCE OF AMMUNITION, MEDICINES AND OTHER RESOURCES DURING THE CIVIL WAR. HUSSEY & LOGAN'S MILL AND GIN FACTORY PROCESSED COTTON FOR CLOTH MAKING AND CORN FOR BREAD AND THEN TRADED IT TO MEXICO FOR GOODS. OTHER WARTIME PLANTS IN TEXAS MADE WAGONS, GUNS, POWDER, SHOES, HOSPITAL SUPPLIES AND CLOTHES!

Top Gun & Legal Legend
Harold W. Nix

- ★ FOUNDING MEMBER OF NIX, PATTERSON & ROACH, LLP
- ★ BORN IN DAINGERFIELD, TEXAS
- ★ CATTLE RANCHING & EMBRYO CALF OPERATOR
- ★ GRADUATED FROM EAST TEXAS STATE COLLEGE (B.S. 1962)
- ★ GRADUATED FROM BAYLOR LAW SCHOOL (LL.B. 1965)
- ★ MEMBER OF DELTA THETA PHI AND THE BAYLOR LAW REVIEW, WHERE HE WAS NOTES AND COMMENTS EDITOR, 1963-1964
- ★ SERVED ON THE SUPREME COURT ADVISORY COMMITTEE ON THE RULES OF CIVIL PROCEDURE, 1982-1988
- ★ PRESIDENT OF THE MORRIS COUNTY AND NORTHEAST TEXAS BAR ASSOCIATIONS (1970-1971)
- ★ VICE PRESIDENT OF THE EAST TEXAS TRIAL LAWYERS ASSOCIATION (1986-1988)
- ★ DIRECTOR OF THE TEXAS TRIAL LAWYERS ASSOCIATION (1978-1989)
- ★ MARRIED TO CAROL ANN NIX AND FATHER OF TWO CHILDREN

"Caddo Pottery"

The Native Caddo Indians were an agricultural society based in East Texas. Being a native Texan and from East Texas, I became interested in collecting and preserving this art form. I have been building my collection of Caddo pottery for a long time and now have the largest collection of Caddo Pottery in the world and one of my prize pieces is on display in the Smithsonian Museum.

About 1200 years ago, Caddo potters began making pottery unique to Caddo because of the particular combinations of material and design. Early Caddo pots were usually made of clay mixed with smashed pottery shreds or sometimes bone. The variety of pottery was immense, but the two designs that stand out as distinctly Caddo are bottles with long, slender necks and "carinated" bottles and bowls, which flare at the bottom and turn inward at the rim.

The first Caddo pottery was discovered about a century ago, and archeologists have had their eye on it ever since. There were dozens of Caddo communities and in each of these communities were a number of potters—generation after generation of pottery making existed over 1000 years. It was not until the late 1800s when there was first a unified Caddo tribe, so the pottery made before this time, although still similar in design, was also unified and had many variations.

It is believed that the Caddo pottery tradition was one created and maintained by women. Generations of mothers and daughters, aunts and nieces, shared the knowledge of pottery making just as the men passed down hunting and weapon making skills to their sons and nephews.

Caddo potters were masters at making two kinds of pottery, fine ware and coarse ware or utilitarian pottery. The coarse wares were ordinary cooking and storage pots made for everyday use, much like the pots you and I would cook with. These were typically made to be plain and sturdy so that they could withstand the heat of the cooking fire.

On the other hand, Caddo fine wares were made to be admired. They were often polished and almost always decorated, to be used in a way that you and I might use fine china; serving food and drink and for special purposes, including religious ceremonies and holidays. The fine wares were also crafted to accompany the dead in the afterlife. Today, it is mostly the fine wares that people collect and admire for their beauty.

NIX PATTERSON & ROACH, LLP

Nelson J. Roach
Attorney at Law

Dear Martana:

Harold Nix was born the son of a poor woodcutter. He had five siblings, and they lived crowded in a small cinder block apartment in a housing project in Daingerfield in deep rural Northeast Texas. Harold never used his humble background as an excuse to be a failure in life. To the contrary, he used his experiences of hard work and humility to develop a strong ambition and a work ethic to match that ambition. Harold used that ambition and work ethic to be the first person in his family to graduate from college and the first person in his family to receive a postgraduate degree.

When Harold received his law degree, he could have quickly become wealthy and successful in a big city representing moneyed interests. However, Harold was not one to abandon his humble roots. He embraced them. Harold developed a genuine love and empathy for people who work hard and play by the rules. So when Harold received his law degree, he came home to Daingerfield, and started using his law degree to make the law work for the people he grew up with -- timber, agricultural, and industrial workers in his home town and the surrounding area.

Harold practiced law with one overriding goal: bring justice to ordinary people. Even as his practice grew and he became more and more successful, his criteria for selecting cases remained the same. The issue was whether someone had a genuine grievance. The question was whether that person's grievance was truly big to the client, not whether it would bring big success to Harold. Consequently, Harold would work just as enthusiastically to make a burial insurance company pay a poor widow a few thousand dollars to bury her husband as he would to make another company pay millions to an industrial worker gruesomely injured by a defective product. As his law firm grew and his material wealth increased, Harold never decreased his focus on protecting ordinary people. In fact, through Harold's leadership, his law firm volunteered to accept all of the legal aid cases in five counties.

In the process of practicing law according to his philosophy of helping ordinary people achieve justice, he became extraordinarily successful. That is not to say that he did not endure many trying moments attempting to hold wealthy and powerful wrongdoers accountable. In fact, his success in helping ordinary people against well-connected and moneyed interests would not go unpunished. As has happened with other lawyers brave enough to bring well-connected, wealthy and influential wrongdoers to justice, Harold had to endure cruel public criticism and ridicule. He never cowered. He never wavered. He persevered, and time and again, in the end, good triumphed over evil.

Very truly yours,

Nelson J. Roach

205 Linda Drive • Daingerfield, TX 75638 • 903-645-7333 • 903-645-5389 Fax
Texarkana, TX 75503 • 903-223-3999 • Shreveport, LA 71101 • 318-425-9255

Where did Navarro County get its name?

THE COUNTY WAS NAMED AFTER TEXAS REPUBLIC LEADER JOSE ANTONIO NAVARRO, A SIGNER OF THE TEXAS DECLARATION OF INDEPENDENCE AND A MEMBER OF THE TEXAS CONGRESS.

Where is the Navarro County Courthouse located?

IN CORSICANA, ABOUT 53 MILES SOUTH OF DALLAS AND HOME OF THE COLLIN STREET BAKERY WHERE THEY MAKE THE WORLD FAMOUS CHRISTMAS CAKE, BETTER KNOWN AS A "FRUITCAKE."

Who designed the Navarro County Courthouse?

JAMES E. FLANDERS DESIGNED THE 1905 HISTORIC COURTHOUSE IN BEAUX-ARTS STYLE OF MARBLE AND BRICK.

What is the Courthouse's most unusual feature?

THE "CALL TO ARMS" STATUE ON THE COURTHOUSE LAWN, WHICH COMMEMORATES THE SOLDIERS OF THE SOUTHERN CONFEDERACY WHO FOUGHT VALIANTLY FOR THEIR STATE.

What is the most famous case tried in the Navarro County Courthouse?

HEROD VS. CITY OF CORSICANA; AN EMINENT DOMAIN CASE. HEROD OWNED THE MOST VALUABLE PROPERTY ON LAKE CORSICANA AND THE CITY CONDEMNED IT FOR USE OF AN INTAKE STATION. THE CITY BELIEVED THAT HEROD'S LAKE LAND HAD LITTLE VALUE; THE MAYOR CLAIMED THE LAND WAS WORTH $500.00. THE CITY REFUSED TO LISTEN TO HEROD AND THE CITY ASSUMED THAT A PREVIOUS APPRAISAL BY THE CITY ENGINEERS APPLIED TO HEROD'S LAKE LAND. THE CITY DECLINED HEROD'S OFFER OF A FREE EASEMENT ON THE LAND RATHER THAN CONDEMNATION. THE RESULT WAS A $2.5 MILLION VERDICT IN FAVOR OF HEROD.

Where do you hang your hat?

I PRACTICE LAW IN DALLAS, TX. MY PRACTICE FOCUSES ON INSURANCE RELATED MATTERS AND SOME PERSONAL INJURY LITIGATION.

Believe it or not!

IN THE 1800S, FENCE CUTTING WAS GETTING OUT OF HAND AND TEXAS RANGERS IRA ATEN AND JAMES W. KING WERE SENT UNDERCOVER TO STOP THE CRIMES. KNOWING THAT FINDING WIRE SNIPERS WAS GOING TO BE LIKE FINDING A NEEDLE IN A HAYSTACK, ATEN PROPOSED ATTACHING DYNAMITE TO THE FENCES. IF SET UP PROPERLY, THE BOMB WOULD EXPLODE WHEN SOMEONE CUT THE WIRE FENCE, SOLVING THE PROBLEM OF FENCE CUTTING. ATEN WAS ORDERED TO DROP THE BOMB IDEA AND HE AND KING WENT BACK ON DUTY ELSEWHERE!

"If you mess with the Bull, you get the horn."

~ MARK'S FAMOUS TEXAS JUSTICE SAYING

"The Visible Man"

A Famous Texas Case as Told by

MARK A. TICER

LAW OFFICE OF MARK A. TICER

Most people would not readily admit that they knew someone on Texas' death row. That was not the case with Joseph Paul Jernigan. It was my privilege to know him and represent him.

Paul was convicted and sentenced to death for the 1981 murder of Edward Hale, a seventy-five-year-old man with a loving family. In 1982, a Navarro County jury voted for death after a trial, including jury selection, which lasted about one week. Jury selection alone in a capital case should have taken weeks, if not months. His own defense counsel even later said that she would not try a dog bite case the way Paul's trial was handled.

Paul and I began our relationship in 1987 after I volunteered for the ABA Pro Bono Death Penalty Project. Texas death row inmates were desperate for representation at that time, so it made little difference that I was barely two years out of law school with no capital defense experience. Paul, knowing all this, was glad to have a lawyer.

From the first time I met Paul in Huntsville, Texas' Death Row, I appreciated and admired his candor, sincerity and accountability. From the outset, he acknowledged his guilt for Mr. Hale's death and a day did not go by that he did not think about Mr. Hale and his family. The focus on Paul's habeas corpus claim was the punishment phase of this trial. His claim had a great deal of merit considering, among other things, that jury selection was alarmingly brief and that one of his trial counsel admitted lack of preparation.

Paul was not only my client, he was my friend. Paul had phone numbers to my home, the family lake house and other spots. He called collect from time to time just to talk. He was aware of family birthdays and was known to send a note or gift he made. Paul used his own money to make my wife a pair of 14kt. gold earrings; he made me a wishing well and a table for my office. He attempted to start an Alcoholics Anonymous Chapter on Death Row. His guards liked him, with one even agreeing to sign an affidavit in support of commutation of his sentence.

Death penalty appeals are an uphill battle. Paul's case was no different. As it became clear that Paul's sentence would

Navarro County Courthouse

be carried out, we talked about death. In a passing comment during one of our conversations, Paul told me that he was going to give his body to science.

What Paul did not know, and of course neither did I, was that the Visible Man project was being developed. The idea of the Visible Man was to put a complete human cadaver on the Internet for teaching and educational purposes. The cadaver would be sliced into razor thin pieces, photographed, digitized, and placed on twenty-three CD ROMs for use on the Internet. It was a massive undertaking and a tremendous scientific feat.

Paul was executed on August 5, 1993. About one year later, I began receiving phone calls and requests for interviews from people all over the world. They wanted to talk to me about Paul. What was the Visible Man like? Who was he? Why Paul? Years later including countless newspaper and magazine writings, journal articles, several books and one foreign film shown on HBO entitled *The Virtual Corpse*, Paul's image lives on. In the HBO

> " . . . 'HE DIDN'T REALLY SAY ANYTHING ABOUT IT... AS FAR AS I KNOW, HE DIDN'T KNOW WHAT THEY WERE GOING TO DO ...ONCE HIS SOUL WAS GONE, IT WAS JUST THE BODY.' "

film that aired in 2003, his brother was quoted as saying, "He didn't really say anything about it . . . as far as I know, he didn't know what they were going to do . . . once his soul was gone, it was just the body." While most only know that the Visible Man was an executed man from Texas, I know the person, the man, the father, the friend, the human being, Paul Jernigan. It was my pleasure to have known him.

Nolan
County Courthouse

"The Red-Handed Rattlesnake Rancher"

A Famous Texas Case as Told by

D. MICHAEL "MIKE" WALLACH
WALLACH, ANDREWS & STOUFFER, P.C.

This is the story of a rattlesnake rancher from west central Texas. While feeding one of his prize pets at work one day, he was bitten on the hand. Reluctantly, he went to a hospital in the nearby big city for treatment in the emergency room. The doctors attending to him wanted to perform surgery to relieve the massive swelling which had resulted from this bite. Instead, he chose to follow the latest trend in South American snakebite treatment which he read about in a sporting magazine i.e., having his buddies hook him up to a car battery in the parking lot to shock the poison from his system. Alas, this mode of treatment was unsuccessful and he was admitted to the hospital for more conventional treatment. However, he was a man of true determination and he did not give up easily on his quest for cutting edge treatment. His wife was caught trying to sneak a stun gun into the Intensive Care Unit for additional home cure treatments!

The rancher eventually went home from the hospital and sought follow-up treatment from another doctor for the long term problems arising from his bite. Although he was bitten on the hand by his own pet rattlesnake, and had spurned certain conventional treatments in favor of some electrifying new one, he ultimately proved unhappy with the result of his subsequent treatment. Of course, this meant that he sued this doctor for his alleged disability in his snake-bitten hand, including the inability to use this hand for a variety of activities of daily work and personal life.

Well, rattlesnake ranching is an outdoor occupation and

you never know who may be watching as you do your job. Ultimately, the rancher was caught "red handed" rather candidly on camera, exhibiting more use of his snake bitten hand than he had been willing to previously admit. After all, he demonstrated, albeit unwittingly, that he was able to stand on the edge of the

> **"ULTIMATELY, THE RANCHER WAS CAUGHT 'RED HANDED' RATHER CANDIDLY ON CAMERA, EXHIBITING MORE USE OF HIS SNAKE BITTEN HAND THAN HE HAD BEEN WILLING TO PREVIOUSLY ADMIT."**

snake pit and weed eat overhanging tree limbs, catch and handle some of those lovely creatures from his pit and perform other more personal activities of daily living with relative ease. The case went away quietly after that revelation.

This was one of the more unique and at times entertaining, cases I have had the privilege of defending. The doctor being sued was my client.

Where did Nolan County get its name?
IN 1881 FROM PHILIP NOLAN, A FAMOUS MUSTANG AND FILIBUSTER. MR. NOLAN IS ALSO PARTIALLY CREDITED WITH HELPING TO FREE TEXAS FROM MEXICAN AND SPANISH RULE.

Where is the Nolan County Courthouse located?
ON THE TOWN SQUARE IN SWEETWATER, TX, HOME TO NINETY ENTRIES ON THE NATIONAL REGISTER OF HISTORIC PLACES.

Who designed the Nolan County Courthouse?
IN 1977, THE ARCHITECTURAL FIRM WELCH AND HAMPTON DESIGNED THE COURTHOUSE IN A MODERNE STYLE WITH A POLISHED GRANITE FACING.

What is the Courthouse's most unusual feature?
ITS UNUSUALLY MODERN ARCHITECTURAL DESIGN THAT IS SAID TO RESEMBLE A FORTRESS.

What is the most famous case tried in the Nolan County Courthouse?
IN 1883, THE RESIDENTS OF SWEETWATER, TX, FOUND OUT THE HARD WAY JUST HOW IMPORTANT A BANK WAS FOR THE GROWING COMMUNITY. IN FEBRUARY OF THAT YEAR, THERE WAS A RAID ON THE TOWN'S SALOON, WHICH WAS RUMORED TO HOLD UP TO $20,000 IN CASH DEPOSITS LEFT BY RESIDENTS. THE RAID RESULTED IN THE MURDER OF THE SALOON'S OWNERS AND THE WOUNDING OF A BYSTANDER. ELEVEN INDICTMENTS WERE HANDED DOWN BY THE NOLAN COUNTY COURT IN THE SALOON ROBBERY ATTEMPT. THE NEXT MONTH THOMAS TRAMMELL AND OTHERS ESTABLISHED A BANK.

Where do you hang your hat?
IN FORT WORTH, TX, WHERE I DEFEND THOSE DOCTORS, NURSES AND HOSPITALS ACROSS TEXAS WHOSE MISFORTUNE HAS MADE THEM DEFENDANT IN A MEDICAL MALPRACTICE CASE. MY OFFICE IS LOCATED IN THE SUMMIT OFFICE PARK, A GOOD COMPROMISE HALFWAY BETWEEN THE MEDICAL DISTRICT AND FORT WORTH'S COURTHOUSE.

Believe it or not!
SWEETWATER IS THE RATTLESNAKE CAPITOL OF TEXAS! IT IS HOME TO THE RATTLESNAKE ROUND-UP EACH YEAR IN MARCH!

Where did Nueces County get its name?

THE COURTHOUSE WAS NAMED AFTER THE SPANISH WORD, NUECES, MEANING NUTS. THE REFERENCE TO NUTS REFERS TO THE PECAN TREES FOUND IN THE AREA BY EARLY EXPLORERS. IT IS ALSO KNOWN AS THE SPARKLING CITY BY THE SEA.

Where is the Nueces County Courthouse located?

THE HISTORIC COURTHOUSE IS LOCATED JUST OUT OF REACH OF CORPUS CHRISTI'S TOURIST DISTRICT, ON THE TOWN SQUARE. IT IS CURRENTLY VACANT.

Who designed the Nueces County Courthouse?

THE 1914 HISTORIC COURTHOUSE AND NATIONAL REGISTER PROPERTY WAS DESIGNED BY HARVEY L. PAGE IN CLASSICAL REVIVAL STYLE IN BRICK. IN 1977, THE COURTHOUSE MOVED TO A NEW MODERN COURTHOUSE BUILDING.

What is the Courthouse's most unusual feature?

THE NEW COURTHOUSE HAS BRONZE WINDOWS WHICH YOU CAN IDENTIFY BY LOOKING AT IT FROM A DISTANCE.

What is the most famous case tried in the Nueces County Courthouse?

SANCHEZ V. PFIZER, THE FIRST REZULIN DIABETES DRUG PRODUCT LIABILITY TRIAL IN THE COUNTRY. WATTS' CLIENT, MARGIE SANCHEZ, WAS AWARDED $43 MILLION IN ACTUAL DAMAGES AND $100 MILLION IN PUNITIVE DAMAGES.

Where do you hang your hat?

IN CORPUS CHRISTI, ALTHOUGH I SPEND A LOT OF MY TIME HUNTING AND FISHING ON MY RANCH IN THREE RIVERS, TX. I BECAME A LAWYER AT AGE 21 AND BY THE TIME I WAS 35, MY FIRM HAD OVER $900,000,000 IN SETTLEMENTS AND OVER $600,000,000 IN VERDICTS. MY FIRM HANDLES COMMERCIAL AND PRODUCTS LIABILITY LITIGATION AND SPECIALIZES IN PERSONAL INJURY CASES INVOLVING DEATH AND CATASTROPHIC INJURIES.

Believe it or not!

THE CORPUS CHRISTI LIGHTHOUSE WAS USED AS A POWDER MAGAZINE FOR THE CONFEDERACY DURING THE CIVIL WAR. WHEN THE UNION ARMY THREATENED INVASION IN 1863, A GROUP OF CONFEDERATE YOUTH DECIDED TO DESTROY THE ARSENAL. THEY FILLED A BUTTER CHURN WITH GUNPOWDER AND PLACED IT BESIDE THE STRUCTURE. THE CHURN EXPLODED, DAMAGING THE TOWER BUT FAILING TO IGNITE THE POWDER INSIDE. AFTER THE WAR, THE LIGHTHOUSE WAS REPAIRED AND REMAINED IN USE UNTIL 1870 WHEN IT WAS CONDEMNED AND TORN DOWN!

"I consider trial by jury as the only anchor ever yet imagined by man, by which a government can be held to the principles of its constitution."

From Thomas Jefferson's letter to Thomas Payne

~ MIKAL'S FAMOUS TEXAS JUSTICE SAYING

"A Soiled Tale of Billion-Dollar Hip Implants"

A Famous Texas Case as Told by

MIKAL C. WATTS
WATTS LAW FIRM, L.L.P.

I was hired by three women who received soiled and defective hip implants from Sulzer Orthopedics. I scheduled my case for trial in Nueces County in September, 2001. Thousands of other claims were filed nationwide and class action lawyers were trying to ram through a secretly negotiated, insider's settlement agreement in a nationwide multi-district litigation case in Cleveland, calling for menial payouts (less than $50,000 each) and huge lawyer fees ($70 million). I refused to agree to the terms and proceeded towards trial.

Sulzer claimed I would bankrupt the deal if I went to verdict. Three days before trial, Sulzer told my clients in mediation that if they did not accept $200,000 apiece, Sulzer's lawyers would file bankruptcy the next day. I told them to go ahead. The next day, Sulzer announced the inadequate nationwide settlement (negotiated with class action lawyer who had taken no depositions at all) and asked the federal judge to issue a writ halting the trial. I tried the case.

After two days of jury deliberations, the jury seemed hung. Sulzer's lawyer began urging my clients to take the paltry amount offered, when the judge announced the jury had a note. It read: "Who gets the punitive damages?" The jury returned a verdict for $15.5 million in actual and punitive damages.

Knowing Sulzer had claimed it would file bankruptcy, I typed up a judgment and urged the court to sign it before Sulzer formally filed for bankruptcy protection. Less than 24 minutes after the verdict came in, Judge James Klager signed the final judgment, preempting Sulzer from undoing the jury's work. The

Nueces County Courthouse

class action lawyers in Cleveland then sued me and my clients to prevent us from executing the judgment. I moved to satisfy the judgment, by having sheriffs' deputies in Hays County, where Sulzer's headquarters were, start seizing the company's property. Sulzer then got the federal judge to issue a writ of prohibition against me and the Hays County Sheriff, preventing us from claiming funds meant for the settlement class.

To keep my clients from getting put at the end of the line, I told Sulzer that I would violate the federal court's order, had a toothbrush ready and to have the U.S. Marshals come get me. I hired a criminal lawyer in Cleveland to enable an attack on the judge's order on appeal. Realizing it could not stop the Cleveland judge's order from being reviewed on appeal, Sulzer's

> "... I TOLD SULZER THAT I WOULD VIOLATE THE FEDERAL COURT'S ORDER, HAD A TOOTHBRUSH READY AND TO HAVE THE U.S. MARSHALS COME GET ME."

lawyers finally relented. My clients were paid in full the actual and punitive damages they were entitled to under Texas law.

Weeks later, Sulzer announced a new billion-dollar settlement, resolving all claims against it nationwide.

Where did Orange County get its name?

ORIGINALLY CALLED MADISON, THE NAME WAS CHANGED IN 1958 FOR THE FRUIT GROWN THERE SINCE THE SETTLEMENT WAS ESTABLISHED.

Where is the Orange County Courthouse located?

ON THE DIVISION STREET IN ORANGE, TX, WHERE THREE PREVIOUS COURTHOUSES HAVE STOOD AND A TIME CAPSULE TO BE OPENED IN 2027 IS BURIED.

Who designed the Orange County Courthouse?

C.H. PAGE & BROTHER FROM AUSTIN, TX, DESIGNED THE MODERNE STYLE HISTORIC COURTHOUSE IN 1937 AND AN ADDITION WAS CONSTRUCTED IN 1960.

What is the Courthouse's most unusual feature?

IT IS MADE OF BRICK, LIMESTONE AND ITALIAN MARBLE AND IS NEARBY THE STARK MUSEUM OF ART; SAID TO BE ONE OF THE BEST MUSEUMS IN THE LONE STAR STATE.

What is the most famous case tried in the Orange County Courthouse?

IN JUNE OF 1974, A MAN WAS ARRESTED FOR ATTEMPTED ARMED ROBBERY OF A CONVENIENCE STORE. WHILE INCARCERATED, HIS BROTHER ATTEMPTED TO BREAK HIM OUT OF JAIL. THE BROTHER WAS IN POSSESSION OF A GUN AND IT WAS BELIEVED THAT THE PRISONER SOMEHOW ENDED-UP WITH A SHOTGUN AS WELL. A GUNFIGHT ENSUED AND THE POLICE CAPTAIN WAS SHOT AND KILLED. IT WAS NOT UNTIL AUGUST THAT BALLISTICS DETERMINED THAT ONE OF THE POLICE OFFICERS HAD ACTUALLY FIRED THE SHOT THAT KILLED THE CAPTAIN. DISTRICT ATTORNEY JIM SHARON PROSECUTED THE CASE AND THE PRISONER WAS SENTENCED TO LIFE.

Where do you hang your hat?

AT THE LAW FIRM OF KROGER, MYERS, FRISBY & HIRSCH, A NATIONALLY RECOGNIZED LEADER IN INSURANCE LAW AND MALPRACTICE DEFENSE LOCATED IN HOUSTON, HARRIS COUNTY, TEXAS.

Believe it or not!

THE THIRD FLOOR OF THE COURTHOUSE ORIGINALLY SERVED AS A DORMITORY FOR IMPOUNDED JURIES AND THE FACT THAT IT WAS ONLY ONE ROOM WAS NOT AN ISSUE, BECAUSE AT THAT TIME THE JURIES CONSISTED OF ONLY MEN, AS WOMEN WERE NOT ALLOWED TO SERVE!

"You can be a bear or a bull, but not a pig."

~ JAY'S FAMOUS TEXAS JUSTICE SAYING

"The Eccentric Physician"

A Famous Texas Case as Told by

JAY D. HIRSCH

KROGER, MYERS, FRISBY & HIRSCH

Hirsch was hired to represent the brother of a general practitioner physician who was on staff at a local hospital in Orange, Texas. The hospital was partially owned by the brother whom Hirsch was representing through a corporation out of Houston, Texas.

The lawsuit began as a physician who had undergone a series of personality changes began acting strangely. It was believed he had actually operated after hours on some animals in the hospital surgical suite. All of his crazy activities were being reported to his brother, who was a partner at the hospital. As a result of the continued irrational conduct, including walking the halls at various times during the night and waking up patients who were not even under his care, my client, the doctor's brother, went to the county judge and asked that the irrational physician be picked-up under a custodial warrant for evaluation and potential treatment for some type of bipolar activity or manic depression. The physician was incarcerated and placed in a private facility away from the hospital, evaluated and found to be manic depressive and required treatment for several months.

After the physician was appropriately treated, he was allowed to resume his work, but he refused to go back to the hospital. He began practicing nearby and then filed a lawsuit against my client, his brother, the corporation who owned the hospital, the chief of staff who was another physician at the hospital and the administrator of the hospital who was also a nurse. The doctor believed that his brother and the hospital were involved in a conspiracy to deprive him of making an honest living and that there was nothing wrong with him and his entire life was being turned upside down by the irrational conduct of those in the conspiracy.

The highlight of the trial included an exchange between the previously detained brother and the caring brother, who had sought out mental help for his brother and initiated the previous commitment proceeding. In the exchange, the doctor referred to his caring brother as "Brutes" in loud tones before the jury. The jury seemed amused at the apparent love-hate relationship between the two brothers. The lawyers appeared self-assured and apparently believed things were going well and that a swift defense verdict would be forthcoming. Deliberations were underway.

Orange
County Courthouse

After three days of proceedings, the jury deliberated for several hours and finally told the judge that they could not reach a verdict. A hung jury! The lawyers were shocked. After the jurors were released, the lawyers were allowed to visit with them about what had happened during their deliberation.

What the lawyers found out during their discussions was that the jury had taken on the responsibility of also deciding an important moral issue. The moral issue involved a "rumored affair" between a staff physician and the nurse administrator. In the juror's mind, this meant that the hospital administrator should be punished for the alleged indiscretion but there simply was not a way to answer the questions propounded to the jury in

> "IT WAS BELIEVED HE HAD ACTUALLY OPERATED AFTER HOURS ON SOME ANIMALS IN THE HOSPITAL SURGICAL SUITE."

The Junkyard Dawg

a manner that would come back with such a verdict. Lawyers who try cases out of the county where they are familiar must know the jury panel or must certainly make some effort to find out the background of the jury panel, including what they might know or perceive about various parties to the litigation.

Six weeks following the trial, various motions were filed in which the judge decided that the case had no merit as a matter of law and dismissed the lawsuit so that a new trial was not necessary. Hirsch certainly learned a lesson of how important it is to be well informed by those who are going to sit on the jury seeking justice in every sense of the word!

Where did Palo Pinto County get its name?

FROM THE SPOTTED OAK TREE WHICH IS PROMINENT IN THE AREA. PALO IS SPANISH FOR TRUNK, WHILE PINTO MEANS PAINTED.

Where is the Palo Pinto County Courthouse located?

IN PALO PINTO, TX, ON US 180, NOT FAR FROM MINERAL WELLS STATE PARK, WHICH WAS ALSO KNOWN AS ROBBERS ROOST IN THE 1800s.

Who designed the Palo Pinto County Courthouse?

PRESTON M. GEREN SR. AND M.A. HOWELL WERE THE ARCHITECTS OF THIS HISTORIC COURTHOUSE IN 1940 WITH CLASSICAL ACCENTS AND A TEXAS RENAISSANCE STYLE IN SANDSTONE. THE PALO PINTO COUNTY COURTHOUSE WAS FIRST BUILT IN 1857 AND RE-MODELED WITH THE STONE RECYCLED FROM THE ORIGINAL 1940 COURTHOUSE.

What is the courthouse's most unusual feature?

THE COURTHOUSE IS AMAZINGLY DETAILED, INCLUDING BRASS DOORKNOBS AND LIGHT FIXTURES ADORNED WITH EAGLES.

What is the most famous case tried in the Palo Pinto County Courthouse?

IN 1996, HELEN MOORE DRUGGED CASEY ELLIOTT WITH MORPHINE AND THEN CUT HIS BODY UP INTO PIECES AND DISTRIBUTED THE PIECES THROUGHOUT FOUR COUNTIES. SHE WAS INDICTED IN PALO PINTO COUNTY AND PLEAD GUILTY TO AVOID THE DEATH PENALTY. THE CASE WAS PROFILED ON THE HBO PROGRAM AUTOPSY.

Where do you hang your hat?

AT THE DENT LAW FIRM IN FORT WORTH, TX, WHERE I SPECIALIZE IN PERSONAL INJURY TRIAL WORK AND AT THE DENT RANCH IN PALO PINTO, TX, WHERE YOU CAN FIND ME ON WEEKENDS HUNTING AND FISHING!

Believe it or not!

THE AREA OF MINERAL WELLS BECAME FAMOUS IN THE LATE 1800s AS A HIDEOUT FOR OUTLAWS TRAVELING BETWEEN FORT WORTH AND FORT GRIFFIN AND AS PEOPLE BEGAN FLOCKING THERE TO RECEIVE THE HEALING BENEFITS OF THE "CRAZY WATER WELL!"

"Never trust a corporation or insurance company to do the right thing."

~ DWAIN'S FAMOUS TEXAS JUSTICE SAYING

"Dangerous & Illegal Rx Drugs"

A Famous Texas Case as Told by

DWAIN DENT
THE DENT LAW FIRM

Keeping the tradition of law and legend, Dwain Dent has pursued corporate and insurance lawbreakers for the citizens of Palo Pinto and North Texas for the past two decades. Most recently he represented Palo Pinto citizens against drug manufacturer Wyeth-Ayres and children from Weatherford and Fort Worth, TX, against the drug manufacturer O'Neal Jones, recovering millions for victims of dangerous and illegal drugs sold to unsuspecting families.

Rachel Eskew died on March 20, 1984, at the age of four weeks. Rachel's mother, Jacque Gibson White, was told that the premature baby's cause of death was kidney and heart failure. It would be eleven more years until White learned the true reason for her daughter's death.

White's only child was born in Weatherford and rushed to Cook Children's Medical Center where she spent each day of her short life in the neo-natal intensive care unit. Like most premature babies, Rachel was born with breathing difficulties. However, doctors at the hospital gave Rachel's mother every glimmer of hope; her survival chances were at least 85 percent.

Rachel died suddenly while being treated in the NICU and her mother was made to feel as though this was a common occurrence among preemies. Despite the doctors' anticipations of Rachel's good health, she had still passed away and her mother did not know what to do besides place the blame for her daughter's death on herself. It was not until 1995 that White could release the guilt from her conscience.

Two years after Rachel's death, Dr. Robert Brown uncovered the actual cause; E-ferol syndrome. E-ferol, a vitamin E solution, although not approved by the FDA, had been given to premature babies in the Dallas/ Fort Worth area as a blindness preventative, causing the death of 38 babies. Brown had studied the effects of E-ferol the year of Rachel's death, even publishing an article in Pediatrics (published by the American Academy of Pediatrics) stating that the effects of the drug were harmful to premature babies. In 1986, Brown reviewed and amended Rachel's original autopsy, officially stating that her cause of death was not lung failure, but E-ferol syndrome.

Brown quickly submitted his findings to the hospital and Rachel's original doctor, even offering to meet with Rachel's parents to

Palo Pinto County Courthouse

discuss the true cause of her death. Ms. White was never told of Dr. Brown's findings.

Nine years after Dr. Brown's findings, Palo Pinto County rancher and Attorney Dwain Dent headed up a lawsuit to extinguish some of the emotional anguish that White and other families in Palo Pinto and Tarrant Counties had been through. Brown fought to punish the manufacturer of the drug, O'Neal Jones, for distributing the drug without FDA approval. A federal lawsuit was also launched to ensure that hospitals must inform former patients and their families if any part of their treatment may have been detrimental to their health. Cook Children's Medical Center adamantly argued that disclosing this information was a breach of doctor-patient confidentiality.

Two executives of the drug manufacturer were criminally prosecuted in federal trials and convicted of fraud and served a six-month sentence in federal prison. Also, as a result of the unnecessary deaths, there was a congressional hearing questioning the country's policies on regulating pharmaceutical drugs.

> "... THERE WAS A CONGRESSIONAL HEARING QUESTIONING THE COUNTRY'S POLICIES ON REGULATING PHARMACEUTICAL DRUGS."

Along with many of the other families affected by the dangerous conduct, Dwain Dent sued the two companies on behalf of Ms. White and her deceased child and won a large settlement. Across, the state of Texas, millions of dollars were procured from the drug companies. White is now an advocate for patient/ family rights. White spent all the years after Rachel's death blaming herself until she knew it was a drug that caused her daughter's death. "I would not have had to live with that guilt so long had I known," she said. Mr. Dent continues to pursue the drug manufacturers on behalf of families across the country.

Parker
County Courthouse

GRANT (LEFT) AND GREG BLAIES

"The Watchdogs of Parker County"

A Famous Texas Case as Told by
GREGORY P. & GRANT D. BLAIES
BLAIES & HIGHTOWER, L.L.P.

Texas is full of high-powered attorneys and landmark cases that have set precedent for the future, not just in Texas, but across the nation. Attorney Greg Blaies certainly knows this type of law first hand, as he has represented many such notable corporations and individuals, including HMOs, airlines and many physicians and hospitals. These are the cases that make the headlines and present the potential for significant exposure.

One of Greg's memorable trials occurred prior to the enactment of the HMO Liability Act, which allows direct suits against health maintenance organizations in healthcare liability matters. Greg represented a local HMO accused of negligence that resulted in the blinding of twin boys.

The plaintiffs claimed that when the boys were born prematurely, the physicians failed to perform screening tests that would have allowed for the twins' premature eye condition to be monitored and then treated timely. The plaintiffs alleged that the retinal defect was a relatively known and common problem for premature babies and that it was standard practice to screen, follow and then treat at the appropriate time in the child's development. The plaintiffs' allegation against the HMO was that it pressured the doctors to cut costs by cutting corners and that its incentives and payment arrangements with the physicians resulted in the physicians failing to timely and properly treat the twins' condition.

Many defendants were involved in this case and in closing argument, the plaintiffs asked the jury for over $120 million. Greg successfully defended and the jury returned a no negligence finding against the HMO. It is worth noting that they were the only defendant in the case who was not negligent. This was a rewarding victory to be sure.

> *"Each person's perception is their own reality".*
>
> ~ GREG'S FAMOUS TEXAS JUSTICE SAYING

The strength of Blaies & Hightower, L.L.P., is that it operates as a team, says Greg, founding partner. "Every person here is important," Greg says, "and as a group we are much stronger than any of us would be individually." It is that team approach to individual cases that has led his group to their litigation success. Greg and his firm were part of a trial team representing one of the word's largest airlines against a software manufacturer that licensed its automated screen scraping software to travel agencies. Those agencies then retrieved fare and schedule data from the airline's website without its consent, allowing travel agents to issue tickets with a lower fare. The airline, through its trial team, successfully brought this suit to preclude cutting edge technology companies from stealing its important business information. This precedent setting case is an example of how legal team work provided justice to their Texas clients.

Greg and his firm have handled litigation for years in the defense of county entities and their elected officials. Greg and his brother Grant are proud to represent Parker County whenever the government is

"THE PLAINTIFFS' ALLEGATION AGAINST THE HMO WAS THAT IT PRESSURED THE DOCTORS TO CUT COSTS BY CUTTING CORNERS . . ."

involved in litigation. The Blaies brother's legal representation of Parker County has specifically included the defense of county commissioners, county judges and the sheriff's department involving claims of civil rights violations, vehicular accidents and wrongful death suits. It is the day-to-day protection of the government and citizens of Parker County that have earned them the trust and respect of the Texas Association of Counties and Parker County.

Not only do they represent Parker County, but the Blaies brothers represent several counties and county officials in Texas. The Blaies' affiliation with the Texas Association of Counties has afforded them the opportunity to protect these county governments and their individual citizens in the courthouse. Most of us take for granted the way in which our local governments function and the positive effect it has on all aspects of our lives. It is attorneys like Greg and Grant Blaies who defend these privileges that very few of us even acknowledge.

Where did Parker County get its name?
FROM ISAAC PARKER, AN EARLY TEXAS LEGISLATOR. THE COUNTY WAS ORGANIZED IN 1855. WEATHERFORD WAS NAMED FOR TEXAS SENATOR JEFFERSON WEATHERFORD.

Where is the Parker County Courthouse located?
THIS HISTORIC COURTHOUSE SITS PROUDLY ON THE SQUARE, AT THE INTERSECTION OF PALO PINTO AND FORT WORTH STREET AND MAIN STREET, JUST THIRTY MILES WEST OF FORT WORTH.

Who designed the Parker County Courthouse?
DODSON & DUDLEY DESIGNED THE HISTORIC COURTHOUSE IN 1886 IN A SECOND EMPIRE STYLE WHICH IS SAID TO BE "ELEGANCE UNEXPECTED ON THE EDGE OF THE TEXAS FRONTIER."

What is the Courthouse's most unusual feature?
IT IS BUILT ENTIRELY OF LIMESTONE. IT FEATURES A FOUR-FACE CLOCK BY SETH THOMAS, ORIGINALLY INSTALLED JULY 24, 1897. IT IS A NATIONAL REGISTRY PROPERTY.

What is the most famous case tried in the Parker County Courthouse?
IN NOVEMBER OF 2003, THREE MEN PUT PARKER COUNTY ON NATIONAL NEWS WHEN THEY ESCAPED FROM PARKER COUNTY JAIL. ONE OF THE MEN, JAMES DOUGLAS HOLDEN, 38, CHANGED HIS PLEA FROM "GUILTY" TO "NOT GUILTY" AFTER BEING EXAMINED BY THE PROSECUTION. THIS WAS THE FIRST TIME DISTRICT ATTORNEY DON SCHNEBLY HAD SEEN A CHANGED VERDICT IN THAT STAGE OF THE PROSECUTION IN HIS SEVENTEEN-YEAR CAREER. HOLDEN WAS FOUND GUILTY OF ESCAPE AND SENTENCED TO LIFE IN PRISON.

Where do you hang your hat?
AT THE FIRM OF BLAIES & HIGHTOWER, L.L.P. IN THE CARTER BURGESS BUILDING LOCATED ON MAIN STREET IN FORT WORTH, TX. THE ATTORNEYS AT B&H HAVE EXTENSIVE TRIAL EXPERIENCE, REPRESENTING ITS CLIENTS STATEWIDE IN BOTH STATE AND FEDERAL COURT, CONCENTRATING IN THE AREAS OF HEALTH CARE LIABILITY, PERSONAL INJURY, GOVERNMENTAL LIABILITY AND COMMERCIAL LITIGATION.

Believe it or not!
ONE OF THE ORIGINAL CONTRACTORS OF THE CURRENT COURTHOUSE SHOT HIS PARTNER TO DEATH AT THE CONSTRUCTION SITE, BUT WAS FOUND NOT GUILTY IN 1888 AFTER HIS THIRD TRIAL. THE FIRST TWO, HELD IN 1885 AND 1887, WERE HUNG JURIES!

Where did Pecos County get its name?

ORGANIZED IN 1872, THE AREA IS NAMED FOR THE PECOS RIVER, WHICH FLOWS ALONG THE NORTHERN BOUNDARY OF THE COUNTY.

Where is the Pecos County Courthouse located?

THE PECOS COUNTY COURTHOUSE IS LOCATED IN FORT STOCKTON, THE COUNTY SEAT, ON CALLAGHAN STREET IN THE TOWN'S COURTHOUSE SQUARE, WHICH IS ALSO HOME TO THE COUNTY'S FIRST SCHOOL, BUILT IN 1883.

Who designed the Pecos County Courthouse?

BUILT IN 1883 WITH STONE IN A CLASSICAL REVIVAL STYLE, THIS IS THE ONLY COURTHOUSE THAT PECOS COUNTY HAS EVER HAD. IT ONCE HAD A DOME REMOVED, BUT A NEW FABULOUS COPPER DOME WAS ADDED TO THIS HISTORIC COURTHOUSE DURING A REMODELING IN 1911-1912 BY ARCHITECT L.B. WESTERMAN.

What is the Courthouse's most unusual feature?

THE COURTHOUSE SQUARE FEATURES THE 1859 "ZERO STONE" WHICH WAS A BASE POINT FROM WHICH ALL WEST TEXAS LAND SURVEYS ORIGINATED.

What is the most famous case tried in the Pecos County Courthouse?

IN 1991, SONIA CACY AWOKE TO SMOKE AND FLAMES IN THE HOUSE. SHE TRIED TO WAKE HER 76-YEAR-OLD UNCLE, BUT THE FLAMES WERE SO INTENSE SHE WAS FORCED OUT OF THE HOUSE. HER UNCLE DIED IN THE FIRE. SHE WAS TRIED FOR ARSON MURDER AND DURING THE TRIAL, THE PROSECUTION SAID THERE WERE TRACES OF GASOLINE ON CACY'S CLOTHES, CONVINCING THE JURY SHE HAD DOUSED HER UNCLE WITH GASOLINE AND SET HIM ON FIRE. CACY WAS SENTENCED TO 99 YEARS IN PRISON. NO OTHER AGENCY, INCLUDING THE FBI, WAS ABLE TO FIND THE TRACE AMOUNTS OF GASOLINE ON CACY'S CLOTHING.

Where do you hang your hat?

AT WALKER SEWELL LLP ON ELM STREET IN DALLAS, TX. AT WALKER SEWELL LLP, WE SPECIALIZE IN ALL TYPES OF CONTRACT, BUSINESS TORTS AND INSURANCE RELATED LITIGATION. YOU CAN FIND US AT WWW.WALKERSEWELL.COM.

Believe it or not!

THE COLORFUL OLD WEST LEGEND, "HANGING JUDGE ROY BEAN," WAS APPOINTED JUSTICE OF THE PEACE FOR PECOS COUNTY IN THE 1880S. ACCORDING TO THE LEGEND, BEAN WAS A FIERY CHARACTER WHOSE PHILOSOPHY WAS "HANG 'EM NOW, TRY 'EM LATER!"

"A well regulated Militia, being necessary to the security of a free State, the right of the people to keep and bear Arms, shall not be infringed."

Second Amendment United States Constitution

~ JIM'S FAMOUS TEXAS JUSTICE SAYING

"A Tribute to Judge Horace E. Resley"

A Famous Texas Case as Told by

JAMES WALKER
WALKER SEWELL LLP

Judge Horace Ernest Resley was born May 9, 1897. Ever patriotic, he joined the Army as a young man of barely 21 in the summer of 1918 and Texas would soon be thankful. During his service he served as an infantryman under General John J. "Blackjack" Pershing in World War I. It was Pershing who led his forces in the Meuse-Argonne offensive of 1918. Resley was among the nearly 3-million-man army that Pershing had to form and train in a year and a half. This, fortunately, was not the end of Resley's run, however. He again served his country during World War II when he was assigned as chief to a 21-man force. They had been assigned to guard the Pacific Air School, which was a cadet training center located on grounds now used by the Pecos County Airport.

After his service in the Army, Resley moved to Fort Stockton in 1928. Wanting to continue his life of public service and dedication to his country, he was named Fort Stockton's City Judge in 1947 and served the citizens of Fort Stockton in this capacity for more than 24 years before he retired in 1971. As city judge, he processed more then 19,500 cases through his courtroom. Through his long tenure, he proved that he was as courageous and strong on the bench as he had been on the battle field. When he stepped down, despite his retirement, he was affectionately known to his friends and colleagues as "The Judge."

Outside of his legal career, Judge Resley never lost his love for firearms that he acquired while in the Army. He was well known throughout his life for his expertise in making and shooting muzzle-loading rifles and pistols. He was a charter

Pecos
County Courthouse

member of the Texas Muzzle Loading Rifle Association and won the Texas State Muzzle Loading Rifle Championship a total of four times, including consecutive championships in 1947 and 1948. In 1958, he placed third in the National Muzzle Loading Rifle Association Championship emerging from a field of more then 1,800 shooters. In 1978, at the age of 81, Judge Resley not only won the 50 and 100 yard target shoots, but he was also named "Muzzle Loader of the Year" at the annual state match held in Brady, Texas.

In addition to the skill he possessed for firing the weapons, he also reconstructed all types of large caliber

> **". . . MUZZLE-LOADING RIFLES WITH A 'RESLEY BARREL' ARE CHERISHED AS SOME OF THE MOST ACCURATE AND BEST MADE RIFLES OF THEIR KIND."**

muzzle loading rifles using a coal forge and a handmade drill press to bore out his rifle barrels. Any parts that required replacement were fabricated by hand. Even the rifle stocks were hand carved when necessary. It could take more than 190 hours to complete a single rifle. Even today, muzzle-loading rifles with a "Resley Barrel" are cherished as some of the most accurate and best made rifles of their kind.

Where did Potter County get its name?

Organized in 1887 "Yellow Brick Road," as Potter County was known, was named for Robert Potter who served as Secretary of the Texas Navy, fighting in the Battle of San Jacinto. He also rallied for Texas' independence and signed the Declaration of Independence.

Where is the Potter County Courthouse located?

In the county seat of Amarillo, TX, named after the nearby creek by Spaniards for the color yellow in Spanish, amarillo.

Who designed the Potter County Courthouse?

Townes, Lightfoot & Funk designed the 1931 Moderne style terra-cotta and concrete Lone star Historic Courthouse.

What is the Courthouse's most unusual feature?

The courthouse was built with funds from the Work Projects Administration in Art Deco style with an unusual doorway with arches and incredible detail.

What is the most famous case tried in the Potter County Courthouse?

After a mistrial in Tarrant County, the Cullen Davis trial was moved to Potter County. There the jury acquitted him of capital murder in the death of his stepdaughter, who was killed in the 1976 shooting at his Fort Worth mansion.

Where do you hang your hat?

At the office of Jackson Walker LLP in Houston, TX, as well as in Dallas, where I specialize in complex litigation, media law and intellectual property and I spend my summers in Canada.

Believe it or not!

Chip used to be a sports writer for The Miami Herald and Philadelphia Inquirer!

"What goes around comes around."
~ Chip's Famous Texas Justice Saying

"Texas Beef Corp. v. Oprah Winfrey"

A Famous Texas Case as Told by
Charles "Chip" Babcock
Jackson Walker LLP

Chip Babcock was on the front page of every newspaper in Texas and the world for representing media mogul Oprah Winfrey in a libel suit filed against her by two cattle feeders in 1996.

The *Texas Beef Corp. v. Winfrey* case originally began at the Potter County Courthouse in Amarillo, TX, after the Oprah show had aired a segment in 1996 about "dangerous foods." Winfrey and her guest, the director of the Humane Society's Eating with Conscience Campaign, raised the question "Could It Happen Here?" in the midst of the break out of the mad-cow disease in England. The comments were in response to the many cattle that were plagued by the disease in England, and the fear that humans were being stricken with the disease, as well.

The meat industry did not like the remarks of Winfrey and one of her guests. Two cattle feeders were outraged at her comments made to millions of viewers all over the world. Oprah's show reaches 20 million viewers a day and one cattleman claimed that because of the broad audience that Oprah reaches, cattle prices dropped severely after the airing of the show and his company lost $7 million because of false statements on the show.

A battle had begun. The lawsuit included claims of libel and the violation of Chapter 96 of the Texas Civic Practices and Remedies Code, which actually confirms liability if someone intentionally circulates false information about a perishable food product.

However, amidst all of the legal commotion, one of the most important events occurred outside the courtroom when Oprah decided to move her show to Amarillo for the duration of

Potter
County Courthouse

the trial. Before she came to town, local sentiment was at best mixed about the case. But once Oprah and her excellent staff arrived they won the town over. "I remember going to see her first show just to gauge local reaction," recalls Babcock. "When she first appeared on stage it was electric. People just jumped out of their seats. It was quite an experience."

> **"CHIP BABCOCK WAS ON THE FRONT PAGE OF EVERY NEWSPAPER IN TEXAS AND THE WORLD FOR REPRESENTING MEDIA MOGUL OPRAH WINFREY IN A LIBEL SUIT FILED AGAINST HER BY TWO CATTLE FEEDERS IN 1996."**

As far as the accusations were concerned, Oprah felt that she was simply opening up a forum for debate about a health issue she thought her viewers and the American public at large wanted to be informed about. Babcock and Winfrey won their case based on our First Amendment Rights set forth in the Constitution of the United States—freedom of speech. Since people have a right to their opinion and to comment on how they feel, Winfrey and her guest won the case based on their right to speak out. This case set a precedent for media/intellectual properties everywhere and Babcock became the "go-to" lawyer on the subject for attorney's state wide and nationally. His notoriety as the "Oprah lawyer" precedes him everywhere he goes.

Presidio
County Courthouse

"Assault Weapons for Drugs"

A Famous Texas Case as Told by
JOAQUIN JACKSON
TEXAS RANGER, RETIRED

The town of Presidio, Texas, lies on the Rio Bravo or Rio Grande River some fifty miles south, southwest of Marfa, Texas, in Presidio County. In 1999, information was received that a subject who we will call Jose was converting semi-auto assault weapons into fully automatic weapons and trading them for narcotics across the River into Ojinaja, Mexico, just across the river. Jose also had duel citizenship which gave him full freedom of movement across the river or international bridge. A search warrant was issued and served on a small adobe house in Presidio. This house originally belonged to Jose's mother, but she was deceased.

Local deputies and federal officers of the Immigration and Border Patrol assisted us in executing the warrant. In conducting the search, several semi-assault weapons were found that had been converted to full automatic weapons and some had silencers attached. In the back room, Jose had a full assortment of parts for conversions and templates laying out a pattern to convert certain weapons. Jose was not at home, but was staying across the river in Ojinaja, as he had homes on both sides.

Working with officers on both sides of the river, arrangements were made to meet with Jose. He said he would meet me at the middle of the international bridge; I was with the Agent in Charge of Immigration at the Port of Entry in Presidio. We approached the middle of the bridge and the agent stopped and said, "Joaquin, I know what you've got on your mind and if you do what I think you plan on doing, I will get fired from my job. I know you are planning to jerk him across the line if he meets us at the

> *"Say what you mean, mean what you say, and tell it like it is."*
>
> ~ Joaquin's Famous Texas Justice Saying

middle." I told him, yes, that was what I was thinking, but I would not do anything to cost him his job. Jose did not show, but I later talked to him in Ojinaja at a café.

Jose finally turned himself in to me and the DEA wanted to brief him as to his narcotic business. He went to work for the DEA to develop narcotic cases with his

"IN CONDUCTING THE SEARCH, SEVERAL SEMI-ASSAULT WEAPONS WERE FOUND THAT HAD BEEN CONVERTED TO FULL AUTOMATIC WEAPONS . . ."

connections and was later caught with cocaine and sent to the federal penitentiary.

After catching Jose, I notified the ATF, the Federal Bureau of Alcohol, Tobacco and Firearms, in reference to the machine guns and silencers possessed by Jose. The Federal prosecutor declined prosecution in this case. The Federal agency sentencing on firearms violations is currently more severe than State law. I believe we do not need more firearms laws, but need to enforce the ones we have.

Where did Presidio County get its name?
In 1875, Presidio County was originally named "El Presidio del Norte," Spanish for the fort of the north.

Where is the Presidio County Courthouse located?
On the town square in Marfa, TX, which was a popular backdrop for Hollywood films in the 1950s and '60s.

Who designed the Presidio County Courthouse?
This 1886 Historic Courthouse and National Register Property built of brick and stone in a Second Empire style was designed by Alfred Giles. The Presidio County Courthouse was rededicated on January 5th 2002 by the Texas Historical Commission's Texas Courthouse Preservation Program.

What is the Courthouse's most unusual feature?
The current courthouse is the only one that Presidio County has ever seen. Built in 1886, it is known for being one of the top preserved courthouses in the state.

What is the most famous case tried in the Presidio County Courthouse?
Frank Brown v. Steve Spurgin; In 2000, the citizens of the 83rd Judicial District voted three times to determine which Democratic candidate, Frank Brown or Steve Spurgin, would be their district attorney. Voters cast their ballots in a March primary, an April runoff and second runoff in August, following a trial alleging improper handling of mail-in ballots. Brown filed suit after losing to Spurgin by two votes in the April runoff. He alleged that Spurgin exerted undue influence on voters and questioned the legality of ballots cast early by elderly and disabled Hispanic voters—some could neither read nor write. The judge voided the election, and a number of the ballots. The voters returned to the polls and Brown won by 41 votes.

Where do you hang your hat?
I worked as a Texas Ranger in Uvalde, TX, for 21 years and another six years in Alpine, TX, before I retired there. I currently do civil Private Investigation and Security work across Texas and New Mexico.

Believe it or not!
If you ever visit Marfa, TX, as evening sets in, you might think you're seeing UFOs in the dusk sky. The truth is . . . no one can really explain what causes the colorful lights that twinkle over the Chinati Mountains. Locals call them the Marfa Lights!

Where did Rains County get its name?

BOTH THE COUNTY SEAT, WHICH IS THE TOWN OF EMORY AND THE COUNTY OF RAINS WERE NAMED AFTER JUDGE EMORY RAINS, A TEXAS LEGISLATOR WHO INTRODUCED A BILL IN THE TEXAS STATE LEGISLATURE ON JUNE 9, 1870, TO CREATE RAINS COUNTY.

Where is the Rains County Courthouse located?

ON THE TOWN SQUARE IN EMORY, TX, GATEWAY TO LAKE TOWAKONI, ONE OF TEXAS' BEST FISHING LAKES.

Who designed the Rains County Courthouse?

THE BRYAN ARCHITECTURAL COMPANY DESIGNED THE COURTHOUSE WHICH WAS CONSTRUCTED IN 1908 FROM WHITE BRICK MANUFACTURED AT THE GINGER BRICK PLANT IN GINGER, TX. THE HISTORIC COURTHOUSE WAS BUILT IN A TEXAS RENAISSANCE STYLE SHAPED LIKE A MALTESE CROSS.

What is the Courthouse's most unusual feature?

WHEN THE 1884 COURTHOUSE BURNED TO THE GROUND IN 1890, THE VAULT, WHICH HOUSED THE COUNTY RECORDS, WAS THE ONLY THING LEFT STANDING. YOU'LL FIND THIS OLD VAULT IN THE NEW COURTHOUSE.

What is the most famous case tried in the Rains County Courthouse?

THE MOST FAMOUS CASE IS THE CASE KEVIN CHAPMAN AND I TRIED WHICH I WILL DISCUSS HERE SHORTLY. HOWEVER, THE SECOND MOST FAMOUS CASE TO BE TRIED IN THIS BELOVED COURTHOUSE IS THE MURDER TRIAL OF J.W. BERGEN. IN DECEMBER, 1916, CLARENCE A. GLASS WAS MURDERED DURING A BANK ROBBERY WHILE WORKING AS A CASHIER AT THE FIRST STATE BANK IN EMORY. AN ARMED ROBBER TRIED TO FORCE GLASS TO EMPTY THE CASH DRAWERS OF THE TIMED SAFE WITHIN THE VAULT. AFTER THREE FUTILE ATTEMPTS TO OPEN THE SAFE, THE ROBBER SHOT GLASS IN THE BACK, KILLING HIM. J.W. BERGEN WAS THE NAMED SUSPECT AND AFTER HIS CAPTURE IN ALEXANDRIA, LOUISIANA, HE WAS BROUGHT BACK TO RAINS COUNTY ON CHRISTMAS DAY, 1916, TO STAND TRIAL. AFTER A SENSATIONAL TRIAL, BERGEN WAS FOUND NOT GUILTY.

Where do you hang your hat?

IN DALLAS, TX, WITH MY PARTNERS IN OUR CRIMINAL LAW FIRM, MY FRIENDS AND MY BELOVED DOGS—JESSIE AND JENNIE.

Believe it or not!

THE DESCENDANTS OF EMORY'S FIRST HOMESTEADERS COMPRISE NINETY PERCENT OF TODAY'S POPULATION IN RAINS COUNTY. EMORY'S POPULATION IS A WHOPPING 818!

"No guts, No glory."
~ DAN'S FAMOUS TEXAS JUSTICE SAYING

"132 Days to Justice"

A Famous Texas Case as Told by

DANIEL K. HAGOOD
FITZPATRICK & HAGOOD
A PROFESSIONAL CORPORATION

In January, 1988, the most famous and longest running trial of any kind to ever occur in Rains County took place. Five co-defendants, three men and two women, were charged with possession of methamphetamine with intent to distribute. Scheduled to last two weeks, the trial became a marathon, lasting into mid-May, 1988.

I was appointed as Special Prosecutor to represent the State in this case and my great and good friend, Dallas County Assistant District Attorney Kevin Chapman, tried the case with me. By the time of the trial, one of the co-defendants, "Doc" Wolfe, had been mysteriously killed by a drug overdose. Not surprisingly, the other four defendants, Tommy Charles Haynes, Christy Lynn Lewis, Tametha Lynne Tarrant and Billy W. Stokes used Doc's death to their advantage by blaming Doc Wolfe at trial.

The facts of the case were pretty simple: all five of the co-defendants were arrested following the June, 1987, discovery of one of the biggest illegal drug labs in Texas history. The drug lab was located in a mobile home north of Emory, Texas. On the day of the arrest, fourteen law enforcement officers surrounded the mobile home, smashing in the front door with an ax. Doc Wolfe and Billy Stokes attempted to escape out the back door while Haynes, Lewis and Tarrant were apprehended in the front room of the trailer where they were standing around a freshly made batch of methamphetamine.

Fifteen pounds of the drug, with a $2 million street value, were confiscated. Also found behind a false wall in a barn adjacent to the mobile home was a larger drug lab with $50,000 worth of laboratory equipment and 55-gallon drums of chemicals used to make the meth. A chemist from the Department of Public Safety testified in the trial that the almost fifteen pounds of methamphetamine was at least 70% pure, which attested to the uncommon skill and sophistication of these drug manufacturers.

The defendants were desperate to win and during the course of the trial a number of death threats were leveled against the participants. However, when a death threat was leveled against Presiding Judge Lanny Ramsay, he called in the Texas Rangers and the law truly came to town that day. Once the Rangers arrived, a great sense of safety enveloped the trial participants

Rains
County Courthouse

(including myself) and I knew that justice would be done in this case.

After eighteen weeks of trial, we argued this case on a Thursday night. The courtroom was packed as both sides exhorted the jury to find for their respective positions. After only 62 minutes of deliberation (45 minutes of which, we later learned, were devoted to consuming the dinner the county catered for the jurors!) the seven women, five man jury found all four defendants guilty as charged. Sentences for the defendants ranged from fifteen to fifty years in prison and a total of $260,000 was fined.

Because of the length of the trial, many of the jurors faced financial hardships and loss to their businesses. The trial lasted over four months and members of the jury were paid only $6 a day by the county. In true Texas fashion, the Rains County community came together to establish the "Love Fund for Jury of Drug Trial" fund. A special bank account was set up in the towns of Emory, Point, Lone Oak and Alba where members of the community

"FIFTEEN POUNDS OF THE DRUG, WITH A $2 MILLION STREET VALUE, WERE CONFISCATED."

donated funds to show their civic pride in appreciation for the members of the jury who had sacrificed their livelihoods in the name of justice.

Since this trial, I have continued to prosecute and represent defendants in high-profile cases across the state in both state and federal court, but I have never had a case of the length or more fraught with difficulty than the case Kevin and I tried in Emory. It will always remain as one of the highlights of my legal career.

Red River
County Courthouse

"Thou Shalt Not Bear False Witness."

"The Price of Liberty"

A Famous Texas Case as Told by
THE HONORABLE JUDGE
JIM LOVETT
6TH DISTRICT COURT

In 1980, after they had passed Rick Holden's rigorous polygraph examination, I agreed to represent three teenagers in a civil rights case against the Red River County Sheriff's office and the Clarksville Police Department. The case arose from a severe beating administered in the local jail and life threats made by the Chief Deputy Sheriff of Red River County on a teenager, accompanied by a conspiratorial cover-up by Clarksville Police Officers.

The next night my law office burned to the ground. Tightly packed files and law books on shelves that fell away from the building during the fire assumed a surreal appearance—looked real until touched—then disintegrated to ash. Nothing remained.

Then a file mysteriously appeared in the ashes two days after the fire. It had been used ten weeks earlier during my successful defense of the "baby killer case" (as the unhappy peace officers named it). So, obviously someone burgled it from my office before the fire and later planted it in the nearly cooled ashes to be found—apparently in an effort to intimidate us. Mail delivered to us that same day included an anonymous and grotesque letter with a message clipped from magazine pages saying: "You saved the baby killer—Your family is next." Signed "Inferno" with a color photo of fire attached for emphasis.

Where could we find help? Surely not from the police, who now appeared to be the arsonists! I, nevertheless, filed the civil rights suit a short time later, joined in the suit by 41 outstanding law firms from across the United States. These firms constituted our only protection from the police!

Shortly after the suit was filed, another anonymous letter was distributed throughout Red River County falsely slandering

> *"Be thankful that Texas law is difficult and demanding. Otherwise, anyone could do this and we would not even be needed!"*
>
> ~ JIM'S FAMOUS TEXAS JUSTICE SAYING

...ne. Tips received indicated its origin to be the police. I hired private detectives and security personnel to investigate and to protect us. The civil rights case was settled a short time later in exchange for establishment of a police review board, cash and a letter placed in the chief deputy's personnel file notifying future potential employers of his violation of the teens' civil rights.

Five years later, and with help from two outstanding FBI agents, one retired (Del Drake) and one active (Jim Blanton), the chief deputy and another deputy, who had been directing traffic during my office fire, were brought to justice for arson, obstruction of justice and violation of my civil rights. The deputy received concurrent state and federal ten-year probated sentences in exchange for his testimony while the chief deputy drew joint federal and state five-year sentences to be served concurrently in the federal prison system.

A year later, federal prison officials from Fort Leavenworth, Kansas, contacted us and advised that the chief deputy had escaped and his wife

> "THESE ROGUE OFFICERS WERE UNWILLING TO LIVE WITHIN THE JUSTICE SYSTEM AND BELIEVED THEMSELVES TO BE 'BULLETPROOF.'"

was missing and warned that they were coming to Texas to kill us. We exchanged gifts, disbanded our Christmas family reunion and scattered immediately. After a month, the former chief deputy and his wife remained at large, so I fortified our home and returned to work in an armored Suburban, which I drove for the next three years until they were apprehended. Their recapture marked the end of a nine-year nightmare and was the result of the story being widely broadcast on television. Thank God for both Deputy U. S. Marshall Dick Schroeder of Kansas and John Walsh, host of FOX's *America's Most Wanted*, or these criminals would still be at large.

These rogue officers were unwilling to live within the justice system and believed themselves to be "bulletproof." Evidence had been discovered during our private investigation showing the chief deputy associating with a major marijuana-grower. However, neither this evidence nor the slanderous letter was ever officially investigated. Enemies remain at large. Life goes on.

As ever, vigilance is the price of liberty!

Where did Red River County get its name?

FROM THE RED RIVER, WHICH SEPARATED IT FROM FRANCE AND THE U.S. THE AREA WAS FIRST CLAIMED BY DESOTO FOR SPAIN IN 1542; SOME 39 PRESENT TEXAS COUNTIES WERE FORMED FROM IT.

Where is the Red River County Courthouse located?

FIRST LOCATED IN THE HOME OF CLAIBORNE WRIGHT ON RED RIVER AND THEREAFTER ON THE CLARKSVILLE SQUARE UNTIL 1885 WHEN IT WAS MOVED TO ITS PRESENT LOCATION TWO BLOCKS NORTH OF THE SQUARE.

Who designed the Red River County Courthouse?

WILLIAM H. WILSON, A DALLAS ARCHITECT. THE COURTHOUSE NOW PROCLAIMS ITSELF AS THE MOST ELEGANT COURTHOUSE IN TEXAS; A CASTLE-LIKE RENAISSANCE REVIVAL, SECOND EMPIRE MELLOW YELLOW LIMESTONE STRUCTURE FEATURING TURRETS, BUTTRESSES, COLUMNS AND A CLOCK TOWER. THE HISTORIC 1884 RED RIVER COUNTY COURTHOUSE WAS REDEDICATED ON OCTOBER 26TH 2002 BY THE TEXAS HISTORICAL COMMISSIONS' TEXAS COURTHOUSE PRESERVATION PROGRAM.

What is the courthouse's most unusual feature?

RESTORATION TO ITS ORIGINAL 1884-5 SPECIFICATIONS AND BEING ONE OF THE OLDEST IN TEXAS.

What is the most famous case tried in the Red River County Courthouse?

IN 1840, DAVID PAGE, A MODERATOR, WAS BROUGHT TO CLARKSVILLE BY THE REGULATORS TO BE HUNG WITHOUT A TRIAL ON THE OLD OAK TREE THAT DATES FROM 1738. ATTORNEY ROBERT POTTER OF CADDO LAKE MADE A POWERFUL SPEECH, IMPRESSING THE CROWD (3,000 ESTIMATED). BUT, THE REGULATORS TIED UP POTTER AND SENT PAGE TO GLORY. TODAY THE OLD TREE IS STILL KNOWN AS PAGE'S TREE.

Where do you hang your hat?

THE 6TH DISTRICT COURT IS COMPRISED OF THREE HISTORIC TEXAS COUNTIES: RED RIVER, LAMAR AND FANNIN, AND THE COURT HAS OFFICES IN ALL THREE COURTHOUSES. THE DISTRICT OFFICE IS MAINTAINED IN CLARKSVILLE, TX.

Believe it or not!

IN 200 LOCAL CITIZENS RAISED IN EXCESS OF $700,000 TO RESTORE THE COURTHOUSE. IN 2001, 6TH DISTRICT JUDGE JIM LOVETT, CHAIR OF THE COMMITTEE FOR COURTHOUSE RESTORATION, RECEIVED THE TEXAS HISTORICAL COMMISSION'S GOVERNOR'S AWARD FOR HISTORICAL PRESERVATION, PRESENTED IN THE TEXAS GOVERNOR'S MANSION WITH ABOUT 200 OF HIS FRIENDS PRESENT!

Where did Robertson County get its name?

FROM STERLING C. ROBERTSON, A LAND CHAMPION AND SIGNER OF THE TEXAS DECLARATION OF INDEPENDENCE AND ONE OF THE ORIGINAL SETTLERS OF TEXAS.

Where is the Robertson County Courthouse located?

IN FRANKLIN, TX, ON THE SQUARE, NEAR THE HISTORIC ROBERTSON COUNTY JAIL.

Who designed the Robertson County Courthouse?

IN 1875, W.T INGRAHAM BUILT WHAT IS NOW CALLED THE HAMMOND HOUSE IN CALVERT. IT IS SAID THAT THIS HISTORIC COURTHOUSE WAS USED ONLY FOR A SHORT TIME. IN 1883, F.E. RUFFINI DESIGNED THE NEWER HISTORIC COURTHOUSE AND BUILT IT OUT OF STONE IN THE SECOND EMPIRE STYLE OF ARCHITECTURE. THIS COURTHOUSE IS ALSO A BEAUTIFUL NATIONAL REGISTER PROPERTY.

What is the Courthouse's most unusual feature?

THE COURTROOM IS LOCATED ON THE THIRD FLOOR OF THE COURTHOUSE BUILDING.

What is the most famous case tried in the Robertson County Courthouse?

JAMES FRANKLIN MCNEILL, SR., HIS WIFE LIBBY AND YOUNG SON, JAMES, JR., MIGRATED TO ROBERTSON COUNTY, TX, FROM ARKANSAS IN THE EARLY 1930S. LIBBY DIED IN 1933, DUE TO WHAT HER HUSBAND SAID WAS AN INJURY THAT TOOK PLACE IN THE BARN WHEN SHE BASHED HER HEAD ON A NAIL. ONE YEAR LATER, JAMES, JR. ALSO DIED SUDDENLY. THE LOCAL AUTHORITIES BECAME SUSPICIOUS AND THE BODY OF JAMES, JR. WAS EXHUMED TO CHECK FOR SIGNS OF ABUSE. JAMES SR. WAS ACCUSED OF MURDER AND HE WAS TRIED IN FRANKLIN, ROBERTSON COUNTY. MCNEILL WAS CONVICTED OF MURDER AND SPENT THE REST OF HIS LIFE IN A HUNTSVILLE PRISON.

Where do you hang your hat?

FORMERLY OF HEARNE AND CALVERT IN ROBERTSON COUNTY, I NOW PRACTICE IN ADJACENT MILAM COUNTY, CAMERON, TX, AT CAPPOLINO, DODD & KREBS, ASSOCIATED ATTORNEYS. FOUNDED OVER FIFTY YEARS AGO BY CHARLES C. "JUDGE" SMITH, WE HAVE CONTINUED TO GROW AND PROVIDE HELP TO PEOPLE IN NEED ALL ACROSS TEXAS.

Believe it or not!

THE GRAVE OF THE LAST CONFEDERATE CIVIL WAR SOLDIER IS LOCATED IN THE MT. PLEASANT CHURCH CEMETERY, ABOUT FOUR MILES SOUTHEAST OF FRANKLIN. THERE YOU WILL FIND THE FINAL RESTING PLACE OF WALTER WILLIAMS (D. 1959), WHO WAS SAID TO BE THE VERY LAST SOLDIER OF THE CONFEDERACY TO DIE!

> *"Injustice anywhere is a threat to justice everywhere."*
> — *Martin Luther King*
> ~ CRAIG'S FAMOUS TEXAS JUSTICE SAYING

"Murder by Gunshot"

A Famous Texas Case as Told by
CRAIG W. BROWN, P.L.L.C.
CAPPOLINO, DODD & KREBS
ASSOCIATED ATTORNEYS

In 1961, Henry Marshall's body was found on his Robertson County farm, pierced with five bullet holes from a .22 caliber rifle. The rifle was found alongside his body, so the coroner labeled the death as a suicide. One highly suspicious fact was that this particular type of rifle was bolt-action, meaning it would have been physically impossible for Marshall to manually move the bolt four times after initially shooting himself and then position the gun at the awkward angle (aimed at his side with his thumb pulling the trigger) that would have been required to shoot himself again and again.

Marshall's family adamantly opposed the suicide ruling. They insisted there was no way he wanted to end his life. He was financially secure, successful in his farming business and a government agriculture investigator. Despite the family's outcries and the suspicious circumstances surrounding the death, Marshall's death certificate listed his cause of death as suicide resulting from bullet wounds.

It soon appeared that Marshall's life was not as quiet as his family believed. Orville Freeman, the Secretary of Agriculture at the time, later revealed that Marshall had been tied to an intense investigation regarding fraudulent business activities of another infamous Texan: Billy Sol Estes.

Billy Sol Estes is known as one of the greatest Texan con-men and in 1961, happened to be the target of Marshall's investigation. A millionaire and prominent figure in his hometown of Pecos, Texas, Estes was both admired and feared. He had solid connections with both local and federal government officials, which propelled him to much of his success. Estes

Robertson
County Courthouse

allegedly ran a heavy cotton allotment scheme in which he, through his government connections, had allocations of cotton requisitioned from other farmers' land and reallocated to his own. Agriculture officials soon became privy to his scheme, which spelled bad news for Estes. Henry Marshall's suspicious death was a major blow to the Estes investigation.

Estes was eventually tried for fraud relating to his business enterprises and imprisoned until 1984. After his release, Estes became friends with Texas Ranger Clint Peoples, who convinced him that he should come forward with information Estes claimed he had implicating Lyndon Baines Johnson in the Marshall suicide case. A Robertson County Grand Jury soon heard Estes' statements regarding the cotton allotment scandal and the death of Henry Marshall. Estes claimed

> **"THE RIFLE WAS FOUND ALONGSIDE HIS BODY, SO THE CORONER LABELED THE DEATH AS A SUICIDE."**

that Johnson ordered Malcolm "Mac" Wallace to "eliminate" Marshall, which resulted in his untimely death. None of Estes' wild claims regarding Johnson were substantiated. Due to his history as a felon, exaggerator and attention seeker, Estes was largely dismissed. Nevertheless, Estes' testimony resulted in Marshall's death certificate finally being changed to read: "Cause of death—murder by gunshot."

Rockwall
County Courthouse

"A Rockwall Legacy"

A Famous Texas Case as Told by
MARY MCKNIGHT
LAW OFFICES OF MARY MCKNIGHT

In exploring the legal and political history of Rockwall County, McKnight was fortunate to be able to speak with former Rockwall attorney (1940-1941) Faire Wade, 87, Kim Wade of Dallas and Judge Brett Hall. They recounted times when "Family Law" in Rockwall had an entirely different twist. The Wade family practiced law and politics in Rockwall County from the early 1920s.

Faire Wade recalls when he was running for County Attorney in 1940 and Congressman Ralph Hall, then a teenager, drove his staff car, a Model T Ford, from farm to farm while the aspiring politician visited local farmers.

During the Hall-Wade era, Earl Wade was County Sheriff and either Reese Wade or Henry Wade Senior was County Attorney/Prosecutor or County Judge. Not only did the Wades oppose each other in elections for County Attorney or County Judge, they were perpetual trial adversaries with "Pappa" Wade, Henry Wade Senior, always for the defense and brother Reese prosecuting. According to Faire Wade, a fist fight in the courtroom sometimes took place with full family participation. Faire Wade was the "peace loving" member of the Wade family as he remembers.

Faire Wade recalls the most memorable case being the murder trial of a prominent farmer from Heath who had too much to drink and shot dead one of his share-croppers. After a heated and much publicized jury trial, Reese Wade, the County Prosecuting Attorney, prevailed and the farmer was sent to prison. Reese won the battle but not the war. Defense attorney, "Pappa" Wade appealed directly to Governor "Ma" Ferguson, who pardoned his client, the farmer, who was freed from prison to return to his farm. Stories were affirmed by Faire Wade of Corpus Christi, Kim Wade of Dallas and Judge Brett Fall of Rockwall, about the adversarial system between "Pappa" Wade and the prosecutor, Reese. "Pappa never thought his clients were guilty," Faire says, "and even if they did do it, they had good reason." Faire said, "Pappa often would accuse either Sheriff Earl Hall, Prosecutor Reese Wade, or both of beating or otherwise unfairly coercing confessions out of those of his clients who admitted they had committed crimes." Pappa Wade once told a jury, in closing argument, following the prosecutor's summation, "You know it's a sad thing. I raised that boy and he's been a liar all his life."

Faire Wade was successful in his campaign for County Attorney in which he ran as a third year law student in 1939 an served until he went into the Army; he was a POW in Germany in WWII.

Henry Wade, Jr. completed law school in 1938 and served as Rockwall County Attorney for two years before joining the FBI. Henry Wade, Jr. was elected Dallas County District Attorney in 1950 and served for more than thirty years.

Ralph Hall was elected to Congress and his son, Brett Hall, currently serves as District Judge in Rockwall County. But

> # "PAPA OFTEN WOULD ACCUSE . . . BOTH OF BEATING OR OTHERWISE UNFAIRLY COERCING CONFESSION . . ."

in this 21st Century "Family Law" has significantly changed. This is not saying present day Rockwall cases have become boring. Quite the contrary; McKnight has been quick to point out and Rockwall is still "small town USA" with all the positives that go with that image. But the characters are still full of color and larger than life. In 2002-2003, McKnight enjoyed two such cases in Rockwall in which one of the parties had been formerly represented by Judge Hall. In 2003, rather than "fist fights" these cases translate into a quiet and appropriate recusal by Judge Brett Hall and a trial without fanfare, a final trial before a visiting judge, and the cast of characters fade into the background.

> ## "There are no 'impossible lawsuits'; just lawyers who get tired and give up."
> ~ MARY'S FAMOUS TEXAS JUSTICE SAYING

Where did Rockwall County get its name?
FROM THE WALL OF ROCK HIDDEN JUST BENEATH THE GROUND THAT RUNS THROUGHOUT THE COUNTY.

Where is the Rockwall County Courthouse located?
IN ROCKWALL, TX, IN THE MIDDLE OF THE TOWN SQUARE, IN THE SMALLEST COUNTY IN TEXAS.

Who designed the Rockwall County Courthouse?
BUILT OF STONE IN 1940, THE IDENTITY OF THE ARCHITECT IS UNKNOWN, BUT THE HISTORIC COURTHOUSE WAS RECENTLY RESTORED BY PHOENIX 1.

What is the Courthouse's most unusual feature?
THE $2.5 MILLION REFURBISHMENT OF THIS HISTORIC COURTHOUSE ENABLED THE STRUCTURE TO NOW SERVE AS A CENTERPIECE FOR THE OLD TOWN SQUARE IN CENTRAL ROCKWALL

What is the most famous case tried in the Rockwall County Courthouse?
FORMER CHIEFS RUNNING BACK BAM MORRIS WAS CONVICTED OF DRUG TRAFFICKING AND MONEY LAUNDERING AND WAS SENTENCED TO SERVE THIRTY MONTHS IN PRISON. THE CASE ALSO INVOLVED ANOTHER FORMER CHIEFS PLAYER AND LEAD TO THE END OF MORRIS' PROFESSIONAL FOOTBALL CAREER.

Where do you hang your hat?
IF I CAN'T BE FOUND AT MY FIRM IN DALLAS, WHERE I SPECIALIZE IN FAMILY LAW, I AM AT CHANDLER'S LANDING IN ROCKWALL, TX.

Believe it or not!
IN THE LATE 1970S, THE GAME WARDEN ARRESTED A FISHERMAN FOR EXCEEDING HIS FISHING LIMIT, HOWEVER THE CASE ULTIMATELY WAS DISMISSED BECAUSE THE EVIDENCE HAD BEEN MISTAKENLY FRIED-UP AND EATEN BY THE JAILER!

Shackelfo
County Courthouse

"The Restoration of Texas Justice"

The Case for Courthouse Restoration as Told by

DALE SELLERS
PHOENIX I RESTORATION AND CONSTRUCTION, LTD.

Justice is the embodiment of the will of the people. It is the assurance that the law will be fair and equitable, impartial and respect the rights of all. The restoration of Texas courthouses is justice on a grand scale—a scale as big as Texas!

After its expansion and restoration, The State Capitol in Austin had rekindled a great source of pride and yet created much controversy. While Austin was booming with growth and newly created jobs, many people felt the project was too expensive, elitist in nature and patently unfair. It would do little for the majority of Texans who rarely, if ever, participated in the "goings on" of Austin. When President (then Governor) Bush championed the Courthouse Preservation Program, he acknowledged Austin may be the heart of our state government, but the counties were the body and soul. They represented the very spirit and diversity of the people that have made this great state what it is today.

With state funding of approximately $150 million dollars as of 2004, new life, jobs and local pride are being restored within the community as well as in the courthouses themselves. Revitalized town squares are once again becoming the center of business and county government. Over 3,000 new jobs have been created in places such as Eagle Pass, Del Rio, Wheeler, Pampa, Albany, Marfa, Newton and Donley.

The Shackelford County Courthouse, as the first

ord

courthouse to be completed under the support, guidance and financial aid of the Texas Historical Commission's Courthouse Preservation Program, represents the beginning of Austin's commitment to Texas counties and their people—an impartial commitment of fairness, equity and respect.

Until you have attended a county commissions' court, it is unlikely you could understand Texas politics, people and justice at the local level. During my first visit to Shackelford Commissioners Court, it became clear these were real people with real jobs and real concerns. Most everyone in attendance was dressed in jeans. There was mud on more than one pair of boots in the room and not an inkling of airs in this group. It was

> ## "WHEN PRESIDENT (THEN GOVERNOR) BUSH CHAMPIONED THE COURTHOUSE PRESERVATION PROGRAM, HE ACKNOWLEDGED AUSTIN MAY BE THE HEART OF OUR STATE GOVERNMENT, BUT THE COUNTIES WERE THE BODY AND SOUL."

obvious that they had interrupted their daily activities to take care of the county's business. From road repairs and animal control to county employee issues and courthouse restoration, their agenda reflected decisions that would affect the lives of everyday Texans.

Phoenix I was one of several companies being considered as the Construction Manager and Contractor for the restoration of their courthouse. I was there to convince these folks to give us the job. The task seemed daunting since our proposal was

---

Where did Shackelford County get its name?
IN 1874 FROM DR. JOHN SHACKELFORD, A SURVIVING SOLDIER OF THE GOLIAD MASSACRE, AS WELL AS THE BATTLE OF 1812 AND A HERO OF THE TEXAS REVOLUTION.

Where is the Shackelford County Courthouse located?
LOCATED IN ALBANY, TX, ON THE TOWN SQUARE, THE COURTHOUSE SERVES AS THE FOCAL POINT OF ALBANY'S DOWNTOWN WHICH IS LISTED IN THE NATIONAL REGISTER OF HISTORIC DISTRICTS.

Who designed the Shackelford County Courthouse?
THE 1883 HISTORICAL COURTHOUSE WAS BUILT BY DALLAS ARCHITECT JAMES E. FLANDERS IN SECOND EMPIRE STYLE OF NATIVE LIMESTONE, WHO ALSO DESIGNED A NUMBER OF OTHER TEXAS COURTHOUSES. THIS TREASURE IS ALSO A NATIONAL REGISTER PROPERTY.

What is the Courthouse's most unusual feature?
IT IS THE FIRST COURTHOUSE TO BE REDEDICATED IN THE TEXAS HISTORIC COURTHOUSE PRESERVATION PROGRAM ON JUNE 30, 2001.

What is the most famous case tried in the Shackelford County Courthouse?
JOHN HENRY SELMAN, A FAMOUS TEXAN OUTLAW TURNED LAWMAN, WAS A SHACKELFORD COUNTY DEPUTY IN THE MID 1870S. KNOWN AS "UNCLE JOHN," THE DEPUTY REVERTED TO HIS LAWBREAKING WAYS AND LED THE "SELMAN SCOUTS," A BAND OF DESPERADOS WHO ROAMED THE SOUTHWEST ACCUSED OF A NUMBER OF MURDERS AND RAPES. UNCLE JOHN WAS SOON CAPTURED BY THE TEXAS RANGERS AND TRIED IN SHACKELFORD COUNTY. HE WAS ULTIMATELY INCARCERATED, BUT HE ESCAPED AND FLED TO MEXICO.

Where do you hang your hat?
WHEN NOT CRUISING ON HIS MOTORCYCLE OR IN HIS HUMMER, DALE IS EITHER AT PHOENIX I IN DALLAS, TX, OR AT RESTORATION SITES ANYWHERE ACROSS THE STATE OF TEXAS.

Believe it or not!
IN SEPTEMBER OF 2001, A FEMALE PRISONER ESCAPED FROM THE SHACKELFORD COUNTY JAIL IN A CAR THAT BELONGED TO THE MINISTER WHO WAS PREACHING SUNDAY SERVICES AT THE JAIL. SHE WAS CAUGHT A FEW DAYS LATER AND RETURNED TO THE PRISON!

Top Gun
Dale Sellers

★ LEFT HIGH SCHOOL IN 1974 TO JOIN THE US NAVY'S NUCLEAR SUBMARINE PROGRAM

★ TRAVELED EXTENSIVELY UNDER THE ARTIC ICE PACK FROM 1976 TO 1978

★ CONFERRED BS OF MECHANICAL ENGINEERING, UTA, IN 1989 AND CONFERRED EXECUTIVE MBA, SMU IN 1997

★ HIRED AS GENERAL MANAGER OF NEOGARD CONTRACT DIVISION OF JONES BLAIR COMPANY IN 1998 AND NEGOTIATED LEVERAGED BUY OUT OF NEOGARD CONTRACT DIVISION IN 1999, GIVING BIRTH TO PHOENIX I RESTORATION AND CONSTRUCTION, LTD.

★ COMPLETED RESTORATION OF JFK MEMORIAL AS DONATION TO CITY OF DALLAS AND DALLAS COUNTY IN 1999

★ 1999, 2000, 2001, 2002 RECIPIENT OF THE SMU-COX SCHOOL OF BUSINESS AND CEO INSTITUTE'S DALLAS 100 AWARDS

★ RECIPIENT OF DALLAS BUSINESS JOURNAL'S PACESETTER AWARD IN 2000

★ PURCHASED SEVERAL ACRES AND A 44,000 SQ. FT. BUILDING IN DALLAS AS PIRC'S NEW HOME IN 2002

★ COMPLETED RESTORATION OF THE SAN JACINTO MONUMENT

★ FOUNDING CIRCLE MEMBER OF PRESERVATION TEXAS

★ NUMEROUS COMPLETED RESTORATION PROJECTS HAVE RECEIVED AWARDS. PROJECTS INCLUDE SHACKELFORD COUNTY COURTHOUSE; DONLEY COUNTY COURTHOUSE; T & P STATION, FORT WORTH; MAGNOLIA LOUNGE, FAIR PARK, DALLAS

several hundred thousand dollars higher than our competition.

The meeting and presentation was conducted in a small room with many people standing and while everyone seemed impressed with our credentials, money issues were obviously a great concern. The single biggest issue was the cost associated with the windows being historically replicated out of long leaf yellow pine. Our competition proposed windows manufactured from materials not approved or acceptable to the architect or THC but at a substantial savings. The commissioners carefully examined samples of both species of wood, but were unimpressed. I exhaustibly explained the technical differences between the wood, but obviously had not convinced several commissioners. Our hopes of landing the project seemed to be fading fast and in shear desperation I asked one of the commissioners, "Just what about 'shit wood' don't you understand?" He put the sample on the table, smiled and said, "That, I do understand." Restoration Architect Kim Williams of The Williams Company, made his recommendation; a vote was taken and Phoenix I was in the courthouse restoration business.

The project was completed early and thousands attended the courthouse rededication which was planned in conjunction with The Fort Griffin Fandangle. In celebration, Phoenix I threw a Texas size barbecue on the courthouse lawn and a good time was had by all. Judge Ross Montgomery remarked, "Our courthouse has always been the pride and joy of Shackelford County and now it is also the pride of joy of the State of Texas".

As I've walked the courthouse squares around the state, I've been fascinated by the historical markers and even more by the stories locals tell. Stories of hangings on the trees in the square bring imagery of life and death into the history of these great places. Travelling on my cycle between courthouses, the loud tempo of Toby Keith and Willie Nelson singing, "Whiskey for my men, beer for my horses," brings visions of cowboy righteousness and Texas Justice as it must have been and as it always should be.

Dale's Favorite Texas Song/Quote

Grand pappy told my pappy back in my days' son
A man had to answer for the wicked thing he done
Take all the rope in Texas—find a tall oak tree
Round up all of them bad boys,
Hang 'em high in the street, for all the people to see,
That Justice is the one thing you should always find.
"Whiskey for my men, beer for my horses"

Toby Keith & Willie Nelson

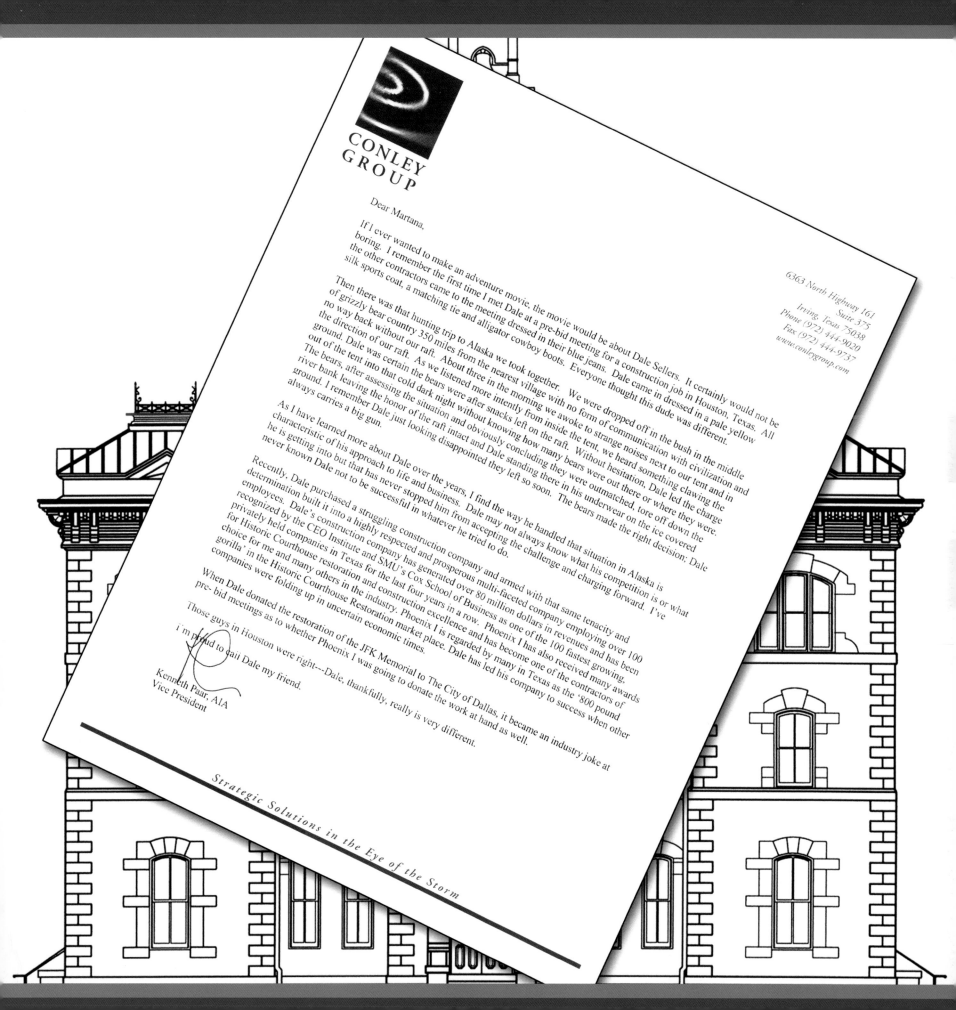

CONLEY GROUP

6363 North Highway 161
Suite 375
Irving, Texas 75038
Phone (972) 444-9020
Fax (972) 444-9737
www.conleygroup.com

Dear Martana,

If I ever wanted to make an adventure movie, the movie would be about Dale Sellers. It certainly would not be boring. I remember the first time I met Dale at a pre-bid meeting for a construction job in Houston, Texas. All the other contractors came to the meeting dressed in their blue jeans. Dale came in dressed in a pale yellow silk sports coat, a matching tie and alligator cowboy boots. Everyone thought this dude was different.

Then there was that hunting trip to Alaska we took together. We were dropped off in the bush in the middle of grizzly bear country 350 miles from the nearest village with no form of communication with civilization and no way back without our raft. As we listened more intently from inside the tent, we heard something clawing the direction of our raft. About three in the morning we awoke to strange noises next to our tent and in ground. Dale was certain the bears were after snacks left on the raft. Without hesitation, Dale led the charge out of the tent into that cold dark night without knowing how many bears were out there or where they were. The bears, after assessing the situation and obviously concluding they were outmatched, tore off down the river bank leaving the honor of the raft intact and Dale standing there in his underwear on the ice covered ground. I remember Dale just looking disappointed they left so soon. The bears made the right decision: Dale always carries a big gun.

As I have learned more about Dale over the years, I find the way he handled that situation is or what characteristic of his approach to life and business. Dale may not always know what his competition is he is getting into but that has never stopped him from accepting the challenge and charging forward. I've never known Dale not to be successful in whatever he tried to do.

Recently, Dale purchased a struggling construction company and armed with that same tenacity and determination built it into a highly respected and prosperous multi-faceted company employing over 100 employees. Dale's construction company has generated over 80 million dollars in revenues and has been recognized by the CEO Institute and SMU's Cox School of Business as one of the 100 fastest growing, privately held companies in Texas and construction excellence and has become one of the contractors of choice for me and many others in the industry. Phoenix I is regarded by many in Texas as the '800 pound gorilla' in the Historic Courthouse Restoration market place. Dale has led his company to success when other companies were folding up in uncertain economic times.

When Dale donated the restoration of the JFK Memorial to The City of Dallas, it became an industry joke at pre- bid meetings as to whether Phoenix I was going to donate the work at hand as well.

Those guys in Houston were right---Dale, thankfully, really is very different.

I'm proud to call Dale my friend.

Kenneth Paar, AIA
Vice President

Strategic Solutions in the Eye of the Storm

Shelby
County Courthouse

1885

LARRY MCNEILL,
JUDGE GUY GRIFFIN
& JUDGE CHARLES MITCHELL

"A Texas Legacy Is Born"

A Famous Texas Case as Told by

LARRY MCNEILL
CLARK, THOMAS & WINTERS,
A PROFESSIONAL CORPORATION

In the first 79 years of the Shelby County Courthouse, attorneys and judges by the name of Davis walked its halls—two were brothers, W.I. Davis, Sr., and T.O. Davis and the third was Tom C. Davis, who began his career before the courthouse was built.

Tom C. Davis was born in 1849 in Terrapin Neck, Shelby County. He was admitted to the Bar, after studying law with Gov. O.M. Roberts in 1875. He then served as County Attorney from 1876-1877, County Surveyor in 1878-1879 and Shelby County Judge in 1894. In 1895, he was appointed to the District Court bench by Governor Culberson, was elected twice to the same post and retired from the bench after ten years.

Because of his prominence in East Texas, Judge Davis was constructively engaged in many of the controversies of his era. He presided over *State v. Mitchell*, a case involving the murder of James Truitt in Timpson; *State v. Buchanan*, in which Davis reluctantly presided over a "race-to-justice" after a sensational manhunt; and *Gibson v. Shelby County*. In Gibson, the builder of the courthouse, J.J.E. Gibson, sought to recover funds expended in building the courthouse as a result of the Commissioner's Court refusal to grant him a delay in laying mortar that he believed would be damaged by freezing weather. Gibson continued the work and bad weather occurred, cracking the walls, requiring Gibson to rebuild. While Judge Davis found merit in the builder's position, the case was reversed on appeal.

His knowledge of the families of East Texas often called him into extraordinary roles such as the time he personally visited Eugene Wall during the Border-Wall-Broocks feud of 1899-1901 in order to avoid the prospect of 200 armed men attacking the town of San Augustine. His counsel and subsequent action on the bench prevented the potential calamity.

> *"If that is the law of Shelby County, this is the constitution that overrules your law."*
>
> *Judge Robert "Three-Legged Willie" Williamson, displaying a gun after a citizen opposed to legal proceedings had stuck a Bowie Knife in the bench saying it was the "law of Shelby County."*
>
> ~ LARRY'S FAMOUS TEXAS JUSTICE SAYING

When Davis retired from his position, he formed a law firm with W.I. Davis. The younger Davis, born in 1885, graduated from the University of Texas School of Law in 1903 and served as County Attorney from 1907-1911. From 1903 until his death in 1960, he was considered one of the most prominent trial lawyers in East Texas, handling both civil and criminal cases, mostly in the Shelby County Courthouse. He was especially recognized for his expertise in land matters, expertise he put into play on many occasions as the attorney for the Pickering Lumber Company, including the sale of 67,000 acres to the USDA that became the Shelby County portion of the Sabine National Forest. It is said that W.I. Davis knew the ownership of every parcel in Shelby County. He kept a map under glass on the top of his desk, penciling in the names of land owners as transfers occurred.

W.I. DAVIS

TOM C. DAVIS

T.O. DAVIS & GEORGE E.B. PEDDY

"IN THE FIRST 79 YEARS OF THE SHELBY COUNTY COURTHOUSE, ATTORNEYS AND JUDGES BY THE NAME OF DAVIS WALKED ITS HALLS . . ."

Although Tom C. Davis died in 1914, the Davis & Davis firm continued because T.O. Davis (1885-1964), younger brother of W.I., joined the firm in 1909. He also served as County Attorney from 1915-1919. Upon the creation of the 123rd Judicial District in 1931, T.O. was appointed District Judge and served in that capacity until 1940.

The Courthouse was the scene of many political events and of all the Davis men; T.O.'s participation in politics was probably the most notable. At various times, he served in local, county and state Democratic Party capacities, at one point holding a position on the Democratic State Executive Committee.

T.O. was the successful attorney in the trial and appeal of a contested election which approved the consolidation of school districts, *Galloway v. Wilburn*, 179 S.W. 2d 540. He was also extremely active in the 1948 U.S. Senatorial campaign of George E.B. Peddy. Peddy, a native of Tenaha, received more than 20% of the statewide vote, but finished third to Coke Stevenson and Lyndon Johnson, whose showing in the controversial run-off election led to the ironical nickname of "Landslide Lyndon."

In the history of the Shelby County Courthouse, there is no firm whose members played such prominent roles in so many different capacities or so long.

Where did Shelby County get its name?
FROM WAR VETERAN ISAAC SHELBY IN 1837, WHO WAS A UNITED STATES REVOLUTIONARY SOLDIER FROM KENTUCKY WHO MADE A NAME FOR HIMSELF BY LEADING MILITIA VOLUNTEERS AT THE BATTLE OF KING'S MOUNTAIN DURING THE AMERICAN REVOLUTION.

Where is the Shelby County Courthouse located?
IN CENTER, TX, ON THE TOWN SQUARE, NEAR THE SHELBY COUNTY MUSEUM LOCATED IN THE 1910 WEAVER-GATES HOUSE.

Who designed the Shelby County Courthouse?
COMPLETED IN 1885, THIS TWO-STORY RED BRICK GABLED ROMANESQUE REVIVAL STYLE HISTORIC COURTHOUSE WAS DESIGNED BY JOHN JOSEPH EMMETT GIBSON, AN IRISH IMMIGRANT. LOCAL TRADITION HAS LONG HELD THAT GIBSON COPIED THE DESIGN FROM A CASTLE IN HIS NATIVE IRELAND. THIS LONE STAR BEAUTY IS ALSO A NATIONAL REGISTER PROPERTY.

What is the Courthouse's most unusual feature?
THE COURTHOUSE HAS A SECRET PASSAGEWAY BEHIND THE COURT'S BENCH THAT LEADS TO A STAIRWAY OUT OF THE COURTROOM, PERHAPS TO PROVIDE A QUICK MEANS OF ESCAPE FOR JUDGES WHO HAVE JUST TRIED DANGEROUS CRIMINALS.

What is the most famous case tried in the Shelby County Courthouse?
THE BILL MITCHELL TRIALS IN 1907-1910 ARE LEGENDARY. AFTER BEING TRIED TWICE FOR THE MURDER OF JAMES TRUITT, BOTH RESULTING IN MISTRIALS, MITCHELL WAS CONVICTED AND SENTENCED TO LIFE IMPRISONMENT. THE FEUD BETWEEN THE MITCHELLS AND TRUITTS SPANNED TEXAS FROM HOOD COUNTY TO SHELBY COUNTY. SEE C. L. SONNICHSEN'S BOOK, OUTLAW, FOR THE COMPLETE STORY, INCLUDING THE ROLE OF JUDGE TOM C. DAVIS.

Where do you hang your hat?
IN AUSTIN, TX, AT THE CLARK, THOMAS & WINTERS' LAW FIRM AND IN TENAHA, A SMALL TOWN IN SHELBY COUNTY, WHERE I PURSUE ONE OF MY GREATEST INTERESTS, TEXAS HISTORY. I AM VERY ACTIVE IN THE TEXAS STATE HISTORICAL ASSOCIATION AND THE SABINE COUNTY HISTORICAL FOUNDATION.

Believe it or not!
SHELBY COUNTY WAS THE LOCALE OF A GREAT FEUD FOUGHT IN TEXAS FROM 1839 TO 1844. RIVALRY BETWEEN TWO GROUPS, THE "REGULATORS" AND THE "MODERATORS," LEAD TO MURDERS, RETALIATIONS AND WIDESPREAD FIGHTING. THE REGULATORS OPENLY DEFIED THE REPUBLIC OF TEXAS AND THREATENED TO OVERTHROW IT. IN 1844, SAM HOUSTON SENT MILITIA TO END THE FIGHTING!

Where did Somervell County get its name?

FROM ALEXANDER SOMERVELL, A MEMBER OF THE TEXAS CONGRESS WHO ALSO FOUGHT IN THE BATTLE OF SAN JACINTO.

Where is the Somervell County Courthouse located?

IN GLEN ROSE, TX, THE THRESHOLD OF THE FAMOUS TEXAS HILL COUNTRY, ON BERNARD STREET; ONE OF THE PREMIER LOCATIONS FOR LIVING THE "RURAL AMERICAN LIFE STYLE."

Who designed the Somervell County Courthouse?

JOHN CORMACK WAS THE DESIGNER OF THE ORIGINAL 1894 HISTORIC COURTHOUSE CONSTRUCTED OF LIMESTONE, WHICH ALSO HAILS AS A NATIONAL REGISTER PROPERTY.

What is the Courthouse's most unusual feature?

THE CLOCK TOWER, WHICH IS PERCHED ON THE ROOF, IS UNIQUE AND DISPLAYS SECOND EMPIRE AND ROMANESQUE REVIVAL ARCHITECTURAL INFLUENCES.

What is the most famous case tried in the Somervell County Courthouse?

FONDLY REMEMBERED AS "LITIGATION AVENUE" IN GLEN ROSE, TX, A DEVELOPER WHO ENDED UP IN COURT ARGUING ABOUT WHO OWNED TITLE TO LOTS ON THE STREET WHERE HE PLANNED A NEW DEVELOPMENT.

Where do you hang your hat?

AT RAGGIO AND RAGGIO P.L.L.C. IN DALLAS, TX. MY THREE SONS, GRIER, THOMAS, KENNETH AND I SPECIALIZE IN COMPLEX FAMILY LAW CASES INCLUDING DIVORCE, CUSTODY AND PROPERTY DIVISIONS. THE FIRM WAS FOUNDED IN 1955 BY ME AND MY HUSBAND, WHO PASSED AWAY IN 1988.

Believe it or not!

EVEN AFTER THE 1960s, WHEN LAWS WERE DIRECTING EQUAL PAY FOR EQUAL WORK AND NO DISCRIMINATION AGAINST WOMEN FOR JOBS, MANY BUSINESS AND LAW FIRMS WOULD NOT HIRE WOMEN AND PAY THEM THE SAME AS MEN. THERE WERE VERY FEW WOMEN LAWYERS IN TEXAS AT THAT TIME, BUT ABOUT SIX DALLAS WOMEN LAWYERS SUED BANKS, AN AIRLINE, A LARGE ACCOUNTING FIRM AND SEVERAL BUSINESSES ALLEGING DISCRIMINATION AGAINST WOMEN BASED ON SEX. THE LAW FIRMS AND BUSINESSES QUICKLY UNDERSTOOD THE MESSAGE AND COMPLIED WITH THE LAWS!

"Success means you have found your niche and used your best efforts to solve the problems."

~ LOUISE'S FAMOUS TEXAS JUSTICE SAYING

"Equal Rights for Women"

A Famous Texas Case as Told by

LOUISE RAGGIO
RAGGIO AND RAGGIO P.L.L.C.

The rights women enjoy today are an evolution in history. From the beginning of time, men have protected women and kept them from harm's way just like in the Squaw Creek Indian Fight, a Civil War frontier victory in the small Texan town of Glen Rose. The women of Glen Rose dressed as men while their sons, husbands and fathers were away to protect them from the raiding Indians. However, later in time, as women became more independent and self sufficient, women needed another kind of protection—the protection of the law to give them equal rights as men.

Carrie Nation was a pioneer and legend who came to Granbury around 1905. She stood almost six-feet-tall and weighed nearly 200 pounds. An ominous figure, she carried with her a hatchet and both men and women were frightened of her. She became concerned about the role of the man in the family and reasoned that when men were controlling the family finances, their drunken behavior was a threat to their wives and families. It was actually her brief marriage to an alcoholic years before that had been the catalyst for Nation's contempt for alcohol. She even described herself as "a bulldog running along at the feet of Jesus, barking at what he doesn't like." Nation felt it was her divine duty to campaign for temperance.

She did not use her axe, but she organized the ladies of the town into the Christian Women's Temperance League. Normally quiet housewives in Granbury held pray-ins in local saloons and forcefully demanded that the sale of liquor should cease. Nation was arrested over thirty times after leading her followers in the demolition of nearly every watering hole in Somervell County.

While Carrie Nation's platform was primarily placed on temperance, The Women's Christian Temperance Union also banded together to promote issues such as health and hygiene, prison reform and even world peace. The WCTU became one of the largest women's organizations in the country and had chapters throughout the U.S. Carrie Nation understood that women banding together for a cause can bring about change.

I, too, continue to practice law and fight for amendments to laws concerning women's rights. I was continually frustrated that even though

omervell
County Courthouse

I was a practicing attorney, my husband still had to sign papers regarding many of our legal matters. Until 1967, married women did not have the same property rights as men. Single women were allowed basic civil liberties, such as the right to make contracts, to sue and be sued, to own and control property, and, if widowed, to have custody of her children. Married women, however, signed over most of their property rights when they signed their marriage certificate. A married woman was required to allow her husband to control the entire joint estate and business affairs.

I fought for change and in 1967 the Texas Marital Property Act reformed state laws affecting married women including property rights. After 1967, both spouses had the right to select their homes and in the event of separation or divorce, mothers retained equal

> **"I FOUGHT FOR CHANGE AND IN 1967 THE TEXAS MARITAL PROPERTY ACT REFORMED STATE LAWS AFFECTING MARRIED WOMEN INCLUDING PROPERTY RIGHTS."**

rights with fathers regarding custody of the children. For the first time, the wife, if employed, acquired the responsibility of providing for a husband unable to support himself; a housewife was not, however, required by law to take a job. The law also recognized the wife's right to retain her birth name after marriage. Finally, the law was equal for both men and women; the Texas Marital Property Act established a basic set of rights for married women. Since the Marital Property Act was enacted, no provision of the code has ever been ruled unconstitutional.

Stonewall
County Courthouse

"The Jury Box
Only Holds Twelve"

A Famous Texas Case as Told by

ROBERT E. HASLAM
THE HASLAM FIRM

In the late 1990s, Mr. Haslam made the acquaintance of Mr. Humberto Rodriguez, who was injured by Brown & Root in Eagle Pass, Texas. Mr. Rodriguez had younger family members who were migrant workers. Three men were standing in line inside Alsup's convenience store, when a car ran through the glass doors of the store and struck the men. Two of the men were seriously injured and went to the local hospital.

When Mr. Haslam filed suit against the driver, the clerk returned it un-filed with "he died" written on it. The man who struck the two men had died from unrelated causes. Mr. Haslam had to file suit against the decedent's widow and the man's estate. The first civil trial in at least ten years was set. Out of 1,176 potential jurors, about 180 showed up! This was the most exciting thing to happen in a long time! The voir dire was interesting. Try to explain suing a widow without mentioning insurance!

The trial lasted all of one day and resulted in a mistrial because Mr. Haslam's local counsel (the only attorney in the county) had once represented the other side; the widow had once faxed something from the attorney's office. The widow didn't even remember it.

After the mistrial, the insurance company settled the claim for just under the policy limits.

The Alsup's convenience store now has heavy metal guardrails in front of their stores, thanks to the Rodriguez family. Hopefully this will not occur again.

This is a great story because it shows the excitement a trial can still bring to a small town!

"Stonewall County newspaper quote "Serving the free State of Stonewall" - interpreted, everyone knows everyone and they do their own thing."
~ ROBERT'S FAMOUS TEXAS JUSTICE SAYING

Where did Stonewall County get its name?
FROM A CONFEDERATE GENERAL DURING THE CIVIL WAR., T.J. "STONEWALL" JACKSON.

Where is the Stonewall County Courthouse located?
THE 1891 COURTHOUSE IS JUST NORTH OF ASPERMONT AND NOW SERVES AS A PRIVATE RESIDENCE. THE MODERN COURTHOUSE IS AT 500 BROADWAY IN ASPERMONT, TX.

Who designed the Stonewall County Courthouse?
ELMER GEORGE WITHERS DESIGNED THE ORIGINAL COURTHOUSE IN 1888, AND ANOTHER IN 1891, BOTH OF WHICH ARE STILL STANDING. THE CURRENT COURTHOUSE WAS BUILT IN 1983.

What is the Courthouse's most unusual feature?
THERE IS A GREAT EMPHASIS ON WWII MEMORABILIA. THE COURTHOUSE ALSO HOUSES THE GOVERNMENT OFFICES AS WELL AS THE COURTROOM, WHICH IS LOCKED MOST OF THE TIME.

What is the most famous case tried in the Stonewall County Courthouse?
DUNCAN V. TEXACO IN THE '60S. THERE WAS AN OIL FIELD ACCIDENT KILLING A WELDER WHEN A RIG BLEW UP. THE SETTLEMENT WAS RUMORED TO BE MORE THAN $25 MILLION. THE JUDGE'S FATHER WAS ON THE JURY AND THE TRIAL ALSO ENDED-UP IN A MISTRIAL.

Where do you hang your hat?
IN FORT WORTH, TX, AT THE HASLAM LAW FIRM. MR. HASLAM IS BOARD CERTIFIED IN PERSONAL INJURY TRIAL LAW BY THE TEXAS BOARD OF LEGAL SPECIALIZATION, AV RATED, THE HIGHEST RATING BY THE NATIONAL SERVICE, MARTIN-HUBBELL.

Believe it or not!
DOUBLE MOUNTAIN IS STONEWALL COUNTY'S BEST-KNOWN LANDMARK. IT IS SO NAMED BECAUSE OF ITS TWO FLAT-TOPPED SUMMITS SEPARATED BY A VISIBLE DEPRESSION. THE MOUNTAIN IS 2,500 FEET ABOVE SEA LEVEL AND CAN BE SEEN FROM MANY PARTS OF STONEWALL, AS WELL AS ADJOINING COUNTIES. THE DOUBLE MOUNTAIN IS SAID TO HAVE BEEN USED AS A LANDMARK FOR SPANISH EXPLORERS AS WELL AS NATIVE AMERICANS AND FRONTIERSMEN FOR CENTURIES!

"OUT OF 1,176 POTENTIAL JURORS, (THE COUNTY POPULATION) NEARLY 15% SHOWED UP."

Where did Sutton County get its name?

SUTTON WAS ESTABLISHED IN 1890 AND NAMED FOR COLONEL JOHN S. SUTTON, WHO WAS A TEXAS RANGER AND CONFEDERATE OFFICER AND WAS KILLED IN THE CIVIL WAR DURING THE BATTLE OF VAL VERDE.

Where is the Sutton County Courthouse located?

ON THE SONORA TOWN SQUARE, AT THE END OF MAIN STREET WHICH HAS BEEN BUSTLING WITH ACTIVITY SINCE THE 1890S.

Who designed the Sutton County Courthouse?

THIS SECOND EMPIRE STYLE HISTORIC COURTHOUSE WAS COMPLETED IN 1891 OF LIMESTONE BY ARCHITECT OSCAR RUFFINI WHO MADE THE 140-MILE ROUND TRIP FROM SAN ANGELO TO SONORA BY BUGGY OR HORSEBACK SEVERAL TIMES A MONTH FOR NEARLY TWO YEARS TO OVERSEE THE WORK OF THIS SPECTACULAR NATIONAL REGISTER PROPERTY.

What is the Courthouse's most unusual feature?

THE ORIGINAL WELL SITE THAT IS STILL EVIDENT ON THE COURTHOUSE LAWN, WHICH DATES BACK TO 1891. A PROUD RECIPIENT OF FUNDING FROM THE TEXAS COURTHOUSE PRESERVATION PROGRAM, THE SUTTON COUNTY COURTHOUSE WAS REDEDICATED ON JUNE 11, 2002.

What is the most famous case tried in the Sutton County Courthouse?

WESTERN FRONTIER OUTLAW, WILLIAM R. "WILL" CARVER, ROBBED TRAINS AND BANKS WITH BUTCH CASSIDY AND THE SUNDANCE KID. HE WAS APPREHENDED ONE NIGHT BY SHERIFF E.S. BRIANT AND HIS DEPUTIES. THE SHERIFF ATTEMPTED TO ARREST THE OUTLAW, BUT HIS FATE DID NOT INVOLVE A TRIAL; HE WAS SHOT AND KILLED. HIS HEADSTONE CAN BE FOUND IN A SONORA CEMETERY.

Where do you hang your hat?

WHEN IT'S NOT ON THE HANDLEBARS OF MY HARLEY DAVIDSON, IT IS AT BRACEWELL & PATTERSON, LLP, HOUSTON, TX, WHERE I MAKE A LIVING AS A TRIAL LAWYER WORKING AT THE ACTUAL DESK OF LEGENDARY OILMAN, SID RICHARDSON OF FT. WORTH.

Believe it or not!

THE CAVERNS OF SONORA ARE CONSIDERED TO BE ONE OF THE MOST BEAUTIFUL AND UNUSUAL CAVES IN THE UNITED STATES AND ARE LOCATED IN SUTTON COUNTY; A STUNNING EXAMPLE OF SOME OF NATURE'S MOST AWE-INSPIRING CREATIONS!

"It is not perfect, but I firmly believe in our jury system for the resolution of disputes."

~ CLIFF'S FAMOUS TEXAS JUSTICE SAYING

"The Valero Precedent"

A Famous Texas Case as Told by

J. CLIFFORD GUNTER

BRACEWELL & PATTERSON

In 1986, a case against Valero was the first take-or-pay case ever tried to a jury. The tale unfolds in Sonora, Texas, located in Sutton County and known as one of the last frontier towns filled with legends of the Old West. Founded in 1885 by pioneer rancher Charlie Adams, this small community began with eighteen houses, three stores and a post office. The town's population grew from 738 in 1904 to an estimated 5,000 to 6,000 people in 1977 due to the great Texas oil and gas boom. Today, Sonora's population is around 3,000, with over 50% being Mexican-American.

Sonora, the only town in Sutton County, is proud of its lively history which includes tales that impeccably embody the Texas spirit: cowboy style fence disputes, rustled cattle, goat raising, frontier trades and natural gas booms. The Valero case represented the spirit of Sutton County and was bigger than their usual tall tales.

Valero Transmission Co. was tried in Sutton County. Both sides set up their headquarters at the Devil's River Motel, practically taking over the motel and the restaurant. Representing Valero in this particular case was the legendary Cliff Gunter who pooled an assortment of existing and new regulatory ammunition to argue

Sutton
County Courthouse

compellingly that the state's oil and gas rules and regulations were, in fact, embodied in the contract between the pipeline and the seller and therefore, the pipeline did not have to take more gas under the contract than its customers could use; known as the pipeline's market demand.

At this time, gas and oil suppliers were considered bullies to the pipeline industry and routinely won in contractual disputes with pipeline companies and other purchasers. If a pipeline buyer such as Valero attempted to cut back on an existing contractual agreement as

> "AT THIS TIME, GAS AND OIL SUPPLIERS WERE CONSIDERED BULLIES TO THE PIPELINE INDUSTRY AND ROUTINELY WON IN CONTRACTUAL DISPUTES . . ."

demand fluctuated, the sellers were able to enforce contracts with intimidating force and general ease. Valero was exonerated and precedence was set that helped ease the crisis in the industry at the time. The jury's findings endured all appeals.

Even the name of Valero's area foreman and, as it turned out, advisor on local jury selection, would be of historical significance; Mr. Whiskey Hill could not have had a more Texan name.

Where did Swisher County get its name?

IN 1890, SWISHER COUNTY HONORED JAMES G. SWISHER AS ITS NAMESAKE, A TEXAS PATRIOT WHO SIGNED THE TEXAS DECLARATION OF INDEPENDENCE.

Where is the Swisher County Courthouse located?

IN THE COUNTY SEAT, TULIA, TX, NEAR THE SWISHER COUNTY MUSEUM.

Who designed the Swisher County Courthouse?

THE ORIGINAL 1909 COURTHOUSE WAS DESIGNED BY ELMER GEORGE WITHERS IN THE RENAISSANCE REVIVAL STYLE IN BRICK. IN 1962, THE ARCHITECTURAL FIRM OF RITTENBERRY AND RITTENBERRY COMPLETELY REMODELED THE COURTHOUSE IN A MODERN STYLE BY ENCLOSING THE BUILDING IN BRICK.

What is the courthouse's most unusual feature?

WHEN THE ORIGINAL COURTHOUSE WAS REMODELED, IT WAS VIRTUALLY ENCASED IN A BRICK VENEER. REMNANTS OF THE ORIGINAL COURTHOUSE CAN STILL BE FOUND IN STORAGE ROOMS AND CLOSETS.

What is the most famous case tried in the Swisher County Courthouse?

IN THE LATE '90S, OFFICIALS LOCKED UP A YOUNG MAN NAMED FELIPE RODRIGUEZ WHO WAS SEVERELY MENTALLY DISABLED—HE COULDN'T EVEN SPELL HIS OWN NAME CORRECTLY WHEN HE SIGNED THE MULTIPLE CONFESSIONS TO BURGLARY AND ARSON PREPARED FOR HIM BY THE SHERIFF AND DISTRICT ATTORNEY. THE DALLAS MORNING NEWS BROKE THE STORY AND QUOTED THE D.A. AS SAYING THE REAL REASON MR. RODRIGUEZ HAD BEEN KEPT IN JAIL FOR TWO YEARS WAS "FOR HIS OWN GOOD." MR. RODRIGUEZ WAS EVENTUALLY RELEASED.

Where do you hang your hat?

AT MY OWN SOLO OFFICE, IN, AMARILLO, TX, WHERE I SPECIALIZE IN CRIMINAL AND CIVIL LAW.

Believe it or not!

THROUGHOUT THE TULIA CAMPAIGN, I GOT USED TO PEOPLE HARASSING ME. ONE DAY, A BIG PICKUP TRUCK FOLLOWED ME. I WAS FED UP, SO I PULLED MY CAR OVER AND GOT OUT. A CAUCASIAN MAN ABOUT FIFTY WITH A CREW CUT AND COWBOY CLOTHES, GOT OUT, AND WALKED OVER TO ME. HE HELD OUT HIS HAND AND THANKED ME FOR WHAT I WAS DOING. AFTER THAT, I LEARNED THAT YOU CAN'T JUDGE A PERSON BY HIS PICKUP—A LESSON I SHOULD HAVE LEARNED A LONG TIME AGO IN WEST TEXAS!

"Simple lawyers in Texas can make a difference."

~ JEFF'S FAMOUS TEXAS JUSTICE SAYING

"The Tulia Drug Trials"

A Famous Texas Case as Told by
JEFF BLACKBURN
ATTORNEY AT LAW

Tulia is the county seat of Swisher County. It has a small population of about 5,000 and is insulated and in the middle of nowhere.

In July of 1999, local cops arrested 39 people on drug dealing charges, most of whom were African-American. The mass arrest was hailed as an example of how a small town could win the war on drugs. The undercover policeman, who made the accusations, Tom Coleman, was called a "hero" and named "Law Enforcement Officer of the Year" by the Governor. Coleman's testimony, and nothing else, caused nearly all those arrested to be convicted and sentenced to prison in short order. With nearly everyone behind bars, the cases seemed to be over.

Then I got involved. Working on a pro bono basis, I began an independent investigation. I found that Tom Coleman, the law enforcement hero, had abused his authority in jobs he had before coming to Tulia, falsified reports and been falsely presented as a credible witness. I decided that a complete miscarriage of justice had occurred in Tulia and was outraged by it.

I then came up with a five-year pro-bono plan to overturn all of the convictions. For the first year, I focused on laying the factual groundwork to discredit Coleman. The next year involved a dramatic confrontation with the State. One case that of Tonya White had not been tried. I took on the case and pulled out all the stops. We were sweating bullets because we knew that we had a hostile jury, a hostile DA and a hostile judge.

Then, just a few days before trial, I discovered a deposit slip that proved my client was in Oklahoma City when Coleman said she was in Tulia. The State was forced to dismiss the case. This was a watershed moment for us. After that, everything broke

Swisher
County Courthouse

wide open. We had proven for good that Coleman really was a liar and that these folks had been falsely convicted. I then joined forces with the NAACP (the National Association for the Advancement of Colored People) Legal Defense Fund. Together, we broadened the fight into an all-out campaign to overturn all of the cases and enlisted firm lawyers to help.

Within a few months of White's case being dismissed, my allies and myself staged a dramatic hearing. We were able to completely discredit Coleman and other policemen. By now, the case had a national crusade for justice. In August 2003, the Governor pardoned everyone convicted in the case.

On the same day that the pardons were issued, we filed a federal civil rights lawsuit against all of the government agencies that had participated in the Tulia fiasco. That suit was settled for $6 million in April 2004. As part of the settlement, the 26-county drug task force that had supervised

> ## "I THEN CAME UP WITH A FIVE-YEAR PRO-BONO PLAN TO OVERTURN ALL OF THE CONVICTIONS."

Coleman was permanently disbanded. Tulia, once a little town in the middle of nowhere, has now become a symbol of injustice and racism.

Now that the cases are over, I view the struggle philosophically: A lot of people thought I was crazy to take these cases on. I think I was lucky. How many times does a lawyer get the opportunity to do the right thing in such a big way? My wife died in April of 2001, just as the cases were beginning to heat up. Rather than become depressed, I threw myself into freeing the Tulia victims. This struggle gave me a whole new lease on life. It brought beauty back into my existence.

Tarrant
County Courthouse

"Officer Good Guy Awarded $1.2 Million"

A Famous Texas Case as Told by

JIM LANE
LAW OFFICE OF JIM LANE

I had known the Fort Worth officer for a long time. He was the kind that was quiet, not flashy and just did his job. I knew he was mad when I first answered the phone: "The SOB sued the company and the guy who saved my life," he hollered. I told him to quiet down and give me a little more information.

He began in rapid fire to explain that he was on routine patrol one night when he made a traffic stop. After approaching the car and talking to the driver, it was apparent to the officer that the driver was intoxicated. After failing the standard field sobriety test, the driver was arrested on suspicion of DWI. The officer hand cuffed the driver and called for a wrecker. It seems that officer good guy listened to the plea of the hand cuffed driver to, "Let me just go over to the near by bushes and relieve myself before the ride downtown." The officer, being the good guy that he is, agreed.

After the driver finished his business, he decided to "run like hell." The "race was on." The officer finally caught the fleeing man and the "fight was on." The bad guy was getting the best of the officer and had managed to get the officer's service weapon out of his holster. In the fight, the officer was beaten severely.

Just as the bad guy was about to shoot the officer, up drives a company man in his truck. Seeing an empty patrol car and no officer in sight, he got out to investigate. Luckily, he heard the fight and began running and screaming at the guy who was on top of the police officer with the weapon. The bad guy heard him hollering and saw him running to help the officer. The bad guy decided to run again. The officer, still holding on to his hand that held the officer's weapon forced the guy to drop the weapon as he got up to run.

Well, that's when it happened—the company man saw the officer lying on the ground with a torn uniform and a bloody face, picked up the weapon, and fired two shots at the fleeing man. Both shots found their mark hitting the bad guy in both legs—the shots were placed like a marksman shoots at his target. It seems that the company guy was a Vietnam Combat Vet and proficient with firearms. The company guy then calmly called dispatch on the officer's radio and two ambulances were on the scene in just a few minutes.

The bad guy goes to jail for attempted capital murder. But, this guy had watched TV and read newspaper accounts of the subway bandit in New York who was shot by law enforcement people, and then sued, and won a bunch of money. Naturally, he decides he has been wronged so he gets himself a good lawyer and they sue the company and the driver. That's what sent the officer into a rage. "What can I do?" he asks over and over—I thought about it and said, "Let's

> ## ". . . HITTING THE BAD GUY IN BOTH LEGS—THE SHOTS WERE PLACED LIKE A MARKSMAN SHOOTS AT HIS TARGET."

intervene in the suit and sue this guy for the exact amount of money he sued the company and driver for." We did.

After a jury trial, the verdict was read in open court. The jury gave the bad guy a goose egg from the company and driver, but the Fort Worth officer was awarded over a million dollars for the beating he took. Of course, the bad guy is penniless, so the officer will never collect a dime. The bad guy had asked the jury to award about 1.2 million in damages—they did, but it wasn't for him, it was against him. The courtroom was full of police officers and as the verdict was read, there was a lot of hoopin' and hollerin'—the judge just let the celebration go on!

Where did Tarrant County get its name?
FROM GENERAL EDWARD H. TARRANT, WHO WAS ALSO A TEXAS RANGER, ORGANIZED TARRANT COUNTY, ALSO KNOWN AS COWTOWN, IN 1850.

Where is the Tarrant County Courthouse located?
ON THE CORNER OF HOUSTON AND WEATHERFORD STREETS IN DOWNTOWN FORT WORTH, WHERE THERE IS STILL A HITCHIN' POST TO TIE-UP YOUR HORSE.

Who designed the Tarrant County Courthouse?
THE ARCHITECTS GUNN & CURTISS ORIGINALLY DESIGNED THIS MASTERPIECE IN 1895. IT IS A MAGNIFICENT RENAISSANCE REVIVAL STYLE HISTORIC COURTHOUSE BUILT OF RED GRANITE, WHICH RECEIVED A TOTAL RESTORATION IN 1983. THIS GEM IS A NATIONAL REGISTER PROPERTY.

What is the Courthouse's most unusual feature?
ITS GRAND RENAISSANCE REVIVAL STYLE OF ARCHITECTURE MAKES THIS LONE STAR BEAUTY A STRIKING STRUCTURE AGAINST THE DOWNTOWN FORT WORTH SKYLINE.

What is the most famous case tried in the Tarrant County Courthouse?
THE T. CULLEN DAVIS MURDER TRIALS IN THE LATE 1970S PUT FORT WORTH IN THE LEGAL MAP. MR. DAVIS HIRED LEGENDARY RICHARD "RACEHORSE" HANES TO BE PART OF HIS DEFENSE TEAM WHICH ULTIMATELY GOT HIM ACQUITTED OF THE CHARGES OF MURDERING HIS STEP-DAUGHTER AND HER LOVER, AND ATTEMPTING TO MURDER HIS ESTRANGED WIFE.

Where do you hang your hat?
AT MY OWN LAW FIRM IN FORT WORTH, TX, AT THE HISTORICAL OUTLAW HOME. THE HOME IS NAMED FOR ITS ORIGINAL OWNER JOHN CALHOUN OUTLAW. I ALSO HAVE AN OFFICE LOCATED IN WEATHERFORD, TX, JUST WEST OF COWTOWN.

Believe it or not!
A BLACK PANTHER USED TO FALL ASLEEP ON THE STEPS OF THE COURTHOUSE, THIS LEGENDARY TALE WAS SAID TO HAVE OCCURRED AS RECENTLY AS THE 1940S!

The Old &

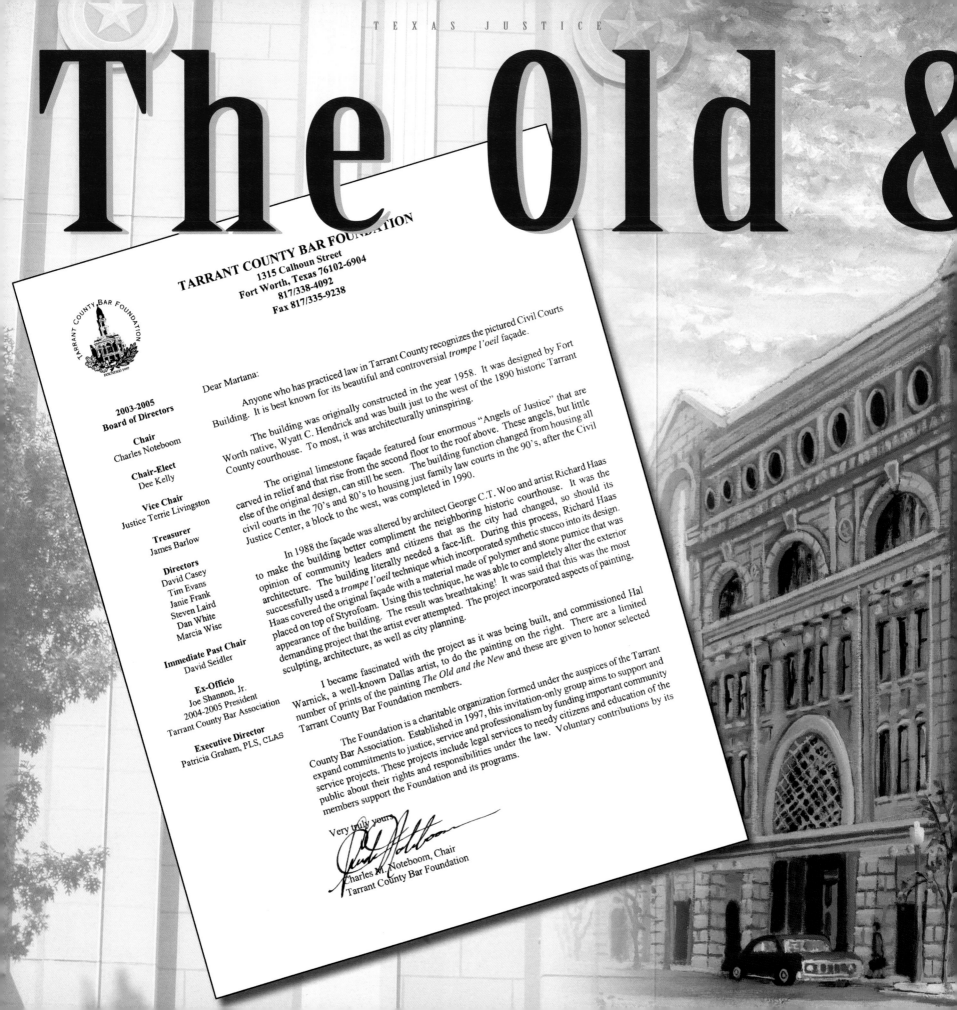

TARRANT COUNTY BAR FOUNDATION
1315 Calhoun Street
Fort Worth, Texas 76102-6904
817/338-4092
Fax 817/335-9238

2003-2005
Board of Directors

Chair
Charles Noteboom

Chair-Elect
Dee Kelly

Vice Chair
Justice Terrie Livingston

Treasurer
James Barlow

Directors
David Casey
Tim Evans
Janie Frank
Steven Laird
Dan White
Marcia Wise

Immediate Past Chair
David Seidler

Ex-Officio
Joe Shannon, Jr.
2004-2005 President
Tarrant County Bar Association

Executive Director
Patricia Graham, PLS, CLAS

Dear Martana:

Anyone who has practiced law in Tarrant County recognizes the pictured Civil Courts Building. It is best known for its beautiful and controversial *trompe l'oeil* façade.

The building was originally constructed in the year 1958. It was designed by Fort Worth native, Wyatt C. Hendrick and was built just to the west of the 1890 historic Tarrant County courthouse. To most, it was architecturally uninspiring.

The original limestone façade featured four enormous "Angels of Justice" that are carved in relief and that rise from the second floor to the roof above. These angels, but little else of the original design, can still be seen. The building function changed from housing all civil courts in the 70's and 80's to housing just family law courts in the 90's, after the Civil Justice Center, a block to the west, was completed in 1990.

In 1988 the façade was altered by architect George C.T. Woo and artist Richard Haas to make the building better compliment the neighboring historic courthouse. It was the opinion of community leaders and citizens that as the city had changed, so should its architecture. The building literally needed a face-lift. During this process, Richard Haas successfully used a *trompe l'oeil* technique which incorporated synthetic stucco into its design. Haas covered the original façade with a material made of polymer and stone pumice that was placed on top of Styrofoam. Using this technique, he was able to completely alter the exterior appearance of the building. The result was breathtaking! It was said that this was the most demanding project that the artist ever attempted. The project incorporated aspects of painting, sculpting, architecture, as well as city planning.

I became fascinated with the project as it was being built, and commissioned Hal Warnick, a well-known Dallas artist, to do the painting *The Old and the New* and these are given to honor selected number of prints of the painting *The Old and the New* and these are given to honor selected Tarrant County Bar Foundation members.

The Foundation is a charitable organization formed under the auspices of the Tarrant County Bar Association. Established in 1997, this invitation-only group aims to support and expand commitments to justice, service and professionalism by funding important community service projects. These projects include legal services to needy citizens and education of the public about their rights and responsibilities under the law. Voluntary contributions by its members support the Foundation and its programs.

Very truly yours,

Charles M. Noteboom, Chair
Tarrant County Bar Foundation

The New

The Civil Courts Building

Where did Titus County get its name?

IN 1846 IT WAS NAMED FOR ANDREW JACKSON TITUS, WHO WORKED FOR THE ANNEXATION OF TEXAS TO THE UNITED STATES, WAS A MEXICAN WAR HERO AND SERVED IN THE TEXAS LEGISLATION.

Where is the Titus County Courthouse located?

ON THE TOWN SQUARE IN MOUNT PLEASANT, ONE OF THE "100 BEST SMALL TOWNS IN AMERICA" THANKS TO ITS ACCESS TO SEVEN LAKES AND A TOWN SQUARE THAT IS SURROUNDED BY HISTORIC BUILDINGS, MUSEUMS AND SPECIALTY SHOPS.

Who designed the Titus County Courthouse?

THE MODERNE STYLE BRICK HISTORIC TITUS COUNTY COURTHOUSE WAS RENOVATED TO ITS 1940S APPEARANCE ACCORDING TO THE DESIGN OF ARCHITECTS EUBANKS-HARRIS, BY PLACING A STUCCO FAÇADE OVER THE ORIGINAL 1895 HISTORIC COURTHOUSE MODERNE EXTERIOR OF BRICK.

What is the courthouse's most unusual feature?

ITS DESIGNATION AS "THE UGLIEST COURTHOUSE IN TEXAS," WHICH LED TO ANOTHER RENOVATION AROUND 1990 THAT RESTORED IT TO ITS 1940S APPEARANCE.

What is the most famous case tried in the Titus County Courthouse?

THE MURDER TRIAL OF JAMES C. ROWLAND, THE ONLY PERSON TO LEGALLY HANG IN TITUS COUNTY UNDER THE WATCH OF "COLONEL BILL" EDWARDS, SHERIFF OF TITUS COUNTY FROM 1871 TO 1882. HE ORGANIZED A VIGILANTE SYSTEM IN THE COUNTY TO COMBAT CRIME FOLLOWING THE CIVIL WAR.

Where do you hang your hat?

IN OCTOBER OF 1993, I RETIRED FROM THE TEXAS RANGERS WITH OVER 29 YEARS SERVICE WITH THE TEXAS DEPARTMENT OF PUBLIC SAFETY. MY WIFE SUZANNE AND I LIVE ON A SMALL RANCH OUTSIDE OF MT. PLEASANT, WHERE WE RAISE, TRAIN AND SHOW CUTTING HORSES. I AM PRESENTLY EMPLOYED BY GUARANTY BOND BANK AS SENIOR CHIEF OF SECURITY OVER ELEVEN LOCATIONS IN THE NORTH-EAST TEXAS AREA AND ANOTHER IN FT. STOCKTON, TX.

Believe it or not!

IN THE1890S, MOUNT PLEASANT HOME TO A LARGE LICENSED DISTILLERY AND HOG FARM. THE HOGS FED ON SPENT MASH FROM THE DISTILLERY AND BECAME INTOXICATED FROM THE RESIDUAL ALCOHOL. BOTH SALOON OWNERS AND PROHIBITIONISTS EXPRESSED DISPLEASURE. ONE GROUP OR THE OTHER DYNAMITED THE DISTILLERY IN 1900, DESTROYING IT AND KILLING MANY OF THE HOGS. NEITHER GROUP CLAIMED RESPONSIBILITY AND TITUS COUNTY WAS VOTED "DRY" IN 1902!

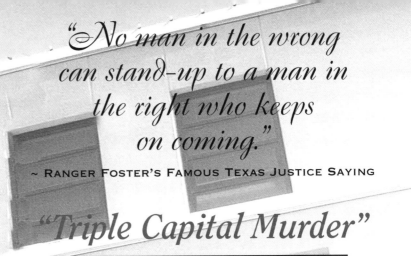

> *"No man in the wrong can stand-up to a man in the right who keeps on coming."*
>
> ~ RANGER FOSTER'S FAMOUS TEXAS JUSTICE SAYING

"Triple Capital Murder"

A Famous Texas Case as Told by
J. BRANTLEY FOSTER
TEXAS RANGER SERGEANT, RETIRED

In May of 1982, I was a young Texas Ranger stationed in Mount Pleasant, Titus County, Texas. I had been involved in several high-profile murder cases in my county, but I never could have expected that I would soon be needed at the local Pizza Hut to assist in a triple capital murder.

Upon arrival to the murder scene, I was met by Chief Sustair of the Mount Pleasant Police Department and Assistant Chief and close friend Conrad Mars, as well as Detective Glen Sisk. We immediately secured the crime scene and began our investigation. The store manager had been beaten to death and was lying just outside his small office. The other male employee was lying partially inside a large cooler face down, with one bullet wound in the back of his head. A female employee was missing, along with cash from the register.

While collecting evidence and taking crime scene photos, I had stopped on several occasions to look at a small dead-end hallway, cluttered with boxes. After removing the boxes, I discovered the missing female employee in a sitting position, her hands clutched in her lap and a claw hammer buried in her head. An autopsy would reveal that she had been shot, her throat cut and beaten with a hammer.

One day while on another investigation, I was contacted by the Mount Pleasant Police Department and spoke with Detective Mike Hatch, an investigator for the Oklahoma State Police. I learned that during an interview with an armed robbery suspect, Calvin Padgett, the suspect had blurted out, "I know who left the hammer sticking in the girl's head at the Mount Pleasant Pizza Hut." No one outside of the investigation team had been informed of the hammer and it had not been published in the media, so we knew Padgett had to have been involved.

Over the next few months, we made a case against Padgett and had him transferred from the Oklahoma State Prison to Texas. During his transportation to Texas, we passed through Ardmore, Oklahoma. Padgett calmly pointed to a motel and said, "That's where I killed the woman in the motel," referring to another case under investigation by the Oklahoma Authorities. Padgett's name would later come up in several more murders in the Fort Worth and northeast Texas areas.

Padgett was eventually tried in Titus County, Texas, by District Attorney Charles MacCobb and Assistant D.A. Chuck Bailey. He was convicted and sentenced to life in prison for one of the crimes. An area newspaper reporter became convinced of and continually

Titus
County Courthouse

protested Padgett's innocence and accused investigators of lying. While Padgett was in the Dallas County Jail, he had developed a relationship with a female by mail and decided to be married. This reporter was so adamant about his innocence that during this ceremony, which was performed over the phone, the reporter was Padgett's stand-in bride.

Padgett eventually plead guilty to a second charge of capital murder and received another life sentence. This plea put an end to the accusations by the press and we also arrested Padgett's fifteen-year-old brother, and a twelve and thirteen-year-old cousin and friend in this investigation. The twelve-year-old had stayed in the car at the crime scene as a lookout, while the other three went inside. He said they were drinking and had driven from their homes in Kilgore to Mount Pleasant looking for something to rob. They spotted the Pizza

> **". . . THE SUSPECT HAD BLURTED OUT, 'I KNOW WHO LEFT THE HAMMER STICKING IN THE GIRL'S HEAD AT THE MOUNT PLEASANT PIZZA HUT.'"**

Hut about closing time and decided that this was their place. Padgett had said the way to commit a perfect crime was to "kill every witness."

Padgett was returned to Lexington Oklahoma State Penitentiary to serve a life sentence, where he contracted HIV. He died in the early 1990s without ever clearing the other crimes that he was suspected of.

My career would lead me to investigate numerous multiple murders, kidnappings and other crimes including the Branch Davidians in Waco, Texas, in 1993, but none ever took the twists and turns of the Pizza Hut investigation.

Travis
County Courthouse

"Misconduct of an Asbestos Company"

A Famous Texas Case as Told by

SCOTT M. HENDLER
THE HENDLER LAW FIRM, P.C.

Ben Baker spent most of his working life as a pipe fitter hanging and connecting industrial pipe at various industrial sites. Part of that job included covering the pipe with insulation, especially where the pipe carried high temperature water and steam for power generation. The insulation contained asbestos, a mineral impervious to fire, heat and virtually indestructible. But asbestos had another, more sinister characteristic: it could be lethal when inhaled.

The cutting of asbestos insulation released asbestos fibers into the air. Throughout his career Ben Baker breathed air filled with asbestos dust, which embedded in his lungs and decades later developed into a fatal cancer called mesothelioma, the signature disease of asbestos exposure.

Owens Corning Fiberglas was (and remains) a leading manufacturer of industrial insulation. From 1953 to 1972, its flagship pipe insulation product was called Kaylo, the principal asbestos product Ben Baker worked with as a pipe fitter. Unbeknownst to him, it would become the instrument of his death.

Lawyers uncovered evidence that Owens Corning had learned as early as the 1940s that the asbestos in Kaylo was dangerous. Incredibly, Owens Corning not only suppressed this information from the public and medical community, it assured workers that Kaylo was safe and even contributed to "worker well-being."

But away from the eye of public scrutiny, Owens Corning was learning of a darker reality. In 1948, a research scientist hired to test Kaylo, wrote to company officials:

I realize that our findings are less favorable than anticipated. However, since Kaylo is capable of producing asbestosis [another

> *"Alexander Hamilton said, 'The first duty of society is justice.' It's as true now as it was then."*
>
> ~ Scott's Famous Texas Justice Saying

potentially fatal asbestos disease], it is better to discover it now in [laboratory] animals rather than later in industrial workers. Thus, the company, being forewarned, will be in a better position to institute adequate control measures for safeguarding exposed employees…

Despite these findings, Owens Corning continued to sell Kaylo without warning people about its dangerous properties. The company also chose not to substitute asbestos with one of the safer substitute products that were available because they were more expensive—company executives placed a higher value on profits than on people's lives.

After repeated studies confirmed the 1948 research results, Owens Corning reluctantly added a vague label in 1966 stating that Kaylo could cause "pneumoconiosis," a word most workers didn't understand. To make this already ambiguous label less conspicuous, it was stamped on the side of the box near the top so that when the top flap of the box was opened, it concealed the label from view. There was no warning in plain view that simply stated the product's dust was dangerous, and potentially lethal if inhaled.

Ben Baker never learned of any of this until after he was diagnosed with mesothelioma, the asbestos cancer that would claim his life. Once he learned the facts, Baker brought suit against Owens Corning and in 1997, the case went to trial, carried forward by his wife and children.

In May of 1997, I and two of my co-counsel, Spencer Parris and Bill Connelly, tried the case in the 345th Judicial District Court of Travis County, Texas. The trial lasted two weeks, during which time the jury heard from

"... COMPANY EXECUTIVES PLACED A HIGHER VALUE ON PROFITS THAN ON PEOPLE'S LIVES."

Ben Baker, who had provided his sworn testimony on video before he died. The jury also learned of Owens Corning's conduct before and during Baker's exposure to its Kaylo insulation. And what the jury heard outraged them. It became clear that if Owens Corning and others in the asbestos industry had acted responsibly, Ben Baker would not have suffered the agonizingly slow and painful death of mesothelioma.

The jury deliberated for two days before returning a verdict of two million dollars in compensatory damages for the Baker family and twenty million dollars in punitive damages. This verdict is believed to be the highest personal injury or wrongful death verdict in the history of the Travis County State Courts. Though the judge ultimately ordered Owens Corning to pay a reduced amount, the jury sent a strong message to this negligent company and others in the asbestos industry that continues to have an impact to this day.

Where did Travis County get its name?
IN 1843, THE REPUBLIC OF TEXAS CONGRESS CREATED TRAVIS COUNTY AND NAMED IT IN HONOR OF WILLIAM B. TRAVIS WHO WAS THE COMMANDER OF THE ALAMO AND DIED IN BATTLE THERE.

Where is the Travis County Courthouse located?
IN DOWNTOWN AUSTIN, TX, THE HOME OF THE UT LONGHORNS, JUST TWO BLOCKS WEST OF THE CAPITAL AND ONE BLOCK WEST OF THE GOVERNORS MANSION.

Who designed the Travis County Courthouse?
BUILT PRIMARILY OF LIMESTONE IN 1930, THIS HISTORIC COURTHOUSE WAS CREATED BY C.H. PAGE & BROTHER IN A MODERNE STYLE. THE ORIGINAL COURTHOUSE WAS EXPANDED TWICE; IN 1959 AND AGAIN IN 1962.

What is the courthouse's most unusual feature?
WHEN THE COURTHOUSE WAS ORIGINALLY BUILT, THE JAIL WAS SITUATED ON THE TOP FLOOR. THIS, HOWEVER, WAS NOT A VERY STRATEGIC MOVE, AS INMATES WHERE ABLE TO CLOG THE TOILETS AND SINKS, FLOODING THE LOWER FLOORS.

What is the most famous case tried in the Travis County Courthouse?
TEXAS V. BEARD IS CERTAINLY ONE OF THE MOST FAMOUS CASES. CELESTE BEARD WAS FOUND GUILTY IN THE MURDER OF HER WEALTHY HUSBAND, STEVEN BEARD, A RICH AND POWERFUL CO-OWNER OF A LOCAL TELEVISION STATION. TRACY TARLTON, CELESTE'S ALLEGED LESBIAN LOVER, PLEADED GUILTY TO THE MURDER OF STEVEN BEARD IN EXCHANGE FOR TESTIMONY AGAINST CELESTE BEARD AND A TWENTY-YEAR PRISON TERM.

Where do you hang your hat?
IN AUSTIN, TX, AT THE HENDLER LAW FIRM, P.C. THIS IS WHERE WE ARE HEADQUARTERED AND WE ALSO HAVE AN OFFICE IN NEW YORK. THE HENDLER LAW FIRM REPRESENTS VICTIMS OF CORPORATE MISCONDUCT IN THE AREAS OF TOXIC INJURY, PHARMACEUTICAL LITIGATION AND COMMERCIAL WRONGDOING.

Believe it or not!
WHEN THE TRAVIS COUNTY BAILIFF'S SIZEABLE PET GOLDFISH PASSED AWAY, HE WAS SO GRIEF STRICKEN THAT THE COURT REPORTER HAD THE FISH STUFFED AND MOUNTED AND PRESENTED IT TO THE BAILIFF AT A LUNCHEON IN THE FISH'S HONOR!

Where did Upshur County get its name?

ABEL PARKER UPSHUR, SECRETARY OF STATE UNDER PRESIDENT JOHN TYLER, WHO REOPENED NEGOTIATIONS FOR THE ANNEXATION OF TEXAS AND DRAFTED THE PROPOSITION IN 1844. THIS COUNTY SEAT IS ALSO KNOWN AS "TATER-TOWN".

Where is the Upshur County Courthouse located?

ON TYLER STREET IN GILMER, TX, HOME OF THE EAST TEXAS YAMBOREE. THE YAMBOREE IS ONE OF THE OLDEST FOOD FESTIVALS IN THE STATE AND CELEBRATES UPSHURER'S LOVE FOR THE SWEET POTATO.

Who designed the Upshur County Courthouse?

ELMER G. WITHERS DESIGNED THE 1933 COUNTY'S FIFTH AND HISTORIC COURTHOUSE IN A MODERNE STYLE DURING THE PEAK OF THE GREAT DEPRESSION. THE DISCOVERY OF OIL NEAR GILMER IN 1937 PAID FOR THE NEW COURTHOUSE.

What is the courthouse's most unusual feature?

THE COURTHOUSE LAWN HAS A HISTORICAL MARKER THAT HONORS EMMA JOHNSON, "SUNBONNET HEROINE" OF EAST TEXAS. AT AGE SIXTEEN, EMMA RODE WITH REBEL GENERAL NATHAN BEDFORD FORREST, SHOWING HIM WHERE HE AND HIS CONFEDERATE MEN COULD CROSS THE RIVER TO FIND FLEEING UNION SOLDIERS.

What is the most famous case tried in the Upshur County Courthouse?

THE TRIAL OF FOUR WOMEN WHO SUED THE BREAST IMPLANT MANUFACTURER, 3M, FOR FAULTY IMPLANTS AND INJURIES CAUSED BY THEM IN 1997 AND WON MORE THAN $1.5 MILLION IN COMPENSATORY AND PUNITIVE DAMAGES. A TEXAS APPEALS COURT LATER REVERSED THE DECISION.

Where do you hang your hat?

I LIVE IN UPSHUR, TX, AND HAVE BEEN PRACTICING LAW FOR THIRTY-SEVEN YEARS. IN THAT TIME, I HAVE BEEN NAMED AS ONE OF THE STATE'S TOP FIVE CRIMINAL LAWYERS, AS WELL AS TWICE NAMED A TEXAS MONTHLY SUPER LAWYER. I CURRENTLY AM WITH MY FIRM, HOLMES & MOORE, P.L.L.C., IN LONGVIEW, TX, WHERE I CONTINUE AN ACTIVE CRIMINAL TRIAL PRACTICE WITH DAVID MOORE.

Believe it or not!

THOMAS W. GILMER, NAMESAKE OF THE GILMER, COUNTY SEAT OF UPSHUR COUNTY, AND ABEL P. UPSHUR, NAMESAKE FOR UPSHUR COUNTY, WERE BOTH KILLED ON FEBRUARY 28, 1844, DURING THE TEST FIRING OF A CANNON ABOARD THE BATTLESHIP PRINCETON NEAR WASHINGTON, D.C!

"Not Guilty."
~ SCRAPPY'S FAMOUS TEXAS JUSTICE SAYING

"East Texas Wildcatters"

A Famous Texas Case as Told by
CLIFTON L. "SCRAPPY" HOLMES
HOLMES & MOORE, P.L.L.C.

The late '50s and early '60s in East Texas became something of a replay of the '30s oil boom, not as a result of the discovery of new oil reserves, but as a result of the "discovery" of a new way of drilling. Though the "whipstock" had been available for years as a legitimate tool for use in controlling the slope or direction which a bore took, it took the felonious genius of new-era wildcatters in East Texas to employ it as a means of stealing the oil reserves of one's neighboring leaseholders. Drilling contractors were thicker than flies on a picnic pie; sinking crooked holes everywhere they could find a vacant mineral estate which bordered producing acreage. It took some time, but thanks to Will Wilson and his special investigating committee (and the Johnny-come-lately assistance of the Texas Rangers), the Railroad Commission cracked down and began wholesale testing of wells to determine their slant.

It's said that cement suppliers and everyone with a vehicle capable of hauling it made fortunes during the thirty days or so of intensive well inspections, the knowing owners of the slant holes busily plugging them ahead of the inspectors. Many criminal charges emanated from this investigation in East Texas, but only one resulted in a conviction—that in Upshur County, by the eminent District Attorney Ott Duncan.

Ott was a legend, not so much for his legal prowess, as for his mode, manner and appearance. He was a slight man, with a bulbous belly about the size of a basketball, always protruding above his low slung trousers and below his neatly buttoned and watch-fobbed vest. He always wore a too-small Stetson silver-belly, perched on the crown of his head. He could turn a phrase with the very best and never met his match in the apt retort. I never saw him try a case with much more than a Big Chief tablet and a double-nought cedar pencil at hand.

The slant-holer who had been indicted by Ott was a typical East Texas "oil man," with strong ties to Kilgore (a very "wet" community 25 miles south of Gilmer). Ott was well aware of Kilgore's reputation as a long-time "wet" area, with many whiskey stores, beer joints, night clubs and even "private clubs" which sold "liquor by the drink." He also knew that Upshur County prided itself as completely dry and true to Baptist "teetotalarianism." The trial was basically uneventful and considering the heavy burden the

Upshur County Courthouse

reasonable doubt standard places on the prosecution, Ott could have been expected to lose. But, his closing argument included the following colloquy, tying his defendant to alcohol and invoking the jury's natural prejudice:

"Ladies and gentlemen, this guy is from over in Kilgore. That's where he did business. That's where he came from. That's where he met up with this other fellow and conspired to steal this oil," [And in a soft voice] "And where did they go? Where did they go?" [Then in an audible whisper] "They went to the Kilgore Club!" [Then in a fainter whisper, as Ott leaned over the jury rail] "And what did they do? What did they do?" [Then in a raspy whisper, expressing disgust] "They had

> "**DRILLING CONTRACTORS WERE THICKER THAN FLIES ON A PICNIC PIE; SINKING CROOKED HOLES EVERYWHERE THEY COULD FIND A VACANT MINERAL ESTATE . . .**"

a drink of HARD LIQUOR!" [Ott then straightened, stepped back, flung his arms in the air, face toward heaven, and shouted] "MACEDONIA, HEAR MY CRY!"

Ott straightened his vest, tucking in his gaping shirt, sat down, folded his arms across his protruding belly and offered a faint smile and a wink toward the judge. The jury was back in no time, convicting the slant-holer as Ott had asked.

No one has a clue what Ott's argument pertained to or why Macedonia was involved. But it worked, the slant-holer got his due, and Ott was re-elected. ⚒

Uvalde
County Courthouse

"100% Sure. Right?"

A Famous Texas Case as Told by
RONALD L. BAIR
THE BAIR LAW FIRM

The use of DNA in court cases is now an everyday occurrence that most people are familiar with. DNA is entered as evidence to both convict criminals, as well as to clear the innocent. This, however, is a relatively new scientific advancement, and in 1990, when Gilbert Alejandro was accused of sexually assaulting an Uvalde County woman, the use of DNA was a novel technique.

The victim, a fifty-year-old woman, had accused Mr. Alejandro, a long-time Uvalde resident, of attacking her in her home where he had been waiting for her to return. The attacker jumped out at her, put a pillow over her face and sexually assaulted her. While the woman testified that she did not get a good look at her attacker, she was able to identify his clothing and ultimately picked him out of a photo i.d. book. The man she pinpointed was Gilbert Alejandro. As his council, Attorney Emmitt Harris told Mr. Alejandro that DNA had been found at the crime scene and that by comparing his own DNA to the sample, he could prove that he was not the attacker and prove his innocence. As Mr. Alejandro strongly professed his innocence, this new science seemed to be the key to his salvation. He readily agreed to provide the sample, which was sent off the Bexar County Medical Examiner, where Mr. Fred Zain conducted the analysis. At that time there was no such a lab in Uvlade.

When the case was taken to trial, both Mr. Harris and his client were confident that this DNA test would prove that they had the wrong guy. When Mr. Zain took the stand to testify about the DNA results, they were appalled. According to Mr. Zain, the DNA was an "exact match" and

> ## "I can't get any corn planted, for fighting Indians."
> ~ Ron's Famous Texas Justice Saying

he was "100% sure" that it was Mr. Alejandro's DNA at the scene. As could be expected, the jury trusted in this evidence and he was found guilty and sent to the State Penitentiary.

For four years, he sat in the penitentiary in disbelief that this had happened. It was in 1994 that someone in the investigation department started to have a funny feeling about the star DNA expert, Fred Zain. An investigation was begun and the skeletons began to come out of the closet! It turns out that Zain had falsely testified in this case and others about DNA evidence. He had repeatedly perjured himself and innocent people were wrongly convicted because of it, Gilbert among them. There were employees who worked with Zain who testified that, in fact, the DNA tests have proved exactly the opposite as to what Zain had claimed.

Attorney Emmitt Harris immediately filled a writ of habeas corpus and demanded a new trial on behalf of his client. The trial was granted, and Gilbert finally had a chance to do it all over again and clear himself of the charges against him. Luckily the D.A. dismissed the case before it even made it to trial, based on the evidence of Zain's false testimony. Finally after four years, Gilbert Alejandro was again a free man.

> ## "BECAUSE OF THE FALSE TESTIMONY OF ONE PERSON, GILBERT ALEJANDRO LOST FOUR YEARS OF HIS LIFE . . ."

Because of the false testimony of one person, Gilbert Alejandro lost four years of his life, the victim never found her real attacker and jurors from the original case were haunted by the result of their actions that they based on false evidence. While Fred Zain was tried in the civil court and found liable, unfortunately Alejandro could not collect from Zain personally due to the statute of limitations and he was not held accountable for his actions. However, Alejandro later accepted a $250,000 settlement from the county for its mistakes.

Where did Uvalde County get its name?
FROM A MISSPELLING OF JUAN DE UGALDE, THE FORMER SPANISH GOVERNOR, KNIGHT AND SOLDIER. OVER THE YEARS, THE NAME METAMORPHOSED INTO UVALDE WHICH WAS CHOSEN AS THE COUNTY SEAT IN 1856.

Where is the Uvalde County Courthouse located?
ON THE TOWN SQUARE ACROSS FROM THE HISTORIC UVALDE OPERA HOUSE.

Who designed the Uvalde County Courthouse?
HENRY T. PHELPS DESIGNED THE COURTHOUSE IN 1927 WITH A TEXAS RENAISSANCE STYLING AND CLASSICAL INFLUENCE IN LIMESTONE AND BRICK. UVALDE COUNTY IS PROUD OF THEIR HISTORICAL COURTHOUSE.

What is the Courthouse's most unusual feature?
THE CLOCK THAT HENRY PHELPS DESIGNED TO BE IN AN UNUSUAL PLACEMENT, RARE AMONG TEXAS COURTHOUSES.

What is the most famous case tried in the Uvalde County Courthouse?
ALTHOUGH THIS INCIDENT WAS NOT TRIED IN THE COURTHOUSE, IT IS THE LEGENDARY TALE OF LAW OFFICER PATRICK F. GARRETT WHO KILLED OUTLAW BILLY THE KID IN 1881. GARRETT CAME FROM ALABAMA AND SETTLED IN UVALDE IN 1869 WHERE HE WORKED AS A FARMER, COWBOY, AND BUFFALO HUNTER, WAS INVOLVED IN RANCHING OPERATIONS AND SERVED AS SHERIFF IN SEVERAL CITIES. HE WAS KILLED IN 1908 IN NEW MEXICO WHEN AN ARGUMENT ESCALATED OVER LAND, BUT MANY PEOPLE BELIEVE THAT THE QUARREL WAS AN EXCUSE TO COERCE GARRETT TO FIGHT. OTHERWISE, IT IS LIKELY HE WOULD HAVE BEEN MURDERED BY AN AMBUSH POSE.

Where do you hang your hat?
IN HOUSTON, TX, WHERE I AM A TRIAL ATTORNEY FOR MY FIRM, THE BAIR LAW FIRM. THE BAIR LAW FIRM HAS A KEEN INTEREST IN HISTORY, AND AS A FOUNDING PARTNER IN THE FIRM, I AM INTERESTED IN PRESERVING TEXAS HISTORY AND BELIEVE THAT UVALDE COUNTY HAS A RICH AND VARIED HISTORY THAT MANY READERS WILL ENJOY FOR GENERATIONS TO COME. I AM COMMITTED TO TRANSPORTATION LAW, EARNING MYSELF MEMBERSHIP IN THE TRUCKING INDUSTRY DEFENSE ASSOCIATION.

Believe it or not!
MR. BAIR HAS PROBABLY TRIED MORE FORKLIFT ACCIDENT CASES THAN ANY OTHER ATTORNEY IN THE STATE OF TEXAS!

Where did Van Zandt County get its name?

FROM ISAAC VAN ZANDT IN 1848, A TEXAS ATTORNEY ELECTED TO SERVE IN CONGRESS AND APPOINTED CHARGE D'AFFAIRS TO THE UNITED STATES IN 1842 BY TEXAS PRESIDENT SAM HOUSTON. VAN ZANDT WAS SEEKING THE OFFICE OF TEXAS GOVERNOR WHEN STRICKEN BY YELLOW FEVER.

Where is the Van Zandt County Courthouse located?

IN THE TOWN SQUARE ON DALLAS STREET OF CANTON, TX, HOME OF FIRST MONDAY TRADE DAYS. SINCE THE 1870s, ABOUT 3,000 DEALERS AND OVER 100,000 SHOPPERS CONVERGE ON THIS SLEEPY LITTLE TOWN FOR ONE OF AMERICA'S LARGEST FLEA MARKETS ON THE WEEKEND PRIOR TO THE FIRST MONDAY OF EVERY MONTH.

Who designed the Van Zandt County Courthouse?

THE MODERNE STYLE HISTORIC COURTHOUSE WAS DESIGNED BY M.T. CLEMENTS, THE FIRM OF VOELCKER & DIXON, IN 1937 OF BRICK. IT WAS THE COUNTY'S FIFTH COURTHOUSE AND WAS CONSTRUCTED DURING THE GREAT DEPRESSION WITH WPA FUNDS TO PROVIDE JOBS.

What is the Courthouse's most unusual feature?

AN EAGLE ON THE LAWN OF THE PRESENT COURTHOUSE, WHICH ONCE SAT ATOP VAN ZANDT COUNTY'S FIFTH COURTHOUSE, BUILT IN 1896. A RITE OF PASSAGE FOR YOUNG BOYS WAS TO SCALE THE COURTHOUSE TO TOUCH THE EAGLE.

What is the most famous case tried in the Van Zandt County Courthouse?

WILLIAM B. "BOME" MOORE FOR MURDERING ALEXANDER BOTTOMS AT THE CIRCUS IN 1870. THE TWO FAMILIES GOT INTO A GUNFIGHT. WITNESSES SAID THAT AFTER BOTTOMS WAS SHOT, BOME WALKED TO HIS BODY, PUT HIS FOOT ON BOTTOMS' CHEST AND CROWED LIKE A ROOSTER. BOME FACED TRIAL IN 1874, BUT WAS FOUND NOT GUILTY.

Where do you hang your hat?

AT PETROFF & ASSOCIATES IN DALLAS, TX. PETROFF HAS BEEN ACTIVE IN THE TRIAL AND APPELLATE COURTS THROUGHOUT THE STATE OF TEXAS, ARGUING CASES IN DALLAS, FORT WORTH, CORPUS CHRISTI AND THE WACO COURT OF APPEALS AND HAS APPEARED BEFORE THE TEXAS SUPREME COURT.

Believe it or not!

ONE OF TEXAS' UNUSUAL STRUCTURES IS "THE SALT PALACE" IN GRAND SALINE, CONSTRUCTED ENTIRELY OF SALT BLOCKS EXTRACTED FROM A LARGE SALT DEPOSIT NEAR TOWN WHICH COULD SUPPLY THE WORLD'S CRAVING FOR 20,000 YEARS!

"Ain't No Hill for a Stepper."

~ KIP'S FAMOUS TEXAS JUSTICE SAYING

"David vs. Goliath: The First FenPhen Case Ever Tried"

A Famous Texas Case as Told by

KIP PETROFF

PETROFF & ASSOCIATES

In the past decade, the diet drug combination known as Fen-Phen gained wide popularity and tremendous publicity as "the magic pill" that helped overweight people effortlessly shed unwanted pounds. This prescription medication was thought by many to be the miracle drug that would save the nation. With heart disease, obesity and many other weight-related disease literally killing people, the diet drug gave many the hope they were looking for. With a healthy diet, exercise and Fen-Phen, even the grossly obese could trim their waistlines and ultimately improve their health. However, as the old adage goes . . . if it sounds too good to be true, it probably is.

In 1997, however, the word was out. Rather than giving people the hope for a healthier life, it was in February of that year that the Mayo Clinic discovered the dangers that Fen-Phen posed to the human heart. In July, the Clinic held a press conference, urging the Food and Drug Administration to investigate the drug and its effects. The FDA took notice and it was only two months later that the drug was removed from the market because it was found to cause valvular heart disease.

The drug maker, Wyeth (American Home Products), which is possibly the 6th largest drug company in the United States, was about to begin what would turn out to be one of the biggest mass torts ever.

American Home Products (AHP) owned rights to market and sell both Pondimin and Redux, two chemically related drugs that were part of the Fen-Phen craze in the mid '90s. AHP had growing knowledge of the adverse effects of the two drugs, but did not warn consumers of the risk of valvular heart disease. It was not until the FDA's official investigation that the company began to warn about the heart dangers associated with the drug. By this time, millions of Americans had tried Fen-Phen to help them lose weight.

Mr. Kip Petroff, along with his partner, Robert Kisselburgh,

an Zandt
County Courthouse

tried the very first individual Fen-Phen "test case" in U.S. history. At that time, Wyeth did not think they were culpable, but history has proven them wrong. Wyeth likened the adverse effects of the drug to those of chemotherapy, as they were lifesaving to those afflicted with obesity and that the benefits of the drug outweighed the disadvantages. As Mr. Petroff described, this was a "David v. Goliath" case. At the trial there were two lawyers, including Mr. Petroff, representing the plaintiff, versus nineteen lawyers representing the drug company at various times throughout the case.

The judge called only 85 potential jurors for the trial in May 1999, but jurors in this type of case have biases for or against big drug companies and healthy-looking overweight people who are unhappy with the results they obtained from diet pills. A jury of unbiased jurors could not be selected. A mistrial was declared. In July of 1999, the judge summoned 500 potential jurors. A jury was then selected and the first Fen-Phen trial was underway.

When the trial began, Judge Tommy Wallace presided. Not

> ## "MR. KIP PETROFF . . . TRIED THE VERY FIRST INDIVIDUAL FEN-PHEN 'TEST CASE' IN U.S. HISTORY."

only was this a landmark trial, but there were so many documents to review and consider, the jury requested room to "spread-out" during jury deliberations. Judge Wallace actually allowed the jury to take over the entire courtroom, which is the second largest in the entire state, so they would have enough room to interpret all of the evidence themselves.

At the conclusion of the trial, Mr. Petroff and his client were astounded when the verdict was read. The jury awarded $23 million dollars to the plaintiff, a landmark verdict and the beginning of a decade of Fen-Phen litigation.

Victoria
County Courthouse

"The Collapse of ENRON"

A Famous Texas Case as Told by

PHILIP HILDER
PHILIP H. HILDER & ASSOCIATES, P.C.

For a while, it looked as if the terrorist attacks of September 11, 2001, and the fighting that followed in Afghanistan would dominate the news for the rest of that year. Then came ENRON and whistleblower Sherron Watkins. No one ever thought that such an elaborate financial scandal could occur in the very heart of America's fifth largest corporation and the one known to be the country's most innovative—but it did. Enron's collapse would become the highest profile white-collar criminal investigation in American history. Hidden debt, false earnings reports and greed beyond comprehension and attorney Philip Hilder had a ring-side seat.

Weeks before the scandal even broke, executives on the inside knew something big was brewing. They began to seek counsel and to prepare for the coming investigation even before the government had time to take formal action. One of those executives was Sherron Watkins, who would soon be known as Enron's whistleblower. It was her internal memo to Enron's former chief executive and chairman Kenneth Lay that opened-up this whole can of worms. The memo to Lay, chairman since 1986, warned him of an elaborate accounting hoax and suggested that Enron would collapse in a wave of accounting scandals—warnings which quickly attracted the attention of investigators.

Watkins is a very astute woman and it not take her long to realize that it wasn't in her interest to be represented by Enron's legal counsel—the very people she thought were complicit in the company's fall (many people at Enron were blind to interest conflicts, but Ms. Watkins wasn't one of them). Following a friend's advice, she contacted Hilder, a savvy former federal prosecutor and congressional aide.

As Watkins began telling Hilder about life at Enron, Hilder was both amazed and concerned for his new client. It sounded to him as though the world's most innovative company might also be the world's most crooked company and that most of the problems and the subsequent cover-up came from the top, with a lot of help from one of the world's most powerful accounting firm and one of the country's leading law firms. The ramifications were enormous. Indeed, it wasn't long before Enron's problems and the greed off its executives eclipsed the war on terror on the front pages of America's newspapers. When a Congressional investigator leaked Watkin's memo to the press, every major national newspaper, television network and cable company came running to her door.

While the cameras rolled and public speculation about Watkins motives abounded, Hilder was working on the inside. It became his role to shepherd Ms. Watkins through a mine field of investigations and hearings, including those with the House Energy and Commerce Committee and the Senate Commerce Committee. The road map outlined by Watkins proved to be invaluable for those striving to unravel Enron's web of deceit and those prosecuting those accused of wrongdoing. Thanks to Watkins, over two dozen individuals have been charged in the scandal to date, with several investigations continuing.

This case certainly changed Attorney Philip Hilder's life, but it is important to note that it also changed the nation as a whole. Many people now demand to know why Enron's false accounting was not spotted sooner. Further, a multitude of American firms, which in the past used aggressive accounting, are now being held accountable for

"WHEN THE INTERNAL MEMO WAS RELEASED BY CONGRESSIONAL INVESTIGATORS, EVERY MAJOR NATIONAL NEWSPAPER, TELEVISION NETWORK AND CABLE-COMPANY CAME RUNNING."

their own misdeeds. Congress even went so far as to pass a new bill aimed at cracking down on corporate fraud. Congress has also ordered a review of US pension regulations, after Enron employees lost billions of dollars because their savings were invested in the company's own stock. Currently, Enron is seeking to salvage its surviving business by spinning off various assets. They have filed for Chapter 11 bankruptcy as well, which will allow them to organize while being protected from creditors. There are those who wonder whether all the lessons from this scandal have been properly learned by people not just inside the company, but throughout America's corporate suites.

"Reasonable doubt at a reasonable price."
~ PHILIP'S FAMOUS TEXAS JUSTICE SAYING

Where did Victoria County get its name?
FROM ITS ORIGINAL NAME, NUESTRA SENORA DE GUADALUPE DE JESUS VICTORIA, LATER SHORTENED TO GUADALUPE VICTORIA AND THEN TO VICTORIA.

Where is the Victoria County Courthouse located?
ON THE CORNER OF GLASS AND CONSTITUTION STREETS IN VICTORIA'S BEAUTIFUL DOWNTOWN DISTRICT.

Who designed the Victoria County Courthouse?
THE ARCHITECT J. RIELY GORDON WAS RESPONSIBLE FOR THE DESIGN OF THIS 1982 HISTORIC COURTHOUSE, AS WELL AS AT LEAST SEVENTEEN OTHERS.

What is the Courthouse's most unusual feature?
ITS ROMANESQUE REVIVAL DESIGN AND REMARKABLE CLOCK TOWER WHICH MAKE THE COURTHOUSE THE FOCAL POINT OF VICTORIA'S DOWNTOWN.

What is the most famous case tried in the Victoria County Courthouse?
PERHAPS THE MOST FAMOUS CASE EVER TO BE TRIED IS CURRENTLY UNFOLDING AS THIS BOOK GOES TO PRESS. A YOUNG MAN BY THE NAME OF RYAN JAMES FRAZIER, AN EAGLE SCOUT AND A BAYLOR UNIVERSITY STUDENT, WAS ACCUSED IN DECEMBER 2003 OF MURDERING HIS FATHER, MOTHER AND BROTHER. THIS CAPITAL MURDER CASE WAS ONE OF THE BIGGEST CASES THAT VICTORIA COUNTY EVER SAW. FRAZIER WAS FOUND GUILTY.

Where do you hang your hat?
AT MY LAW FIRM IN HOUSTON, TX, WHERE WE SPECIALIZE IN DEFENDING WHITE COLLAR CRIMINAL CASES AND CONDUCTING INTERNAL INVESTIGATIONS.

Believe it or not!
PREHISTORIC FOSSILS OF MAMMOTHS, HORSES, CAMELS, SLOTHS AND BISON OF THE LATE PLEISTOCENE ERA HAVE ACTUALLY BEEN UNEARTHED IN VICTORIA COUNTY!

Where did Wichita County get its name?

IT WAS NAMED AFTER THE WICHITA RIVER AND THE WICHITA INDIANS WHO RESIDED THERE IN 1882. INDIAN TROUBLES DELAYED ORGANIZATION OF THE COUNTY FOR MANY YEARS.

Where is the Wichita County Courthouse located?

AT THE INTERSECTION OF 7TH AND LAMAR STREETS IN WICHITA FALLS' HISTORIC DISTRICT.

Who designed the Wichita County Courthouse?

THE WICHITA COUNTY COURTHOUSE WAS BUILT IN 1916 USING THE CLASSICAL REVIVAL DESIGNS OF BOTH FIELDS & CLARKSON AND SANGUINET & PATE. THE BUILDING UNDERWENT EXTENSIVE REMODELING IN 1961 AND AGAIN DURING THE 1980s BY MICHAEL KOEN, WHEN THE BEAUTIFUL OLD COURTHOUSE WAS HIDDEN BY GLASS AND CONCRETE.

What is the most famous case tried in the Wichita County Courthouse?

A DIVORCEE WENT TO COURT WHEN THE FATHER FOUND THAT THE MOTHER—A CHRISTIAN—WAS TAKING THEIR DAUGHTER TO THE METROPOLITAN COMMUNITY CHURCH—A PROTESTANT DENOMINATION MINISTERING PRIMARILY TO GAYS AND LESBIANS. THE JEWISH FATHER CONTENDED THAT THIS WAS A VIOLATION OF THEIR 1998 DIVORCE SETTLEMENT. JUDGE KEITH NELSON AGREED WITH THE FATHER THAT THE DAUGHTER COULD ONLY BE TAKEN TO "MAIN LINE CHURCHES." THE RULING WAS LATER OVERTURNED BY THE COURT OF APPEALS.

Where do you hang your hat?

I LIVE ON TESTA ROSSA RANCH, APPROXIMATELY TEN MILES NORTH OF HENRIETTA IN CLAY COUNTY, TX. I PRACTICE IN WICHITA FALLS AT THE LAW FIRM OF MORRISON & SHELTON, WHERE I TRY A BROAD ARRAY OF CIVIL CASES ARISING OUT OF THE OIL AND GAS BUSINESS.

Believe it or not!

WICHITA FALLS IS HOME TO THE WORLD'S SMALLEST SKYSCRAPER. IT STANDS ONLY FOUR STORIES HIGH AND IS ONLY ONE ROOM WIDE!

"Gunfighters didn't charge by the bullet. Lawyers shouldn't either."

~ LONNY'S FAMOUS TEXAS JUSTICE SAYING

"Red River Litigation"

A Famous Texas Case as Told by

LONNY D. MORRISON
MORRISON & SHELTON

The case that came to be known as "Red River Litigation" was filed by Robert ("Saltwater") Helton, a lawyer born in 1913, who represented several Wichita County, Texas, riparian landowners in a lawsuit against the Bureau of Land Management and other agencies of the federal government, as well as several substantial defendants. Their claim was that they had acquired title, under the doctrine of accretion, to approximately 1,000 acres of public lands in the Red River valley adjacent to the riparian lands of the Texas landowners.

The cast included an interesting group of characters. Sarah T. Hughes was presiding in the Wichita Falls federal court where the case was filed; Eldon B. Mahon represented the interests of the United States government; Robert K. Pace, renowned oil and gas lawyer, and I together represented the primary oil company defendants.

From the first moment, Judge Hughes considered the case to be without merit. She granted a motion to dismiss for want of jurisdiction, based upon the inclusion of the United States as a necessary party and the absence of consent by the Sovereignty to be sued. Saltwater Helton did not wait to complete the ensuing appeal before he initiated another action in the same court, seeking damages as a result of an alleged trespass. When the Fifth Circuit Court of Appeals affirmed the ruling of Judge Hughes and the Supreme Court of the United States denied the appeal, the defendants were feeling pretty good about the case. After all, they reasoned, if a party can't sue the United States government for a determination of title, how could such party sue for damages as a result of trespass since, inevitably, a trespass case would require proof of title? So much for that theory of defense. . .

While the dismissal of the land title claim in the first case was still on appeal, Judge Hughes took up the second case, which sought damages for trespass. Judge Hughes was predisposed to believe that if the first case was without merit, the second case was frivolous. She promptly granted a motion to dismiss, but Saltwater Helton perfected yet another appeal to the United States Court of Appeals. This time, much to the surprise of the defendants and Judge Hughes, the dismissal was reversed and the case was remanded for trial. The Court of Appeals reasoned that trespass (as asserted in the second

Wichita
County Courthouse

case) was a tort, not a land title action and the Federal Tort Claims Act, intended to make the federal government responsible for the negligence of its employees, constituted a consent by the federal government to be sued for the tort of trespass.

At the time of the remand, I was a young lawyer with just a few years experience. Conveniently, I lived next door to Saltwater Helton. We spent many an evening together debating the facts of the case, the law and what the law should be. Ultimately, the two of us, as good friends, settled the differences of our clients. The United States government, the oil and gas lessees and the Texas landowners entered into a Consent Judgment unitizing all of the leases as if they were a single property and providing for the payment of royalty to the clients of Saltwater Helton. I met with John Mitchell, then the Attorney General of the United States (who became notorious in Watergate), to obtain the required consent to the reduction of the government's royalty.

"THE HISTORY OF THIS CASE SHOULD ENCOURAGE ALL LAWYERS TO NOT BE EASILY DISSUADED WHEN THEY SUFFER PROCEDURAL SETBACKS AND TO FIGHT DOGGEDLY, AGAINST ALL ODDS, FOR JUSTICE . . ."

The history of this case should encourage all lawyers to not be easily dissuaded when they suffer procedural setbacks and to fight doggedly, against all odds, for justice as they see it. Saltwater Helton, a high spirited, tobacco-chewing lawyer who celebrated his 91st birthday in 2004, lives in Wichita Falls and is frequently mentioned at bar association and other gatherings of North Texas lawyers.

Williamsc
County Courthouse

"Casey Goes To Bat"

A Famous Texas Case as Told by
EDWIN J. "TED" TERRY
EDWIN J. TERRY LAW FIRM, P.C.

In a remarkable case of Texas history, Mr. Terry represented a man in a custody case who held several traits unique to Texans: self-determination, fearlessness, passion and he also wore high heeled cowboy boots and a hat with a large, rather menacing looking rattlesnake on it. The case may be called, "Casey Goes To Bat."

Mr. Terry's client, a large man of about 6'6" and 280 pounds was embroiled in a custody battle with his

> ## "THE JUDGE EVEN BROUGHT A GUN TO THE COURTROOM TO PROTECT HIMSELF AND THE JURY."

deceased wife's parents. During the course of this trial, Terry's client allegedly made a bomb threat against the courthouse, which led to his arrest in front of the jury. And if this weren't enough drama for television, during the jury trial, the client's mother came into the room and removed her false teeth and demonstrated how she had French-kissed the court appointed psychiatrist the Saturday before the jury trial started.

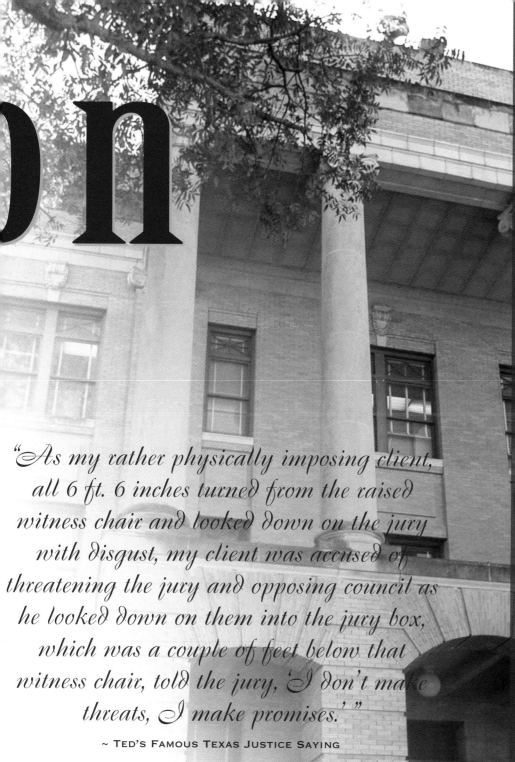

on

> *"As my rather physically imposing client, all 6 ft. 6 inches turned from the raised witness chair and looked down on the jury with disgust, my client was accused of threatening the jury and opposing council as he looked down on them into the jury box, which was a couple of feet below that witness chair, told the jury, 'I don't make threats, I make promises.'"*
>
> ~ TED'S FAMOUS TEXAS JUSTICE SAYING

With Mr. Terry's client making various threats against both the judge and the jury, things became heated. The judge questioned the client as to whether he was making threats. The client looked directly at the jury, leveled a finger and coldly stated, "Your Honor, I don't make threats; I make promises." The judge even brought a gun to the courtroom to protect himself and the jury.

This goes to show that divorce law is unique in Texas, in that it is the only state that provides for a jury trial in divorce proceedings. Attorneys across the United States and the world find Texas divorces and custody cases astonishing.

Where did Williamson County get its name?
FROM ROBERT MCALPIN WILLIAMSON, WHO LOST THE USE OF HIS RIGHT LEG BELOW THE KNEE. HE WALKED WITH A WOODEN LEG INSTEAD AND HE TOLD THE TEXAS LEGISLATURE ABOUT BUFFALO HUNTING IN THE PROPOSED NEW COUNTY. THE COUNTY WAS ORGANIZED IN 1948.

Where is the Williamson County Courthouse located?
ON THE CORNER OF ROCK AND EIGHTH STREETS IN GEORGETOWN, TX—THE RED POPPY CAPITAL OF TEXAS.

Who designed the Williamson County Courthouse?
IN 1911, CHARLES H. PAGE & BROTHER, AN ARCHITECT FROM AUSTIN, TX, AND A FOUNDER OF THE LEGENDARY AUSTIN CONSTRUCTION FIRM BROWN & ROOT DESIGNED THIS HISTORIC COURTHOUSE IN A BEAUX-ARTS STYLE OF STONE AND BRICK. THIS IS A NATIONAL REGISTER PROPERTY.

What is the Courthouse's most unusual feature?
THE STONE TRIPLE-ARCHED ENTRYWAYS ON ALL FOUR SIDES OF THE COURTHOUSE LEADING TO THE GALLERIES. THERE IS ALSO A FIGURE OF JUSTICE SITTING ATOP A LARGE COPPER DOME WHICH HAS LARGE CLOCK FACES ON ALL SIDES OF THE DOME.

What is the most famous case tried in the Williamson County Courthouse?
THE DISBARMENT TRIAL OF A LAWYER, IT LASTED MANY WEEKS AND FEATURED A NUMBER OF PROMINENT LAWYERS AS WELL AS A NUMBER OF JUDGES. THIS LAWYER WAS BOTH BRILLIANT AND DEMENTED AFTER THE MULTI-WEEK JURY TRIAL; THE JURY DISBARRED HIM.

Where do you hang your hat?
IN AUSTIN, TX. I AM BOARD CERTIFIED IN FAMILY LAW BY THE TEXAS BOARD OF LEGAL SPECIALIZATION. IN ADDITION, I AM ALSO THE PAST PRESIDENT OF THE AMERICAN ACADEMY OF MATRIMONIAL LAWYERS, TEXAS CHAPTER, AS WELL AS THE SECRETARY OF THE INTERNATIONAL ACADEMY OF MATRIMONIAL LAWYERS, U.S.A. CHAPTER.

Believe it or not!
ONE RAINY DAY, ROBERT WILLIAMSON'S HORSE LOST ITS FOOTING AND FELL WITH HIM WHILE CHASING BUFFALO DURING A HUNT. THE HORSE SCAMPERED OFF, BUT WILLIAMSON'S WOODEN LEG WAS STUCK IN THE MUD, SO HE COULD NOT GET UP. THIS STORY WAS ONE THAT MADE HIM WELL-KNOWN!

Where did Wise County get its name?

IN 1856, FROM HENRY A. WISE, A U.S. CONGRESSMAN FROM VIRGINIA WHO ACTUALLY NEVER LIVED IN TEXAS, BUT WAS KNOWN TO BE A STRONG SUPPORTER OF THE ANNEXATION OF TEXAS. ALSO KNOWN AS, "EIGHTER FROM DECATUR," THE COUNTY SEAT OF WISE,— GAMBLING EPITHET OF THE DICE THROWERS THAT CAME IN ON THE TRAINS.

Where is the Wise County Courthouse located?

IN DECATUR, TX, JUST WEST OF THE TEXAS TOURIST CAMP, TEXAS LUNCHROOM AND PETRIFIED WOOD GAS STATION. BONNIE AND CLYDE SUPPOSEDLY STAYED IN ONE OF THE CABINS FOR A FEW NIGHTS AT THE TEXAS TOURIST CAMP.

Who designed the Wise County Courthouse?

TEXAS STAR, J. RIELY GORDON OF NEW YORK, DESIGNED WISE COUNTY'S HISTORIC COURTHOUSE IN 1896 ROMANESQUE REVIVAL STYLE, USING PINK TEXAS GRANITE ON THE EXTERIOR AND VERMONT MARBLE IN THE INTERIOR. OUR COURTHOUSE HAS BEEN PROCLAIMED AS ARCHITECTURALLY PERFECT!

What is the Courthouse's most unusual feature?

THE TEXAS GRANITE USED TO BUILD THE COURTHOUSE WAS SHIPPED FROM BURNET COUNTY WHERE EACH STONE WAS PRE-CUT AND THEN NUMBERED. THIS IS A NATIONAL REGISTER PROPERTY.

What is the most famous case tried in the Wise County Courthouse?

THE SHARON GREEN CRIMINAL TRIAL. HER HUSBAND WAS TRIED & CONVICTED ON SEVERAL SERIAL MURDERS IN THE FORT WORTH AREA. SHARON WAS FOUND NOT GUILTY. THE CASE WAS WRITTEN ABOUT IN <u>BLOOD RUSH</u> BY PATRICIA SPRINGER.

Where do you hang your hat?

I AM THE FOUNDING PARTNER AT SIMPSON, BOYD & POWERS, P.L.L.C., LOCATED IN THE HEART OF NORTH CENTRAL TEXAS, WHERE I SPECIALIZE IN CIVIL TRIAL. IN 26 YEARS OF PRACTICE, I HAVE OBTAINED JURY VERDICTS FOR MY CLIENTS TOTALING NEARLY $1 BILLION.

Believe it or not!

ON APRIL 19, 1897, A SPACE SHIP CRASHED INTO A WINDMILL, BURSTING INTO PIECES IN AURORA, TX, LOCATED IN SOUTHEAST WISE COUNTY. AS THE DEBRIS WAS SEARCHED THROUGH, THE BODY OF A SMALL ALIEN WAS SUPPOSEDLY DISCOVERED AND THE TOWN'S PEOPLE GAVE THE ALIEN A PROPER BURIAL IN THE AURORA CEMETERY!

"I would be a good judge, if I am any judge at all."

Kinky Friedman's campaign slogan when he ran for JP in Kerrville, Texas.

~ MIKE'S FAMOUS TEXAS JUSTICE SAYING

"Misdemeanor Murder"

A Famous Texas Case as Told by
MIKE SIMPSON
SIMPSON, BOYD & POWERS, P.L.L.C.

It all started with a call from an investigator who worked for a local oil company who wanted to visit with me. My practice consisted of high profile civil cases including a $488-million jury verdict in an anti-trust case, a $204-million verdict in an environmental contamination case and several million-dollar personal injury jury verdicts. Although I had prosecuted criminal cases in my early law career and defended people accused of crimes in the past, I was no Perry Mason.

I had read about an alleged murder of a man's girlfriend that occurred in our small town. The facts appeared to be conclusive that the young man murdered his girlfriend during a domestic dispute, as set out by the local newspaper. This was the first murder that had occurred in this small town in the last sixty years. It happened in the silk stocking district of our community.

The facts that the investigator had uncovered in his brief investigation were far different than the account relayed to the local newspapers. The paper was quick to point out that the accused and the deceased had an argument the day of the murder that prompted our client to make the first call to 911. During this visit, the deceased was questioned by police and examined by paramedics but refused any treatment or transfer to the hospital. The papers failed to point out that after the argument, my client was jailed and, therefore, could not have been responsible for any subsequent injuries sustained by the deceased.

Further, the police failed to disclose to the newspaper that the deceased had continued partying with a couple doing cocaine and drinking alcohol after my client's arrest and just minutes before a second 911 call was placed stating that the deceased was unconscious. The police never directed their investigation at the couple that was with the deceased in the final moments of her life. In fact, the whole case was reminiscent of a John Grisham novel because the wife of the couple, who was the "best friend" of the deceased, committed suicide just weeks after the deceased was

Wise
County Courthouse

murdered. Supposedly, the deceased was having an affair with the husband. The husband left for parts unknown.

I called on an old, battle scarred criminal defense lawyer out in Gainesville, Jimmy Jack Hatcher, to help us. Attorney Mike Carrillo and legal assistant Kayla McComis would head up the investigation of the case, Jimmy Jack would handle the Motion Practice and I would shape the trial strategy.

Trial was set to begin almost a year to the date of the murder. The prosecution described our client as a woman beater and laid the groundwork to convict him. Then it was our turn and we gave the facts. The girlfriend was partying with another couple and moving throughout the house where there was ample opportunity for her to have sustained the lethal blow to her head, which was the cause of her death. Our client happened to be in jail at this time.

Fearing a defeat, the State asked the jury not to find the defendant guilty of murder (a maximum sentence of life), but to

> "... THE WHOLE CASE WAS REMINISCENT OF A JOHN GRISHAM NOVEL ..."

find him guilty of aggravated assault. This would carry a maximum sentence of 20 years in prison.

With the limited existence of high crime in our community, the stakes were high and the prosecution was out for blood. As the jury filed in, you could read nothing from their expressions. The charge was read, the verdict was unanimous. Our client was found innocent of aggravated assault and was allowed to pay a fine of $500 for simple assault.

Wood
County Courthouse

"Run for the Border"

A Famous Texas Case as Told by
DALE LONG
THE LAW OFFICE OF DALE LONG

In early February of 2002, Charles Alan Hammer was arrested in Las Cruses, New Mexico, after he was found driving the car of an elderly Quitman woman whose slain body had been found the week before. Janie Marie True, an 83-year-old retired missionary, had been found by a family member who came to check on her after she did not answer her phone. Her throat had been cut and she had been left to die. She had last been seen the day before chatting to her neighbors as she checked her mail.

Hammer was soon apprehended by Las Cruses, New Mexico, and police when he attempted to cross the border into Mexico. True's 1991 Chevy Lumina had been reported stolen after her body was found. Las Cruses police immediately notified Quitman Police Chief Bill Wansley. FBI officials arrived promptly at the scene to survey the car and any other evidence. Hammer was arraigned in New Mexico for other charges not pertaining to the murder, but was not initially a suspect in the case. Following an autopsy report from the Southwest Institute of Forensic Sciences, Hammer was called in for questioning and quickly became the prime suspect in the case.

Six months later, after being extradited to Wood County to face charges of murder, Hammer plead guilty to the slaying, a charge of capital murder. His confessions were numerous; three written confessions and one oral videotaped confession. His plea bargain agreement ensured that he would plead guilty to capital murder and two other charges and serve at least seventy years in prison before the possibility of parole, while avoiding the death penalty.

> *"With a proper explanation, the jury will get it right."*
> ~ DALE'S FAMOUS TEXAS JUSTICE SAYING

"THE FAMILY RESTED ASSURED THAT HAMMER WOULD NEVER AGAIN BE OUT IN SOCIETY."

While the state was pursuing the death penalty, the victim's family consented to the plea bargain.

Judge Timothy Boswell, the defense, as well as the victim's family all wanted the murderer to pay for his crime. The family was not against the death penalty, but felt that Janie Marie True would have been compassionate to her killer and they wanted to best fulfill what they believed would have been her wishes. And the family rested assured that Hammer would never again be out in society; his capital murder charges specified that he would not be eligible for parole for forty years, while his additional aggravated robbery charges added another thirty years to that. The agreement also stated that Hammer would waive his rights to any appeals. This was a case where justice was truly served.

Where did Wood County get its name?
THE COUNTY WAS ORGANIZED IN 1850 AND NAMED AFTER GEORGE T. WOOD, WHO WAS THE GOVERNOR OF TEXAS FROM 1847 TO 1849.

Where is the Wood County Courthouse located?
THE COURTHOUSE IS LOCATED IN QUITMAN, TX, ON THE SQUARE, FIVE MILES FROM THE LAKE FORK RESERVOIR, WHICH BOASTS 300 MILES OF SHORELINE.

Who designed the Wood County Courthouse?
IN 1925, C.H. LEINBACH DESIGNED THIS CLASSICAL REVIVAL-STYLE HISTORIC COURTHOUSE WHICH IS BUILT OF BRICK. AN ADDITION WAS BUILT BY THE COUNTY IN 1949 AS WELL AS EXTENSIVE REMOLDING IN 1976, 1979 (REMOVE COMMA) AND 1981.

What is the Courthouse's most unusual feature?
MOST OF THE ORIGINAL PIECES WERE LOST DURING THE RENOVATIONS, BUT THE OLD MARBLE STAIRCASES AND BLACK AND WHITE TILE STILL REMAIN FROM THE 1925 BUILDING.

What is the most famous case tried in the Wood County Courthouse?
C.E. CHAMBLEE KEPT A TEN-YEAR DIARY IN WHICH HE STATED THAT HE DID NOT WANT HIS ADOPTED SON TO INHERIT ANY OF HIS ESTATE. AFTER MR. CHAMBLEE COMMITTED SUICIDE, MR. AND MRS. CHAMBLEE'S ADOPTED SON DIED AND THEIR GRANDSON CONTESTED THE WILL IN TWO SEPARATE TRIALS. IN THE END, THEIR GRANDSON WAS AWARDED $300,000 OF THE $4 MILLION ESTATE AND THE REST WAS GIVEN TO THE UNIVERSITY OF TEXAS AT TYLER.

Where do you hang your hat?
AT THE LAW OFFICE OF DALE LONG IN TYLER, TX, AND I PRACTICE LAW IN EAST TEXAS. I HAVE MAINTAINED LAW OFFICES IN TYLER FOR THE PAST 35 YEARS AND AM ENGAGED IN THE GENERAL PRACTICE OF LAW INCLUDING MATTERS CONCERNING INJURIES TO THE PERSON, GENERAL LITIGATION, CORPORATE AND BUSINESS AFFAIRS AND REFERRALS TO HIGHLY SPECIALIZED FIRMS.

Believe it or not!
THE OLD SETTLERS REUNION WAS FIRST ESTABLISHED BY JAMES L. RAY IN 1898 AND IS STILL HELD ONCE A YEAR ON THE FIRST WEEKEND OF AUGUST IN QUITMAN AT JIM HOGG PARK. IN TRUE TEXAN STYLE, ON THE SATURDAY OF THE FESTIVAL, THERE IS A FIDDLING CONTEST!

"The Art of Restoring Texas Historical Courthouses"

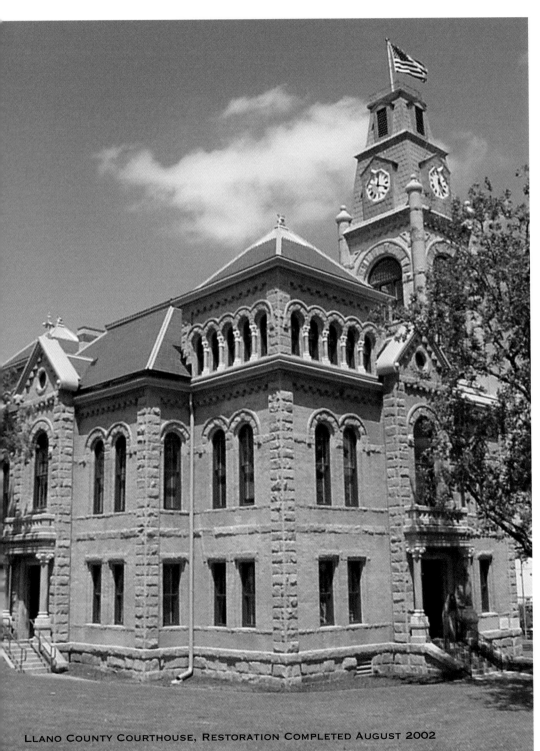

LLANO COUNTY COURTHOUSE, RESTORATION COMPLETED AUGUST 2002

In 1998, Texas Historic Courthouses landed on the list of "America's 11 Most Endangered Historic Places" by the National Trust for Historic Preservation. This was recognition of their often severe state of deterioration, abandonment, as well as their architectural, social and historical significance. The "endangerment" was a function of the lack of funds and a plan to save them. We applaud the Texas Legislature and then Governor George W. Bush for creating the Texas Historic Courthouse Preservation Program in 1999. With hundreds of millions of dollars being awarded, now over thirty Historic Courthouses are being restored and Rededicated.

"PHOENIX I IS A PROUD SPONSOR OF THE TEXAS HISTORIC COURTHOUSE PRESERVATION PROGRAM & PRESERVATION TEXAS."

Phoenix I has proudly participated in over twenty Historic Courthouse restorations. The artistry and detail that goes into the restoration of a Historical Courthouse is a passion for Dale Sellers, President and CEO of Phoenix I Restoration and Construction, a sixth-generation Texan. Dale emphasizes, "We take great pride in what we do, how we do it and with whom we do it." His leadership, knowledge, passion and vision have drawn the very best artisans, master craftsmen and entrepreneurs in their fields to his team. Their dedication to community, restoration and

Phoenix I
Restoration and Construction, Ltd.

preservation are more than just words or ideals—they are the heart and soul of Phoenix I.

Dale is happy to share his passion by providing a glimpse into the behind the scenes process of restoring a Lone Star legend. From bidding a historical courthouse project to matching the original hardware of a doorknob; from casting plaster to match an existing column to finding the rare woods of the original structure—he will introduce you to the artistry of Historic Courthouse restoration.

Texas Historic Courthouse Restoration
as Told by Dale Sellers

My introduction to courthouse restoration begins with my first love and passion, the Shackelford County Historic Courthouse, Rededicated on June 30th, 2001, by the Texas Historic Courthouse Preservation Program. Shackelford County was Phoenix I's first Historic Courthouse Restoration Project. As you tour through the art forms and departments in the following pages, you will see the artistry that is involved and meet some of the people who make quality restoration happen. I am proud of the dedication to excellence these artists and professionals exhibit so that future generations of Texans may enjoy the Lone Star state's Historic Courthouses.

Another restoration project close to my heart is undoubtedly the restoration of the JFK Memorial, shown here in the photo. In fact, I along with employees of Phoenix I, donated the restoration of the JFK Memorial at Dealey Plaza to the City of Dallas and Dallas County.

DALE SELLERS
PRESIDENT AND CEO

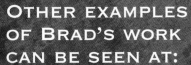

JOHN B. WILSON BUILDING-
REPLICATION AND INSTALLATION
OF BALUSTRADES AND NEWEL
POST CAPS

OTHER EXAMPLES OF BRAD'S WORK CAN BE SEEN AT:

DONLEY COUNTY COURTHOUSE

GRAY COUNTY COURTHOUSE

HARRISON COUNTY COURTHOUSE

LAMPASAS COUNTY COURTHOUSE

LLANO COUNTY COURTHOUSE

PARKER COUNTY COURTHOUSE

PRESIDIO COUNTY COURTHOUSE

SHACKELFORD COUNTY COURTHOUSE

ROCKWALL COUNTY COURTHOUSE

WHEELER COUNTY COURTHOUSE

JOHN B. WILSON BUILDING, DALLAS, TX

KIRBY BUILDING, DALLAS, TX

MASON BANK, MASON, TX

PRESBYTERIAN HOSPITAL, DALLAS,
SHIU FOUNDATION

ROSA MEXICANA RESTAURANT,
NEW YORK CITY, NY

EMERIL LAGASSE RESTAURANTS,
NEW ORLEANS, ORLANDO

WATER COLOR INN,
SANTA ROSA BEACH, FL

PHOENIX STUDIOS

Brad Oldham is the Division Manager of Phoenix Studios and comes from a family of seven generations of Texans. Although Brad was actually born in California, he has lived in Texas most of his life. He has been profiled in many business and architectural magazines across the country, including *Architectural Digest*, with *Conde Naste Travel, Platinum*, and the *Dallas Business Journal*. Brad is truly an extraordinary artisan. One of the traits that warrant the extraordinary characteristic is the many mediums in which he works: clay, plaster, cement, canvas, wood, glass, ceramic tile, resins, bronze, brass, copper, aluminum, stainless steel, white metals, zinc and steel alloys, as well as many plating and oxidizing finishes.

His artistry is brilliantly displayed in the clay models carved to reproduce and cast eleven eagles, each with a 6' 4" wingspan, and the 7' Lady of Justice, for the 1901 Harrison County Courthouse in Marshall, Texas. The replication of fourteen different colors of 109-year-old lead-glazed hearth tiles on the Donley County Courthouse was extremely challenging. Current day health standards dictated the use of non-leaded glazing, compounding the difficulty on matching the color and gloss of the tiles.

Many courthouse restoration projects involve the restoration and replication of deteriorated artifacts as well as the

replacement/reproduction of irreparable or missing elements. Brad has replicated door and window hardware elements with such a degree of accuracy that on many projects even architectural experts couldn't tell the original pieces from replicas. He has also created period hardware for structures from which the original hardware was missing and no evidence of the design could be found. ADA approved hardware has also been designed and manufactured to compliment the original hardware where required.

Brad closes the circle between the specialty trades of Phoenix I's other artisans and assures that whatever element or medium it's made from, Phoenix I craftsmen can repair or replicate it.

BRAD OLDHAM
DIVISION MANAGER

STRUCTURAL & ORNAMENTAL
STEEL

Keith Ashmore, Manager of the Ornamental and Structural Steel Division, is out of his element when he's not on the jobsite welding or scheming how to transform an architect or engineer's intent into reality. The jobs that no one else wants, can't figure out how to do or are scared to do are what keeps Keith excited. Keith's work goes far beyond just being a challenge; it's about feasibility and possibilities. "Typically, these old buildings are literal 'tender boxes,' and the key is often not just how to do the work, but how to do it safely."

Many courthouses have endured significant structural damage from fire, poor foundations, poor workmanship, poor materials, inadequate designs, owner modifications, and of course, Texas tornados and storms. Due to major weather damage, the entire tower of the Lampasas courthouse previously had bracing added that protruded into the original courtroom ceiling. As part of the restoration, Keith had to install new steel reinforcement in the original attic space. Keith had to temporarily support the entire tower during the load transfer. Lasers, movement monitors and control lines were used to ensure the structure was not damaged. The released deflection of the old repair steel trusses was over two inches compared to that Keith's newly installed steel trusses, whose deflection which was less than 1/2 of an inch.

In the Red River County Courthouse, the huge wooden beams and trusses had suffered "creep" over the years and the tower was in real jeopardy of collapsing. Keith's crews installed support bracing over 44-feet long to stabilize the structure.

Keith's desk is made from twisted steel rebar that he removed from a crumbling foundation and recovered long leaf yellow pine. It's not just a job; it's a love of what you do. Even when he's at the office, he's still close to his courthouses.

It's often not the most visible part of the project, but its Keith's work that assures the courthouse will last another hundred years.

KEITH ASHMORE
DIVISION MANAGER

OTHER EXAMPLES
OF KEITH'S WORK
CAN BE FOUND AT:

BOSQUE COUNTY COURTHOUSE

BURNET COUNTY COURTHOUSE

DONLEY COUNTY COURTHOUSE

ELLIS COUNTY COURTHOUSE

GRAY COUNTY COURTHOUSE

LAMPASAS COUNTY COURTHOUSE

LLANO COUNTY COURTHOUSE

LEE COUNTY COURTHOUSE

MAVERICK COUNTY COURTHOUSE

NEWTON COUNTY COURTHOUSE

PARKER COUNTY COURTHOUSE

RED RIVER COUNTY COURTHOUSE

ROCKWALL COUNTY COURTHOUSE

VAL VERDE COUNTY COURTHOUSE

WHEELER COUNTY COURTHOUSE

BALL-EDDLEMAN-McFARLAND HOUSE,
FORT WORTH, TEXAS

Phoenix I Texas County Courthouse Restoration Projects Include the Following:

1. Bosque County Courthouse
ArchiTexas, Restoration Architect

2. Burnet County Courthouse
Eleven Thirteen Architects, Restoration Architect

3. Donley County Courthouse
Volz & Associates, Restoration Architect

*4. Ellis County Courthouse
ArchiTexas, Restoration Architect

5. Gray County Courthouse
ArchiTexas, Restoration Architect

*6. Harrison County Courthouse
ArchiTexas, Restoration Architect

7. Lampasas County Courthouse
Komatsu Architecture, Restoration Architect

8. Lee County Courthouse
Architects Rabe + Partners, Restoration Architect

9. Llano County Courthouse
Volz & Associates, Restoration Architect

10. Newton County Courthouse
Wharry Engineering, Restoration Architect

11. Parker County Courthouse
Cauble, Hoskins & Loose, Restoration Architect

12. Presidio County Courthouse
The Williams Company, AIA, Restoration Architect

*13. Red River County Courthouse
ArchiTexas, Restoration Architect

14. Rockwall County Courthouse
ArchiTexas, Restoration Architect

15. Shackelford County Courthouse
The Williams Company, AIA, Restoration Architect

16. Cameron County Courthouse
Roberto J. Ruiz, Restoration Architect

*17. Lamar County Courthouse
ArchiTexas, Restoration Architect

18. Maverick County Courthouse
Ford Powell & Carson, Restoration Architect

19. Val Verde County Courthouse
Volze & Associates, Restoration Architect

20. Wheeler County Courthouse
Wharry Engineering, Restoration Architect

*subcontractor

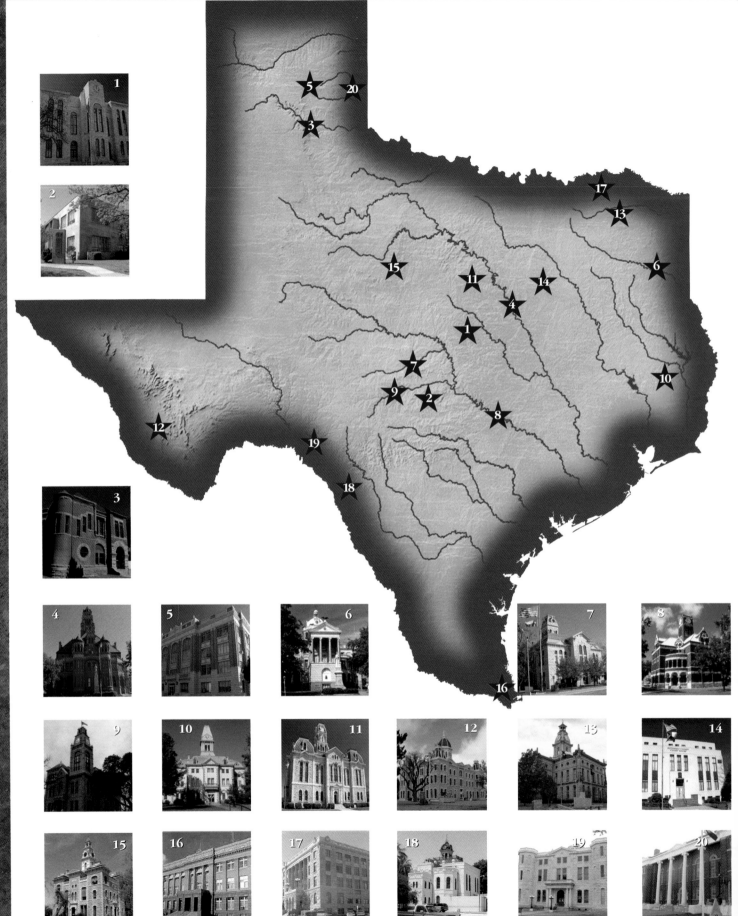

ESTIMATING & PRE-CONSTRUCTION

Estimating and preconstruction services provide the glue that binds the other divisions together. Although Phoenix I does many facets of the work in-house, many times local subcontractors are available and can offer additional value to the owner. The Estimator pre-qualifies subcontractors assuring that Phoenix I consistently offer the best value achievable, while also ascertaining that all the scopes are clearly defined and not duplicated by any of the subcontractors. Courthouse restoration can't be bid competently by the plans and specifications alone. Our Estimator personally visits all jobsites and conducts detailed visual and picture surveys of the buildings to ensure the incidental work is picked up and that pre-existing conditions are well-documented.

Our experience and reputation for thoroughness and accuracy have led many historical architects to hire Phoenix I for our services during the design and development phases to ensure their projects are "buildable" and within budget. We identify each and every item in our estimate. During the course of the project, the subsequent cost is captured in the accounting system, providing a feedback loop that ensures virtually each estimate is more accurate than the previous ones, and a "real costs" database unequalled in the industry. We have provided costing information to the Texas Historical Commission to assist them in assessment of future projects.

MASONRY & PLASTER RESTORATION

Our Masonry and Plaster Restoration Division possesses comprehensive knowledge of old-world construction and repair techniques, as well as modern technology and material advances. Members of our team are experts at determining the composition and condition of existing plasters and substrates. Historical plasters were commonly made of clays, gypsums, limes or Portland cements and often had additives that included animal hair for reinforcement, along with other elements such as malt, urine, beer, milk and eggs. Recognizing the limitations and advantages of these varied materials and substrates is critical to the success of the replication and blending of old and new materials. Often, an old photograph or small broken and crumbling pieces are the only available record of the original art. A carving must be made from which he can form and cast clay molds to recreate the original elaborate pieces.

Masonry restoration scopes include stone patching and replacement, tuckpointing and cleaning.

Whether the project includes an elaborate ceiling, arched entryways, ornamental column capitals, scored plaster walls, or stone and masonry repairs, each is a source of pride.

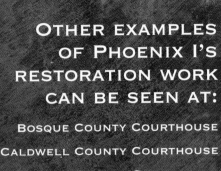

ROOFING & FLOORING

Our Flooring and SPF Roofing Division's discernment and eye for detail has proven to be a key asset to Phoenix I and our clients. Many historic courthouses were built utilizing materials whose "art form" has been lost in the last century. The hallway floors of the Presidio County Courthouse were originally hand trowelled with a wood fiber, limestone, sand and cement mix. The finish lacked the necessary durability to withstand heavy boot traffic and, over the years, sand that was constantly tracked in from the surrounding desert had taken its toll. The floors were repaired utilizing a modified polymer concrete overlay. They were then stained and waxed, replicating the original colors, patterns and textures, while greatly enhancing the durability of the original finish.

Notice was taken that one area that 'stained-out' differently from the rest of the floor. It was immediately rumored to be bloodstains from some misfortunate character over a hundred years ago. The Gray County Courthouse utilized a poured linoleum system that hasn't been commercially produced in many decades. An epoxy compound system was formulated and installed to provide the owner with a long term, durable floor, while replicating the color, sheen and texture of the original linoleum.

COMMERCIAL COATING & PAINT

Most of the courthouses over the years have had literally dozens of coats of paint added to the walls and original stained woodwork. The stripping, refinishing and blending in the new work and patches to match the old is an art in and of itself.

One of the most challenging projects for our Commercial Coating and Paint Division to date has been The T&P Terminal Lobby in Fort Worth. Built in 1931, deemed the "Sistine Chapel ceiling" of Fort Worth by restoration architect Bob Adams of Gideon Total architectural firm, this project really showcased the extent of the paint division's decorative talents. Based on displays from the 1925 Paris Exposition, French-style fountains, stair-stepped pyramids called ziggurats, and dolphins are amid the motifs on the ornate 30-foot ceiling. Phoenix's elaborate stenciling, gold and silver leafing, as well as oil glazings, highlight the intricate detail of the art deco treasure.

FAR LEFT: RESTORED TURRET AT THE PRESIDIO COUNTY COURTHOUSE. RIGHT AND BELOW: THE "LADY OF JUSTICE" WITHOUT HER SWORD AND SCALES AT THE PRESIDIO COUNTY COURTHOUSE.

ARCHITECTURAL METALS

While our team completed the restoration of the Presidio County Courthouse, we were able to restore the Goddess of Justice who overlooks the county from atop the cupola of the courthouse. Multiple coats of paint and misguided attempts at repairs were stripped from her metal. Her hand, which had been severed at the wrist, was repaired and reattached, prior to covering her with a new protective coating. Originally, she held a sword in one hand and the scales of justice in the other. However, local folklore has it that some years ago, a disgruntled cowboy recently released from jail, blasted them out of her hands with his Sharps rifle, proclaiming from the courthouse steps, "There is no justice in Presidio County." Due to the historic events involving their removal, these elements were not replaced. Sometimes knowing when not to restore something to its original state is as important as knowing how to restore it.

Other contributions to the restoration of these symbols of Texas justice include restoration and replication of historic pressed metal ceilings found in several courtrooms, decorative metal elements such as cornices, entablatures and finials, as well as flat-seamed copper roofing, turn-coated stainless steel and standing-seam metal roofing.

OTHER EXAMPLES OF PHOENIX I'S ARCHITECTURAL METAL WORK CAN BE SEEN AT:

DONLEY COUNTY COURTHOUSE

ELLIS COUNTY COURTHOUSE

JEFF DAVIS COUNTY COURTHOUSE

LAMPASAS COUNTY COURTHOUSE

LLANO COUNTY COURTHOUSE

ROCKWALL COUNTY COURTHOUSE

SHACKELFORD COUNTY COURTHOUSE

BELLE HOUSE RESTORATION, RICHARDSON, TX

FORT DAVIS TOURIST WELCOME AND VISITOR CENTER, FT. DAVIS, TX

LEGEND AIRLINES, DALLAS, TX

MASON BANK, MASON, TX

MEYERSON SYMPHONY CENTER, DALLAS, TX

SANTA FE DEPOT, TEMPLE, TX

WILL ROGERS AUDITORIUM, FT. WORTH, TX

CONTRIBUTORS

Ashley Bennett

Born and raised in Springfield, Missouri, Ashley moved to Dallas in 1997 to attend Southern Methodist University where she earned a B.A. of Art History and a second B.A. in French. She went on to teach archeology in Italy and later continued her French studies in Paris. Upon returning to The States, the decision to come back to Dallas was an easy one. She tracked down legal eagles to interview and pen their cases. Ashley is currently pursuing her law degree at Southern Methodist University and plans on following in the footsteps of our Texas Legal Legends.

Santiago "BO" Botello III

A Lone Star flag waving salute to Bo for kicking off the graphics for the book with big beautiful ideas; and who is a fun loving Latino that finds chocolate simply irresistable…cheers!

Denise Brooks

Although originally born in the Texas panhandle, Denise, a fifth-generation Texan, has been in Dallas for so long (since 1970, but she didn't want me to tell you that) that she is a true Dallasite. When she's not hard at work at Red Bandana Publishing, Denise is busy at home with her Texan menagerie consisting of her husband, Clay; children, Cody and Casey; pit-bull, Rocky; cat, Scratch; parakeet, Oliver and a plethora of fish too numerous to count.

Brooks Fitch

Brooks arrived from the East Coast twenty years ago, simply expecting an interesting and rewarding two years. But "Big D" suprised him when he discovered the pride, positive energy and passion of Texas and Texans. The *Texas Justice* project has given him appreciation for not only the people and the architecture of the Texas Historic Courthouses, but also the colorful history that we have come to know as *Texas Justice*.

MDVC Creative

MDVC Creative Inc. was responsible for the layout and design of *Texas Justice*. Located in Dallas, MDVC is a well-oiled fusion of business analysis, consulting, marketing, design and writing. The company is known for its unique zebra-striped exterior, as well as its speed, economy and ingenuity in crafting creative problem-solving solutions. In addition to its core staff, MDVC is also home to "The Boss," its live-in feline mascot and pawed muse.

Kelly Roberts

A true Texas yellow rose living in the Austin Hill country and an editorial pioneer for Texas Justice. A big Texas thank you!

Karla Setser

A true Texan at heart and quite the adventurer, Karla toured over 150 of the Lone Star State's counties and courthouses in search of "Tall Tales" for "Texas Justice." In the process, she learned a lot about the pride Texas attorneys and judges have in their state and in their work. The stories she heard were creative, inspiring and whip crackin' (motivating!). She even got a bruise on her head as she was touring a courthouse attic. Karla was born in Houston and followed the man of her dreams to Tarrant County in 2002. With a background in marketing and public relations, Karla is well suited to promote something she is extremely proud of— Texas and her county courthouses!

Sarah Toler

Born in Texarkana (on the Texas side), Sarah is a proud Texan whose friends in Sydney, Australia, simply referred to her as "Tex." She lived in Sydney while getting her B.A. in Communications from The University of Technology, Sydney, and has since traveled across the Asian and European continents. Sarah is extremely happy to be back in Texas after five years away, mostly due to the fantastic music scene in Dallas. When without pen and paper editing and writing on *Texas Justice*, you can find Sarah at a club listening to live music, at home strumming on her guitar or adoring her niece, Madelyn, and nephew, Brayden.

PHOTOGRAPHERS

George Brainard

A sixth-generation Texan, George was raised in Austin. He graduated from the University of Texas at Austin in 1993 with a BA in Studio Art. For many years George led a double life of photographer by day and singer by night. He fronted a seven-piece swing band in the late 90s, recording three CDs of original songs and touring the country. In 1999 George gave up the nightlife to focus exclusively on his photographic career. He does primarily commercial, corporate and music photography. He has shot over thirty CD covers and has shot assignments for *Rolling Stone Magazine, The New York Times* and *The Times of London*. His corporate and commercial clients have included Motorola, Dell, IBM, AMD, Purina, Schlotzsky's and record companies too numerous to mention. He is currently working on a documentary film about the slam poetry phenomenon around the nation. More of his work can be seen at www.georgebrainard.com.

Patty Foppen

Patty has made a transition from one side of the lens to the other—after modeling for eighteen years, she has become a first-rate photographer, specializing in black & white and environmental portraits. While working on *Texas Justice*, Patty came across a truly Texan twist of fate. While photographing Steve Laird at the Hunt County Courthouse, she discovered that both photographer and subject were from the same small Texan town of Greenville. Even more uncanny was the discovery that poised on the courthouse walls were plaques of two very notable Texan World War II veterans, Patty's father and Steve's father, positioned just feet away from each other. When she's away from the camera, Patty loves to travel to the Caribbean, her favorite spot outside of Texas.

Sylvester Garza

Originally hailing from Corpus Christi, this now Houstonian photographer has taken photos for the likes of Houston House and Home, Shell, and Chevron Texaco, as well as Red Bandana Publishing. The proud dad of 11-year-old twins, Sylvester is also a talented musician and martial arts guru who is not afraid to use this latter skill on difficult subjects during a photography assignment. Sylvester was awe inspired by many of the amazingly restored courthouses. "They are just so beautiful." Most memorable to Sylvester was the remarkably restored Grimes County Courthouse.

Danny Piassick

Danny is a photographer who works to the beat of a different drummer. Whether it is his artistic good looks, the drums he plays in one of his rock 'n' roll bands or one of the motorcycles he roars around town on, it is certain that this native Dallasite is one of the best photographers out there. Danny has an eye for beauty, having shot some of this country's more beautiful homes and homeowners for both local and national magazines, numerous books and advertisments. Danny jumped at the chance to visit Historic Texas Courthouses. "I love what I do, the places I get to go and the people I meet." When he's not shooting, he's either checking out Dallas' music scene or rough-housing with his three dogs.

Scot Smith

A second-generation professional photographer, Scot R. Smith graduated from Louisiana Tech University in 1979 with a BFA in Photography and earned his master's degree in 1993. After working for Thurman C. Smith Photography and Skipworth, Inc., he established Smith Photographic Services, Inc. in 1982. He has eight times received the prestigious Kodak Gallery Award and twice received the Fuji Masterpiece Award. His prints and transparencies have won honors at Southwestern Photographers Association's print competitions.

Mark Umstot

Mark is a Texas photographic artist wanting to push the limits. After being born and reared in Lubbock, Texas, he spent time throughout the state and then headed overseas to Spain, back to the United States into Connecticut and New York City. After 9/11, it was time to head back to Texas. Being a lover of all things unique, he likes to echo that characteristic in his work and use ordinary folks to break the mold of typical photography. Since returning to Texas, he opened a studio catering to anyone wanting an imagemaker who does something different, something special, something better. When Mark isn't photographing something different, he volunteers at his daughter, Alex's school and goes to the movies with his wife, Paula. He loves to be identified as a Renaissance man, with interests in quantum theory/physics/mechanics, riding motorcycles and reading any non-fiction, scary books and people's minds. See more at www.umstot.com.

ACKNOWLEDGEMENTS

The verdict is in . . . Martana, Brian Carabet, Brooks Fitch and Karla Setser would like to tip their hats to the following Texans and those with Texas-sized hearts for their time, insight and wisdom; for providing some outstanding cases and Texas tales—most of which we can print!

A TEXAS-SIZE THANKS TO . . .

DeDee Bellomy and Rhonda Spencer of Phoenix I, Molly DeVoss, Jimmy Rainey, Becky Purvis, Gay Arney, Kathleen Reichert, Pam Burns, Elise Sartwelle and Thomas Sartwelle, Carmen Barrera Ramirez , Lynn Dickson, Linda Dickerson, William Alexander, Neil D. Anderson, Kim J. Askew, John Barr, Ted Brabham, Debbie Branson, Harold F. Entz, Lisa Garza, Don Godwin, Robert Goodfriend, Foster Green, William R. Gustavson, Brian Hail, James J. Hardt, Jimmy L. Heisz, Tom Helfand, Michael S. Holmes, Rhonda Hunter, Darrell Jordan, Michael McCullough, Larry McNeil, John Mitchell, John E. Mitchell, Lonny D. Morrison, Robert C. Prather, Gerald J. Reihsen III, Marcus Ronquillo, Judge William F. Sanderson, William C. Shaddock, Donna Smiedt, Kyle Steele, Charles P. Storey, Cheryl Wattley, Mikal Watts, Ward White, Atty. William Whitehurst, Tom Alexander, J.D. Bucky Allshouse, Vic Anderson, Mike Andervett, Sonia Aube, John Aycock, Jim Barlow, John Barr, Ray Bass, Daniel Barrett, David Berg, Matt Blevins, Robert Bliss, Joe Bobbitt, Bob Bodoin, Sue Boggs, William Book, David Botsford, Art Brender, Daryl Bristow, Mayor Euline Brock, David Brooks, Ernest Cannon, Ruben Castillo, David Chappell, Jerry Cobb, Dan Cogdell, Paul Coggins, Gregory Cokinos, C.C. Kit Cooke, Richard Corbitt, B.C. Cornish, Jim Cowles, Rob Crain, Tom Cunningham, Anita Cutrer, David Davis, Don Davis, John Davis, Mark Davidson, Bill Dawson, Beale Dean, Dick DeGuerin, Sylvia DeMarest, Larry DePlaza, Carol Dinkins, Tieman "Skipper" Dippel, Frank Douthitt, James Doyle, Sharon Easley, Bill Eggleston, Gary Elliston, Cadelario Elizondo, Carolyn Farb, H. Dustin Fillmore, Douglas Floyd, Jan Woodward Fox, Donn Fullenweider, Michael Gallagher, Terry Gardner, Jim George, Robin Gibbs, Hal Gillespie, H. Lee Godfrey, Dan Goforth, Gerald Goldstein, Bob Goodfriend, Jay Gray, Dicky Grigg, Mike Handy, Rusty Hardin, Senator Chris Harris, Mike Harrison, John David Hart, Jayne Hawkins, Joseph Hawthorn, Craig Haynes, David Haynes, Albon Head, Mike Head, Joseph Heard, John Hart, Graham Hill, Robert Hinton, Rod Hobson, Lisa Hoppes, Mike Hull, Rhonda Hunter, Kevin Isern, Steve Johnson, Randy Johnston, Rhonda Jolley, Charles Jordan, Darrell Jordan, Darrell Keith, David Keltner, Kerry Kilburn, Skip King, Steve King, Carol Chapman Kondos, Ronald Krist, Cathy Lamboley, Jim Leahy, Jack Little, Roy Longacre, Joe Longley, David Lopez, Gilbert "Buddy" Low, Mike Lynn, Clem Lyons, George Mackey, Matt Mankin, Pat Maloney, Stephen Malouf, John Marshall, Chris Martin, Kimberly Mayer, Levi McCathern, Randy McClanahan, Arch McColl, Robert McCoy, Mike McCurley, Tom McDade, Don McFall, Mike McKool, Harriet Miers, Frank Mitchell, Mike Moncrief, Bruce Monning, Jim Moriarty, Gerry Morris, Steve "Cowboy" Murrin, George Parnham, John Odam, Bill Ogden, Cynthia Orr, Richard Orsinger, Mike Park, Alice Oliver-Parrott, J.D. Pauerstein, Michael Perrin, Jim Perdue, Michael Pezzulli, Yvonne Puig, Kelly Puls, Kirk Purcell, Wayne Reaud, Joe Reynolds, Marc Richman, John Roach, George Robinson, Celina Romero, Martha Rose, Richard Sayles, Katherine Scardino, Mike Schattman, Charles Szalkowski, J. Shelby Sharpe, John Shepperd, Laurel Sheridan, Toby Shook, Jim Showers, Lewis Sifford, Mark Singleton, Bill Slusser, Broadus Spivey, James Stanley, Linda Steele, Tom Stollenwerck, Tom Stumpf, Steve Sumner, Steve Susman, Steve Suttle, Mack Ed Swindle, Charles Szalkowski, Blake Tartt, Robert Thackston, Mike Thomas, Terry Tottenham, Lannhi Tran, Walter Umphrey, Jay Vogelson, Bill Wade, Ronnie Walker, Wayne Ward, Michael Ware, Sherron Watkins, Sarah Weddington, Mark Werbner, David West, Keith Wheeler, Bill Whitehurst, Nancy Wooldridge, Bill Wischkaemper, Marie Yeates, Steve Zager, Wanda Irby for research on the old 1910 Baylor courthouse, Gary King of Castle Mailing, Macy Jaggers for her legal eagle editing, Jared Hokema-Cameron County, Rick Vanderpool for his Lone Star passion, Mavis Kelsey, Sr. and Donald Dyal -The Courthouses of Texas, Kate & John Troesser of www.texasescapes.com, Brett Cameron and Ted Lerich of www.texascourthouses.com & all the other Texans across the Lone Star State who saddled up and rode the extra mile for us!

Order Books by MARTANA

TEXAS MEN
Big Guns, Rising Stars & Cowboys

$49.95

Foreword by Larry Hagman

The men of The Lone Star State are heroic and notorious, capturing imaginations worldwide with tales of bull riding, cattle rustling and Texas black gold. *TEXAS MEN* captures the essence of these cowboys with interviews and photos highlighting each man's unique contribution to Texas. The rugged individualism of these men is portrayed through stories of Texas billionaires, cattle barons and even film and music stars!

TEXAS WOMEN
Trailblazers, Shining Stars & Cowgirls

$49.95

Foreword by U.S. Senator Kay Bailey Hutchison

Texas' Top Lone Star Ladies are showcased through photography and personal interviews saddled up with a real life "Tall Texas Tale" told by one of the cowgirl's favorite pals. From a Texas Ranger to a Dallas Debutante, *TEXAS WOMEN* has got 'em all!

TEXAS JUSTICE
The Legacy of Historical Courthouses

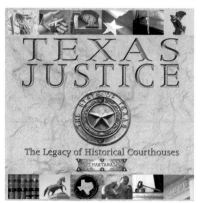

$49.95

Foreword by Richard "Racehorse" Haynes

In the heart of every Texas county seat sits a symbol of the Texas heritage of freedom, prosperity and protection for all Texans; our Historical Courthouses. These Lone Star beauties and the lawyers, judges and Texas Rangers who walk their halls tell the tales of crime and passion; love and war; murder and innocence. *TEXAS JUSTICE* unveils nearly 100 of Texas' 254 county courthouses and the sometimes remarkable, sometimes infamous cases that have taken place within their historic walls. And these courthouses have witnessed it all; from Old West deaths by hanging, to the modern twelve-man jury, it is all represented in famous cases told by Texas law legends!

RED BANDANA Publishing

RED BANDANA PUBLISHING
25 HIGHLAND PARK VILLAGE, 100-140
DALLAS, TX 75205
214-459-1217
FAX ★ 214-853-5425
TOLL FREE 1-866-MARTANA
E-MAIL ★ SALES@MARTANA.COM
WWW.MARTANA.COM

"Thou Shalt Not Bear False Witness."

Photography Credits

Principal Texas Justice Photography By

Cover-Top Row (L-R): Danny Piassick, Mark Umstot, Danny Piassick, stock photo, Sylvester Garza, Danny Piassick

Cover-Bottom Row (L-R): Sylvester Garza, Danny Piassick, Sylvester Garza, Phoenix I, Charlie Elizade, Danny Piassick

George Brainard: Cover-Limestone, 22, 23, 52, 53, 70, 71, 142, 143, 144, 145, 146, 147, 148, 149, 182, 183, 206, 207 (small), 218, 219

Patty Foppen: 32, 33, 50, 108, 109, 110, 111 mural, 169, 173, 179, 212, 213, 221

Sylvester Garza: 6, 18, 19, 30, 74, 75, 88, 89, 102, 122, 123, 131, 135, 175, 197

Danny Piassick: Back Flap, Introduction-Martana, Back Cover, 4, 10, 20, 21, 42, 43, 44, 45, 46, 47, 48, 49, 56, 57, 58, 59, 60, 61, 62, 63, 64, 65, 66, 67, 68, 69, 72, 73, 84, 85, 104, 105, 112, 113, 114, 115, 120, 121, 124, 125, 138, 150, 152, 153, 155, 161, 162, 166, 167, 170, 171, 184, 193, 194, 195, 200, 201, 214

Scot Smith: 36, 38, 39, 78, 79, 106, 107, 132, 133, 156, 157, 158, 159, 180, 181, 190, 191, 204, 205, 208, 209, 222, 223, 240

Mark Umstot: 54, 55, 90, 91, 100, 101, 118, 119, 127, 128, 129, 198, 199, 216, 217

Additional Texas Justice Photography & Art By

Ackerman McQueen: 176

Courtesy of Roy R. Barrera, Sr.: 24, 25, 26, 27, 28, 29

Courtesy of Michael Caddell and Cynthia Chapman: 140, 141

Neil Caldwell: 137 drawing

Brett Cameron & Ted Lerich of www.TexasCourthouses.com: 31, 48, 51, 76, 111, 116, 126, 134, 139, 154, 160, 164, 168, 172, 173 courthouse, 174, 177, 178, 179 courthouse, 192, 193 courthouse, 196, 215

Charlie Elizade: 25, 210, 211

Courtesy of Vic Feazell: 144 (small)

General Land Office Archives & Records, Texas, National Map Company, c. 1920: 2

John Glowczwski: 40, 41, 80, 81, 82, 83, 92, 93

Scott Newton: 165

Elaine Martin of www.rootsweb.com: 163 (small)

Courtesy of Bill Messer: 23 (small)

Michael O'Brien: 136 (Reprinted with permission from the March 2004 edition of The American Lawyer, copyright 2004 ALM Properties, Inc. All rights reserved)

Courtesy of Phoenix I: 177, 186, 187, 188, 189, 224, 225, 226, 227, 228, 229, 230, 232, 233, 234, 235

Jimmy Rainey: 220, 221 (small)

Steve Satterwhite: 77

Senate Media Services: 207

Richard Stockton: 34, 35

Wesley Treat: Old Rip-64

Kate & John Troesser of www.TexasEscapes.com: 20, 130, 151, 185 (TXDoT 1939)

Rick Vanderpool: Cover-Star Seal, 86, 87, 98, 99

Hal Warnick: Tarrant County Civil Courts building, 202, 203

Amy Weber: 115, 116 (small photo)

Courtesy of Mr. and Mrs. Dan Wendt: 93 (small), 94

Courtesy of The University of Houston: 95